TESTS I
OVERSEAS STUDENTS

Accompanying this book, and available from the Publishers:

TESTS IN ENGLISH FOR OVERSEAS STUDENTS—Cassettes

TESTS IN ENGLISH FOR OVERSEAS STUDENTS

Maureen J E Kassem
BA (Hons) FIL (Fr)

Stanley Thornes (Publishers) Ltd

© M J E Kassem, 1982
Illustrations © Stanley Thornes (Publishers) Ltd 1982

All rights reserved. No part of this publication may be reproduced, stored in a retrieval system or transmitted in any form or by any means electronic, mechanical, photocopying, recording or otherwise, without the prior written permission of the copyright holder.

First published in 1982 by
Stanley Thornes (Publishers) Ltd
Educa House
Old Station Drive
off Leckhampton Road
CHELTENHAM GL53 0DN
England

British Library Cataloguing in Publication Data

Kassem, Maureen J E
   Tests in English for Overseas Students.
   1. English language — Examinations
   2. English language — Study and teaching —
   Foreign students
   I. Title
   428'.2'4076   PE1128.A2

ISBN 0-85950-464-4

Typeset by Permanent Typesetting & Printing Co., Ltd. Hong Kong
Printed in Great Britain at the Pitman Press, Bath

Contents

Preface   viii

WRITTEN TESTS

The Circle	1
Convection	3
The Spectrum	4
Garden Implements	5
Experiment to Demonstrate the Percentage of Oxygen in the Air	7
The Gemini Twin	8
How to Make an Omelette	9
Friction—Part 1	10
How to Grow a Potato Plant	12
Parts of a Bicycle	13
Exterior Parts of a House	15
Dolphins	17
Victorian Jewellery	20
Disposable Ballpoint Pen	22
Sedimentology	23
Experiment to Show How Clouds Form	25
Camels	26
Levers	29
The Arch	33
Windows	35
Friction—Part 2	37
The Anemometer	39
Experiment to Show the Effect of Heat	40
Chinese Architecture	42
The Cuckoo	46
The Amoebae	48
The Pagoda	50
Castleton	57
Lasers	58
Ants	63
The Crocodile	65

Petersfield	68
Barrows	71
The Field Survey	76
Angiosperms and Gymnosperms	79
Angiosperms	82
Heredity	86
The Sonnet	89
The Scarab	94
Chemotherapy	96
The Dangers of Chemotherapy	99
Communicating across Outer Space	101
Cosmic Covers	103
Castles—Part 1	104
Charles Darwin	108
The Aneroid Barometer	111
Stonehenge	113
Comets	118
Pointing and Jointing	123
By-products of Timber	128
Swallow Showers	133
Hand Tools in Woodwork	134
The Miniature	139
Little Oakham Hall	141
Ashton University	145
Castles—Part 2	148
Skenfrith Castle	156
Flour Milling	158
The Solar System	162
The Earth	170
The Greenhouse	175
Ribblesdale House	182
Windmills and Watermills	186
Probing the Universe	197
Rose Cottage	205
Bacteria and Viruses	209
Bonding	219
Bodiam Castle	225
The Development of Archaeology	227
Exeton	230
The Methods of Excavation	232
Pyramids and Ziggurats	238
The Process of Excavation	248
Ancient Jewellery	252

Gold	270
Dale Village	273
The Lion	275
A Landmark in Archaeological History	277
The Mastaba	282
Bricks and Bricklaying	289
Allergies	301

AURAL TESTS

Traffic Accident	305
The Life Cycle of the Frog	306
Blakeley Castle	307
St. Dane's Church	309
The Regional Exhibition Centre	311
Bees—The Honey Bee	313
The Honey Bee Community	315
The Castes of the Honey Bee	317
The Worker Bee	319
A Neolithic Settlement Complex	321
Iron Age Village Complex	323
Roman Forts	327
The History of the Horse	330
The Horse—Parts of a Horse	331
The Horse—Colours	333
The Horse—Breeds	336
Wiring-Up a Three-Pin Plug	339
Screws, Nails and Bolts	342
Castleburgh	347
St. Mary's Church—Inside	350
St. Mary's Church—Outside	352
Buttresses	354
Triangles	360
Neolithic and Bronze Age Pottery	366
Gears	371
The City of Norwich	374
Civilisation and the Natural World	377

Preface

Usually, when an overseas student comes to Britain to study, he does so because he hopes to go on to higher education at a university or a polytechnic. However, in order to be accepted at a university and at some polytechics, the student must provide evidence that he has reached a satisfactory standard in English language. The requirement varies according to the university he has applied to and also depends on the subject he has decided to study there. For example, if he has decided to study medicine, pharmacy or physiotherapy, then it is usual for him to be asked for a pass in the General Certificate of Education in English Language, but for most other courses there are two certificates which are acceptable—the Cambridge Proficiency Examination (or the CPE) and the University Entrance Test in English (The Test in English, Overseas) of the Joint Matriculation Board. The Cambridge First Certificate is not considered acceptable. Most colleges in Britain, therefore, offer courses leading to the CPE or the JMB but there are difficulties. Both examinations are demanding and require a high standard in English but the CPE requires about two years of preparation after First Certificate level and this is not possible when the student comes to Britain on a one-year 'A' level course; there is simply not enough time. Even for the student on a two-year 'A' level course, there is not enough time, especially during the second year. The GCE 'O' level examination is far beyond the language ability of the average student from overseas.

The JMB is an examination which is completely different from any other examination in English. It is unique. It is an examination in two parts, the first a written test of 2½ hours and the second a listening test of about 40 minutes. It is different because it tests the way you use your English to perform a variety of tasks or solve problems. You will be required, for example, to translate data presented to you in one medium into another; you may perhaps be given a description in words of a building such as a house and you could be asked to draw a plan of it. Alternatively, you may be presented with the drawing of a house and asked to describe it in words. You may be asked to interpret a graph, a chart or a table using words, or you may have to give the steps in the process of making something or describing a series of events. The listening test has similar aims—to test your understanding of shapes, events, processes and so on. In order to be successful in the examination, you have to pass both written and aural papers.

Colleges entering students for the JMB found very little difficulty with the time element but they found that there was no suitable text available for their students to use. Past papers could be used but only once as they often had to be drawn on, and there were not always past papers available. For this reason, I wrote material of my own to be used with my students which I presented in booklet form but the students said that they preferred a textbook of their own which they could work from. When I learned from other teachers in other colleges that their students also wanted textbooks, I decided to put my material together into a book which the student could use for his own needs. Here it is—a student textbook and workbook in one. In it there is a wide range of questions on several subjects studied at the higher education level which test the student's understanding of written information and his ability to express his understanding of other information presented visually. In most cases the subject is outside the student's own field of study. Each question has been very carefully researched and checked and in the case where a town does not exist, such as Castleburgh or a house such as Rose Cottage or a university such as Ashton University, the technical and historical data is accurate.

A few listening tests have been added which can either be read to you by your teacher or played on a cassette which accompanies the book. I must add that many of the tests, both written and aural, are longer and more demanding than the JMB tests which are conducted under examination conditions. The tests in this book can be done with the aid of a dictionary. Your teacher can prepare you for them beforehand and you can take as much time as you like to solve them. All of the questions in the book have been pre-tested on my own students who enjoyed doing them and gave me useful advice when it was clear that there was not enough detail given or when the instructions themselves were not specific enough. I am grateful to them for this and would like to pay tribute to those students who worked through the questions. I hope that you will enjoy doing the questions as much as they did.

Maureen J.E. Kassem

WRITTEN TESTS

The Circle

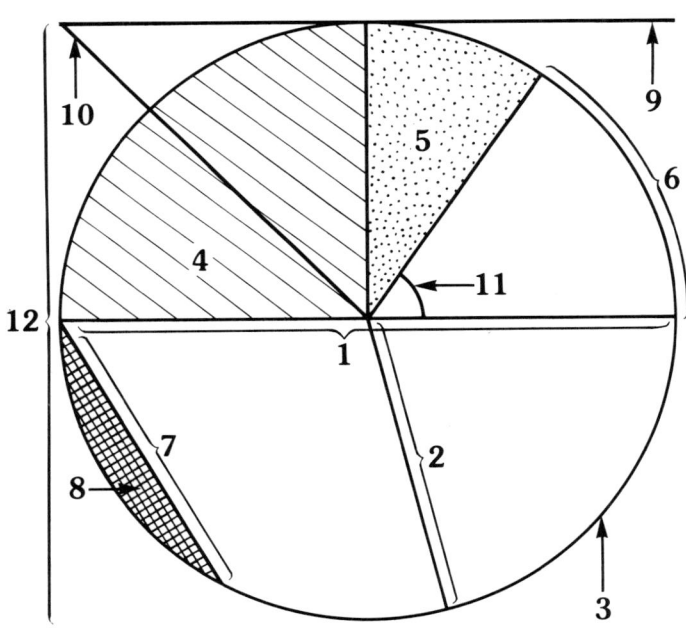

Read below the definitions of the properties of a circle and then complete the table overleaf with the appropriate definition.

Circle A curve through points which are all an equal distance from the centre; a perfectly round plane figure

Circumference The boundary-line of a circle and the total length of its perimeter

Diameter A straight line passing directly through the centre of a circle

Chord A straight line joining any two points on the circumference of the circle but which does not pass through the centre

Segment The area within the circle that is cut off by the chord

Radius	A straight line from the centre of a circle to its circumference
Arc	Any part of the circumference
Radian	An angle at the centre of a circle formed by an arc equal in length to the radius
Sector	The area of a circle between two radii
Quadrant	A sector formed by two radii at right angles to each other
Tangent	A line outside the circle touching the circle at one point but not intersecting it. The tangent to a circle is perpendicular to a radius at the point of contact and produces a right angle
Secant	A straight line from the centre of a circle through one end of an arc to the tangent from the other end

1		7	
2		8	
3		9	
4		10	
5		11	
6		12	

Convection

Current is a word we give to the movement of water and convection the word we give to the passage of heat through a liquid or gas by means of currents. We can illustrate convection currents by means of a simple experiment with potassium permanganate ($KMnO_4$) which, when added to water, turns it pink. Describe the experiment by referring to the diagrams below.

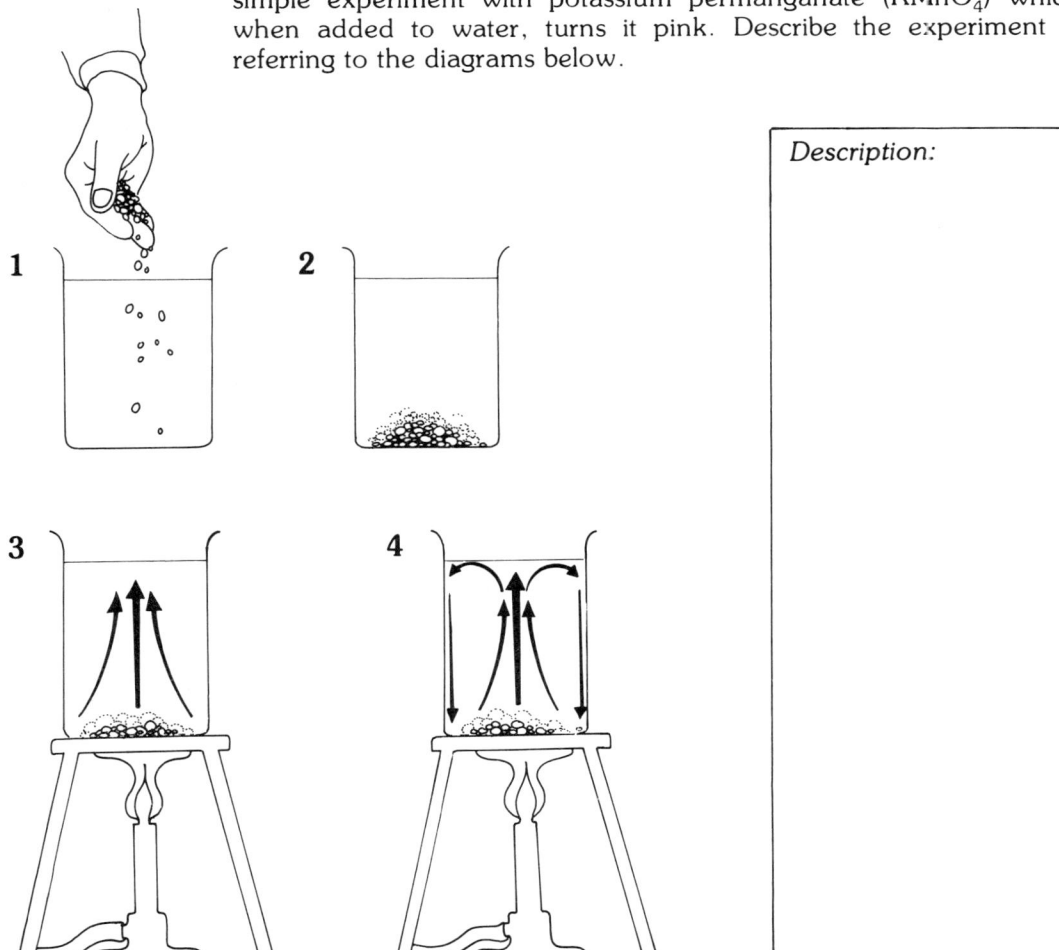

Description:

The Spectrum

Read the passage below and insert the correct alternative in the space provided.

Sir Isaac Newton, in 1672, was the first to use a triangular prism to **1** ____ that white light could be split up to give a spectrum of colours. He placed a prism in the path of a narrow beam of sunlight which was **2** ____ into a dark room through a small hole in a window shutter. On the other side of the prism he placed a screen on which he was able to observe a band of colours **3** ____ the colours of the rainbow, in the same **4** ____ in which they occurred in the rainbow. This band of colours is called a spectrum and comprises seven colours—red, orange, yellow, green, blue, indigo, and violet. Newton, however, was at first uncertain whether the prism lent the colour to the light or whether it separated colours that were **5** ____ in the light, so he performed a further experiment. He made a small slit in the screen on which the spectrum was projected, allowing a beam of a certain colour to pass through it. Then a second prism was placed in the path of the beam which **6** ____ no colour change when it was deviated. By this Newton ascertained that sunlight was a mixture of various colours, which were separated by the prism. His theory was **7** ____ by yet another experiment in which he placed a second prism behind the first, which had already **8** ____ the light into its **9** ____ colours. The second prism was placed in an exactly reversed position which, by deviating the coloured rays to unequal extents in the reverse direction, brought them into the same path so that a ray of white light **10** ____ .

1	A	reveal	B	survey	C	allow	D	concentrate
2	A	infiltrated	B	dilated	C	migrated	D	admitted
3	A	supplanting	B	matching	C	reverting	D	keeping
4	A	sequence	B	mobility	C	design	D	event
5	A	estimated	B	included	C	evolved	D	inherent
6	A	underwent	B	processed	C	exposed	D	neglected
7	A	verified	B	disproved	C	operated	D	calculated
8	A	advanced	B	moved	C	dispersed	D	attracted
9	A	arranged	B	component	C	following	D	peripatetic
10	A	equalised	B	emerged	C	culminated	D	perceived

Garden Implements

Read below the definitions of garden implements and then complete the table overleaf with the appropriate definition.

Dibber	A small wooden stick fitted with a horizontal bar and having a pointed end used for making holes in the soil for planting seeds
Secateurs	A pair of pruning clippers or shears with curved blades, usually held in one hand when used for trimming plants
Trowel	A short-handled flat or scoop-shaped tool often used for lifting plants
Shovel	A scooping and digging tool with a long handle and a broad, slightly curved steel blade
Spade	A tool with a long handle and a very sharp, straight-edged cutting blade, usually flat and rectangular, used for digging holes and cutting turf
Draw hoe	A tool with a long handle and a sharp metal blade set at right angles to it. It has a chopping action and is used for breaking up the surface-soil and for cutting weeds
Shears	A clipping instrument with two pivoted blades meeting as in a pair of scissors. Its long handles are held in both hands when trimming hedges
Rake	An implement consisting of a pole with a metal crossbar toothed like a comb at the end. It is used for drawing grass or hay or for smoothing loose earth
Dutch hoe	An implement with a sharp blade set on a U-shaped base in the same plane as its handle. Its sliding motion dislodges small weeds.
Fork	A fork is used for digging and breaking up lumps of soil. It consists of a long pole at the end of which are a number of long metal prongs

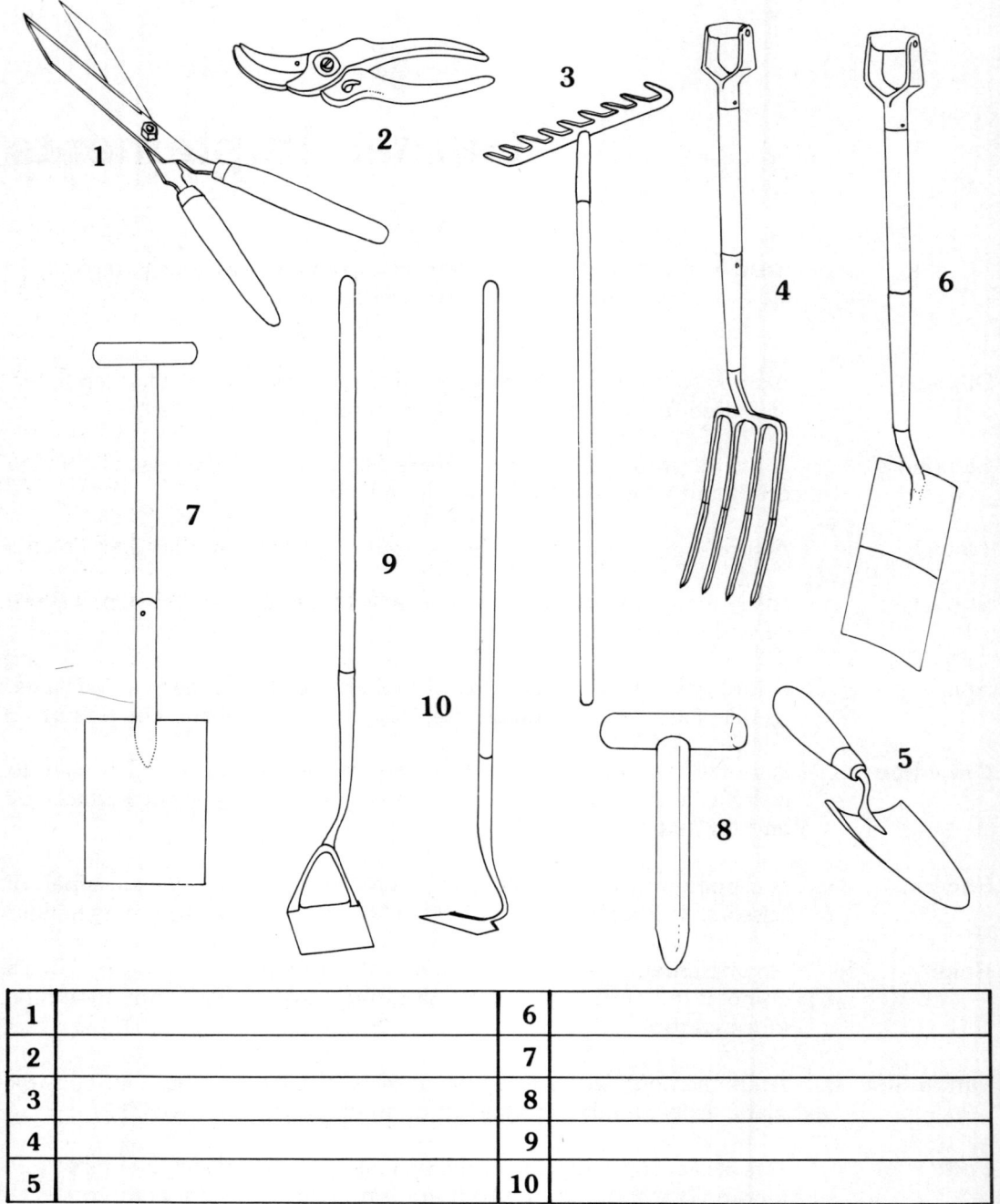

1		6	
2		7	
3		8	
4		9	
5		10	

Experiment to Demonstrate the Percentage of Oxygen in the Air

Up to the middle of the 18th century, air was thought to be a simple elementary substance of which all other gases were modifications, but it is now known that air is a mixture of gases consisting of approximately 4 volumes of nitrogen to 1 of oxygen, with small quantities of carbon dioxide, water vapour, and other gases. We know that oxygen is important not only for respiration in animals and plants but also for supporting combustion, that is, substances need oxygen to burn, and without its presence combustion cannot take place. We can prove that air is composed of about one-fifth of oxygen by a simple experiment.

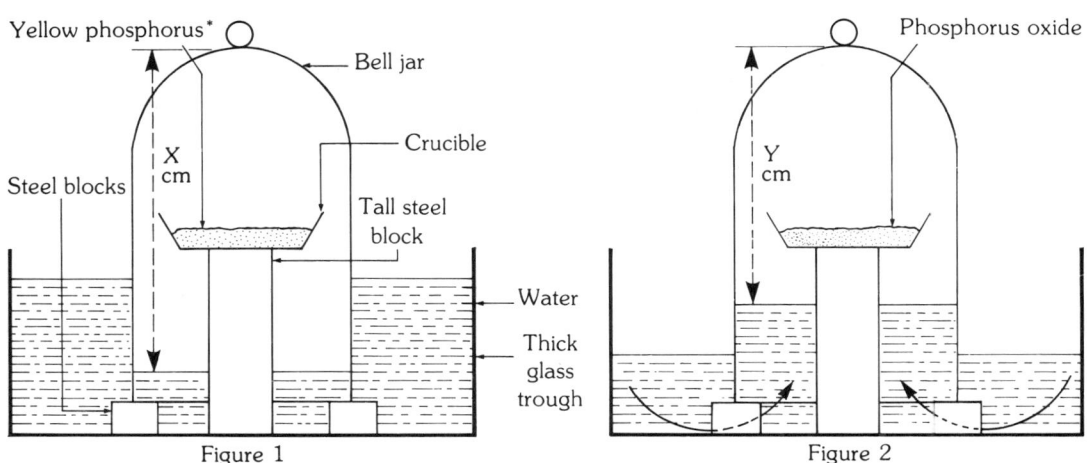

Figure 1

Figure 2

*Phosphorus is dangerous because it burns the skin. Contact with the skin must be avoided.

Describe the experiment by referring to the diagrams above.

The Gemini Twin

Read the passage below and then write a factual account of the Gemini Twin Travelling Clock-Radio, disregarding any advertising jargon.

Begin the day the Gemini way! Yes, you can begin the day the space-age way with our wonder device, the Gemini Twin Travelling Clock-Radio. Just imagine being able to wake up in the morning at any time you want to, anywhere you choose to be, to the sound of your favourite music or radio programme. You can with Gemini. Thanks to our fully battery-operated radio, you can take your Gemini anywhere and you can set the programme the night before so that when you wake up with the firm, yet gentle buzzer, your day will begin just the way it should.

Gemini is the alarm clock of tomorrow, a combined clock and radio. Thanks to its heart, a tiny chip of quartz, which beats more than 4 million times every second, it is accurate to within 60 seconds a year and with its luminous hands and markers, can be read even in the dark. The radio has both AM and FM bands and with its fold-away aerial you can pick up VHF transmissions. Yet in spite of all this, the Gemini is very small and light—it weighs only 500 g even with its simulated leather case, and measures only 18 cm in length, 4 cm in depth and is a mere 8 cm wide. It can easily fit into your briefcase, handbag or pocket. Can you ask for more? Yes! For just over £20, including postage and packing, you can be the proud owner of this remarkable little gadget. Fill in the coupon now and within four weeks it will be yours. If you are not absolutely delighted with Gemini, you can return it and we will refund you in full, with no questions asked.

How to Make an Omelette

Look at the diagrams and write a set of instructions on how to make an omelette. Use the following list to help you: basin; whisk; eggs; salt; pepper; butter; frying-pan; fork; plate.

Friction—Part 1

Put the missing word in each line in the space provided and indicate the place in the line from which it is missing by using the symbol /.

1 _____ Whenever one surface moves over another, a force set up which
2 _____ resists the movement. We call force friction and it always
3 _____ acts such a direction so as to oppose the motion. Friction
4 _____ be found in every machine, where it is responsible for reducing
5 _____ efficiency; it arises because surface is completely smooth
6 _____ and the roughness one surface catches on that of the other.
7 _____ The use of lubricants the machine bearings can lessen the
8 _____ friction when the lubricant, grease or blacklead, forms a
9 _____ film on each surface keeping roughness apart from that of the
10 _____ other surface to some degree, it is not possible to completely
11 _____ remove it. In general, the force opposes the motion is slightly
12 _____ greater one surface starts to move over another than after the
13 _____ movement started; this is why it requires a greater force to
14 _____ start a body moving than keep it in motion. Friction always
15 _____ acts in such a direction as to oppose the force tending
16 _____ produce the motion, adjusting so that it is equal to the force
17 _____ producing the motion. To this point it is called static friction.
18 _____ The point is reached beyond which friction cannot increase and the
19 _____ force tending to produce the motion exceeds, motion begins. Once
20 _____ motion has begun, the sliding friction is than the static friction and
21 _____ independent the surface area of contact, although it is proportional

22	_____	to the reaction between the two surfaces. If double the mass carried
23	_____	on one surface, for example, we shall double sliding friction;
24	_____	if we halve mass, sliding friction is also halved. It is possible
25	_____	to lessen the effects friction by using a simple device; it is
26	_____	commonly known that it is much to move a heavy object if
27	_____	it is mounted on wheels rollers because in such bearings
28	_____	the surfaces do not slide but roll one another, and rolling
29	_____	friction is considerably less sliding friction. It can be
30	_____	seen, therefore, that engineers fully understand the laws of
31	_____	friction. Although it often causes effort to wasted, friction plays a
32	_____	useful part our physical world, because without it, any body standing
33	_____	on a slope slide down because there would be nothing to counteract
34	_____	its motion, and without a force exerted the direction necessary
35	_____	stopping the motion of wheels, brakes could not operate.

How to Grow a Potato Plant

Look at the diagrams below and explain simply how to grow a potato plant.

You Will Need:

one or more potatoes with large eyes
one or more jam jars
bag of potting compost
cocktail sticks
plant pot(s)
wooden stake(s)
sharp knife

Parts of a Bicycle

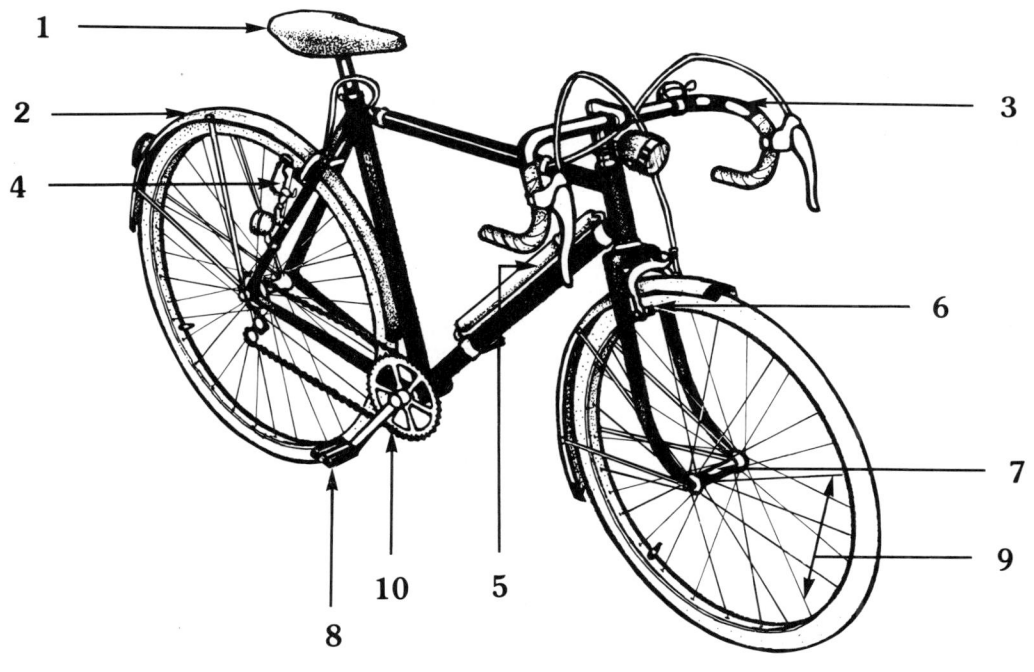

Read below the definitions of parts of a bicycle and then complete the table overleaf with the appropriate definition.

Dynamo	A device which converts mechanical energy into electric energy
Mudguard	A hood covering the wheels of a cycle to protect the rider from being soiled by mud
Saddle	A rider's seat, either on a horse or on a vehicle
Brake-block	A rubber pad pulled into contact with the rim of a wheel, checking its motion

Pedals	Foot levers in a machine		
Hub	The central part of a wheel rotating on an axle and from which spokes radiate		
Pump	A cylindrical device which is used to raise water or inflate tyres by moving a rod up and down		
Spokes	Bars radiating from the hub of a wheel to its rim		
Chain-wheel	A circular disc with pointed teeth which fit into holes in a chain along its edge		
Handlebar	A steering bar on a bicycle with a handle at each end which the cyclist grips		

1		6	
2		7	
3		8	
4		9	
5		10	

Exterior Parts of a House

Read below the definitions of exterior parts of a house and then complete the table overleaf with the appropriate definition.

Gable	The triangular portion of a wall between the enclosing ends of a sloping roof
Facia board	A board or plate covering the ends of roof rafters
Dormer	A small window with a gable, projecting from a sloping roof
Eaves	The lower part of a roof projecting beyond the face of the wall

Downpipe	A vertical tube made of plastic or metal which conveys water from the gutters of a roof to a drain
Patio	A concrete or slabbed area at the rear of a house used for sitting out
Lintel	A horizontal timber or stone member that spans an opening over a door or window
Ridge	The apex of a sloping roof running from end to end
Flaunching	A concrete bed for pots on the top of a chimney
Sill	Shelf of stone, metal, tiles, or wood at the foot of a door or window
Pointing	The final mortar laid between a course of bricks
Flashing	Thin strips of metal inserted into brickwork over the tops of windows or around chimneys to prevent the entry of water
Air brick	An open brick inserted into the wall of a house to permit currents of air to circulate and prevent the growth of fungus
Gutter	A horizontal, shallow trough of plastic or metal which collects water from a roof surface and prevents it from entering the house at the eaves
Verge	The terminating edge of a roof at a gable end

1		9	
2		10	
3		11	
4		12	
5		13	
6		14	
7		15	
8			

Dolphins

Put the missing word in each line in the space provided and indicate the place in the line from which it is missing by using the symbol /.

1 an   The dolphin, or short-toothed whale, is / aquatic mammal which
2 of   belongs to the order / Cetacea, as do porpoises and large whales.
3 from   All members of the order, the dolphin surfaces / time to time
4 are   to take in air. There / two main types of dolphin—the marine
5 first   dolphin and the freshwater or riverine dolphin; the / are found
6 but   in all warm and temperate seas, / the latter are restricted to rivers,
7 other   estuaries, and lakes. A few species inhabit / types of environment.
8 between   There are a few differences / marine and riverine dolphins—marine
9 in   dolphins are gregarious and enjoy living / groups, whilst the long-
10 more   nosed riverine dolphins are found in groups of / than a dozen.
11 and   Marine dolphins have conical teeth, a standard dorsal fin / fused
12 both   neck-bones, whilst the riverine dolphins are provided with / conical
13 a   and molar teeth and separate neck-bones. They also have / low
14 most   dorsal fin. The largest and / beautiful dolphin of all, with its
15 the   dramatic black and white markings, is the voracious killer whale, /
16 in   male reaching up to 9 metres / length; it is the only dolphin
17 on   species to feed / warm-blooded aquatic mammals. There is, however,
18 and   no evidence that it kills human beings. It is docile / amenable
19 on   to training when in captivity. Other dolphins feed / squid and fish.
20 been   Marine dolphins have / loved and feared by all people connected
21 from   with the sea / the earliest times and have been prominent in legend, folk-

17

22. on — lore, and art. They have been represented coins, and the heir to
23. but — the French throne not only had the dolphin in his coat of arms
24. and — was called Le Dauphin after it. However, sailors fishermen
25. be — have killed the dolphin where they consider it to a threat to
26. were — their livelihood, and off the coast of Japan, thousands killed
27. be — every year. Dolphins are considered to highly intelligent; in fact,
28. more — they are thought to be much intelligent than a dog. They have
29. in — been taught not only a number of tricks which they perform zoos
30. yet — and aquaria they have also been used in a variety of scientific
31. by — experiments, replacing human divers. They communicate producing
32. through — high-pitched vocal sounds and 'see' a system of echo-location.
33. for — The Atlantic bottle-nosed dolphin, example, is sensitive to sounds
34. very — of high frequency—up 120 kHz. This system of echo-location
35. is — particularly useful to the Ganges dolphin of India which is blind
36. by — and finds its food poking in mud with its beak. The species is also
37. in — unusual that it swims on its side. In both physiology and behaviour
38. of — the dolphin resembles us very much: it is fond company,
39. to — enjoys play and is very affectionate, especially its young. It
40. a — can convey its emotions vocally and can emit wide variety of
41. to — high-pitched noises which appear be specific for each animal.
42. than — Males are larger females and the young, born after a gestation
43. natural — period of one year and 16 months, are nursed underwater by their
44. on — mothers for up to two years, depending the species. Some dolphins
45. as — live for between 20 and 25 years, and others can live long as 50.

18

QUESTION

Decide whether the following statements are true or false according to the passage, then complete the table.

		True	False
1	The killer whale eats men.		✓
2	Marine dolphins enjoy being with other dolphins.	✓	
3	The riverine dolphin feeds on aquatic mammals.		✓
4	The bottle-nosed dolphin cannot see.		✓
5	Marine dolphins have molar teeth.		✓
6	Riverine dolphins have fused neck-bones.		✓
7	All riverine dolphins swim on their sides.		✓
8	Each dolphin appears to have its own special voice.	✓	
9	Dolphins carry their young for at least a year.		✓
10	Baby dolphins are independent of their parents after being born.		✓

Victorian Jewellery

Read the passage below and insert the correct alternative in the space provided.

The dominant flavour of the Victorian **1** _____ was bourgeois and their jewellery was no exception. The Victorians were **2** _____ fond of jewellery and wore it a great deal, but most of the finest examples, being of precious metals, have long since disappeared. What remains has a charm of its own and is today highly popular among collectors, although it is made of relatively inexpensive materials, such as coral, ivory, jet (a deep black, polishable stone), paste (a glass containing a proportion of lead oxide which could be cut to **3** _____ real gems), and pinchbeck (an alloy of copper and zinc which looked like gold). Enamelled ware was popular with the Victorians and, following the Queen's love of her estate at Balmoral in Scotland, there was a **4** _____ for cairngorms, natural crystals found in the Scottish Highlands and fashioned into buckles and brooches, set in silver. The Victorians were a very sentimental people as can be seen in their art and exemplified in the novels of Dickens; and this is **5** _____ in their jewellery, which is largely of a memorial and sentimental character. Most Victorian women were in mourning for a large part of their lives, and in the early part of the Queen's reign jet was used **6** _____ in the form of earrings, necklaces, brooches and bracelets, all rather large and heavy. Later, jet was to be **7** _____ by amber and plain gold. Jewellery was also made out of the hair of the beloved or the mourned one. In addition, lockets, with a miniature of the loved one (inferior in **8** _____ to the miniatures of the 18th century) on the one side and his hair under a glass panel on the other side were popular, as was shell jewellery, especially in the form of cameos. Functional jewellery in the form of bracelets, stick pins, buckles, rings, scarf-pins and combs was widespread. Other favoured **9** _____ were Indian and Egyptian, following the colonisation of India and the archaeological discoveries in Egypt, respectively. There are still countless pieces of enamel jewellery available that reflects a great deal of artistry and design without being expensive. To **10** _____ Victoria's fiftieth anniversary as Queen a special type of enamel, particularly bright and translucent, was created and is remarkable for its beauty and delicacy of workmanship.

1	A	century	B	epoch	
	C	time	D	decade	
2	A	excessively	B	so	
	C	partially	D	almost	
3	A	imitate	B	appear to	
	C	repeat	D	deviate	
4	A	anger	B	rage	
	C	delight	D	interest	
5	A	for example	B	referred to	
	C	written	D	reflected	
6	A	only	B	completely	
	C	widely	D	many	
7	A	taken in	B	extended	
	C	taken up	D	replaced	
8	A	workmanship	B	working	
	C	building	D	function	
9	A	variations	B	plans	
	C	motifs	D	ideas	
10	A	report	B	depict	
	C	celebrate	D	register	

21

Disposable Ballpoint Pen

Study the diagram below and write a paragraph on the following:
(a) outline the background to the development of the ballpoint pen from its first invention, expanding the information which is given in note form;
(b) describe the appearance of the disposable ballpoint;
(c) describe how the ballpoint works from the diagram given.

Background

1888   John Loud (an American) invented the first ballpoint pen. A clumsy model. Had ballbearing at end of tube—used for marking leather and fabrics. Patent allowed to expire.

1938   Two brothers, László and Georg Biró (Hungarian nationals)— László a painter, sculptor and journalist and Georg a chemist—patented a ballpoint pen more workable than previous models.

1939   World War Two breaks out— Biró brothers move to Argentina and license their invention to many countries. Now ballpoint widely used in Britain.

1942   The U.S. Army Quartermaster commissions a pen that will not leak in high-flying aircraft. Ballpoint pen recommended. Since then, pen has become cheaper and disposable type very popular with students as no refill required.

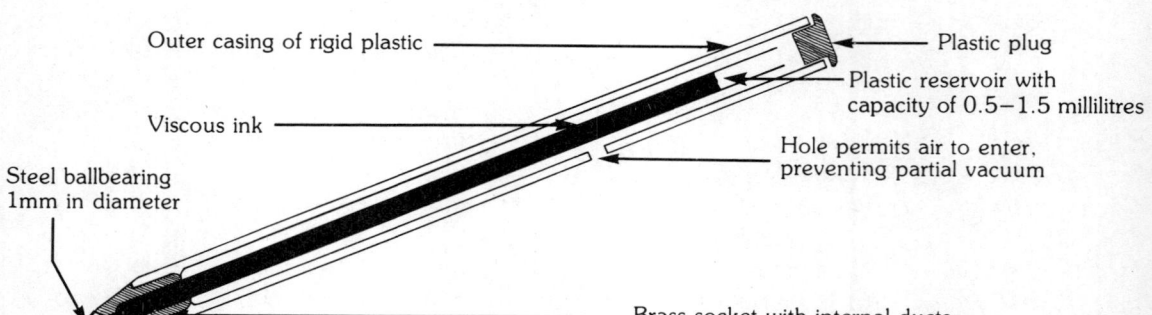

Sedimentology

Read the passage below and insert the correct alternative shown overleaf in the space provided.

Sand is a collection of particles of rock, **1** _____ feldspar and quartz, that are formed as a result of natural erosion of rocks by winds, extremes of temperature, glaciers, and moving water. Sand grains have been **2** _____ throughout the Earth's history to cover vast areas of the planet, forming deserts. It is possible to grade sand according to the particular size of the grain into fine, medium, coarse, and very coarse grains: fine-grained sand has particles 0.125–0.25 mm in diameter; medium-grained sand has particles with a diameter of between 0.25 and 0.5 mm; coarse sand has grains with a diameter of between 0.5 and 1.0 mm, while very coarse sand has grains of 1–2 mm diameter. When sand grains are carried by the wind, they **3** _____ with each other, becoming scratched in the process. The resulting surface grooves can be **4** _____ under an electron microscope. The microscopic evidence makes it possible to trace the characteristics of winds, **5** _____ from those of today back to those of the distant past, because the grains of sand lying in desert regions have been lying there for millions of years. Some sedimentologists in the United States have recently made detailed studies of the grooves on the surface of the grains: they created artificial sand by crushing natural rock, then rotated it so that the grains abraded each other as they would have done naturally, under a variety of wind speeds. The scientists **6** _____ that there was a relationship between the speed of the wind and the spacing between the grooves on the sand particles: when the wind speeds were low, the grooves were closer together; and when they were high, they were wider apart. The groove patterns could be changed fairly rapidly as soon as the wind conditions altered, the most recent wind speed always being the final one to be recorded. If sand is **7** _____ from a known prehistoric site, it is possible to **8** _____ wind conditions of the time, since the sand will not have been **9** _____ to winds of a later period. For example, sand obtained from such sites in Britain known to have suffered a hot, dry climate has **10** _____ wind speeds of about 60 m.p.h., which is higher than wind speeds in similar desert environments today.

1	A	likely	B	besides	
	C	chiefly	D	most	
2	A	made	B	growing	
	C	deposited	D	formed	
3	A	meet	B	collide	
	C	clash	D	bump	
4	A	maintained	B	observed	
	C	regarded	D	illuminated	
5	A	extending	B	bending	
	C	reversing	D	returning	
6	A	accounted	B	deduced	
	C	invented	D	collected	
7	A	allowed	B	undermined	
	C	dissected	D	excavated	
8	A	imagine	B	gather	
	C	determine	D	consider	
9	A	subjected	B	responsible	
	C	situated	D	defined	
10	A	signalled	B	allowed	
	C	indicated	D	provided	

Experiment to Show How Clouds Form

Read the passage below and then study the diagrams. Now write a short description of an experiment to show how clouds are formed.

Clouds are formed when the Sun causes water on the surface of the Earth to evaporate into water vapour. When the vapour meets a body of cold air it condenses to form millions of droplets which are suspended in the atmosphere and fall as rain when they become larger and so heavier. We can illustrate this by a simple experiment.

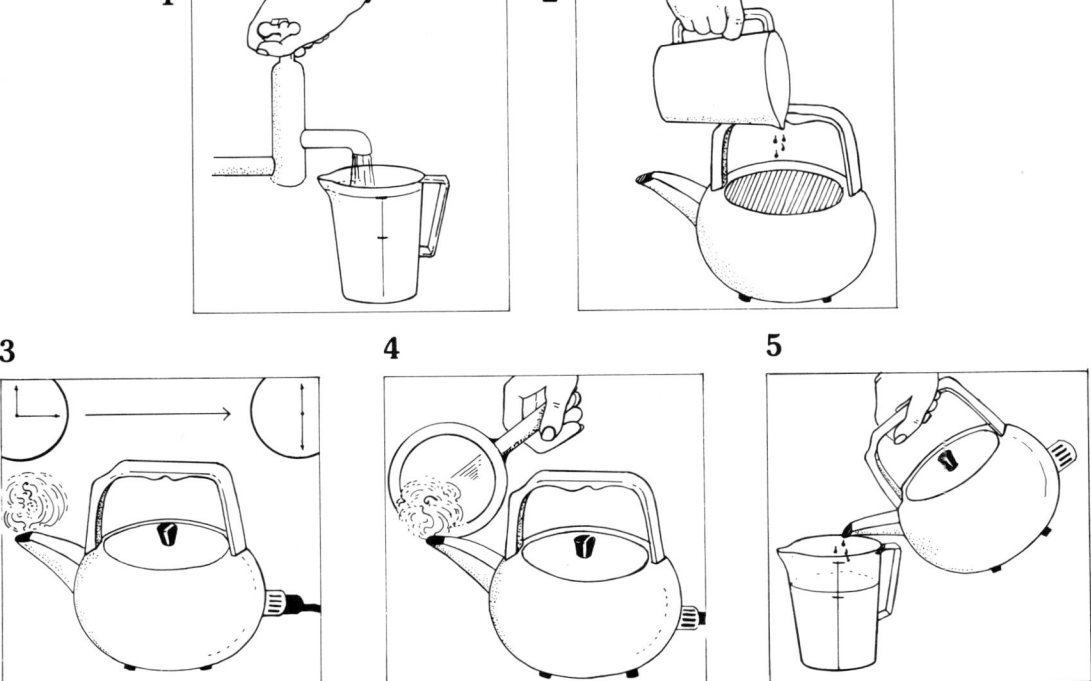

Camels

Put the missing word in each line in the space provided and indicate the place in the line from which it is missing by using the symbol /.

1 _____ The camel is a hoofed mammal belonging the class of ruminants but
2 _____ differs other members of the group in the way it chews its cud
3 _____ and by the fact that it has a third incisor tooth its upper jaw.
4 _____ It also has three stomachs. Most ruminants usually chew a short time
5 _____ on one side of the mouth before switching the other side, but camels sh
6 _____ the cud continuously their lower jaw makes a wide sweep across its
7 _____ upper teeth and then again. It also differs from other quadrupeds in
8 _____ the way it moves the two legs of one side simultaneously of alternately.
9 _____ Its red blood cells resemble those of other mammals in that they have
10 _____ nuclei but also, these are oval instead of round. Camels once populated
11 _____ the land masses of the world with the exception of Australia, they were
12 _____ introduced there in 1860. The earliest camels, which appeared North
13 _____ America the Eocine period, 40 million years ago, were much smaller
14 _____ than the camels of today, but 10 million years ago they had become
15 _____ gigantic in stature. About one million years, camels spread westwards
16 _____ into South America, Asia, and Europe, and southwards into Africa, the
17 _____ then disappeared everywhere in central Asia and the hotlands of
18 _____ the Arabian peninsula. The llama, alpaca, guanaco, and vicuña all
19 _____ close relatives of the camel with the latter two—found the Andes—
20 _____ the ones as yet to remain undomesticated. The only camels existing
21 _____ today are two domesticated species, descendants of the camels

22	_____	ancient Babylon, one thousand years Christ: the bactrian camel of
23	_____	central Asia, of which there are still wild herds roaming the Gobi
24	_____	desert, and the dromedary or Arabian camel. Types are characterised
25	_____	by elongated necks, small ears and long legs, their feet evenly divided
26	_____	two toes connected by a thick membrane. Their feet have padded
27	_____	leathery soles but they do have a horned hoof. On their chests, ankles
28	_____	and knees camels have a pad hard skin which cushions them when they
29	_____	lie down and variety has a cleft upper lip with both canine and incisor
30	_____	teeth in the upper jaw. The camel has no gall bladder. Varieties of camel
31	_____	are of great economic value their owners, providing milk, meat, leather
32	_____	and wool which is very warm yet light to wear. Camel dung the only fuel
33	_____	readily available in the desert. The bactrian camel, which native to all
34	_____	parts central Asia, is stronger and more sturdy than its Arabian counter-
35	_____	part, short legs which help it climb in difficult mountain terrain and
36	_____	a long, shaggy coat which is windproof and waterproof. It has humps
37	_____	of fatty tissue, one situated on its shoulders and the over its hind-
38	_____	quarters. Excluding its hump, the bactrian camel just under two metres
39	_____	in height. The dromedary is taller the bactrian camel and has a single
40	_____	hump which acts, like of the bactrian camel, as a food reserve. They store
41	_____	fat in their humps, and their metabolism is that they can conserve water.
42	_____	Contrary to public opinion, camels do store water in their humps. When
43	_____	camels are in good condition, the hump, which has bony substructure,
44	_____	is firm and large, but when the animal is debilitated, it becomes flabby
45	_____	loose. There are two varieties of dromedary—the heavier beast burden
46	_____	is capable of carrying a load of 181.5 kg for an average of 40 km day;
47	_____	and the racing camel, slighter build, which can travel up to 100 km
48	_____	in a single day. Arabian camels feed mostly grain which they
49	_____	supplement eating green vegetation. They are ideally suited to desert
50	_____	conditions with their broad feet which do sink into the sand and their

51 _____ nostrils which they can close completely—the hairs filtering the air
52 _____ during a sandstorm. The camel's eyes have a double row interlocking
53 _____ lashes which provide additional protection the sand. Camels are
54 _____ able to withstand extremes of temperature and can for long periods
55 _____ without food or water. They drink, they can take in up to 68 litres.

QUESTION

Decide whether the following statements are true or false according to the passage and then complete the table.

	True	False
1 All ruminants chew their food in exactly the same way.		
2 Camels do not have hoofed feet.		
3 There are two types of Asian camel.		
4 Every camel in the world today is domesticated.		
5 The Arabian camel is taller than the Asian camel.		
6 The camel has a history of more than 40 million years.		
7 The camel moves like all other quadrupeds.		
8 The camel has teeth like all other ruminants.		
9 The earliest camels were gigantic in size.		
10 In the distant past, there were camels on every continent.		

Levers

1

A lever is a very important and *ancient* mechanism, which makes it possible to move a *load* by means of a smaller effort. It is a very simple machine whose invention was of as great an *importance* to primitive societies as the wheel, and without a knowledge of its use the magnificent pyramids of the Nile valley and the Bronze Age monuments at Stonehenge in southern Britain could never have been *constructed*. Basically, the lever is a rigid beam pivoted at a fulcrum so that the force applied to it by a man (the effort) may be used at another point along the beam to shift a load placed on it. Levers can be divided into three groups according to the relative positions of the load (L), the effort (E), and the fulcrum (F), which is *the point at which the lever turns*.

Class one lever The fulcrum is somewhere between the load, on one side, and the effort applied to it on the other. Let us write it EFL or LFE.
Class two lever The load is somewhere between the effort, at one end of the lever, and the fulcrum at the other. Let us write it ELF.
Class three lever The effort is somewhere between the fulcrum, at one end of the lever, and the load at the other end. Let us write it FEL.

The lever may either be used to *amplify* force, or to amplify *velocity*. The force which a lever applies to a load is increased when the load is nearer to the fulcrum than the effort is, so it is much more *effective* to apply the effort as far away from the fulcrum as possible. The amplification in the effort is called the mechanical advantage and is calculated as the ratio of the load to the effort. Provided that these two forces are parallel, and that the friction at the fulcrum is negligible, this is the same as the ratio of distances along the lever, i.e. the ratio of distance from fulcrum to effort, to distance from fulcrum to load. For example, an effort of 10 newtons applied 1 metre from the fulcrum would *exert* a force of 20 newtons on a load situated 0.5 metres away from the fulcrum. However, if the lever rotates when this effort is applied, the load will move only half as far and at half of the velocity of the effort.

2

The lever principle also amplifies movement. In a simple lever like the see-saw, with the fulcrum at the centre, if one end moves a certain distance, then the other will move the same distance, but if the fulcrum is nearer to one end than the other, the two ends will move different distances, the ratio being the lengths from each end to the fulcrum. A small movement can produce a much larger movement. In a see-saw having a shorter and longer end, the longer end of the see-saw would move farther than the shorter end when a load is applied to the shorter end.

Levers can also amplify velocity: whilst the two ends of a lever may move through different distances, they are, at the same time, travelling at different velocities, the ratio being the same as between the distances travelled. An excellent example of this is the conventional typewriter. The movement of the keys is relatively slow and short but this movement is *converted* into the rapid movement of the typebars, whose ends will travel between eight and ten times the distance moved by the keys.

QUESTION 1

Complete the table below to show the class of lever each drawing represents.

1		6	
2		7	
3		8	
4		9	
5		10	

1 Scissors

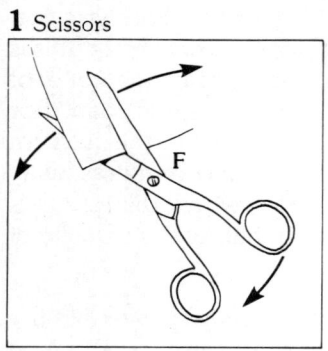

2 Aneroid-barometer pointer

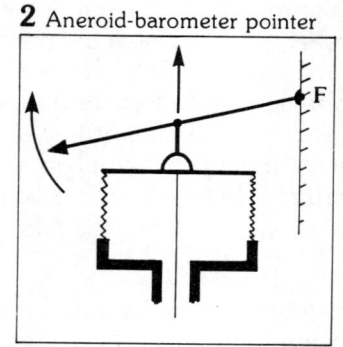

3 Paper punch

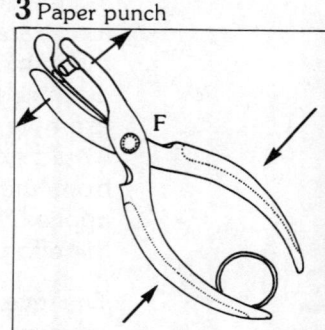

4 Crowbar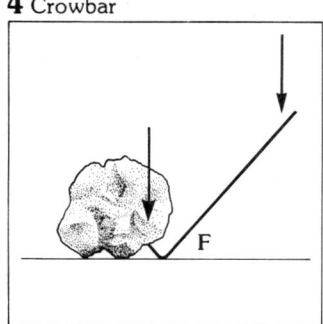

5 Steam safety valve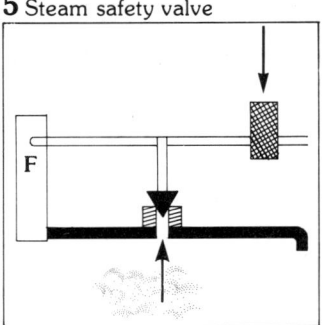

6 Pump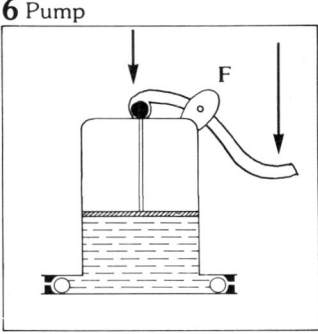

7 Tongs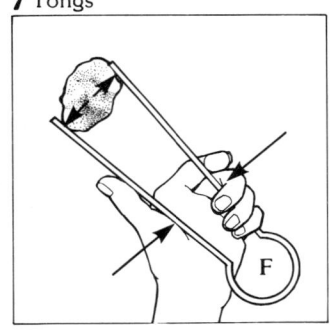

8 Wheel barrow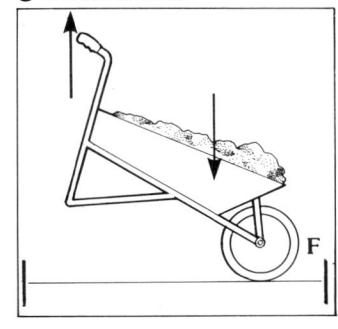

9 Nutcracker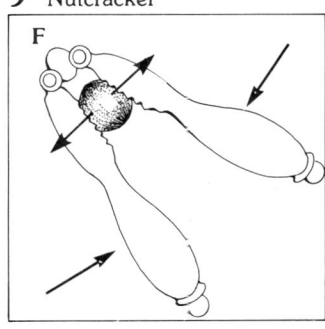

10 Beam balance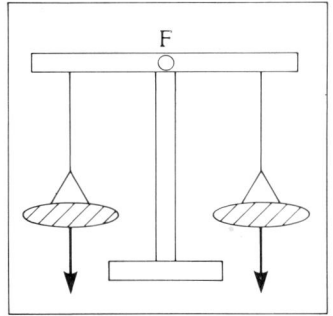

QUESTION 2

In the passage there are ten words and phrases set in italics. Give their correct meaning in sequence from the list of definitions given to you below.

1 ....   6 ....

2 ....   7 ....

3 ....   8 ....

4 ....   9 ....

5 ....   10 ....

machine   productive
expand   weight
apply   balances
rotate   built
old   changed
pivot   designed
speed   significance
hinge

The Arch

Read below the definitions of terms used for an arch and then complete the table with the appropriate definition.

Voussoir	An individual, wedge-shaped block of stone or brick, used to construct an arch or vault
Intrados	The term given to the underside edge of an arch when seen in elevation
Lintel	A beam of wood, stone, brick or reinforced concrete which spans a door or window opening horizontally
Rise	The vertical distance between the springing-line and the highest point in the ceiling or soffit
Bed joints	The mortar joints between the voussoirs
Crown	The highest point of an arch where the keybrick or keystone is placed
Extrados	The outer curve of an arch
Haunch	The name given to the lower part of the arch from the springing-line midway to the crown
Soffit	Another word for the underside of an arch
Span	The distance between the supports of an arch, beam, or roof
Springer or springer-point	Is the lowest unit or voussoir of an arch from where the curve starts
Keystone	The topmost, central stone in an arch, usually placed last
Face joints	The cross joints between voussoirs in arches
Springing-line	The horizontal line drawn through the two springer-points
Striking-point	The centre point of the springing-line from where the voussoirs radiate

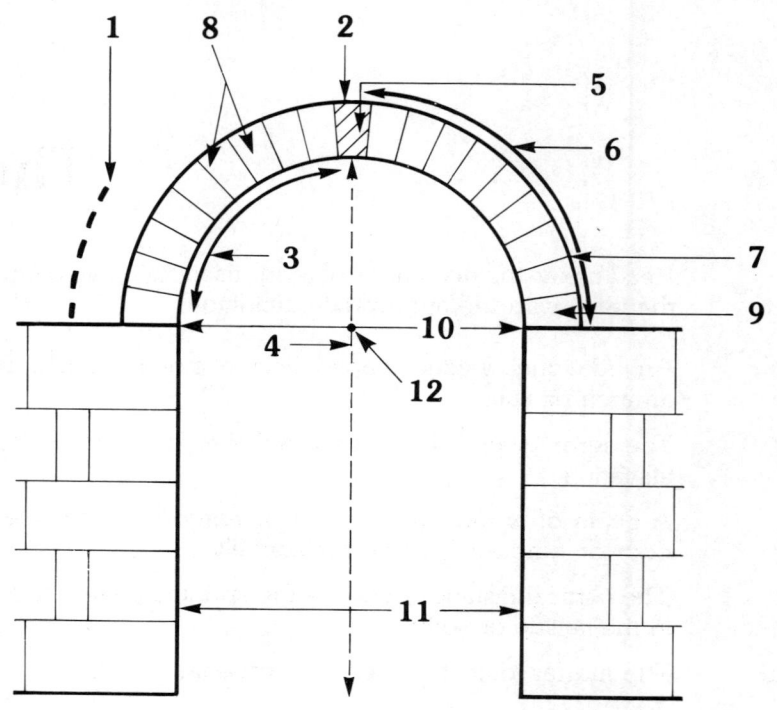

1		7	
2		8	
3		9	
4		10	
5		11	
6		12	

Windows

Read below the definitions of parts of a window and then complete the table with the appropriate definition.

Head	The upper part of the frame of a window
Transom	The horizontal dividing member of the frame of a window
Reveal	The internal or external distance between the plane of a door or window and the face of the wall through which it is cut
Hinge	A movable joint of steel or wrought iron which hangs a door or window on to a side-post or frame allowing it to pivot
Glazing bars	Members which divide a sash horizontally or both vertically and horizontally into smaller panes (lights)
Casement	A window in which the opening lights are hinged at the side and open like a door
Jamb	The vertical member of the outer frame of a window or door
Sill	Shelf of wood or stone at the foot of a window or door
Drip moulding	A projecting moulding over the head of a window or door designed to throw off the rain
Ventlight	A casement window that is hung from the top
Pin plate	A piece of metal with an upright pin screwed to the sill which engages with the hole of a peg stay to keep a casement open
Mullion	A vertical post which divides a window into separate lights
Sash	A frame which holds the glass in the window and may be fixed, pivoted, hinged or sliding
Casement fastener	A metal fastener screwed to the vertical upright (stile) of a sash with a pivoted handle whose projecting point engages in a slotted plate screwed to the frame so that the window can be fastened
Oriel	A bay window projecting from a wall above ground level and supported by projecting blocks of stone (corbels)

Peg stay A metal bar holed at intervals of about 50mm. It is pivoted to a pinplate which is screwed to the inside face of the bottom rail of a casement to keep it open

Fixed sash A glazed sash which does not open

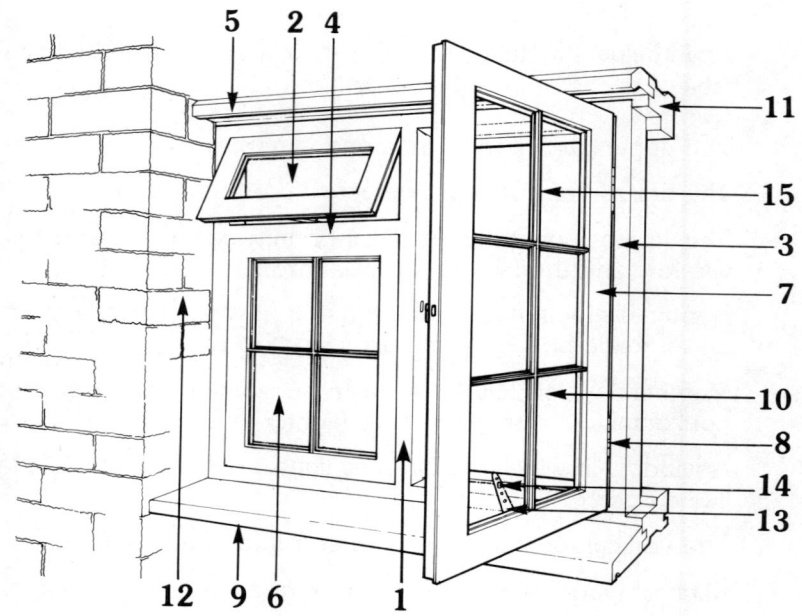

1		9	
2		10	
3		11	
4		12	
5		13	
6		14	
7		15	
8			

Friction—Part 2

Complete the following passages using the appropriate number of words.

When we attempt to slide one body over another we shall see that there is always a certain amount of resistance to the motion. We call this resistance friction, and *its amount depends on the types of surfaces which are in contact with each other* as well as the weight or load which forces them together. *No surface is perfectly smooth, and the rough surface of one body may catch on the other, increasing the friction.* The area of the body makes no difference. An easy way to illustrate this point is to take a block of wood, say 20 cm × 15 cm × 10 cm, with two smooth, long sides and two smooth, short ones, the other sides being left rough. If we place the block on to a smooth planed board and attach a dynamometer to it we shall see that ... (Use between 65–70 words.)

1

We can illustrate that the friction is independent of the area of contact of the sliding surfaces by a further experiment ... (Use between 35–40 words.)

2

If we place another block of wood of similar dimensions on top of the first one, doubling its weight, we would note that the reading on the dynamometer would be twice as high; were we to place two more blocks on top of the first two, we would see that the reading on the dynamometer was four times as high. This illustrates the second law of friction which is ... (Use between 35–40 words.)

3

The Anemometer

An anemometer is an instrument for measuring the strength and direction of the wind as it passes an observation point during a specific period of time. By referring to the diagram below indicate what the most widely used type of anemometer consists of, describe its construction and how it works.

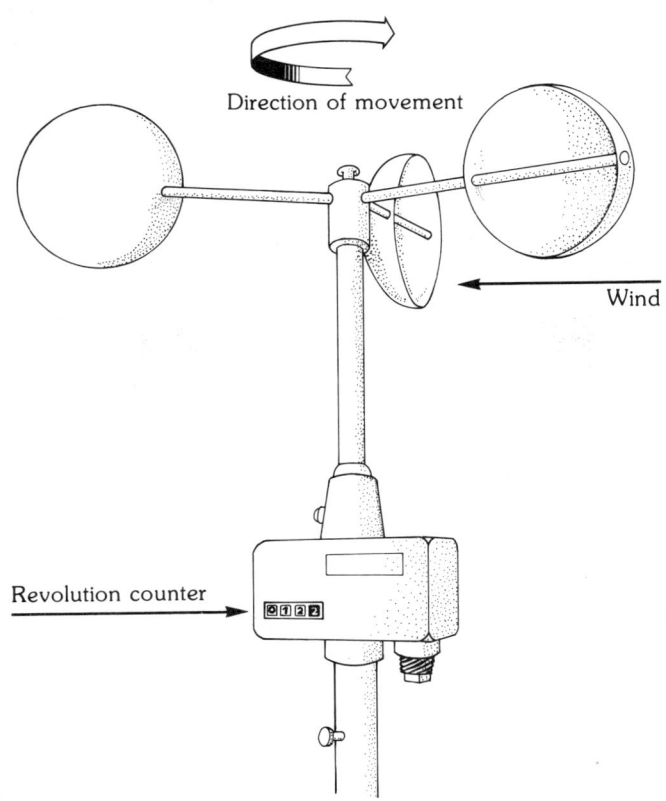

Direction of movement

Wind

Revolution counter

Experiment to Show the Effect of Heat

When heat enters a body, a number of results can follow: the temperature of the body may rise; it may change its state, such as being converted into a liquid or vapour; chemical changes may result; or the body may expand in size. Different bodies can also expand unequally

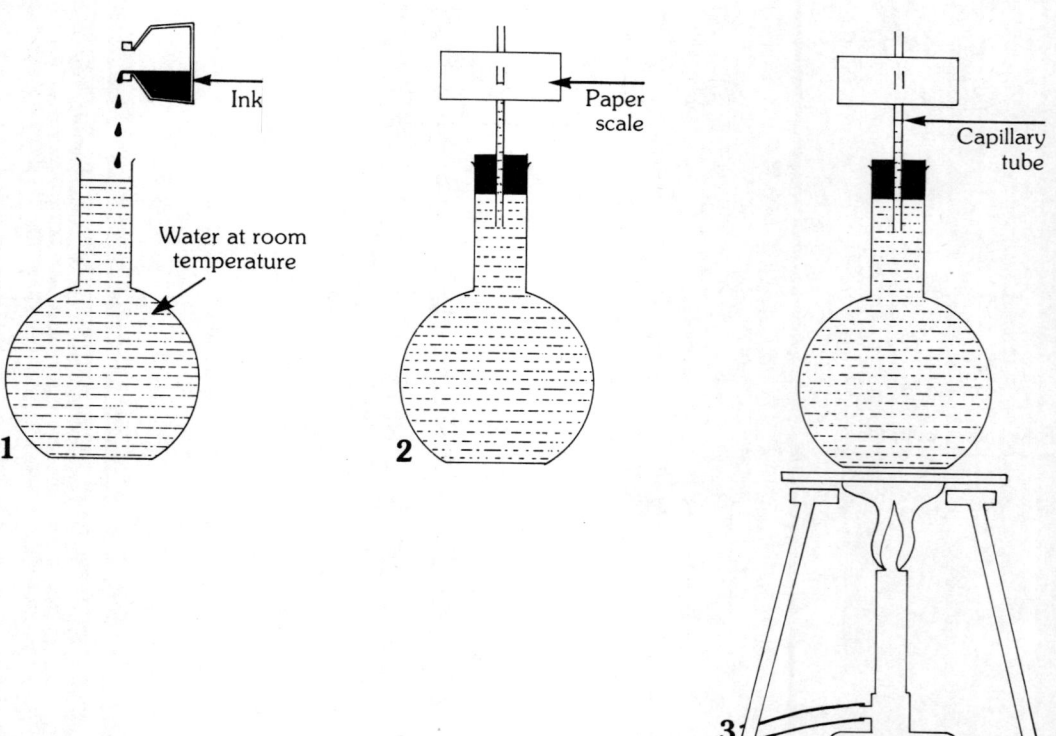

even when equally heated. There is a simple experiment which demonstrates that bodies expand when heated and that they may expand and contract unequally. Describe the experiment by referring to the diagrams 1–6.

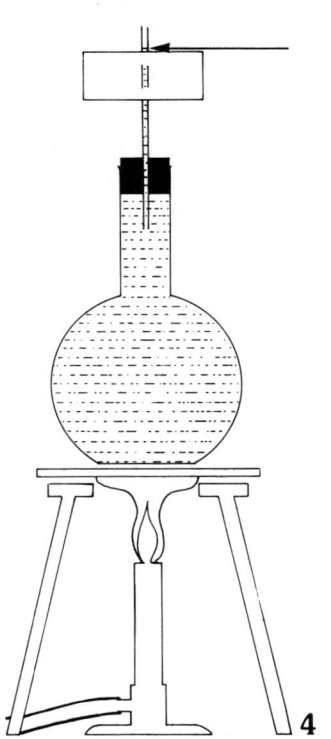

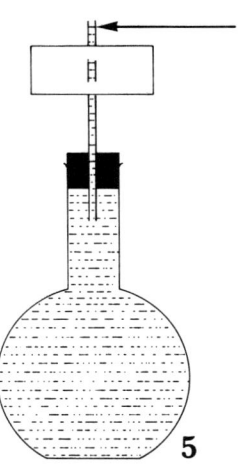

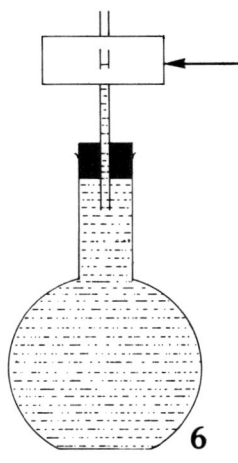

41

Chinese Architecture

1

The Chinese have never been regarded as great architects and have not seen architecture as an art form as we have in the West. They are famous rather for their fine drawing, painting, calligraphy, porcelain, carving and sculpture. It is *seldom* that old or substantial buildings are found in China and only a few pagodas date back beyond the sixteenth century. For over 23 centuries the Chinese people have *restricted* themselves to the same modest designs in their architecture. There are no grandiose palaces or imposing temples in China as there are in western countries and there are several reasons for this. If any fine structures existed they have now *perished* as they were mostly built of wood and in addition, unlike most great nations of antiquity, the Chinese have lacked a hereditary aristocracy or ruling class, a powerful priesthood and a wealthy and vigorous central government. In this respect they were *unique*. In other countries it has been precisely such institutions that have commissioned and encouraged the building of temples, churches and palaces as well as the creation of fine music and sculpture. When compared with the architecture of the West, Chinese buildings seem fragile and delicate, not solid or secure and this is probably because the fear of earthquakes must have been constantly present. Moreover, there was in Chinese architecture no distinction made between public and private building, the rich or the poor, the religious or the secular so there were no great country houses or palaces or temples. There were, furthermore, strict laws controlling the size and scope of domestic buildings depending on a man's rank so most of the people had to be content with homes of modest size, usually of one storey. All buildings, with the possible exception of those in difficult terrain, had to follow two *cardinal* rules—a perfect symmetry of plan and a rigid orientation on a north–south axis. This meant that the buildings were *uniform* in plan with the doorway of every dwelling on the southern side and never at the gable end, with other buildings arranged at right angles to it, irrespective of its size or the rank of its owner. The outer walls of the buildings would be of brick, tiles would cover the roof and the inner walls and columns would be of timber.

2

The basic unit of Chinese architecture is the walled courtyard which, like all Chinese buildings, is entered from a gateway in the centre of the south wall. Facing the gateway at the rear of the courtyard is the principal building, the main hall, which is rectangular in shape and stands with its broad side facing the gateway. It usually stands on a low terrace of masonry with a carved wooden rail at the top and is reached by a short flight of steps placed centrally. Along each side of the courtyard at right angles to the main hall are ranged symmetrically proportioned *subsidiary* buildings, each occupying its own cube of space. Most houses of modest means have two such units, one behind the other, consisting of ancillary rooms on the same axis, the first unit being used for guests and business of a domestic nature, the other for private family quarters. *Further* units can be added if necessary, sometimes being added to left and right but at all times conforming to the same symmetry. Rectangular windows are evenly spaced on either side of square-headed doors which are themselves flanked by wooden pillars. The most important feature of Chinese building is the roof which is concave in section and very steeply pitched, with boldly projecting up-tilting angles and highly ornamented ridges of brightly-coloured, glazed tiles formed in an S-shape and set in mortar. On the upturned angles of the roof there are *grotesque* animals such as fish and dragons in bright colours, and the bamboo frames to the roof are similarly painted. An unusual feature of such roofs is that they do not depend upon the walls for support—the walls have no constructive value at all—but rest upon timber uprights. Unlike the roofs in the West, too, Chinese roofs have no internal triangular supports but consist of a system of rigid rectangular trusses of bamboo. Another unusual feature is that the timber uprights supporting the roof are fitted under it once the roof has been positioned—not the other way round—and are fitted into the roof beam. This gives the pillars the unique characteristic of having no capital. If the courtyard is the basic unit, then the city itself is a composite checkerboard of such units on a much larger scale, each unit being surrounded by a wall and the entire city then being contained within a perimeter wall. Symbolic square-headed gates or entrances are to be found on every south wall and on each axial *intersection*. The main streets run along the cardinal points of the compass, whilst the central thoroughfare runs directly north—south on the main axis.

QUESTION 1

a) Draw a house of one unit as it would look from above, according to the description given in the passage.

b) Draw the main hall as it would look from the front as described in the passage.

QUESTION 2

In the passage there are ten words set in italics. Give their correct meaning in sequence from the list of definitions given to you below.

1 ....   6 ....   mis-shapen   essential
                                         alone   junction
2 ....   7 ....   rare   limited
                                         larger   secondary
3 ....   8 ....   still more   crumbled
                                         died   unvarying
4 ....   9 ....   beautiful

5 ....   10 ....

QUESTION 3

Decide whether the following statements are true or false according to the passage and then complete the table.

	True	False

1 The Chinese are accomplished painters.
2 The walls in Chinese houses support the roof.
3 Chinese houses are entered from the north.
4 The roof has particular importance in Chinese buildings.
5 Architecture is an important art form to the Chinese.
6 The Chinese have had a ruling upper class.
7 The possibility of earthquakes has influenced Chinese building.
8 The Chinese are free to design their homes.
9 The roof in a Chinese house is constructed like a European one.
10 The roof in a Chinese house is put in place before the walls.

The Cuckoo

Put the missing word in each line in the space provided and indicate the place in the line from which it is missing by using the symbol /.

1 _____ The cuckoo is found in most parts the world, being more numerous
2 _____ in tropical countries like Africa and India in temperate climates
3 _____ like Britain and Europe. The tropical varieties are gaudy colour
4 _____ and much larger than the European cuckoo; the Plantain Eaters tropical
5 _____ Africa, example, can be up to 91 cm long with crests on
6 _____ their heads, long tails and brilliant green and blue plumage. Common
7 _____ cuckoo is 31 cm in length and its plumage slate-grey in
8 _____ colour with strongly barred white underparts. Juveniles and females,
9 _____ may be more red-brown in colour. Flight the cuckoo resembles a hawk
10 _____ flying rapidly and low open ground, and can easily be identified by
11 _____ its small head and pointed wings. The cuckoo hunts food in trees
12 _____ and on the ground, very fond of insects and caterpillars. It does
13 _____ not winter in Britain but in Africa and returns here spring when it
14 _____ is a welcome visitor, for we hear those first characteristic notes
15 _____ of the male bird, we know that spring has last arrived. He sings
16 _____ the beginning of July and then flies off to Africa, but the female's
17 _____ song is different and there are fewer females males. The female
18 _____ is rarely loyal to her mate and can be mated to several birds once.
19 _____ Each season she lays one and two dozen eggs, each one in a different
20 _____ nest, working a particular territory and selecting type of host parent,
21 _____ laying the type of egg resembling of the host parent. Having laid

22 _____ her egg, the female cuckoo then leaves it to reared by the host parent,
23 _____ who has no idea of what has happened. The parasitic cuckoo in nest
24 _____ then gets fatter and fatter it becomes so large that the host parent
25 _____ sometimes has to stand its back to feed it. Although it is
26 _____ able to fly three weeks, it remains in the nest where the host parents
27 _____ feed it for a further three to four weeks. The small cuckoo a
28 _____ hollow in its back and manoeuvres the other fledglings in a way that
29 _____ they are balanced its back before being tipped out of the nest to
30 _____ perish on the ground. Leaving the nest, the young cuckoo soon
31 _____ migrates, following the same migration route instinct that its
32 _____ parents followed just two months. Not all cuckoos are parasites,
33 _____ however; the American cuckoo, together some ground cuckoos in
34 _____ India and Australia, build their nests and do not depend upon
35 _____ other birds to bring up their young at tremendous cost.

QUESTION

Decide whether the following statements are true or false according to the passage and then complete the table.

	True	False
1 The cuckoo is more plentiful in Europe than in tropical countries.		
2 European cuckoos are smaller than tropical ones.		
3 The cuckoo remains in Europe during the winter months.		
4 There are more female than male cuckoos.		
5 The male and female cuckoos have identical songs.		
6 The female cuckoo has only one mate.		
7 The baby cuckoo does not accompany its parents.		
8 The baby cuckoo leaves the nest after three weeks.		
9 Not all cuckoos are parasitic.		
10 The common cuckoo begins to sing in July in Britain.		

The Amoebae

Put the missing word in each line in the space provided and indicate the place in the line from which it is missing by using the symbol /.

1	_____	Although complex in structure than viruses and bacteria, the
2	_____	amoeba is one of the simplest animals and belongs the sub-kingdom
3	_____	of Protozoa. It is a unicellular organism, the largest of is
4	_____	just visible to the naked eye and consists naked protoplasm
5	_____	known cytoplasm in which lies a granular nucleus, spherical in shape,
6	_____	which controls normal metabolic processes. The protoplasm surrounded
7	_____	by a relatively rigid outer layer of ectoplasm. The amoeba contains
8	_____	a contractile vacuole pulsating space, which is responsible for
9	_____	pumping out water has entered the animal by osmosis. Amoebae
10	_____	move protruding part of the cytoplasm and then flowing into the
11	_____	protrusion, which is called a pseudopodium. Extending the pseudo-
12	_____	podium in the direction, the amoeba can reverse. It catches food
13	_____	by surrounding organic particles its pseudopodia and absorbing it
14	_____	by any part of its protoplasm; waste matter be disposed of by any part
15	_____	of its protoplasm. A few amoebae reproduce sexually most reproduce
16	_____	asexually by binary or multiple fission when cytoplasm and nucleus
17	_____	divide upon maturity, resulting a transparent or slightly yellow
18	_____	organism. One dissects an amoeba so that one half contains the
19	_____	nucleus, half will continue to live and reproduce in the usual way
20	_____	but the half which consists merely of protoplasm will die soon
21	_____	after. If, a nucleus from another amoeba is placed inside it,

22 _____ it will continue to grow and reproduce normally. The amoeba has
23 _____ legs, no stomach, no intestine and no sense organs; but
24 _____ is capable movement and is sensitive to light, heat and toxic
25 _____ substances. Amoebae can found wherever there is adequate moisture
26 _____ and are often found in stagnant water. General, they are harmless
27 _____ and there are some parasitic forms living the bodies of other
28 _____ animals: Entamoeba, which has contractile vacuole, unlike the
29 _____ amoeba, is an allied genus and lives in human intestine.
30 _____ *Entamoeba coli* is harmless but *Entamoeba histolytica*, rife the
31 _____ tropics, causes amoebic dysentery. Nearly the diseases caused
32 _____ by Protozoa are tropical diseases and include sleeping sickness
33 _____ malaria, spread by the tsetse fly and mosquito, respectively. Amoebic
34 _____ disease, probably spread by bite of sandflies, is dumdum fever or
35 _____ kala-azar, which enlarges the spleen liver and often results in death.

────────────────────────────────────── QUESTION ──────

Decide whether the following statements are true or false according to the passage and then complete the table.

		True	False
1	Amoebae are less complicated in structure than viruses or bacteria.		
2	The majority of amoebae reproduce sexually.		
3	The amoebae have legs.		
4	In general, amoebae are harmless.		
5	Entamoebae have a contractile vacuole.		
6	*Entamoeba histolytica* is common in the tropics.		
7	Kala-azar is often a fatal disease.		
8	*Entamoebae coli* live in the human body.		
9	All amoebae are parasitic in character.		
10	Sleeping sickness is spread by the mosquito.		

The Pagoda

1 A pagoda is a religious building or monument peculiar to the Far East and an essential ingredient of Buddhism. It is not actually a temple but a depository for relics of the Buddha or of saints. Its main purpose is to remind the people of the life and work of their great teacher and allow them to offer gifts in thanksgiving. There are two main prototypes of pagoda or shrine—the Indian type, which is the forerunner of all pagodas; and the Chinese. The Indian type is to be found in India, Ceylon, Java, Burma and Thailand; the Chinese type is found in China, Japan and Korea. The Tibetan pagoda is a vertical version of the Indian type. It is the Indian stupa which is the original model for all pagodas: in pre-Buddhist times, the stupa was a communal place of worship, being a relic or funerary mound. The typical stupa was dome-shaped and surmounted by a square stone railing within which stood a broad stone platform topped by a thin, tapering mast on which were mounted three equidistant stone discs, diminishing in size from the base. At the foot of the stupa was a raised processional stairway, reached by a flight of steps from ground level. A low stone balustrade, into which four square-headed ceremonial gates were admitted at the cardinal points of the compass, enclosed the entire structure, which was said to represent the cosmos. Eventually the mound was incorporated into Buddhist rituals and its earlier purpose, that of a memorial to a king or saint, was forgotten. Out of the many hundreds of stupas built in India, only a few now remain, the most famous being the Great Stupa of Sañchī, in what was once the province of Bhopal. It was built in the 3rd century BC by the emperor Ashoka and enlarged the following century by the Andhras people, who embellished it still further in the late 1st century BC. It was 3201 cm in diameter and 1280 cm high.

2 The largest and most celebrated stupa in the world is the Borobudur of Java which was built in the middle of the 9th century. It looks like a ziggurat and consists of a hemispherical dome surmounted by a conical stone steeple upon which are mounted three equidistant discs, diminishing in size from the bottom. The dome is almost 11 metres in diameter and stands upon three concentric terraces. These form the basis for 72 smaller stupas with a statue of the seated Buddha in each, slightly bigger than life-size. The lowest and broadest of these terraces is encircled by 32 stupas while the middle and upper ones have 24 and 16 respectively. The entire stupa complex stands upon a massive, square, double pedestal, 153 metres in length, cut into four receding galleries whose walls are decorated with relief panels for a total length of over 5½ kilometres. There are altogether 504 figures describing scenes from the life of the Buddha along the walls. The terraces above the galleries have no relief decorations. The galleries and terraces can both be reached by four stairways leading up the centre of each side of the building from the ground, coinciding with the cardinal points of the compass, the entrance on the east being considered the most important. The stupa is entered from this stairway. The visitor ascends from gallery to gallery and walks round following the direction of the sun's movements so that at all times the inner wall of each gallery will be on his right hand side. The interior of the stupa, however, where there is an unfinished statue of the Buddha, cannot be entered from the outside.

3 Development has brought wide differences in the design of the pagoda in different countries and regions of the Far East; from the early Indian stupa, the hemispherical mound developed an increasingly high cylindrical base until the emphasis was changed to the vertical in China, Japan and Korea. A typical Tibetan pagoda is shaped like a bottle and consists of a pedestal of four diminishing square tiers topped by a tall circular drum which entirely covers it. Surmounting the drum is another square tier of the same size upon which stands the dome, topped by a short, truncated spire with the familiar discs equidistantly arranged along it. In Burma, bell-shaped pagodas can be found in every village, on hill tops and along overgrown paths in the jungle. Built of brick, they are usually plastered and painted white, but, with the exception of a few very important pagodas, they are not maintained, being allowed to fall into disrepair; the essence of such pagodas is in their construction, and once this has been accomplished they are forgotten about. The most important Burmese pagoda is the Shure Dagôn, a bell-shaped, gold-plated pagoda to be found in Rangoon.

4 In China, Korea and Japan there is an entirely different type of pagoda, based on the Chinese watchtower design supporting a number of storeys of diminishing proportions. In the Japanese variety, which has a remarkable delicacy of structure, the pagoda has five storeys and looks like a gabled box, each storey being covered by a sloping, projecting roof tiled in unglazed tiles of natural earth colours. The upper part of the roof is terminated by a gable placed vertically above the end walls, and there are pendants hanging from the gable ends. On the ground floor, which is reached by a short flight of steps, images and shrines are housed, while the upper storeys, each with its own balcony, are used as look-out posts. Crowning the entire structure is a tapering spire with a number of discs arranged along it.

Chinese pagodas, from which the Japanese are derived, are built of timber, or brick and timber and have a number of storeys, ranging from 3 to 15, although the most popular has 13. The storeys, always built in odd numbers, have roofs with elaborate curved edges, not gentle like the Japanese variety, and are crowned with projecting cornices. The tapering mast, with its discs, tops the structure. With its brilliantly tiled and coloured roofs and their ornate, hooked edges, the pagoda seems the most typical Chinese building, but the spire is a direct borrowing from the ancient Indian model. Although initially of religious significance, the Chinese pagoda—square, circular, or polygonal—has a more secular appeal, being more concerned with the superstition of fêng-shui than orthodox Buddhism, unlike the Japanese pagoda, which has a specifically religious purpose.

QUESTION 1

a) Draw the typical Indian stupa described in the passage, as it would look from the front.

b) Draw the Tibetan pagoda described in the passage, as seen from the front.

c) On the outline of the Borobudur given to you, draw and label the following: pedestal, 1st gallery, 2nd gallery, 3rd gallery, 4th gallery, plateau, 1st terrace, 2nd terrace, 3rd terrace and main stupa. Include the smaller stupas and mark the stairways, add an asterisk (*) to the main stairway.

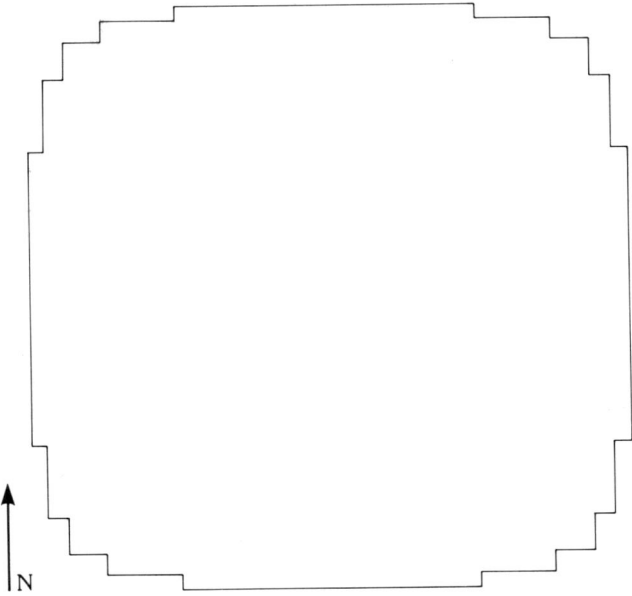

QUESTION 2

Here is a list of words from the passage. Other words are used in the text in place of these words and have the same meaning. Next to each word below, write the word or words which fulfils this function. The first word has been done for you.

1 building . . . . . . structure . . . . . .
2 spire . . . .
3 foot . . . .
4 elaborate . . . .
5 flight of steps . . . .
6 diminishing . . . .
7 memorial . . . .
8 celebrated . . . .
9 surmounted . . . .
10 platform . . . .
11 forerunner . . . .
12 tier . . . .
13 railing . . . .
14 type . . . .
15 significance . . . .
16 curved . . . .

QUESTION 3

Look at the diagrams of Japanese and Chinese pagodas opposite and overleaf. Some of them are described in the passage. Decide which are accurately drawn Chinese or Japanese pagodas and complete the table below. If they are not described in the passage, use an X.

Number	Type/name	Number	Type/name
1		6	
2		7	
3		8	
4		9	
5		10	

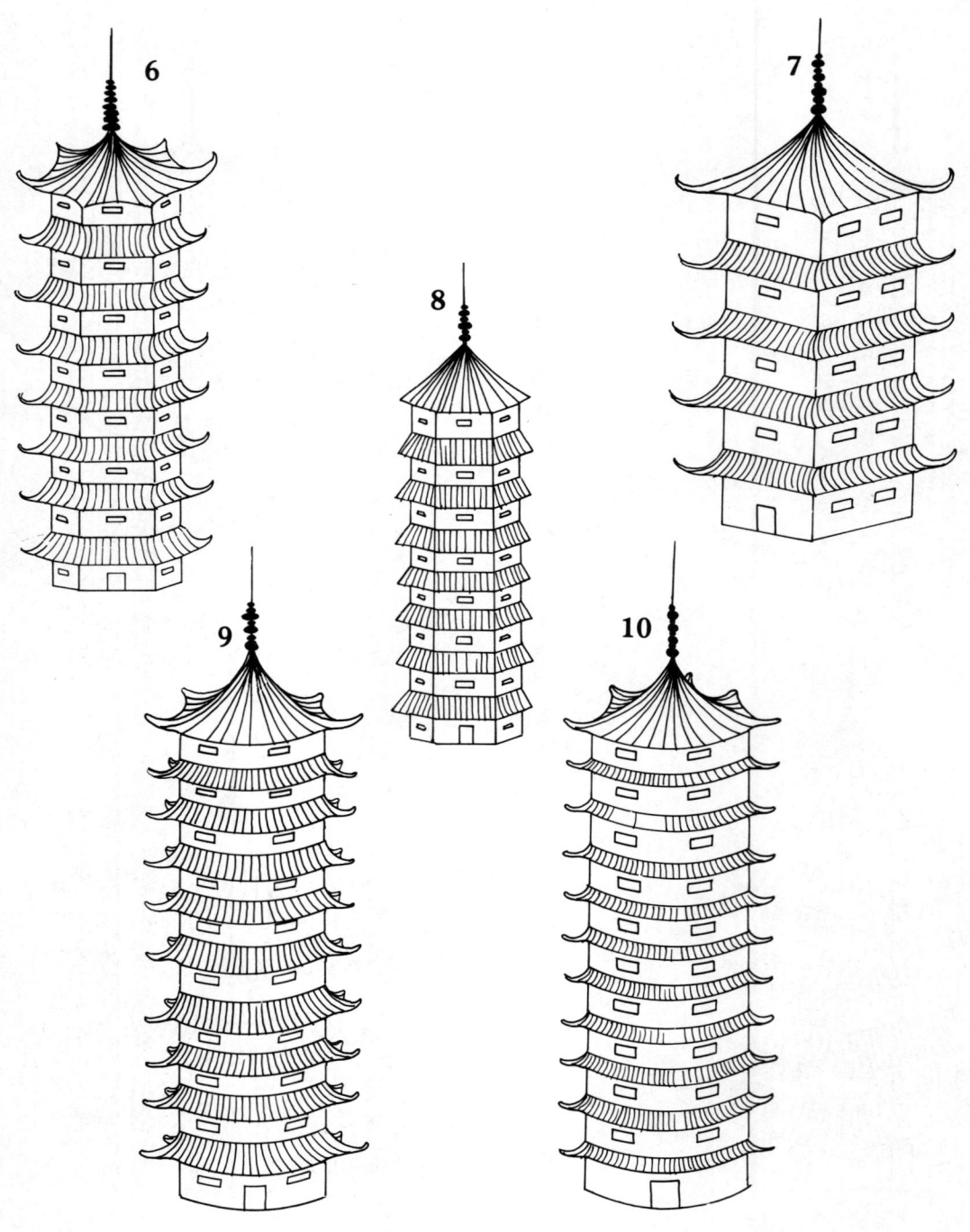

Castleton

Give a description of Castleton from the information given in the four diagrams below.

1700
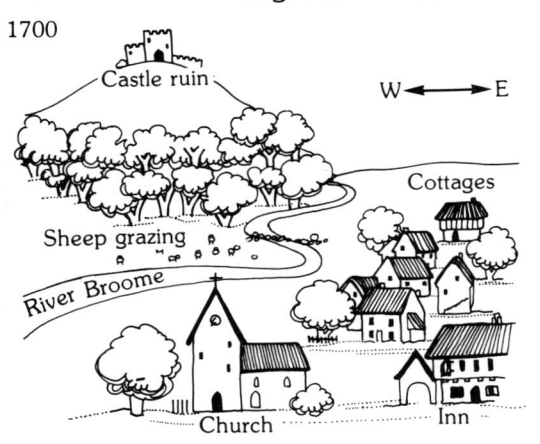

1850
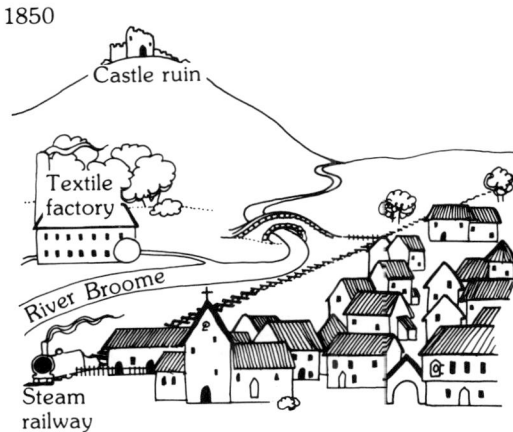

1960
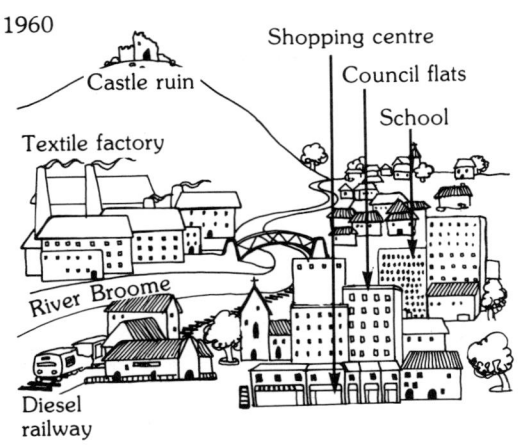

2000
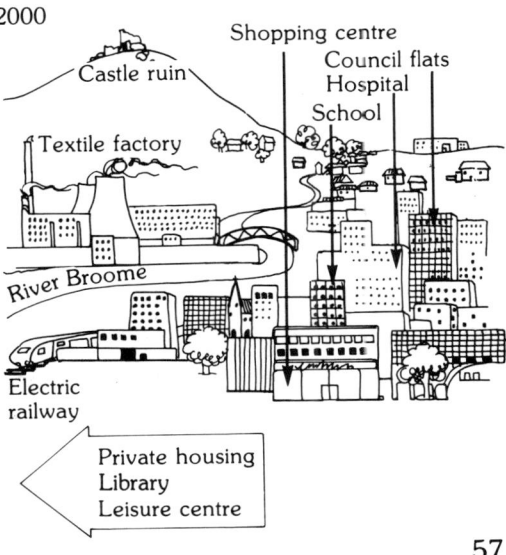

57

Lasers

Put the missing word in each line in the space provided and indicate the place in the line from which it is missing by using the symbol /.

1 _____ The word 'laser' is an acronym 'light amplification by stimulated
2 _____ emission of radiation' and is a device produces an intense
3 _____ beam of electromagnetic radiation a precisely defined wavelength.
4 _____ The light produced a laser is very different from other light, which
5 _____ radiates independently in many directions from the atoms which produc
6 _____ in the laser, the light produced is coherent—that
7 _____ that the atoms radiate step with each other and in the same
8 _____ direction, producing waves of equal length. Laser light one
9 _____ colour, sunlight, which has seven. Every atom consists of
10 _____ a central mass nucleus containing positively charged protons and
11 _____ negatively charged electrons which move in a hierarchy orbits
12 _____ around the nucleus and represent the atom's energy levels. The
13 _____ electrons are close to the nucleus, atom possesses the least
14 _____ possible amount energy—it is said to be in its ground state—but if the
15 _____ radius increases, then the atom becomes excited. Heat is applied it
16 _____ also causes the atom to become excited, and when there a change
17 _____ one energy level to another, there is either emission or absorption
18 _____ of electromagnetic radiation of a particular frequency. If
19 _____ atoms are in the higher energy state the lower state, more emission
20 _____ than absorption occurs and the atom emits of its energy content
21 _____ as light energy. Among the common laser types are ruby and crystal
22 _____ systems, and gas lasers. The gem stone, ruby, is crystal

23	_____	of aluminium oxide in which some of the aluminium atoms replaced
24	_____	chromium atoms—it is these which give the stone its rich colour—
25	_____	and when heat is applied to the crystal a flash lamp, the chromium
26	_____	atoms absorb the light energy and become excited; the excited
27	_____	they become, in fact, the more energy they radiate. Ruby
28	_____	crystal has a pair of parallel mirrors on end, one of them half-silvered.
29	_____	The light emitted the chromium atoms is reflected
30	_____	and forth in the direction of the mirrored ends, becoming more
31	_____	and intense as it does so. This causes the ruby to become hot
32	_____	so it is necessary to apply a coolant. The light which is
33	_____	travelling the axis between the mirrors builds up until it passes
34	_____	out the half-silvered end as a powerful beam of coherent light,
35	_____	stronger that produced on the surface of the Sun. Gas lasers
36	_____	have the advantage crystal lasers in that they can be operated
37	_____	continuously for long periods. The first gas laser contained mixture
38	_____	of helium and neon and was operated the passing of an electric
39	_____	current through the gas mixture, which energised the gas atoms
40	_____	excited states from which emission be stimulated. The radiation
41	_____	from the stimulated gases was then reflected and forth in the gas chamber
42	_____	increasing its intensity as it did so. Nowadays, argon and
43	_____	krypton mixture is used, where the emitted light appears white
44	_____	is in fact composed several colours. Lasers have a number of
45	_____	applications in different fields activity; very hard substances
46	_____	such diamond and steel can be cut and welded in seconds without
47	_____	the need any physical contact; with a flash of bright light
48	_____	lasting only one-thousandth of a second, the laser is to weld
49	_____	a detached retina in the human eye. This is particularly effective
50	_____	operation there is extreme accuracy and no bleeding since the
51	_____	laser also cauterises. Lasers also be used for the measurement of time

52	_____	and space, since the light they produce coherent: tiny pulses of light
53	_____	can be divided small parts—in fact, Russian scientists
54	_____	have produced pulses of laser light will last only a picosecond;
55	_____	that is, the time which light travels three-tenths of a millimetre,
56	_____	just one-thousand-millionth of a second. Measuring distances,
57	_____	the laser has told us how the Moon is from Earth. On one Apollo
58	_____	mission, the astronauts up a reflector on the Moon to catch laser
59	_____	beams projected from the Earth and them. By measuring the time
60	_____	it took for the beam to travel and back (light travels at about
61	_____	300 000 km second), the precise distance could be calculated.
62	_____	There are photographic applications of lasers; the light beam
63	_____	is divided, one of the beams strikes the object and the the
64	_____	photographic plate that when the beams again converge, the
65	_____	image produced is three-dimensional and be viewed from every
66	_____	side. This hologram is used in entertainment realistic images
67	_____	are produced which can amuse or frighten spectators, it has an
68	_____	important part to in crime detection when crucial fingerprints can
69	_____	be viewed from all directions. The technique is especially important
70	_____	medicine, when tissues and organs can seen in greater detail than
71	_____	with X-rays. The hologram also has industrial uses, when can
72	_____	detect metal stress and fatigue with superb clarity. Important
73	_____	technological advance could be the use lasers in communication:
74	_____	the frequency of a laser beam is much than radio frequencies,
75	_____	and since the amount of information that can carried by a wave
76	_____	of electromagnetic radiation increases as frequency increases, it
77	_____	be possible for a laser to carry as much information 80
78	_____	million T.V. channels! It is also considered the laser has the
79	_____	potentiality for storing information when a number of coloured dots
80	_____	be imprinted on to a crystal which will change colour exposed to a laser

| 81 | _____ beam. The information can then read by using a weaker beam.
| 82 | _____ There are also destructive military uses the laser: laser
| 83 | _____ guns have developed which could shoot down an inter-continental
| 84 | _____ ballistic missile or aircraft from great distances. Has also
| 85 | _____ been suggested that energy may be produced, sufficiently powerful
| 86 | _____ lasers can be made, by thermonuclear fusion; if frozen pellets
| 87 | _____ hydrogen are bombarded a pulse of laser light, their temperature
| 88 | _____ can be increased to over 10 million degrees centigrade. Pellets
| 89 | _____ then vaporise and expand, producing a simultaneous equal implosion
| 90 | _____ which compresses the hydrogen so that thermonuclear fusion takes.

QUESTION

From the information given in the passage, and the diagram shown overleaf, complete the table below, using the following words:

mirror
half-silvered mirror
gas mixture
gas tube
electrodes
emitted beam

1	
2	
3	
4	
5	
6	

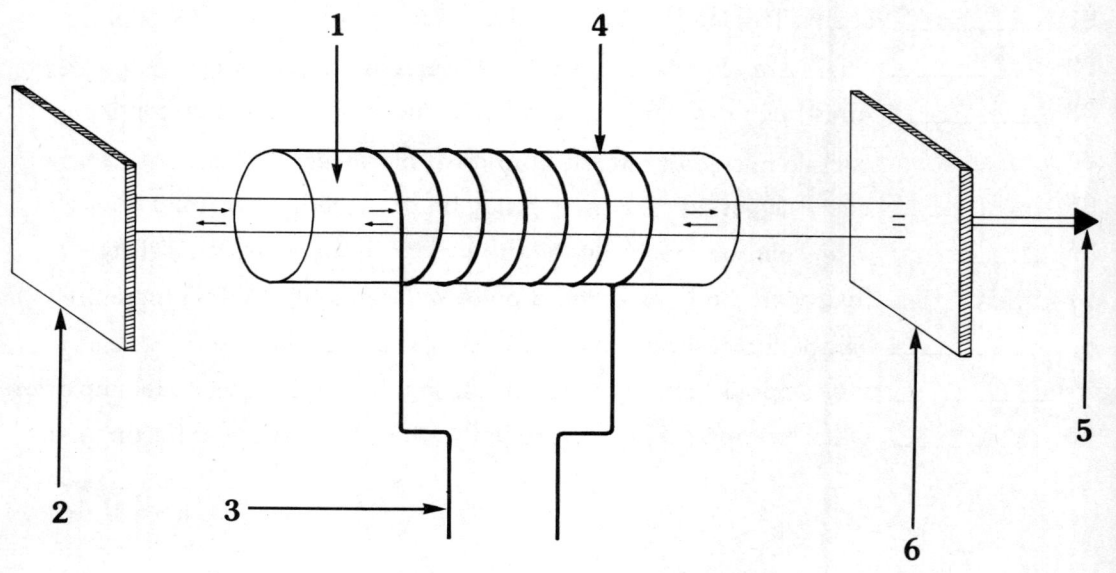

Ants

Read the passage below and insert the correct alternative given on the next page in the space provided.

There are 3500 species of ants, 41 of them to be found in Britain. They belong to the order Hymenoptera, as do wasps and bees. They are highly social insects, living in **1** _____ of varying size and development, easily recognisable by their petiole or waist between their abdomen and chest. Ants **2** _____ sugary or saccharin matter and it is on this account that some ants farm aphids or greenfly which **3** _____ a sweet substance called honeydew on which the ants feed. There are three basic **4** _____ of ants: the females or queens, the males, and the workers—who are neuter in gender although in some cases they can have a separate group of larger workers, called soldiers, as is the case with the harvesting ants, which defend the nest and **5** _____ the heavy work. The male ants are only seen at certain times of the year; they have wings and after the mating flight they leave the nest and never return. The queen has wings but after mating she rubs them off with her legs. She can live for up to fifteen years, still laying eggs that were fertilised during the **6** _____ mating flight. Some species of ants make slaves of other ants: the workers carry out slave raids during which they attack workers of other species and carry off the pupae. Still more ants collect grains of corn which they store for food. The South American leaf-cutting ants completely **7** _____ trees of their leaves which they carry off to their nests. After some time, the leaves develop a fungus which the ants eat. Other ants are cannibalistic and prey on their fellows. The most primitive ants may form nests with only a few individuals but wood ants can have nests housing as many as 100 000 ants. The carnivorous army ants do not build nests as they are nomadic in habit, travelling in armies of up to 150 000 strong. The higher and more **8** _____ species of ants are vegetarian. Termites, which **9** _____ the tropics, are sometimes called white ants: they closely **10** _____ ants both in their habits and in the construction of their homes but they belong to the order Isoptera, which is a different insect order. There are only two species of termites in Europe and none at all in Britain.

1	A	civilisations	B	communities	
	C	gangs	D	unions	
2	A	dislike	B	produce	
	C	experience	D	delight in	
3	A	hide	B	cause	
	C	secrete	D	eat	
4	A	parts	B	fractions	
	C	castes	D	units	
5	A	help	B	assist with	
	C	avoid	D	rescue	
6	A	last	B	initial	
	C	recent	D	eventual	
7	A	shave	B	undress	
	C	denude	D	uncover	
8	A	deceptive	B	bigger	
	C	industrious	D	sophisticated	
9	A	overflow	B	suffice	
	C	abound in	D	fill in	
10	A	resemble	B	identify	
	C	rhyme with	D	copy	

──────────── QUESTION ────────────

Decide whether the following statements are true or false according to the passage and then complete the table.

1 The queen ant disposes of her wings.
2 Ants belong to the same family as wasps.
3 Worker ants are female.
4 Male ants stay to guard the nest.
5 Some ants eat each other.
6 All ants build nests.
7 White ants belong to the same family as bees.
8 Britain has no termites
9 Ants live in organised colonies.
10 There are many termites in tropical countries.

True	False

The Crocodile

Put the missing word in each line in the space provided and indicate the place in the line from which it is missing by using the symbol /.

1. __to__ The first vertebrates/be true land animals were the reptiles, which
2. __ago__ appeared in the Mesozoic period, 225 million years/. The present-
3. __and__ day reptiles include snakes, lizards, turtles, tortoises, crocodiles/
4. _____ alligators. The largest, heaviest and intelligent of the reptiles
5. __was__ today is the crocodile. Once it/ distributed world-wide but now it
6. __in__ is almost extinct in many areas. The true crocodile is found mainly/
7. __of__ tropical and sub-tropical parts/the world although the alligator is
8. __River__ found in the waters of the Mississippi/ and in China; the gavial
9. __to__ found in India and the cayman is restricted/ South America. There
10. _____ are 20 recognised species of crocodile and /live in water, either in
11. _____ swamps and rivers, as is the case with the estuarine crocodile of Asia,
12. __is__ in the open sea. The crocodile/ a large triangular head and a long
13. __on__ snout, its length depending /the species. With its elongated body
14. __like__ the crocodile looks/ a lizard (which is why the alligator is so-called,
15. __that__ for the word/ comes the Spanish meaning 'lizard'). The body of a
16. __by__ crocodile is covered/ bony plates, heavy on its back but, apart from
17. __Most__ the cayman, smaller and softer on its underside. A crocodile spends/
18. __of__ of its time in the water, although it can travel long distances /land
19. __are__ and can even run! Its legs/ short and stumpy with curved, webbed toes
20. __the__ making it very clumsy out of /water. Its hindlegs are very strong,
21. _____ its forelegs are degenerate and indicate that the crocodile, which the

65

22 _____ last living link with the reptiles of prehistoric times, is nearest
23 __with__ ✓ living relative of birds. Its powerful jaws and *constantly* replaced
24 __is__ ✓ conical teeth, the adult crocodile a *nocturnal predator*, feeding on
25 _____ waterfowl, fish and mammals. It has the reputation of being a man-
26 __not__ ✓ eater, the crocodile usually does kill man, apart from the ferocious
27 _____ estuarine crocodile of Asia. Crocodiles are adapted to life in the
28 __which__ ✓ water; their long powerful tail acting as a paddle they can
29 _____ swim with ease and their sensory organs are placed on their
30 __so are__ heads, well above the water-line. The crocodile's nostrils
31 __will__ provided flaps which prevent water from entering and it is able
32 __to__ ✓ to breathe underwater thanks a membranous flap at the back of the
33 _____ throat. It is also able to see underwater of a transparent membrane
34 __a__ ✓ and flap which cover its eyes. Unlike the hearts of reptiles, the
35 __into__ ✓ crocodile's heart is divided four chambers and it has a muscular
36 __from__ ✓ partition separating its heart and lungs its chest cavity.
37 __as__ ✓ The crocodile cannot move its tongue, it is fixed to the floor of
38 ____✓_____ its mouth. Crocodiles do not live for more than 40 years in
39 __as__ ✓ captivity, they are known their *longevity*: Nile crocodiles have
40 __been__ ✓ known to live for over a hundred years. We have all seen pictures
41 __the__ ✓ of large numbers of crocodiles sunning on the banks of rivers but
42 _____ this does suggest that the crocodile is a *gregarious* animal—on the
43 __it__ contrary, it lives alone and has a strong sense territory which
44 __in__ ✓ it defends roaring and bellowing fiercely. The crocodile lives
45 _____ a burrow which is dug almost horizontally just above the water-
46 _____ line of the river bank, *terminating* a chamber where the crocodiles
47 __all__ ✓ of northern latitudes spend the winter sleeping. They are
48 __when__ about 10 years crocodiles are sexually mature and they measure
49 _____ a metre and a half in length; when they emerge the egg,
50 __the__ baby crocodiles measure only 20–25 centimetres they

66

51 ____and____ grow by about 30 centimetres *annually* they become fully
52 _____ adult. Growth then *decreases* although it stops throughout the life
53 _____ of the animal, which can eventually reach over 9 metres. Female
54 ____this____ crocodile lays 20 and 90 eggs at once and either buries
55 ___out or__ them in sand builds a nest of grass or reeds in the river bank
56 ____for____ where she guards them 3 months until she hears them squeaking
57 ___that____ inside their shells. She removes the debris has hidden them and
58 _____ helps them to leave the eggs. Having so, she leaves them to
59 _themselves_ *fend for*. Of the four groups of Crocodilia, the cayman and the
60 _____ gavial least resemble the crocodile proper the alligator closely
61 ___apart___ resembles it. It is difficult to *distinguish* them, because
62 ____the____ of their teeth: the fourth tooth on side of the lower jaw of
63 _____ the alligator fits a socket in the upper jaw so that it cannot
64 _____ be seen when its mouth is closed, the crocodile has a groove instead
65 _____ which still allows the teeth to seen even when the mouth is closed.

──────────────── QUESTION ────────────────

In the passage, there are 15 words set in italics. Give their correct meaning in sequence from the list of definitions given to you.

1 ....   9 ....   length   identify
2 ....   10 ....   lessens   take care of
                                         night   nose
3 ....   11 ....   increases   spread
                                         inadequate   squat
4 ....   12 ....   long life   regularly
5 ....   13 ....   daytime   limited
6 ....   14 ....   yearly   confuse
                                         hunter   ending in
7 ....   15 ....   sociable

8 ....

67

Petersfield

Look at the map of Petersfield opposite and write a paragraph on each of the following:

―――――――――――――――――――――――― **QUESTION 1** ――

Direct your friend from the bus station to the hospital. He will be going on foot after he gets off the bus at the bus station in Clifton Road.

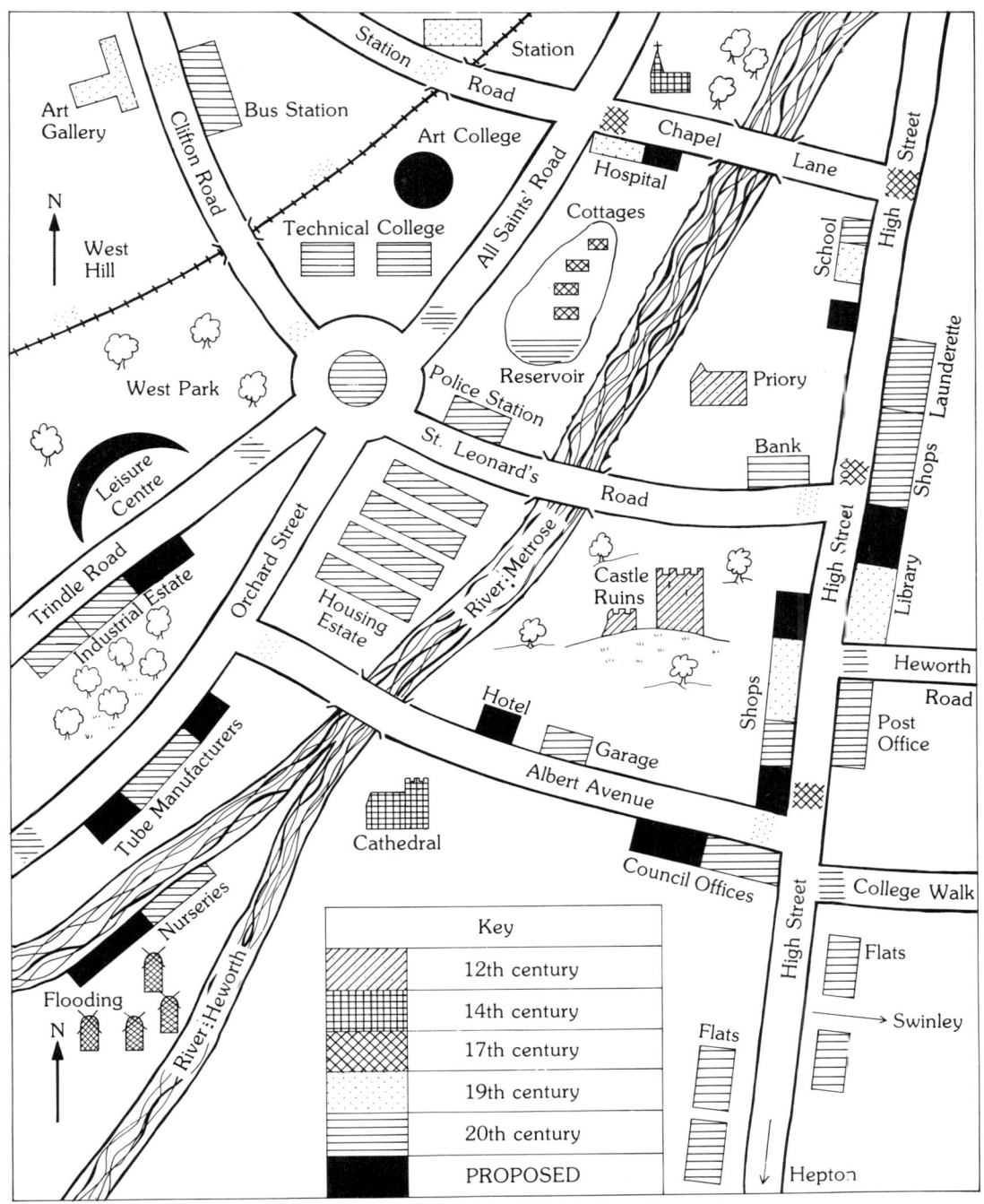

QUESTION 2

Describe the development of Petersfield from the 12th century up to the present day.

QUESTION 3

Describe how Petersfield will look by the following century.

Barrows

1 A barrow is a mound of earth or stone covering one or more burials, and in Britain barrows have been constructed by different groups of people from 2500 BC until the late Saxon period, when the practice ceased.

2 The bodies were interred in a hole or prepared grave in the ground, in a subterranean chamber dug into the ground, on the surface of the ground, or in a structure built above the ground, covered with soil and turves. The burials were accompanied by grave offerings and funerary rituals: for example, a ditch may have been constructed around the base of the mound which, especially in the chalk lands of the south of England where most round barrows are to be found, would have indicated the ritual colour significance of the white ditch and the bright green mound above it; some burials celebrated the changing seasons of the year and some others show that human sacrifice took place. These satellite burials have human remains placed in a subordinate position at the edge of the mound and were evidently interred simultaneously with the primary burial, otherwise they would have been inserted into the mound from the top. Grave offerings often indicated the trade or profession of the dead man; some graves contain the bodies of women, others of men; and objects recovered from Bronze Age barrows such as amber from the Baltic countries, pendants from Saxony, pins from central Europe and faience beads from Greece attest to a flourishing trade network between Britain and Europe and that there were contacts made with the more advanced civilisations of the Near East.

3 Some important changes in the burial ceremonies took place during the Bronze Age. Earlier, during the Neolithic period, burials had been communal in long low barrows or chambered tombs but by the second millenium BC this practice was abandoned and the dead were interred either singly or in small family groups in unchambered round barrows, of which there were many different types. Initially, the dead were inhumed, the entire body being placed in the barrow with funereal offerings, but by 1550–1400 BC cremation became the predominant method, the ashes being stored in urns of crude pottery. Round

4

barrows are much less impressive than the earlier Neolithic long barrows and at one time existed all over Britain, but ploughing has destroyed and disfigured many of them, and today they are confined largely to upland areas like wolds, moors, and the chalk downs of southern England.

Round barrows have many forms; for example, there is the **nuclear** type, where a number of subsidiary barrows surround a central main mound, or the **linear** type, which consists of a long line of separate barrows. Some other barrows appear to have no specific pattern and are scattered at random. These are called **dispersal barrows**. However, archaeologists have placed round barrows into the following categories.

The Bowl Barrow — The commonest type of burial mound, and it can be found all over Britain. It is shaped like an upturned bowl or basin and can be found with or without a ditch. If there is a ditch, then it is placed very near to the edge of the central mound with occasionally a low bank on the outer perimeter. The bowl barrow varies in size from 609–915 cm in height to 915–4572 cm across. It belongs to the late Neolithic period.

The Bell Barrow — Usually found in the chalk areas of southern England, this consists of a central mound surrounded by a ditch which is placed far from the edge or rim of the mound and is itself encircled by an outer bank or flat ledge which is very low. With a diameter in excess of 4572 cm, this barrow was reserved for the bodies of warriors, as can be seen from the battle-axes placed inside.

The Disc Barrow — This contained no weapons and, from the household items found, was probably meant for the womenfolk. Found largely in the chalk lands of southern England, this low mound had a surrounding ditch and, at some distance away, a high bank enclosed the entire structure.

The Pond Barrow — A scooped-out, concave burial place dug out of the chalk. It had no ditch but a high bank encircled it. Usually between 915–3658 cm in overall diameter, the pond barrow is relatively rare.

The Saucer Barrow — This is also fairly rare. It consists of a central very low mound, rather like an upturned saucer, and is surrounded by a ditch. A high bank completes the structure.

The Ring Barrow — This is a variant of the Bronze Age disc barrow and closely resembles it in construction except that it has no central mound. It is commonly found in the Thames valley and the north of Britain.

The Platform Barrow A Bronze Age barrow which closely resembles a bowl barrow but it is low and flat-topped and also has no encircling bank.

Roman Barrows Usually the tombs of rich traders or merchants. They have a steep conical outline with a flat top and are to be found in the south-east of Britain. They have a ditch but no bank.

The Saxon Barrows The last remnants of burial mound culture in Britain. They have two main types, the large, steep conical mound type and the group of small low mounds, clustered together. There is a ditch around the base of the conical mound, but no bank.

──────────────────────────────── QUESTION 1 ────

Look at the diagrams of round barrows overleaf—they are NOT drawn to scale—and complete the table below according to the classification given above.

1		6	
2		7	
3		8	
4		9	
5		10	

──────────────────────────────── QUESTION 2 ────

Decide whether the following statements are true or false according to the passage and then complete the table.

	True	False

1 Neolithic burial mounds were constructed for single bodies.
2 All round barrows follow an identical structure.
3 Barrow burials continued after the Saxon period.
4 The Neolithic period precedes the Bronze Age.
5 Neolithic burial mounds are rectangular in shape.
6 Dispersal barrows are arranged in uniform groups.
7 Bodies were usually burned before burial prior to 2000 BC.
8 Agricultural practices have contributed to the destruction of barrows.
9 Women were interred in disc barrows.
10 Satellite burials probably included human sacrifice.

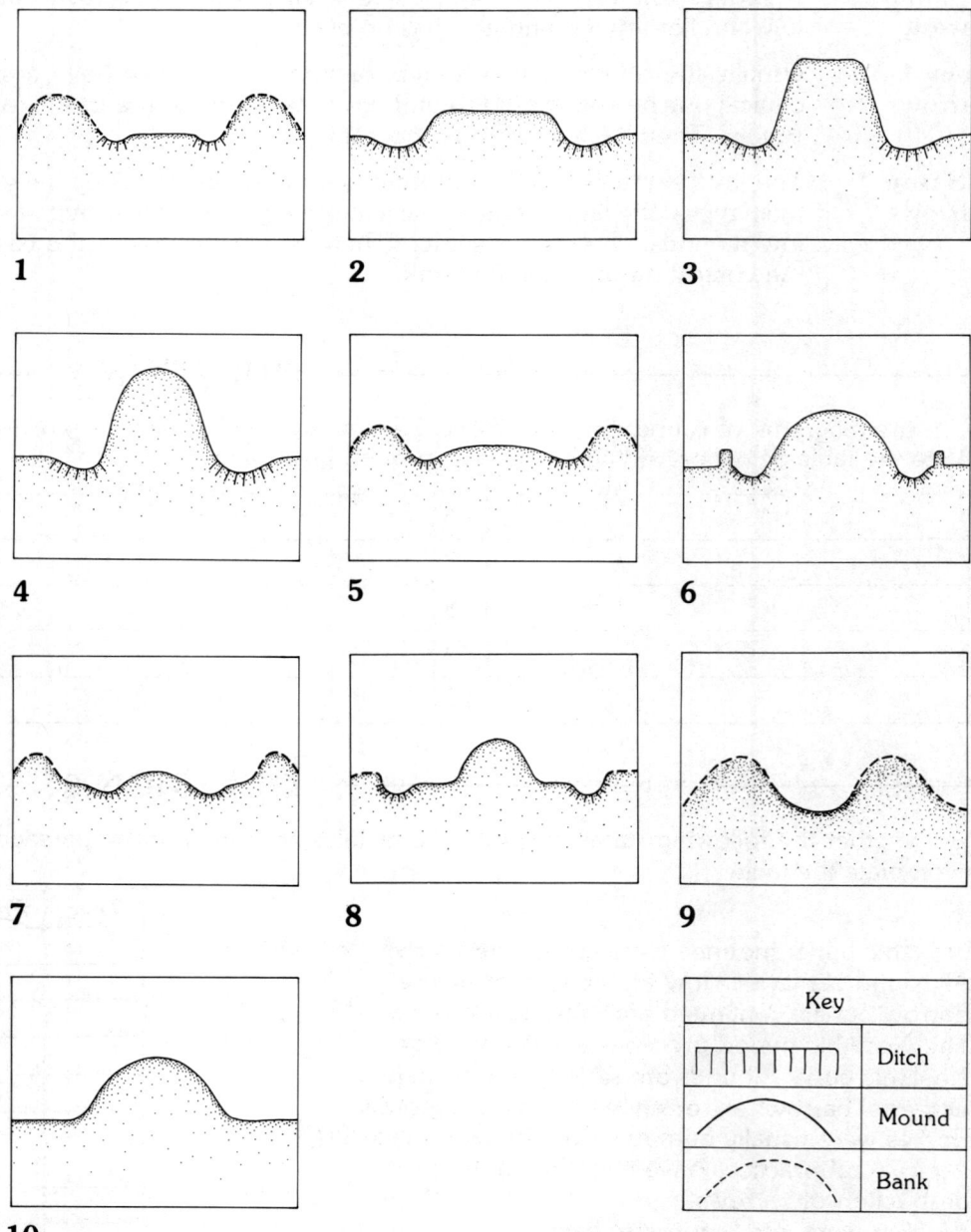

─────────────────────────────────── **QUESTION 3** ───────

Here are three main forms of round barrow. From their position relative to each other, determine what type they are and complete the table.

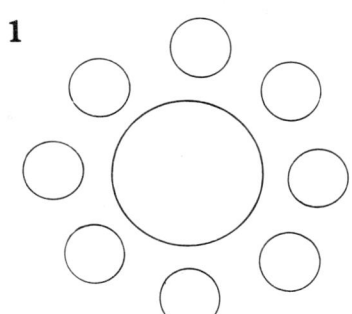

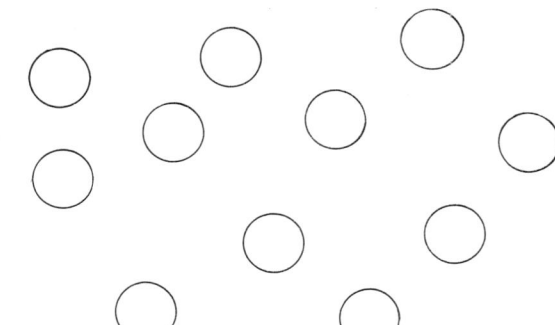

1	2	3

─────────────────────────────────── **QUESTION 4** ───────

Give the word or phrase in the passage which is equivalent in meaning to the following:
(The paragraph numbers are given.)

1	stopped .... (1)		**6**	provide evidence .... (2)
2	ceremonies .... (2)		**7**	at first .... (3)
3	importance .... (2)		**8**	most common .... (3)
4	obviously .... (2)		**9**	restricted .... (3)
5	at the same time .... (2)		**10**	particular .... (4)

75

The Field Survey

Put the missing word in each line in the space provided and indicate the place in the line from which it is missing by using the symbol /.

1 __of__ A fundamental part archaeology, which consists of the searching
2 __with__ for and recording of sites any actual digging, is the field
3 __than__ survey which, although less precise the detailed excavation,
4 _____ is the less essential. It records data which is still available
5 __after__ without the costly undertaking of excavation, which is, all, only
6 __the__ a comparatively small part of the entire process. First stage
7 _____ in a field survey is the preparation of good base-maps which
8 _____ more detailed distribution maps will later compiled, and it
9 _____ comprises the reconnaissance entire areas of the country, both
10 _____ the ground and from the air, to establish the degree or likelihood
11 _____ various types of settlement and culture areas of archaeological interest.
12 _____ Suggestive place names can often provide clues as to the location of
13 _____ ancient road; or geographical features such rivers could indicate trade
14 _____ routes; hills would offer defence a site, while the availability of fresh
15 _____ water and pasture land would attracted early settlers. It is connections
16 _____ like these enable the archaeologist to complete his preliminary research
17 _____ proceeding to the next step, which is the systematic survey, when, on
18 _____ detailed distribution maps, different symbols are made use of demonstrate
19 _____ extent of various types of site or monument or implements and their
20 _____ geographical or geological relationship to other. Areas with light soils,
21 _____ for example, would most likely have been populated prehistoric peoples

22	_____	as they only the simplest of tools and this could be plotted on the
23	_____	distribution map, items of jewellery can provide other vital evidence.
24	_____	Earliest Anglo-Saxon invaders to visit Britain were accustomed to
25	_____	wearing very crudely made brooches or pins while the ones wore much
26	_____	more sophisticated and elaborate ornaments. Showing the range of
27	_____	each brooch type on the distribution map, it make it possible for
28	_____	the archaeologist to establish the positions of both early and
29	_____	the succeeding settlements a nation-wide basis. In addition to work on
30	_____	ground aerial photography forms an integral part
31	_____	of the field survey programme, being employed where it is possible to
32	_____	obtain accurate data from the ground alone. Consists of both low-flying
33	_____	photography, is, at altitudes up to 350 metres, which records individual
34	_____	sites and monuments considerable detail; and higher level
35	_____	or vertical photography where, several thousand metres up,
36	_____	a series of overlapping exposures records extensive territory
37	_____	than isolated aspects of it. Aerial photography basically looking
38	_____	for three main features which provide evidence archaeological sites:
39	_____	crop marks, stunted growth could denote underlying structures or lush
40	_____	growth, old ditch; soil marks, invisible at ground level, would indicate
41	_____	soil disturbance; shadow marks on an apparently level site would
42	_____	appear as highlights or shadows and may be burial mounds. The
43	_____	preliminary investigation been completed both from the air and from
44	_____	the ground, the real interpretative work done in the laboratory, where
45	_____	data is classified and recorded very thoroughly means of different
46	_____	symbols and placed on to maps and reports showing the geographical
47	_____	and geological distribution of whole culture areas. Cumulative
48	_____	evidence will prove to be enormous value, not only to the archaeologist
49	_____	of today to those archaeologists of the future as they seek to fit
50	_____	together the whole history man from his primitive and remote past.

QUESTION

Decide whether the following statements are true or false according to the passage and then complete the table.

		True	False
1	Prehistoric peoples settled in clay areas.		
2	The field survey does not include digging.		
3	Place names are a valuable guide in field surveys.		
4	Vertical photography gives full details of particular sites.		
5	The systematic survey precedes the base-map.		
6	Successive settlers in Britain wore roughly made jewellery.		
7	Distribution maps have greater detail than base-maps.		
8	Symbols are used on base-maps to indicate where tools were found.		
9	Low-flying photography records details up to 500 metres.		
10	Vertical photography takes place at several thousand metres.		

Angiosperms and Gymnosperms

From the information given in the table below, write a description of Angiosperms and Gymnosperms. The opening sentence has been written for you on page 81.

Angiosperms   **Gymnosperms**

Angiosperms	Gymnosperms
General Characteristics	
Usually herbaceous, annual or biennial.	Plant usually woody and perennial.
Description of leaves	
Deciduous, wide, soft and large.	Evergreen, narrow, stiff needles.
Fruit, flowers	
Flowers short-lived, coloured and bisexual.	Cone-bearing; cones unisexual as a rule.
Wood structure	
Has true vessels.	Lacks true vessels.
Fertilisation	
Unusual for more than one embryo to develop from each egg. Fertilisation occurs soon after pollination.	Many embryos can develop from one egg but only one survives. Seeds can be shed unfertilised. Fertilisation takes place between several weeks and 14 months after pollination.

Pollination	
Pollen grains carried by wind or insects to female ovule.	Pollen grains carried by wind to ovule of female cone.
Location of seeds	
Enclosed in fruits.	Carried on upper part of scale leaves.
Pollen grains	
Contain only pollen-tube nucleus and 2 germ cell nuclei.	Contain tissue of 2–48 cells.
Condition of embryo sac	
Does not contain tissue.	Filled with tissue before fertilisation.
Number of egg cells	
One only.	Between 2 and 100.
Stamens	
Stamens present.	Stamens absent.
Food stored	
In new tissue.	In former embryo-sac tissue.

There are many important differences in characteristics between the two groups of seed-bearing plants, the Angiosperms and the Gymnosperms, in their structure, methods of pollination and fertilisation, and in the length of their lifecycle.

Angiosperms

1 There are two groups of seed-bearing plants, Angiosperms and Gymnosperms, which *differ from* each other in a number of respects. The larger of the two groups is the Angiosperms which has at least 250 000 species distributed throughout the world, and apart from natural vegetation, the vast majority of our crops and garden plants fall into this category. Angiosperms first appeared during the Cretaceous period, 135 million years ago, and from their fossil remains appear to have looked very much like varieties that exist today; they are the *dominant* land flora of our world and can be found growing in *every* type of habitat. Some Angiosperms are very small while others are enormous trees; some climb, others live in water; some types are succulents, others parasites. Most Angiosperms possess chlorophyll. The sophisticated mechanisms of seed *dispersal* and germination have *ensured* the survival of the Angiosperms; some seeds, for example, have hairs attached to them or wings so that they can be carried by the wind; others are sticky or provided with hooks so that they can be carried by animals; yet more have a flotation device which enables them to be carried by water. There is also a wide variety in the size of their seeds—some seeds are so minute that they can only be seen with the aid of a microscope, while others are quite large. The double coconut weighs up to 18 kg! The botanist John Ray, in the 18th century, divided the Angiosperms into two divisions; those possessing only one seed leaf and having their flowers arranged in groups of three and their leaves with parallel veins are called monocotyledons, while those with two seed leaves and their flowers in groups of four or five and their leaves with net veins, dicotyledons, the latter being the larger group.

2 There are several different patterns of flower groupings or inflorescences in Angiosperms which appear very confusing at first, but closer examination shows that there is in fact a basic structure for each pattern. Firstly, the inflorescences can be classified according to the behaviour of the main axis; if it *terminates* in a flower bud then its growth will be *arrested* and any further growth will be from subsidiary branches. This is termed a cymose or closed inflorescence. If the main axis goes on growing and the lateral branches bear the flowers, it is termed a racemose or open inflorescence.

3

The flower clusters provide a particularly beautiful variety of branch system and can be distinguished according to their degree of branching into simple or complex; the simplest is the single terminal flower, like the daffodil, while some plants combine their patterns, like the horse-chestnut whose main axis is racemose and whose subsidiary branches are cymose. In many inflorescences, the flowers are small and insignificant but the plant compensates by making them very numerous and compound. Often the leaves, too, are suppressed and give rise to inconspicuous **bracts**. Let us examine the different patterns of inflorescences in Angiosperms. Firstly, the **raceme**. This is a type of inflorescence in which the flowers are attached to the main axis or **peduncle** by short stalks or pedicels of equal length, and placed in *spiral* succession at equal distances along an unbranched main axis. A hyacinth is a raceme. A **panicle** is like a raceme but the pedicels or stalks bear more than one flower; it could be described as a branched raceme, and oats are an example. When the flowers occur in flat-topped clusters, as in hawthorn, the inflorescence is called a **corymb** and the flat-top is achieved because the lower pedicels are very long while the upper ones are very short. When all the pedicels arise from the same point on the main axis, the formation is called an **umbel** and there are two types, **simple** and **compound**. With the simple type each **pedicel** leaves the main axis from one central point, giving the plant head the look of an open umbrella; in compound umbels, several simple umbels spring from one central point, each with its own flower formation. The **spike** has no lateral pedicels and its flowers, which can be large or small, are sessile, that is, they have no pedicels but are attached directly to the main axis, a gladiolus being an example. The **spadix** must not be confused with the spike: it is a raceme in which the flowers are small, sessile and insignificant but it is distinguished by a swollen, fleshy axis and surrounded by a **spathe**, a large curling bract which *partially* or entirely encloses the flowers. The arum lily is a spadix. If the axis is enlarged and flattened or curved to form a *receptacle* for its crowded sessile flowers, it is a **capitulum** and often looks like one large flower, as is the case with the daisy. A catkin is a type of raceme in which the inflorescence is long and *pendulous*, the flowers have no petals but are downy and **sessile** and adapted for wind pollination. The **cyme** is a type of inflorescence where the main axis terminates in a single flower which is the first to develop and whose subsidiary axes may also have flowers but their pedicels will be shorter than the main axis. There are two types of cyme, **monochasial** and **dichasial**. The former is distinguished by having only one lateral bud while the latter continues to grow by means of two opposite lateral buds.

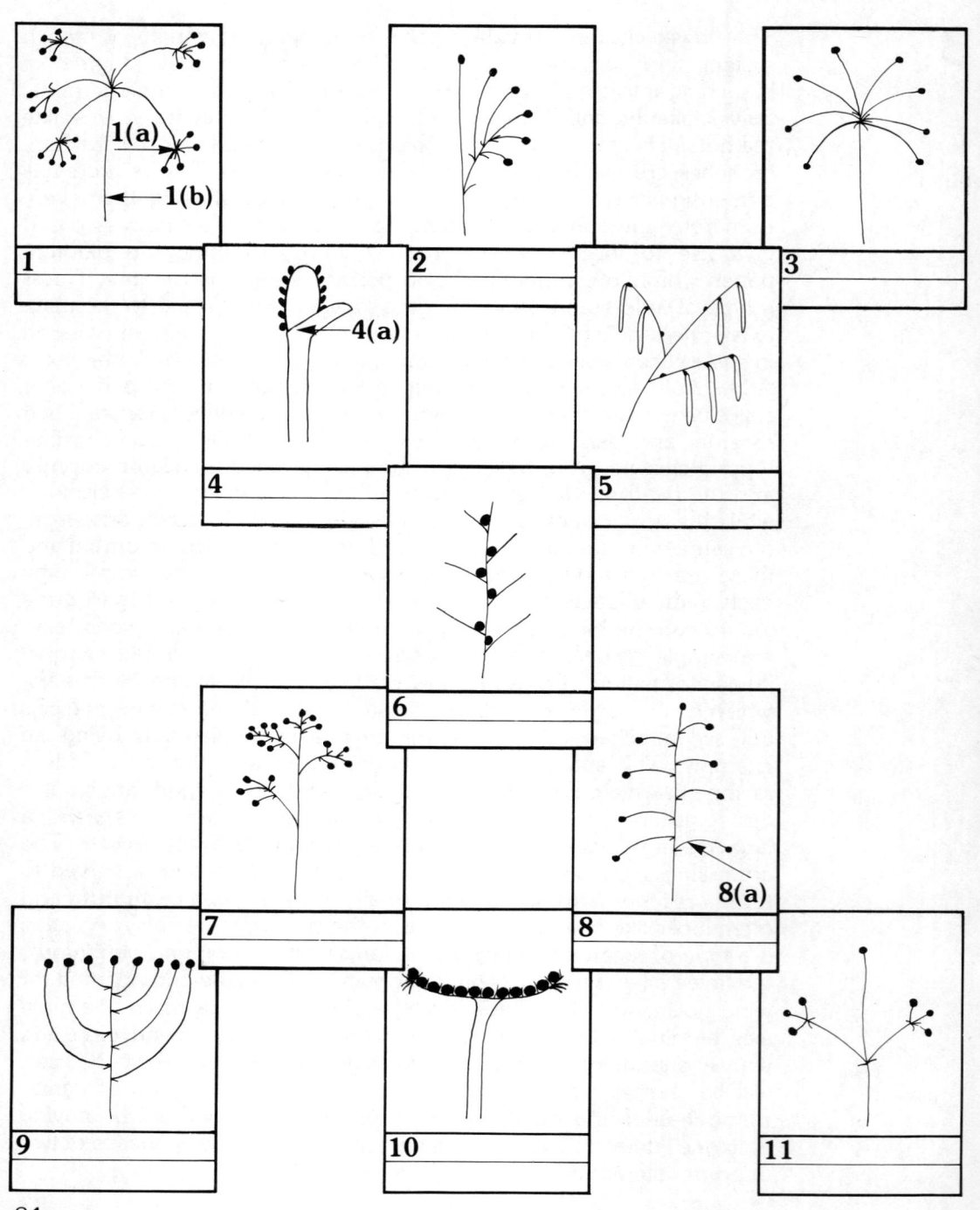

QUESTION 1

From the information given in the passage and the diagrams on the previous page, fill in the table below.

1		6	
1(a)		7	
1(b)		8	
2		8(a)	
3		9	
4		10	
4(a)		11	
5			

QUESTION 2

In the passage, there are ten words set in italics. Give their correct meaning in sequence from the list of definitions given to you.

1 ....   6 ....
2 ....   7 ....
3 ....   8 ....
4 ....   9 ....
5 ....   10 ....

stopped   distribution
hanging   construction
determined   container
contrast with   prevalent
in part   totally
thick   collected
develops   helical
ends

Heredity

Read the passage below and insert the correct alternative shown on pages 87 and 88 in the space provided.

The **1** ____ of transmitting various peculiarities of bodily form or structure or physical or mental activity from parent to offspring is called heredity, and the scientific study of it is called genetics. The information is transmitted in a chemical code by means of the genes, the **2** ____ units of heredity which are to be found arranged in particular positions along the length of chromosomes, the thread-like bodies composed of proteins and DNA which are found in the nucleus of every animal and plant cell containing the characteristics of the species. The nucleus, by virtue of DNA, controls not only the pattern of reproduction but also the metabolic processes of the cell. DNA, or deoxyribonucleic acid, is structurally a long chain of smaller chemical **3** ____ called nucleotides, each one consisting of a combination of one of several (usually four) nitrogenous bases with a sugar and phosphoric acid; the hereditary information contained in the genes is dependent on the order in which these nitrogenous bases are arranged along the DNA molecules. DNA itself consists of two intertwining helices which separate during cell division, each half ending up in a new cell as part of another spiral. The number of chromosomes is **4** ____ for every species of animal and plant life and are normally found in pairs: human beings have 23 pairs, a cat 17, a mouse 20, a fruit fly 4 and a potato 24 pairs. Every individual begins life as two cells, one from each parent, carrying half the number of chromosome pairs; therefore in humans, 23 chromosomes are derived from one parent and 23 from the other. Each gene in a chromosome has its partner on the other chromosome in the pair: the one which transmits a characteristic to the offspring is called the dominant gene and the one which does not is called the recessive gene. Dark hair, dark eyes, and tallness are all dominant genes while blond hair, blue eyes, and shortness are recessive genes, the **5** ____ of which in the offspring can be determined by the laws of heredity, the numerical patterns of which were founded in the mid-1860's by the Austrian botanist and monk Gregor Mendel from his study of the pea plant. Mendel **6** ____ from his researches that the characteristics passed from parent to offspring were in pairs, of which only one would emerge and that in **7** _____ ratios; some would be dominant but others would be hidden to emerge at some future date, possibly as mutant or abnormal characteristics. Our genetic make-up therefore seems to follow a pattern; if two true tall people, for example, were to breed, their children would all be tall; were two true short people to breed, their children would be short; if a true tall person bred with a true short person, the children would again be tall because tallness is a dominant characteristic, but the children of such people will pass on either tallness or shortness—out of every four children, one will transmit tallness, one shortness and two will transmit either characteristic. The laws of heredity determine the sequence. With humans, however, there is great variety in gene combination because there is rarely breeding between close relatives, but a **8** _____ in this variability is found in animals whose matings are deliberately controlled, as in the case of thoroughbreds, where constant features are required. In the vast majority of animals and higher plants, sex is determined by a special sex chromosome pair. In humans these are the X chromosome and the Y chromosome. Human males have XY chromosome pairs and females XX—all ova are X but sperms can be X or Y. There should, therefore, be an equal number of male and female babies born; but this is not so, because the Y-bearing sperms are more efficient in fertilisation. Inherited characteristics can be undesirable or even dangerous: eye **9** _____ like short-sightedness, cataracts, and blindness can be inherited, as can certain types of deafness. One in four deaf-mutes inherited their condition. Susceptibility to rheumatism, tuberculosis, and various skin diseases may be inherited as a result of the genetic **10** _____ of the individual to form a resistance to them; epileptic individuals in families with a history of epilepsy constitute one-third of all cases. There is a 10% probability that the epileptic will transmit the disease to his children. Certain mental illnesses such as schizophrenia and manic-depressive insanity have a tendency to be genetically transmitted, while inherited defects in certain organs can result in goitre, gastric ulcer, diabetes, or asthma in the unfortunate offspring. Down's syndrome, commonly called mongolism, is a relatively common congenital disorder caused by a chromosome abnormality which is increasingly likely as the prospective parent grows older.

1 A advantages   B principle
    C observation   D reason

2 A small   B important
    C clear   D elementary

3	A	fragments	B	parts	
	C	qualities	D	sorts	
4	A	commonplace	B	indefinite	
	C	specific	D	special	
5	A	coming	B	emergence	
	C	number	D	list	
6	A	introduced	B	collected	
	C	deduced	D	deducted	
7	A	original	B	predictable	
	C	significant	D	negative	
8	A	pattern	B	rule	
	C	analysis	D	reduction	
9	A	defects	B	problems	
	C	illnesses	D	faults	
10	A	refusal	B	inability	
	C	pressure	D	misbehaviour	

— QUESTION —

Decide whether the following statements are true or false according to the passage and then complete the table.

	True	False
1 Epileptics form 10% of the population.		
2 There are fewer baby girls born than boys.		
3 Parents over a certain age have an increased risk of having an abnormal baby.		
4 The number of chromosomes is fixed in each species.		
5 Human ova can bear either X or Y chromosomes.		
6 Mental illness is always inherited.		
7 Controlled breeding restricts genetic variety in a given species.		
8 There is a greater number of male chromosomes in each species.		
9 Both types of gene transmit information to the offspring.		
10 Chromosomes are found in every animal and plant cell nucleus.		

The Sonnet

1 A sonnet is a poem of fourteen lines, each line consisting of ten syllables, two of which constitute one foot. It has a set rhyme scheme and movement, depending on whether it is the original Italian or Petrarchan model, first established by the 13th century Italian poet Guittone of Arezzo and later perfected by the great Petrarch, who died in 1374; or the Shakespearean or Elizabethan model which was adapted to suit the English language, being a variant on the Italian original. Both forms show the sonnet to be serious and reflective in tone, having great concentration of language, structure and feeling.

2 The Petrarchan model is perfectly suited in its structure to the flowing cadences of the Italian language and consists of an octave of eight lines and a sestet of six, rhyming ABBA, ABBA; and CDE, CDE respectively, although there are often variations in the sestet, for example, CDCDCD, a structure favoured by John Milton. Whatever the rhyme scheme in the sestet, however, the Italian sonnet form always maintains the division into octave and sestet, making in effect two poems expressing different aspects of the same idea. There would never be two closing lines or couplet as in the Shakespearean model. The first eight lines state the proposition of the poem and the last six its resolution.

3 It was in the early 16th century that the Italian sonnet was introduced into England by Wyatt who, in publishing his *Songs and Sonnets* in 1565, performed a great service to English poetry, not only by presenting a new verse form (although he did not strictly adhere to the Italian model) but showing how it could be used as a vehicle for expressing personal emotion. Four years after Wyatt's *Songs and Sonnets* were published, twenty-six sonnets were issued by Spenser, now acknowledged as the true father of the English sonnet tradition. However, it took some time for the verse form to be completely accepted, and it was not until the last decade of the century that English poets, influenced more by the contemporary French sonnet than the original Italian one, were confident enough to use it, with varying degrees of success. Without doubt, the most gracious and sincere were those of Sir Philip Sydney, whose *Astrophel and Stella*, written between 1580–84 and published in 1591, introduced the sonnet sequence, where a number of sonnets were connected in theme, each following on from the other.

4 The Elizabethan or Shakespearean sonnet was so-called because the greatest writer to use the form was Shakespeare himself. This model retains the break in thought between the octave and sestet like the Italian one but otherwise differs in construction, having a rhyme scheme of ABAB, CDCD, EFEF for the first three quatrains and a closing couplet, GG. It is this last couplet which changes the whole character of the form and is the main thought division of the poem. Some of the finest religious poems in the English language are the *Holy Sonnets* of John Donne but the date of their composition is uncertain: some scholars believe them to have been written prior to 1615. Eventually the sonnet tradition in England fell into decline and became exhausted and insincere until its revival by John Milton, the first great English poet to use the original Italian form, in the middle of the 17th century. In his hands, the sonnet achieved a grandeur and dignity, and he abolished the pause at the end of the octave. He never used it to express romantic love or fleeting emotional moods but rather to describe his spiritual mood or make a political comment.

5 For a century and a half, the sonnet form received scant attention from English poets until it reappeared in the first decade of the 19th century in the poems of Wordsworth, who again preferred the Italian form and was strongly influenced by Milton; and the sonnets of the tragic John Keats, written four years before his early death in 1821, are very memorable. Dante Gabriel Rossetti, himself of Italian ancestry, was a Victorian poet who used the sonnet to good effect in his sonnet sequence *The House of Life*, written between 1848–81, chiefly inspired by his wife; while Elizabeth Barrett Browning's *Sonnets from the Portuguese*, a sonnet sequence addressed to her husband, was published for the first time in 1850.

6 Of all forms of poetic art, the sonnet remains the most difficult to write; within the short space of fourteen lines, the poet, whichever model he selects, must condense his subject while at the same time adhere to the appropriate rhyme scheme and structure. With its compact and precise form and its economy of expression, the sonnet avoids loose and disjointed thought and even after over four hundred years it continues as a challenge and a joy to poet and reader alike.

QUESTION 1

Put the following sentences into chronological sequence as described in the passage.

		Step	
A	The first decade of the 19th century sees a sonnet revival.	1	
B	Twenty-six sonnets establish the English sonnet tradition.	2	
C	A Victorian sonnet sequence is completed.	3	
D	The sonnet sequence appears for the first time in England.	4	
E	The Italian sonnet form is rescued from decline by a master poet.	5	
F	The sonnet form is born in Italy.	6	
G	A new verse form is introduced into England from abroad.	7	
H	Sonnets inspired by a husband are published.	8	
I	A dying poet uses the sonnet to good effect in his last years.	9	
J	The sonnet form is perfected in Italy.	10	

QUESTION 2

The table below represents the Shakespearean sonnet form, and certain rhymes have been given to you. Using the words in the boxes, write in the appropriate rhyme in the column at the end. Begin with the words in group 1, then go to the second group, and so on until your sonnet is complete. The first line has been written already.

Line	1	How can I tell you of my sudden
	2	
	3	
	4	
	5	
	6	
	7	
	8	
	9	

joy
ought
allow
fade
state

(Continued overleaf)

10	
11	
12	
13	
14	

	gladly
	eyes

Group One   : thought;   annoy;   joy;   ought.
Group Two   : allow;   fade;   shade;   brow.
Group Three : fate;   state;   gladly;   sadly.
Group Four   : arise;   eyes.

--- **QUESTION 3** ---

Show the rhyme sequence of the Petrarchan sonnet by using the words in the groups as you did in the previous question, and indicate the thought division by using the symbol *. The first line has been given to you.

Line 1	Never believe that I have been
2	
3	
4	
5	
6	
7	
8	
9	
10	
11	
12	
13	
14	

untrue
dear
new
fear
speed
old
save

Group One   : near;   untrue;   you;   dear.
Group Two   : bear;   new;   fear;   do.
Group Three : speed;   cold;   deed;   save;   have;   old.

QUESTION 4

Complete the following Petrarchan sonnet as it would have been written by Milton and indicate the thought division of the poem by using an asterisk (*). The second line has been given to you.

Line	1		
	2	Though ages pass, my faith in God is	strong
	3		
	4		might
	5		
	6		long
	7		
	8		night
	9		years
	10		
	11		bears
	12		throne
	13		
	14		alone

Group One   :   strong;   light;   wrong;   might.
Group Two   :   song;   night;   fight;   long.
Group Three: bears;   years;   gone;   throne;   alone;   hears.

The Scarab

Put the missing word in each line in the space provided and indicate
the place in the line from which it is missing by using the symbol /.

1 _____ The dung beetle, *Scarabaeus sacer,* was sacred the ancient Egyptians, for
2 _____ it was an emblem of the resurrection. Just under 3 cm in length,
3 _____ the dung beetle lives for up two years, feeding on the droppings of
4 _____ animals. It lays its eggs in dung (which it then rolls a ball and pushes
5 _____ into a hole) or in the body of a dead beetle, the young will eventually
6 _____ emerge. The ancient Egyptians saw this miraculous; the ball of dung
7 _____ represented the sun which was rolled daily the sky by the Divine Force,
8 _____ and in the insect's life cycle they saw life coming of death. Its image was
9 _____ carved into ornament called a scarab, initially made of stone, glazed blue
10 _____ or green, later during the Middle Kingdom, between the 11th and 12th
11 _____ Dynasties, was carved obsidian and amethyst with an inscribed gold base.
12 _____ Many scarabs were made of wood or soapstone and the 18th Dynasty,
13 _____ which included the reigns of Amenophis IV and Tut-Ankh-Amon,
14 _____ was customary use blue glass. Gold and silver scarabs were rare. The
15 _____ commonest function of the scarab was as a seal or ornament, its underside
16 _____ was flat and engraved a device or inscription, initially the name of a god
17 _____ which the wearer believed protect him from harm as well as indicate that
18 _____ he held an important position. Sometimes the seal was attached a metal
19 _____ ring by a swivel. In funeral ceremonies, the scarab was inserted the cavity
20 _____ left by the heart. It was usually made of basalt and its underside carved into
21 _____ the shape of the insect's legs. The Late New Kingdom, between the 21st

22 _____ and the 25th Dynasties, a large winged scarab would be laid the breast of
23 _____ the mummy. Scarabs had appeared as early the 1st Dynasty, about
24 _____ 3000 BC, and by the Middle Kingdom become intricate and expensive, but
25 _____ by the Late Period, between the 25th and 30th Dynasties, had degenerated
26 _____ charms. They disappeared entirely under the Ptolemies. Many specimens
27 _____ have been found in Cyprus, Crete, Rhodes, Greece, Syria and Italy but the
28 _____ crudity of the hieroglyphs and the fact that there was division of the wing
29 _____ cases show them to copies and not the genuine Egyptian scarabs. Those
30 _____ made by the Hyksos before they invaded Egypt are the famous copies.

──────────────────────── QUESTION 1 ────

Decide whether the following statements are true or false according to the passage and then complete the table.

1. Gold and silver scarabs were very common.
2. There were few scarabs left in Ptolemaic Egypt.
3. The earliest scarabs were made of precious stones.
4. Scarabs used as ornaments had carved legs.
5. In 4000 BC scarabs were used as charms.
6. Wooden scarabs were usually used in funeral ceremonies.
7. The scarab's main use was as a seal or ornament.
8. Scarabs for the dead were different from those for the living.
9. It is easy to identify fake scarabs.
10. *Scarabaeus* beetles live on the bodies of animals.

True	False

──────────────────────── QUESTION 2 ────

Give the word or phrase from the passage which is equivalent in meaning to the following: (they are in sequence).

1. holy ....
2. ultimately ....
3. likeness ....
4. use ....
5. fixed ....
6. fitted ....
7. complicated ....
8. declined ....
9. samples ....
10. authentic ....

Chemotherapy

Put the missing word in each line in the space provided and indicate the place in the line from which it is missing by using the symbol /.

1. _____ Chemotherapy is the treatment disease by the administration of a
2. _____ chemical compound, often synthetic, by means of which pathogenic
3. _____ harmful bacteria are killed or prevented from multiplying. Compounds
4. _____ are called bacteriocidal or bacteriostatic respectively. Science of
5. _____ chemotherapy born in 1909 when Paul Ehrlich, an American biologist,
6. _____ discovered a compound of arsenic destroyed the spirochaetes of syphilis
7. _____ He called it Salvarsan and the next 40 years it was the standard
8. _____ treatment for disease until it was replaced by penicillin. Penicillin
9. _____ was discovered in 1928 Sir Alexander Fleming and was, thanks to the
10. _____ production techniques of Florey and Chain, available sufficient quantity
11. _____ in 1940 to used for clinical purposes. It was to save the lives of
12. _____ thousands of Allied soldiers the Second World War. In 1935 Domagk
13. _____ noted the bacteriostatic properties the red dye Prontosil, which was
14. _____ synthesised as early as 1908, but antibacterial properties had not
15. _____ been known. It, Domagk developed the first of the sulpha drugs, which
16. _____ prevent bacteria like pneumonococci and streptococci from spreading.
17. _____ The drugs were soon found to have side effects; patients developed a
18. _____ rash, others headaches lesions in the mucous membranes. A few died.
19. _____ The bacteria cause gonorrhoea became resistant to it. Penicillin
20. _____ took the place of the sulpha drugs and found to be effective against
21. _____ a number of diseases but because it was protected by patent, it became
22. _____ cheap and easily available and people, particularly in United States,

23	_____	took it every minor ailment until resistant strains began to appear.
24	_____	It was found that certain Gram-negative bacteria not respond to it
25	_____	that septicaemia, gonorrhoea and diseases of the urinary tract could
26	_____	be treated with penicillin. Streptococci and staphylococci developed
27	_____	resistance the drug and certain micro-organisms produce the enzyme
28	_____	penicillinases which breaks down penicillin. Vibrio resistant, as were fungi,
29	_____	viruses and the tuberculus bacillus. 1944 the antibiotic streptomycin
30	_____	obtained from fungus-like bacteria and found to be effective against some
31	_____	Gram-negative bacteria and tuberculosis. Was excellent news but still
32	_____	some bacteria resisted antibiotics so the search continued for a
33	_____	broad-spectrum antibiotic that would effective against a wide range of micro-
34	_____	organisms. In late 1940's, the first three broad-spectrum antibiotics—
35	_____	Chloromycetin, Aureomycin and Terramycin—were marketed
36	_____	the United States and the emphasis began change as the pharmaceutical
37	_____	companies competed each other in the production and marketing of
38	_____	new drugs. Eventually the parent compound penicillin, penicillic acid,
39	_____	was isolated and, by adding new side chains to it, became possible
40	_____	to produce many semi-synthetic types of the drug soon
41	_____	flooded the market. The law of patents as applied to drugs that
42	_____	the inventor of a drug a monopoly in its manufacture and distribution,
43	_____	so rival companies would direct their research find an imitation
44	_____	of it altering its molecular structure slightly before giving it a
45	_____	new name. And again, variants have been introduced which have little
46	_____	therapeutic justification. There was considerable disquiet Britain at the
47	_____	American monopoly of the pharmaceutical industry, and in reports
48	_____	from 1960 to 1964 the Committee of Public Accounts declared that
49	_____	average profit made by the American companies was nearly 73%, the
50	_____	profit was 40% and the highest 98%. The companies claimed theirs
51	_____	was a high-risk business and, in case, they put back any profit into

52 _____ research. Their opponents denied; they maintained that the profits were
53 _____ lavished on promotion still more drugs and that such massive production
54 _____ served the commercial interest of the companies than the therapeutic
55 _____ needs of the public. It would appear that research has been on
56 _____ discovering drugs that cure disease rather into providing drugs
57 _____ that remove the symptoms of disease. This clearly shown in diabetes
58 _____ where most research had been devoted the production of anti-diabetic
59 _____ drugs, a variant on the one before until, in the 1950's in Germany,
60 _____ the oral anti-diabetic drug Tolbutamide was found to be effective
61 _____ treating the effects the disease; but the companies immediately
62 _____ began to look for variants of concentrating on finding the cause of the
63 _____ disease. We can only hope the emphasis in the pharmaceutical
64 _____ industry will be more on the prevention and curing of disease
65 _____ its causes than the commercial advantages of product development.

──────────────────────────────── QUESTION ──────

Put the following sentences into chronological sequence as described in the passage.

		Step	
A	The first of the sulpha drugs is discovered.	1	
B	An effective anti-diabetic drug is found.	2	
C	Prontosil Red is synthesised.	3	
D	The first broad-spectrum drugs appear in the United States.	4	
E	The first antibiotic is produced in quantity.	5	
F	An antibiotic is found to be effective against tuberculosis.	6	
G	Arsenical compound used in the treatment of syphilis.	7	
H	The first semi-synthetic penicillin drugs are produced.	8	
I	The pharmaceutical companies are under scrutiny in Britain.	9	
J	Penicillin is discovered.	10	

The Dangers of Chemotherapy

Put the missing word in each line in the space provided and indicate the place in the line from which it is missing by using the symbol /.

1 _____ There was great excitement streptomycin was found to cure tuberculosis
2 _____ and tetracycline seen to be effective the treatment of typhus, but it was
3 _____ later discovered that, although a patient could successfully treated for
4 _____ tuberculosis, were he to transmit it another patient then the latter would
5 _____ developed a resistance to the drug; and that streptomycin caused
6 _____ problems associated hearing and balance. Tetracycline has been found
7 _____ to concentrate in the teeth and bones and to cause liver dysfunction
8 _____ well as being toxic to the foetus during pregnancy. Are many thousands
9 _____ of chemical compounds used in the treatment of disease unfortunately
10 _____ pathogenic organisms show a remarkable adaptability these agents
11 _____ employed them; they become gradually resistant until they are no longer
12 _____ affected by the drug. The drug companies respond producing a new
13 _____ substance which will eventually produce more resistant strains thus
14 _____ the cycle continues. The dangers of antibiotic therapy are emergence
15 _____ of supra-infections by resistant bacteria; example, bacteria may be
16 _____ destroyed in the intestine which are harmful to man but which keep
17 _____ down potentially pathogenic bacteria, resulting the spread of harmful
18 _____ bacteria and disease. When certain broad-spectrum antibiotics given
19 _____ orally, they cause fungoid infections the mouth, the gastro-intestinal
20 _____ tract and the upper respiratory tract. Doctors, nurses and dispensers
21 _____ handle antibiotics have developed contact dermatitis; administered

22	_____	intravenously, some antibiotics have caused acceleration the brain
23	_____	waves, others, retardation; there appears to be interference the
24	_____	absorption of essential food factors like vitamin B in intestine.
25	_____	Irritability of the mucous membranes the intestine causing vomiting
26	_____	and nausea is another side effect. It is facts these which make us
27	_____	wonder the chemotherapeutic revolution is rather a step backwards.
28	_____	Outbreaks of epidemics in hospitals are unavoidable risk
29	_____	nowadays; indeed, there are over a hundred year in parts of the
30	_____	United States, which is the most over-medicated, over-vaccinated
31	_____	over-operated society in world. We must accept that people in
32	_____	societies which are over-exposed drugs will develop diseases
33	_____	resistant to them, and side effects from them; it is illusion that a
34	_____	new drug will not cause resistant strains to develop—it is inevitable
35	_____	process. The misused drugs of all, however, are the
36	_____	tranquillisers, stimulants and barbiturates; some recent figures that
37	_____	75% of suicides in Britain caused by deliberate use of barbiturates,
38	_____	while 80% of accidental deaths were caused by their use, majority being
39	_____	young children. Every year many animals die to enable new drugs be
40	_____	marketed when they are necessary, and doctor and patient alike are
41	_____	confused by the sheer numbers of new drugs the market; the doctor
42	_____	is pressure from both his patients and the drug companies to put
43	_____	new drugs use, while some medical journals—which should be watch-
44	_____	dogs for the public and a source information for the doctor—are them-
45	_____	selves dependent on the drug companies income from advertising.

Communicating across Outer Space

Complete the following passages using the appropriate number of words.

The planets of the Solar System appear to shine but in fact they only reflect the light of their star, the Sun, and have no light of their own. We know that light is necessary for providing the conditions necessary for living things.

1   We must therefore assume that . . . (Use 30–35 words.)

If planets are formed when stars condense, then there must be thousands of millions of planetary systems in our Galaxy alone, and our Galaxy is only one of millions. It is almost certain therefore, that Man is not alone and that there must be other intelligent beings in the Universe. The best way of establishing contact with such beings would be to send out a series of radio signals from a radio telescope and wait for a response.

2   The surest plan would be to . . . (Use 30–35 words.)

Even if we assume that our signals would be travelling at the speed of light . . . (Use about 35 words.) (*Speed of light* = 300 000 km per second; *nearest star* = α Centauri, 417.5 million million km distant.)

3

Assuming that these other intelligent beings were scientifically as well or better developed than ourselves, when they picked up these radio signals they . . . (Use 30–35 words.)

4

Cosmic Covers

Read the following advertisement about Cosmic stretch covers and write a simple factual account for inclusion in a consumer magazine. You must disregard any advertising jargon.

Has the upholstery on your furniture reached the stage when you can't bear to live with it any longer? Don't worry, just fill in the coupon below and leave the rest to us. Within three weeks, you could be the proud possessor of a brand-new three-piece suite except that only the covers will have changed. Yes, you will surprise your family and be the envy of your friends at very little cost. Our superb stretch covers will fit your suite to perfection whatever shape it is because we have a range of over 60 standard furniture styles to choose from, from contemporary to Jacobean or Queen Anne, and there is bound to be one that will be exactly what you are looking for. We have some fantastic patterns to choose from, too, with bright floral designs or plain if you prefer, in 45 colourways. If you are prepared to pay just that little bit extra, you could enjoy our luxury range of thick tapestry-look covers or our sumptuous velvet-look sculptured covers, all in easy-care man-made fibres. All of our covers are washable, in fast colours and will never shrink. You can forget about ironing, too. Nothing could be easier. All of our stock is backed by an unconditional guarantee so there is no need to worry. Take advantage of our exclusive offer today and you will be glad that you did.

Castles—Part 1

Read the definitions of features in castle architecture below, look at the diagrams on pages 105–107 and then complete the table with the appropriate definition. Should any feature not be described, put X.

Machicolation	A parapet built out from the wall on stone corbels allowing the base of the wall to be covered when attacked. A permanent version of a hoarding
Merlon	The solid part of a parapet between two crenelles
Bailey	A castle courtyard containing stables and other outbuildings and surrounded by an outer defence
Hoarding	A wooden gallery erected on beams projecting from the parapet enabling defenders to protect the base of the wall in cases of attack
Curtain	A length of wall between towers in mediaeval architecture
Allure	The wall-walk behind the battlements or parapet
Shell keep	The crowning ring of high walls around a motte
Pierced merlon	A narrow slit cut into a merlon to enable arrows to be shot
Drawbridge	A bridge covering a gatehouse with a hinge at one end permitting it to be drawn up for defensive purposes
Motte	A steep, conical mound of earth, natural or artificial, with a castle on the top and a related bailey
Vice	A spiral staircase set within the thickness of the wall
Portcullis	A heavy lattice grating of timber or iron sliding in vertical grooves in a wall to protect a doorway. Frequently found behind a drawbridge
Archère or loophole	A slit cut in the wall of a castle so that arrows could be shot through
Coursière	A wooden roof over a wall-walk
Crenelle	A gap between the merlons on a parapet

Solar   A private room for the lord of a castle and his family
Palisade A fence of wooden stakes
Parapet   A protective screen on top of a wall or tower made of alternate merlons and crenelles
Keep   The inner tower of a castle

1		9	
2		10	
3		11	
4		12	
5		13	
6		14	
7		15	
8		16	

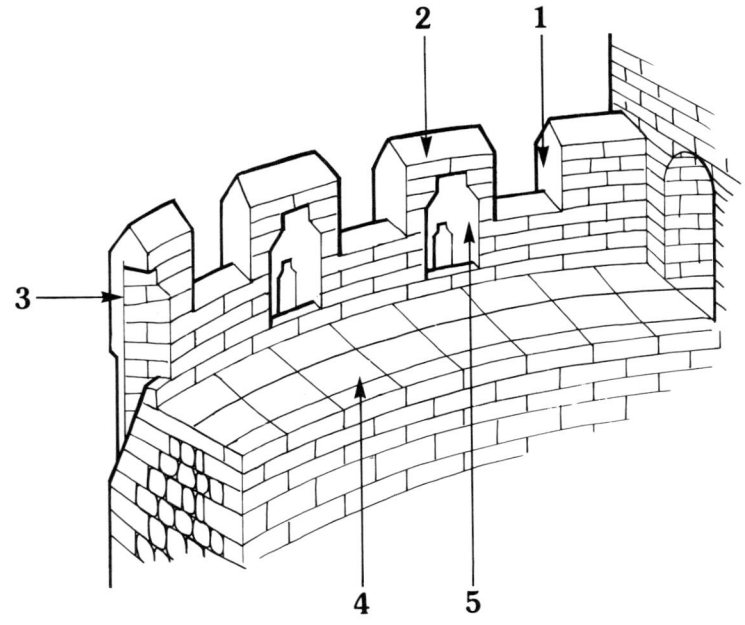

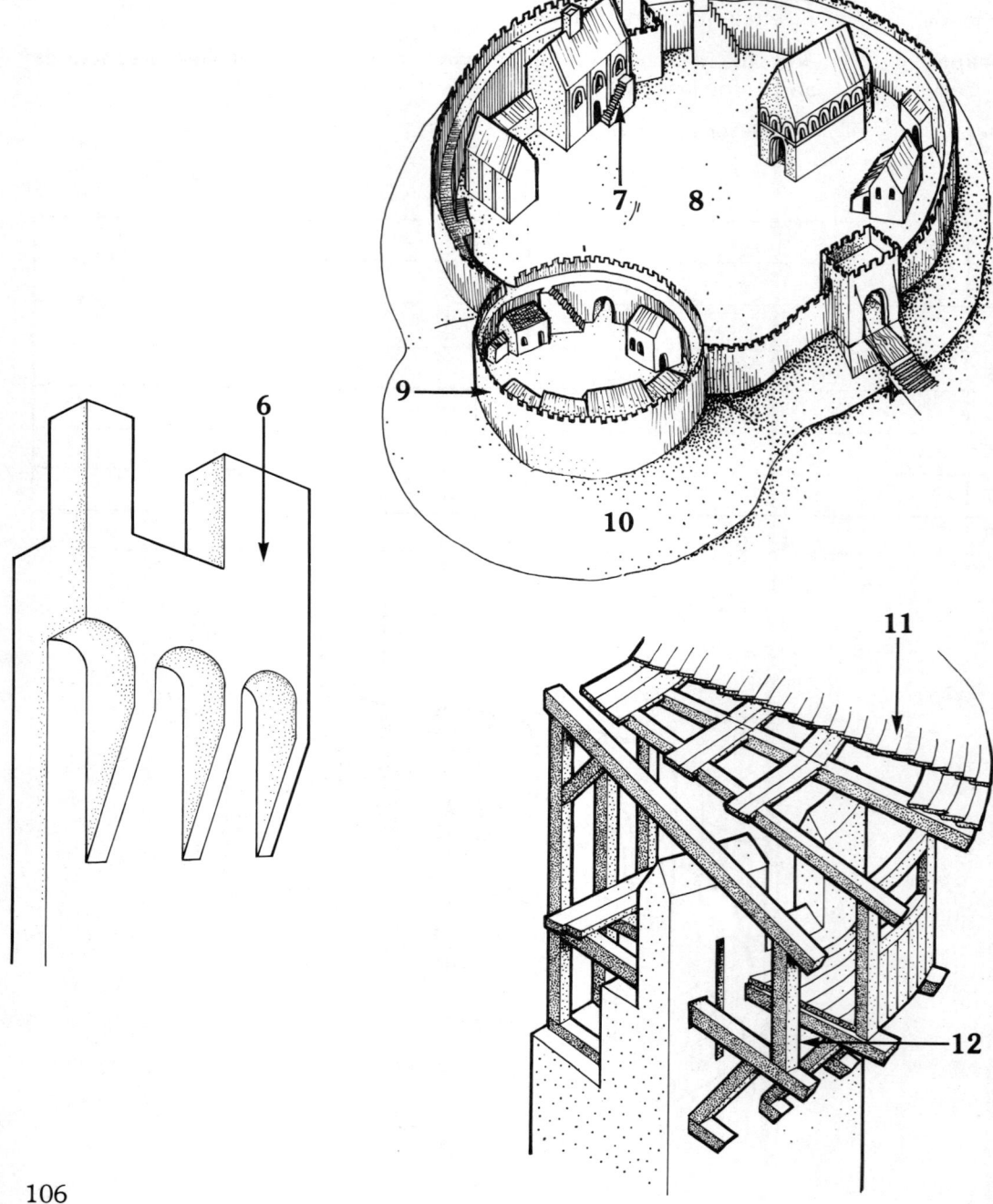

Charles Darwin

Put the missing word in each line in the space provided and indicate the place in the line from which it is missing by using the symbol /.

1 **had** — Charles Darwin already / abandoned his medical studies at Edingburgh
2 **had** — and / graduated in theology from Cambridge, at his own expense, he
3 **he** — applied for the position of naturalist on H.M.S. Beagle, in 1831 / was
4 **and** — ready to set sail for a five-year expedition to South America / the Pacific.
5 **No** — / One could have foreseen that the result of Darwin's diligence and
6 **to** — dedication in his researches during the expedition were / become one of
7 **of** — the great intellectual signposts of our modern world, for our way / thinking
8 **of** — has been radically altered as a result of Darwin's theory / Natural Selection
9 **On** — which grew out of his observations. / The voyage, Darwin kept a journal
10 **under** — his researches which was published in 1839 / the title of *The Voyage of the*
11 **to** — *Beagle* and which contained his great constructive theories later / be
12 **work** — published more fully in his monumental / *The Origin of Species* in 1859—
13 **from** — the ideas themselves and the speculations which developed / them were
14 **earlier** — born on the Beagle several years / . The collection of information from
15 **place** — the expedition convinced him that the evolution of life had taken / over
16 **the** — millions of years. His was the first real attempt to collect all /
17 **of** — evidence scientifically, and no other satisfactory explanation / all the
18 **has** — facts he presented / yet been proposed. The year prior to the publication
19 **had** — of *The Origin of Species*, Darwin / received an essay from A.R. Wallace,
20 **the** — a naturalist working at / time in Malaya, in which he outlined theories on
21 **to** — evolution identical / Darwin's own. The situation was resolved, however,
22 **by** — / Darwin's friends Lyell and Hooker, who insisted that a joint paper be

23 _____ read in London the Linnean Society in July of that year. The publication
24 _____ of his *The Origin of Species*, which is said to sold out in one day, was
25 _____ issued the following year and the controversy began. In it, Darwin
26 _____ that life of all kinds and at all times shown great variety, but a
27 _____ variety which striking similarities of form and pattern can be traced:
28 _____ that varieties of life adapt to their particular environments, leading us
29 _____ to suppose that there was a gradual change evolution in all living things.
30 _____ In all forms of life, Darwin proposed, offspring are produced of which
31 _____ only a few will live to maturity—those fitted to their environment.
32 _____ These survivors will turn pass on these features, which enabled them to
33 _____ survive, to their offspring. He further stated that some members of
34 _____ a species differ from others in any way gives them an advantage, then
35 _____ they are more to survive. Darwin further propounded that environments
36 _____ themselves were stable over long periods of time so the characteristics
37 _____ which best fitted the individual to continue exist would gradually
38 _____ adapt the species to fit the new conditions. These theories him many
39 _____ enemies, many of saw his work as an attack upon their religion, raising
40 _____ the question of the very existence of God or the need Him. In 1860,
41 _____ for example, there was a very angry and emotional scene the meeting
42 _____ of the British Association for the Advancement of Science Oxford, when
43 _____ Darwin was ridiculed. Some prominent scientists defended however,
44 _____ but he was to spend the of his life meeting the criticisms levelled
45 _____ at him. In 1868 published his *Variation of Animals and Plants under*
46 _____ *Domestication,* in which he proposed inheritance might be passed on
47 _____ from parents to their offspring; then, spite of growing ill health,
48 _____ he produced *The Descent of Man* in 1871, which excited enquiry Man's
49 _____ ancestry, the book produced nothing like the effect of *The Origin of*
50 _____ *Species* so many years before. He made a notable contribution, year
51 _____ after, to psychology and laid the fundations the science of ethology

52 _____ with his *Expressions of the Emotions in Man and Animals* but health
53 _____ was failing and he suffered a heart attack within the year. He to suffer
54 _____ another in April 1882 which killed him and he buried in Westminster
55 _____ Abbey. Since his death, theologians have accommodated to the idea of
56 _____ evolution by saying that it was idea unfolding in God's mind all the
57 _____ time, they do not explain why it should have taken so long to develop.
58 _____ We cannot, either, assume the idea of any plan of cosmic progress, can
59 _____ fill us with optimism for the future of Man; and we can still guess at the
60 _____ true significance of this life on earth and what, anything, it means.

--- QUESTION ---

Put the following sentences into chronological sequence as described in the passage.

A There is an angry scene at Oxford.
B Darwin graduates in theology.
C Darwin receives a letter from a fellow naturalist.
D Darwin is buried.
E Darwin takes his medical degree.
F The science of ethology has its beginnings.
G Darwin reads his independent theories to a group of scientists.
H Darwin publishes a best-seller.
I Darwin sets out on an expedition.
J Darwin's ideas on inheritance are issued.
K Darwin's theories on Man's origins are published.
L Darwin's journal is issued in book form.

Step	
1	
2	
3	
4	
5	
6	
7	
8	
9	
10	

The Aneroid Barometer

Look at the diagram of an aneroid barometer below and then complete the description of how it works. (Use about 60 words.)

An introductory sentence has been written for you on page 112.

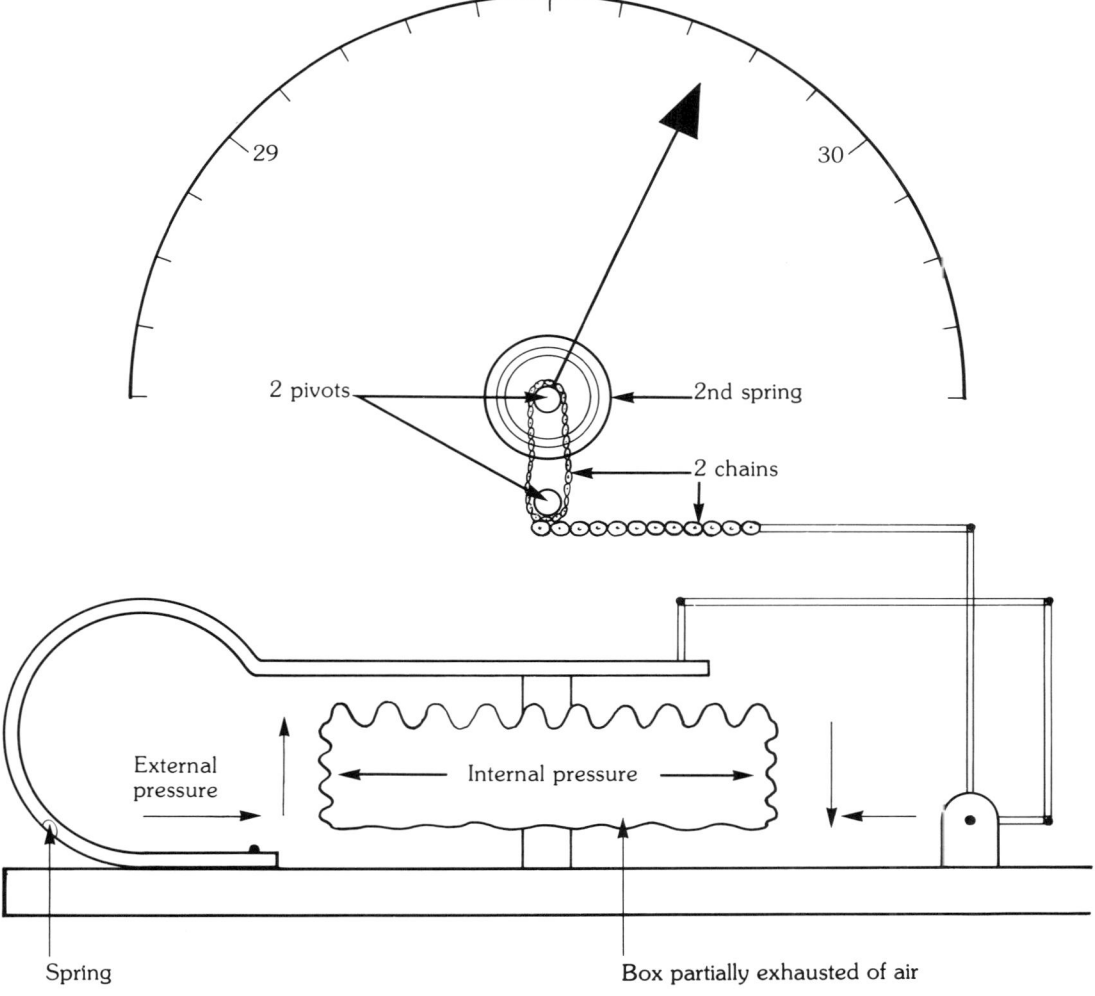

The aneroid barometer measures atmospheric pressure and is the kind of barometer that does not depend on the use of mercury or other liquids. It is used for aircraft altimeters and consists of . . .

Stonehenge

1 The most remarkable and perplexing prehistoric site in Europe is that of Stonehenge, a megalithic monument dating from the Stone Age and early Bronze Age, which stands on the chalk downs of Salisbury Plain in Wiltshire. The monument displays techniques of construction known only to the Mycenaean and Minoan Mediterranean cultures at the time and so poses an important question: did the builders of this prehistoric monument have trade links with the Mediterranean peoples? Certainly there were carvings discovered on two of the stones, of a hafted dagger and axeheads, with a pattern found on Mycenaean work at this time. The most noticeable features of the monument are the remains of four concentric rings of upright stones, alternately of sarsen—a hard, grey, local sandstone—and an igneous rock called bluestone, a speckled blue-green stone from the Prescelly Hills in Pembrokeshire, West Wales, more than 321 km from the site and probably brought by raft along rivers. The stones were shaped with primitive stone or bronze tools and raised without any form of mechanical aid. When the monument was completed nearly 4000 years ago, it had an outer ring of 30.5 metres in diameter comprising 30 sarsens topped by continuous lintels of shaped stone curved to meet the circumference of the circle. Within the ring of sarsens was a ring of much smaller blocks of Prescelly stone. The inner circuits were both horseshoe shaped and aligned with the axis of the monument. The outer one consisted of five enormous sarsen trilithons or free-standing structures crowned by a lintel which graduated in height with the largest, 9.15 m high, in the curve of the horseshoe, whose opening aligned with the axis of the monument and faced the entrance to the north-east. The innermost circuit of all were bluestones and enclosed the Altar Stone, a flat oblong sandstone slab 4.88 m long, whose long sides ran parallel to the entrance. From the Altar Stone the eye would have been drawn to a 6 m tall upright sarsen, just outside the gap in the enclosing ditch. This was the Heelstone, over the top of which the sun would rise every year on June 21st—the longest day of the year, when it would be at its most northerly point on the horizon. There were two further sarsens placed outside the Aubrey pits at the entrance of the avenue, exactly in front of the Heelstone, the more easterly of which is called the Slaughter Stone. The circle of pits (called the Aubrey pits after John Aubrey who discovered them in 1666) surrounded the monument on its outer perimeter; they have been found to contain incinerated human remains. Beyond the pits was an embankment and outer ditch. Between the Aubrey circle and the outer sarsens of the monument were two concentric rings of socket holes, the Y and Z holes respectively, the latter being the inner circuit. The holes, 30 in the Y circuit and 29 in the Z, were meant to house encircling rings of bluestone. The construction of Stonehenge took place over a period of 500 years, from 2000 BC to 1500 BC, and we can divide the stages into three, each one including a separate culture. The first people to be associated with the monument were Neolithic farmers who came to Britain about 2200 BC. They were followed some 500 or so years later by the Beaker people, who were sun worshippers, and these in their turn were succeeded by the Bronze Age Wessex people of about 1500 BC, whose dead are buried in barrows within walking distance of Stonehenge.

2 The earliest site at Stonehenge, which we will call the late Neolithic, consisted of a circular embankment nearly 2 m high with a mean diameter of 98 m, and surrounded by an outer ditch, both ditch and embankment being broken on the north-east by a single entrance, just over 12 m wide. On either side of the entrance an avenue with parallel ditched banks, its axis coinciding with the axis of the monument, stretched directly north-east. The Heelstone, which stood in its own shallow ditch, was a few metres away from the entrance to the Avenue and the 56 Aubrey pits containing human remains closely encircled the embankment on its inner side.

3 The Beaker people began to develop the monument in about 1700 BC. They began by setting in place two concentric rings of bluestone uprights with diameters of 22.5 metres and 26.2 metres respectively within the centre of the site, and so arranged that their entrance aligned with the Heelstone, the only stone structure of the earlier period of development. At the same time, the Avenue was extended by several metres until it turned eastwards to meet the river Avon. During the Wessex period of occupation there were three sub-divisions of development of the site, which began with the dismantling of the bluestone outer circles and the remodelling of the entire monument with the introduction of the ring of upright sarsens capped by continuous stone lintels. Following this, the bluestones were dressed and re-erected with lintels in an oval setting near the centre of the monument, coincident with the final position of the horseshoe of bluestones. The two concentric circles of Y and Z holes were dug to house the remaining bluestones but were never completed. In the last phase, the oval arrangement of bluestones was removed and replaced by five sarsen trilithons while at the same time four equidistant station stones (of which two now remain) were erected just inside the embankment and almost in line with the Aubrey pits. If lines could be drawn through these stones, they would converge in the centre of the monument through the Altar Stone. The station stones were followed by the two sarsens placed at the entrance-way fronting the Heelstone.

We do not know why Stonehenge was built: it is a great archaeological puzzle. It has been suggested that it was a temple for sun worship or an observatory for studying the heavens. Certainly key locations on the site such as the station stones and the Altar Stone show correlations with both solar and lunar positions, and there are twenty-four such correlations on the site. The sun rises over the Heelstone on the morning of the summer solstice and from anywhere else on the axis; and on the afternoon of the winter solstice, the sun sets in the archway of the great central trilithon. A British astronomer, G. Hawkins, has demonstrated that the full moon in midwinter is eclipsed over the Heelstone three times in a cycle of fifty-six years. He has also proposed the theory that the Aubrey pits originally held a set of markers which were moved around annually by one hole so that they could record eclipses. We do not know whether or not he is right. It has also been suggested that Stonehenge was a sacrificial temple but no reliable deduction can be made about its real purpose. It remains to puzzle us.

QUESTION 1

Use the following key for all plans:

Embankment	
Ditch	V V V V
Bluestones	✳ ✳ ✳ ✳
Trilithons	𝝥
Sarsens	⌑
Aubrey pits	AP
Y holes	Y

Z holes	Z
Slaughter stone	S
Altar stone	AS
Avenue	A
Heelstone	HS
Station stones	SS

a) Draw a plan of Stonehenge as it would have looked from above during the Neolithic period.

↑
N

b) Draw a plan of Stonehenge as it would have looked from above during the Beaker period.

↑
N

c) Draw a plan of Stonehenge from above as it would have looked at the end of the Wessex period.

↑
N

─────────────────────── QUESTION 2 ───

Put the following sentences into chronological sequence as described in the passage.

		Step	
A	A ring of sarsens with lintels on top is set up.	1	
B	Two concentric rings of bluestone uprights are set in place.	2	
C	Bluestones are replaced by sarsen trilithons.	3	
D	Aubrey makes a discovery.	4	
E	Neolithic farmers arrive in Britain.	5	
F	The Slaughter Stone is laid.	6	
G	The bluestones are taken down.	7	
H	Y and Z holes are dug to house extra bluestones.	8	
I	An earthwork is constructed.	9	
J	An oval setting of bluestones is arranged.	10	

Comets

1 Man has always regarded comets with awe, fear and superstition because they appear so suddenly and dramatically in the sky. Called 'kometes aster' or 'hairy star' by the ancient Greeks, comets are *nebulous*, celestial bodies composed of swarms of metallic particles orbiting in elliptical, parabolic or hyperbolic paths around the Sun. In 1750 there was only one comet known, but since then there have been increasing numbers of sightings: in 1800 there were two known; in 1850, three; in 1900, five; in 1950, eight; and by 1975, there were eleven known. Comets consist of a head or coma which is the brightest part, a nucleus, which is the only solid part with a diameter *ranging* from 1.6 km to 48 km and sometimes one or even two tails—very bright and up to millions of kilometres long. The space behind the nucleus and inside the tail is known as the hollow cone. The tails appear to be straight but they are in fact curved and are only seen when the comet is closest to the Sun at perihelion. It used to be thought that the tail was produced by the pressure of sunlight on the comet, but it is now believed that it is produced by the combined action of the solar wind (a continuous cloud of ionised hydrogen originating from the Sun) and the inter-planetary magnetic field. The tail always points away from the Sun so that it always *precedes* the comet as it recedes into space.

2 The physical appearance of a comet depends on its distance from the Sun: when it is farthest (aphelion)—when it can extend even beyond the orbit of Pluto—it is very faint but as it approaches the Sun, it gets gradually brighter until at perihelion—when it can be as near as a few million miles to the Sun—it is at its brightest. The ultraviolet light of the Sun melts the nucleus of the comet, releasing huge volumes of ionised gas which carries away the icy particles of the nucleus, producing the head or coma of the comet. Bessel, the German astronomer, *devised* a theory in 1836—two years before he observed stellar parallax and set new standards of accuracy for positional astronomers—that explained comet tails: he said that a repulsive force acted on the comet particles and varied their gravitational attraction.

3 Although only minor constituents of the solar system, comets have a *complex* history and are undoubtedly the oldest and best preserved material in it, probably *critical* in its early development. There are three main areas in the study of comets: the discovery of new comets and the recovery of periodic comets; the measurement of their orbits and position in space; and a study of their physical aspects. Although there is a lot we do not yet know—for example, we do not know whether it would be possible to pass through a comet nucleus or its outer regions—there is much we have learned, largely as a result of the efforts of amateur astronomers, about comets and their behaviour. We know that they seem to originate at the edge of the solar system and move in closed orbits; we know there are two types of comet, classified according to their orbital period. Comets less than 200 years old are called short-period comets, those over 200 years old are called long-period comets. Some comets have elliptical orbits, others parabolic or hyperbolic. Newton interpreted the orbits of comets as parabolas, deducing that each one was appearing for the first time. Halley, however, showed that some at least were periodic, returning after a number of years. He determined the orbit of the first periodic comet which bears his name. He deduced that the five comets which had appeared from 1378 to 1682 were successive returns of the same comet. Halley's Comet, first seen in 1682, has an orbit of 76.09 years. The date of April 13th 1759 was given as its perihelion passage, with a month either side for error. It returned in December 1758 and reached perihelion on 12th March 1759; in 1835 it returned again, within three days of the date *predicted*, and appeared yet again in 1910. After Halley's death in 1742, it was shown that the comet had made twenty-nine appearances since 239 BC and that it was probably not only the comet *depicted* on the Bayeaux tapestry in connection with the Norman Conquest of England in 1066, but also the comet that terrified the Christians three years after the Turks captured Constantinople in 1453. Halley's Comet, the brightest of all the comets, will next reappear in 1986.

4 The shortest orbit of any comet is that of Encke's Comet, first seen in 1786—it has an orbit of just 3.30 years. Encke was a pupil of the German mathematician and astronomer Gauss who, in 1809, constructed a method for computing any type of orbit, improving on a rather *limited* method used for computing parabolic orbits published twelve years earlier. Gauss also won fame when he showed how to rediscover the lost asteroid Ceres in 1801.

5 Short-period comets move mainly in direct orbits that lie close to the mean plane of the solar system and are often referred to as belonging to the family of Jupiter, because they have aphelion distances close to the orbit of that planet. They rarely have *conspicuous* tails and can sometimes *disintegrate*, causing showers of meteoric particles. Comets that have a hyperbolic orbit are usually seen only once and do not reappear; others, like Halley's Comet are elliptical in orbit and the date of their next appearance can be calculated. Periodic comets are rich in gas because they have lost the dusty outer layers of their nucleus and are also quite bright, unlike the dust-rich new comets. The behaviour of the comet nucleus suggests that there may be two types—one a uniform icy conglomerate which eventually dissipates, and the other a nucleus with a central core of heavy, compacted stony material which eventually loses all its gas, leaving behind a rocky body.

6

It was believed in Graeco-Roman times that comets were phenomena restricted to the upper atmosphere of the Earth, but in the late 15th and early 16th centuries it was shown that comets were far more distant than the Moon. The greatest naked-eye astronomer, Tycho Brahe, demonstrated that a comet he observed in 1577 must be more distant than the Moon because it showed no shift in its position through parallax, nearer planets showing a more noticeable apparent shift in position. Then Sir Isaac Newton observed that the comet Kirch discovered in 1680 moved in an orbit around the Sun in accordance with his theory of gravity, but the first person to study the spectra of comets was the Italian astronomer Donati in 1864; he discovered several comets, including the one of 1858 which bears his name. Dr William Wollaston had found dark areas in the spectrum of the Sun in 1802, and spectroscopic analysis really began in 1861 with a much-improved spectroscope designed by Bunsen and Kirchhoff; then in 1868, Sir Norman Lockyer discovered helium in the solar spectrum. In 1881, the first photographic spectrum of comets revealed a strong ultraviolet emission and a continuous spectrum was recorded showing the strongest lines of the solar spectrum. Later on there was a study of comet tails. Near the turn of the century it became possible to observe the constituents within a comet with the aid of the wide-field view of the objective prism. Our present knowledge of comets is *derived* from these early pioneering observations, solely visual until the beginning of the present century.

7

Comets are named after their discoverers with up to three names *permitted*; then the year of discovery is given, followed by a lower-case letter giving the order of discovery (or recovery in the case of periodic comets), e.g. 1979 a, 1979 b, 1979 c, and so on. Permanent designations are eventually *allotted* in the order of perihelion passage; the first comet to pass in 1979 would be called 1979 I, the second 1979 II, and so on, using upper-case Roman numerals. Sometimes there may be a difference between the preliminary and the *definitive* designations as comets can be discovered long before or long after their perihelion passage. A short-period comet will be prefixed with the letter P and may be followed by an Arabic number showing that the same person has discovered two or more periodic comets. If a lost periodic comet is seen again, then the name of the recoverer is added; some comets are named after the observer who discovered their periodic habit. Should there be a multi-observation of a comet at the same time, then an impersonal name, e.g. Northern comet, is given.

QUESTION 1

Put the following statements into chronological sequence as described in the passage.

A   Donati gives his name to a comet.
B   Comet Kirch is discovered.
C   The first photographic spectrum of a comet is recorded.
D   The first periodic comet is noted.
E   It is decided that comets can be more distant than the Moon.
F   The first record of a comet is made in the ancient world.
G   Comet tails are explained by a German astronomer.
H   The appearance of a comet terrifies Christians.
I   The first study of the spectra of comets is made.
J   The shortest orbiting comet is seen for the first time.

Step	
1	
2	
3	
4	
5	
6	
7	
8	
9	
10	

QUESTION 2

In the passage there are 15 words set in italics. Give their correct meaning in sequence from the list of definitions given to you (overleaf).

1 ....   3 ....
2 ....   4 ....

5	....	11	....
6	....	12	....
7	....	13	....
8	....	14	....
9	....	15	....
10	....		

break up   represented
forecast   invented
follows   decorated
conclusive   measuring
set out   essential
forbidden   results from
goes ahead of   narrow
cloudy   intricate
allowed   distinct

QUESTION 3

Here is a list of five hypothetical comet sightings. Give each one its full title as described in the passage.

1 This short-period comet was discovered by Ian Jenkins in 1978 when it was the second comet to reach perihelion that year. Jenkins already has two other observations of comets to his credit.

2 This short-period comet was recovered by Neal Thomas thirty years ago and was re-discovered by W. Henry in 1970, when it was the first comet to reach perihelion that year.

3 This comet was seen in 1963 by a large group of astronomers at Cambridge university who decided to give it the name of the university. It was the fourth comet to pass perihelion that year.

4 This comet was particularly brilliant, which gave it its name. It was seen for the first time in 1974 by several observers who later discovered that it was the ninth comet that year to pass the Sun.

5 This comet has only just been observed by W. Homer in 1981, when it was the second comet to be observed. Its perihelion date has yet to be calculated.

Pointing and Jointing

Pointing and jointing are terms used in brickwork to describe the surface finish of bed joints (horizontal) and cross joints (vertical) and have a similar function, that of sealing *crevices* to prevent moisture penetration and to give a pleasing appearance to the brickwork face. They are, however, different methods and have different characteristics. Pointing is the term used when the original bed and cross joints of a brick wall are raked out to a depth of approximately 12 mm, *dampened*, and filled with a new mortar, possibly of a different colour, texture and density from that used to lay the bricks; it is done after the brickwork has been completed in the case of new work or when the mortar joints in old walls have crumbled allowing moisture to penetrate. Jointing is the term used when the joint is formed as the work proceeds course by course while the mortar is in its plastic stage. Each method has its advantages and disadvantages: Pointing is neater than jointing, it keeps the face of the brickwork cleaner and the bricks more clearly defined, especially if they are sand-faced and regular in shape. It is also easier to maintain the *consistency* of colour, texture, and density as smaller quantities of mortar are used. This is not so with jointing, as large quantities of mortar are required and variations are *bound to* occur; however, the finish is much stronger as there can be no failure of adhesion since the joint is an integral part of the mortar bed. It is also quicker and cheaper than pointing. The choice of joint in both pointing and jointing depends on a number of factors; for example, whether the brickwork is internal or external, whether it is functional or decorative, whether it is to repair old brickwork, or whether it is to be rendered over once completed. The type of brick used will also determine the finish of the joint: with sand-faced bricks, the joints must not be trowelled smooth as the total effect must be one of roughness of texture, and extra care must be taken to avoid smearing and staining the brick as it is very porous. If an old brick wall is being repointed then great attention must be paid to the density of the mortar mix; if, again, engineering bricks are being used, a severely trowelled smooth joint would be necessary. The tools used in pointing and jointing are the pointing rule, which is a straight length of wood with a bevelled cutting edge and two small pieces of wood on each end to give *clearance* between it and the wall. The bevelled edge is placed along the edge that requires trimming and a pointed knife with its tip bent at right angles, called a frenchman, is drawn along it causing the *surplus* mortar to fall between the wall and the rule. There are two trowels used in pointing and jointing, the dotter and the bed jointer, the former used for cross joints and the latter, as it is larger, is used for better effect on bed joints. The hawk is a square-shaped piece of wood about 225 × 225 mm with a handle attached at right angles to it from beneath. It carries the small amounts of mortar necessary when repointing. Flush joints can be converted into keyed or tooled joints by drawing a specially shaped tool along the joint; this can be a jointer, a flat piece of steel varying from 60 mm to 125 mm in length, fastened in a wooden handle and used for square recessed joints, the jointer being of the same thickness as the width of the joint; or it could be a home-made tool such as a piece of electrician's conduit or mild-steel rod; even a piece of wood can be used to avoid damaging the arrises of the bricks.

Here is a selection of types of pointing and jointing:

Weather-struck joint
These are used on external work, usually with smooth-faced, machine-made bricks. The joint is formed as the wall is in the process of being built when the mortar is semi-stiff, and the *inclined* blade of the trowel is drawn across the bed joint to give an angle of 60° or more, depending on the effect required. The bed joint will then slope slightly inwards either from the lower edge of the upper brick or from the upper edge of the lower brick, the horizontal joint recessed under the brick above. Vertical jointing is done first by pressing the point of a trowel down each centre joint to produce a V section, then the bed joints are made. The bevel allows rain water to run off the top edges which have been sealed smooth by the trowel. This joint must never be used with rough-textured bricks as its joint is too smooth and, as the top arrises of the course are straight, the joint would accentuate any inaccuracy in the lower edges should they be uneven.

Weather-cut joint
These are identical to weather-struck joints but the mortar is allowed to project at the bottom of the bed joint and at one side of the cross-joint.

Struck joint
Striking the joints in the *reverse* direction, that is, sloping them inwards from the top, is not recommended for outside work as it forms a ledge on which water can collect, damaging the arrises and allowing damp penetration. This is a struck joint and is used on internal walls where a decorative appearance is required. The lower edge of the bed joint is struck back as the work progresses.

Flush joint This is a flat joint finished with a rough texture and lies flush with the brickwork. It is the commonest joint because it is the quickest. The mortar is pressed into the joint and when semi-stiff is rubbed in one direction with a clean piece of sacking or, lightly brushed with a soft brush, so that the flat joint has a rough texture and not trowelled smooth. It is a good joint to use where smooth-faced brickwork is desired.

Recessed or sunk joint This is not often used but can be extremely effective, creating shadow effects with textured bricks, whose sharp arrises can be accentuated. It is for internal use only but could be used outside if the bricks are very hard, but there is a strong risk of damp penetration and damage to the arrises as a result of weather action. The recess, square in profile, can vary in depth. It is formed by raking out brickwork joints for approximately 12 mm from both top and bottom edges of the bricks with a pointed piece of metal, then smoothed with a tool the same width as the joint.

Tooled or rounded joint Also called bucket-handled joints, these are formed while the wall is in the process of being built and when the mortar is semi-stiff. It is a form of recessed joint but semi-circular in profile, the size of its curve being determined by the diameter of the tool used. If a narrow indentation is required, then a convex piece of steel rod can be drawn along the joint. For a wider curve, a thicker, rounded jointer could be used, fitting the width of the joint.

Projecting joint This is used when the inside of a wall is to be plastered over. It is formed by allowing the mortar to project between the bricks for the entire width of the joint so that it will provide an excellent key for plaster which will be applied later.

Tuck pointing This is used in *renovating* old brickwork whose joints are defective and whose arrises are ragged. New mortar is pushed into the joint after the old mortar has been raked out and then trowelled flush with the brickwork. Then, when the mortar is semi-stiff, a deep groove is made along the centre of each joint and the entire wall coloured as required, prior to the application of the tuck mortar. This is a mixture of lime, putty and silver sand. It is applied to the indented joint so that it projects from both top and bottom edges by about 3 mm. Its final appearance is that of narrow, white projecting joints which look very neat but require skill in application, since all vertical joints must be plumb with each other and maintain a correct appearance.

Bastard tuck pointing This is more *durable* than tuck pointing but less attractive. The shape of the joint is exactly the same but the projecting bands are of the same material as that on the bed joints and contain no putty and silver sand.

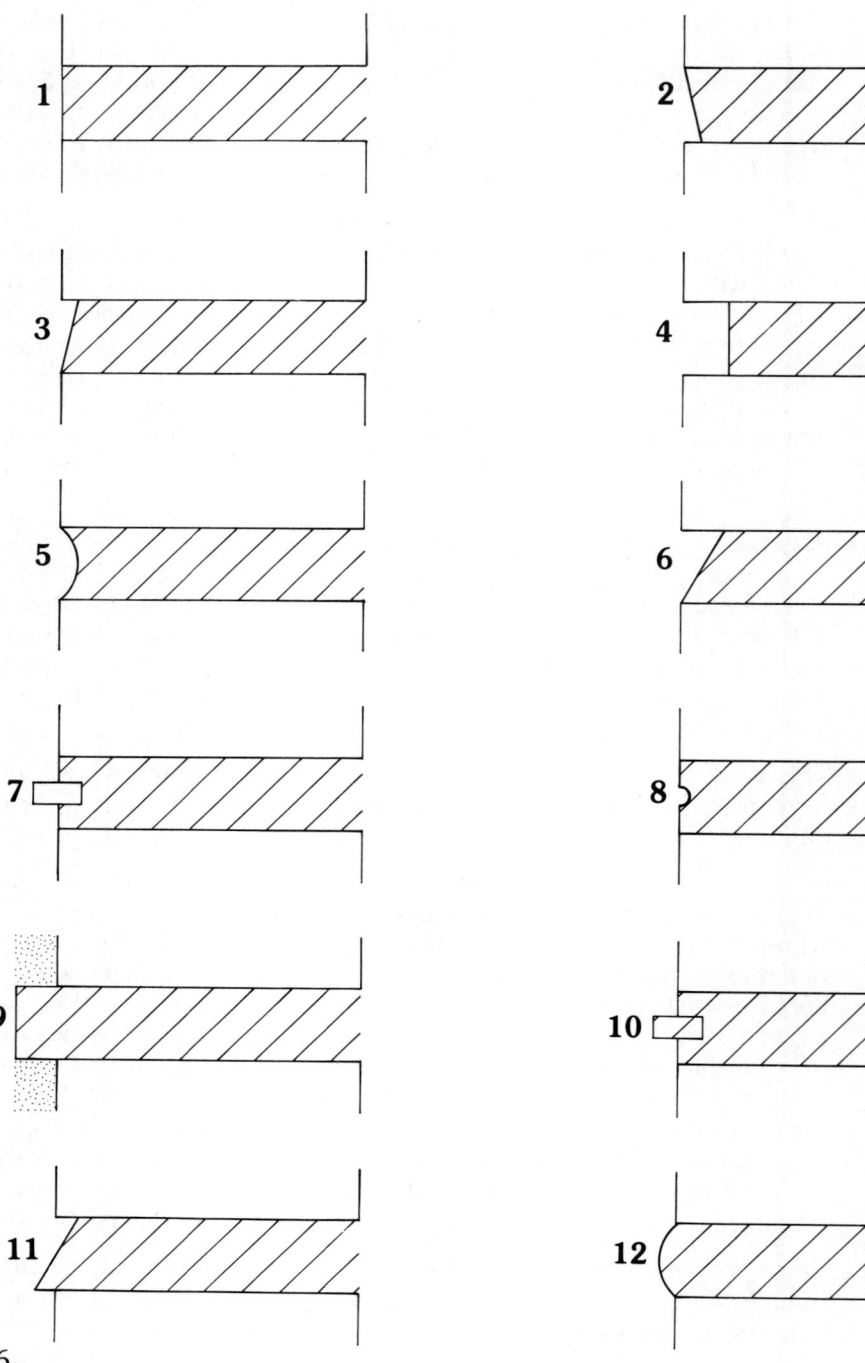

QUESTION 1

Look at the diagrams of the various types of pointing and jointing on the previous page. Decide, from the descriptions given, which type is which and complete the table. Should any type not be described, put X.

1		7	
2		8	
3		9	
4		10	
5		11	
6		12	

QUESTION 2

Some words in the passage are italicised. From the list of words given to you in the box below give the italicised word which most closely resembles it in meaning. If there is no suitable definition given in the box, put X in the space. Please follow the words in the box in the order in which they are written.

1	9		sharp
			lasting
2	10		sloping
			difficult
3	11		liable to
			same
4	12		space
			unlikely to
5	13		cracks
			uniformity
6	14		unnecessary
			opposite
7	15		bricks
			renewing
8			fixed

By-products of Timber

Wood was used for building purposes as early as 8000 BC and has continued to be exploited by man for centuries. Although there are more than 20 000 species of timber in the world and 25% of its land area is covered by forest, there is a shortage of timber of all kinds, largely because there has, until recently, been little attention paid to the conservation or protection of certain species, and comparatively few species are commercially cultivated. With the development of forestry, where trees are bred by the most efficient means, and wood technology where intensive research has been made into ways and means of improving timber utilisation, more timber and timber products are available for use. Some important by-products of timber are hardboard, plywood, chipboard, battenboard, blockboard and laminboard.

Hardboard is made from highly compressed softwood pulp, and if properly sealed can be painted, papered or laminated. It is manufactured in several different grades, one of which is suitable for exterior use. It has one smooth and one textured face and can be glued or pinned to a wooden framework or can be used to face a panelled door.

Plywood is another important by-product of timber. It is a highly versatile material and is made by the cementing together of a number of sheets of veneer or layers of wood of three or more pieces, the grain of each successive piece running at right angles to the next, giving strength and stability, whilst avoiding contraction, expansion and splitting. The manufacture of plywood began in 1793 when a patent was granted to Dr Samuel Bentham for a machine which would cut veneers, and at the same time the use of adhesives was introduced. The greater the number of veneers, the stronger the plywood, but there must always be an odd number of sheets used in each bonding: an even number will suffer tensions created by the glue which will cause warping or twisting, so there can never be a 2, 4, 5, 8, or 10 ply: but by putting two veneers one on each side of the centre core, the tensions are equalised and no warping can take place provided that there is no wetting of the material and that there is no excessive heat. New veneers can be added in pairs to the basic 3 ply, building up to 11 ply. Ply is graded according to the quality of its outer veneers; grade A indicates that there is no blemish, B means there are slight markings on the veneer, BB means there are dead knots and other faults like repaired areas. AA indicates that both sides of the veneer are perfect, while B/BB, the common grade, means that there is one sound side but one side with repaired faults. Thick veneers are called constructional veneers, and it is these that are used in the manufacture of plywood; the thinner veneers are used for decorative purposes. Plywood can be used for many purposes, just as solid timber, and can be jointed like solid wood provided it is thick enough. If dampened, it can be curved, although the grain of the outside ply should be across the curve rather than with it for a tighter curve. It also bends best when it is thin. It should be cut with a fine saw, being scored with a knife across the grain prior to sawing to prevent splitting. It is also advisable to drill holes into the ply rather than screwing in direct, as the material is prone to splitting, and the use of screw cups will prevent the screw from sinking in too far. Ply should be laminated with a waterproof bond if it is to be used in damp conditions and a special marine ply is used for boat building. Because the edges of ply are prone to chipping and wear badly, all edges should be protected with lipping or rounded off.

3

Chipboard is also made from wood. It consists of resin-coated particles of wood chips and wood shavings bonded together under pressure and heat. It is sandwiched between veneers and used for work tops and mass-produced furniture. It is made in thicknesses of 4–40 mm, the most common being 12, 18 and 22 mm. The fibres of chipboard criss-cross so that the board has a similar strength in all lateral directions, but the vertical structure is layered. It is strong and will not warp, but must be supported at the edges as it will sag under its own weight over a span of about a metre. Most chipboard is made in three or more alternating layers of fine and coarse particles with the fine particles on the faces. It is for interior use only and must never be used in damp conditions. It can be jointed like solid wood but must never be jointed edge to edge as this is a weak point in the bond, unless it is supported. Chipboard machines well, although the resin in it wears the cutters after a time. It will take pins, nails and screws except on its edges when they will pull out unless the board has been lipped with solid timber. Nor should one screw into chipboard but through it. It must be stored either flat or in a vertical position to avoid distortion. Some chipboard is sealed ready for painting or veneered with plastic for shelving or work tops.

4 **Blockboard** is more than twice the cost of chipboard and is made by taking random lengths of timber or small blocks of wood joined together with bonding agents under high pressure and faced with single or double sheets of veneer. The core is placed in such a way as to create inner strength and runs the length of the sheet, making it stronger in its length than its width. It is for interior use only and commonly used for making table tops, cupboards, wardrobes, and doors. Usually one side has a good veneer and one of a lower grade but the grain will always run across the width. It must be stored flat or in a vertical position to prevent warping and should it require painting, then both sides must be painted as tensions will result, and the board will twist. In order to conceal the core construction of blockboard and to provide fixing for screws, the exposed edges need to be lipped with solid timber.

5 **Battenboard** is a variation of blockboard and contains relatively wider pieces of timber. It is used in major construction work.

Laminboard is made from lengths of plywood placed vertical to the top and bottom veneers. Its core strips are narrower than those of blockboard, otherwise it is constructed in exactly the same way. It has the advantage over blockboard in that it is stronger and usually has a better quality surface veneer. It is rarely more than 9.5 mm wide.

QUESTION 1

Look at the diagrams opposite and overleaf. In the table below give the name of the wood product described. If a diagram does not fit any of the descriptions put X. Then decide whether the products in the last six diagrams are being correctly or incorrectly used.

1		9	
2		10	
3		11	
4		12	
5		13	
6		14	
7		15	
8			

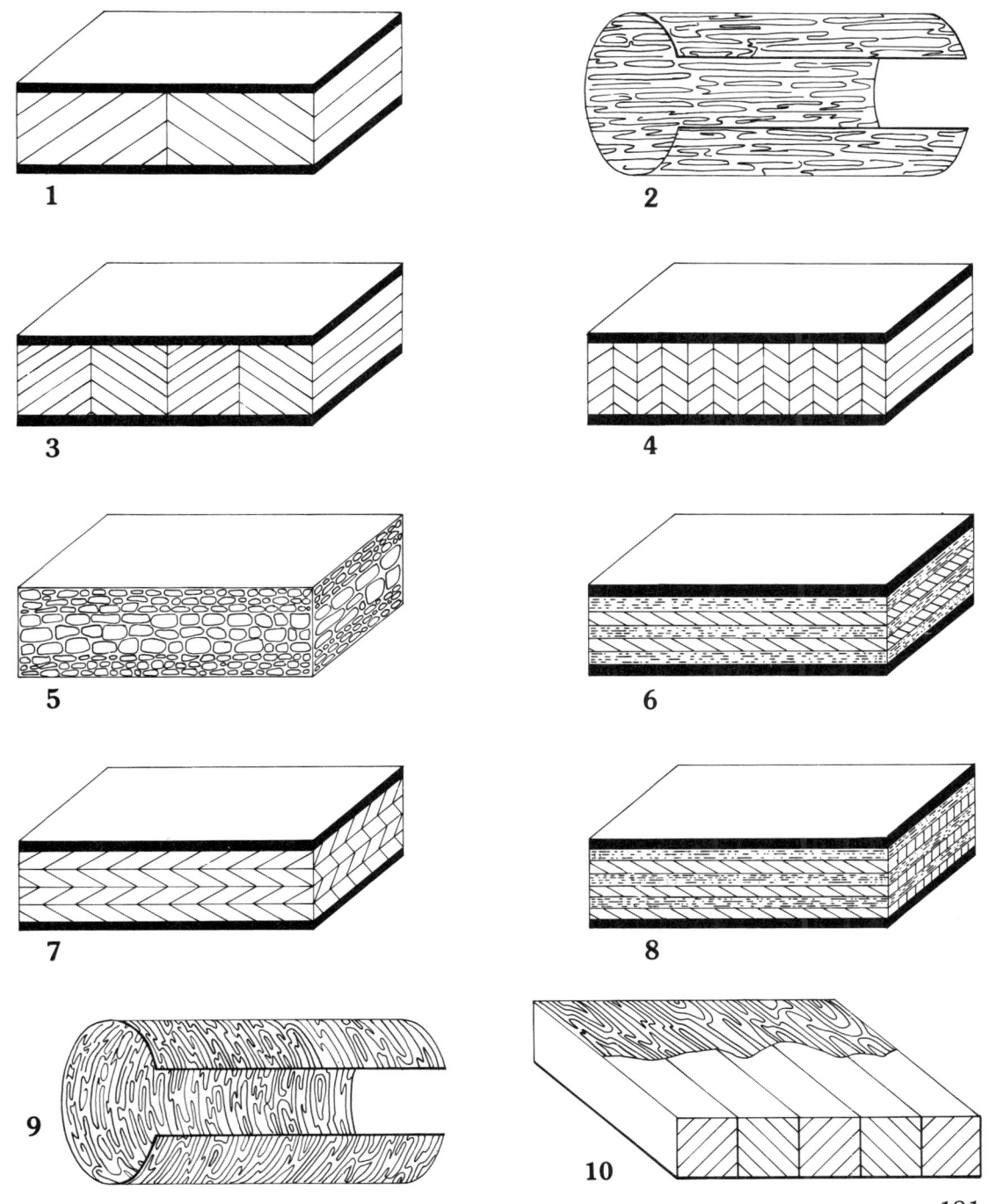

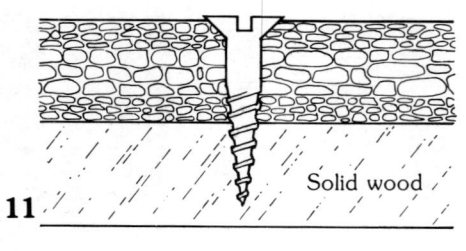
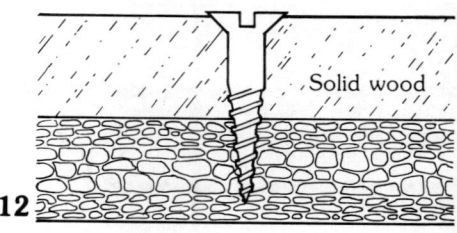
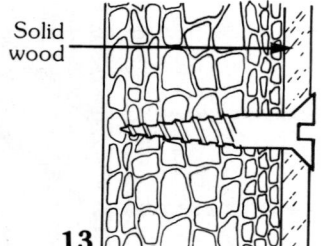
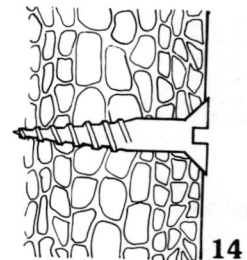
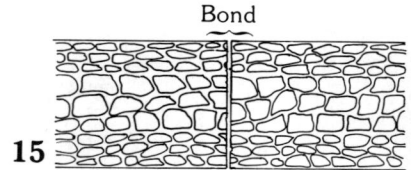

QUESTION 2

Give the word or phrase from the passage which has the same meaning as the following: (the paragraph numbers are given.)

1 outside . . . . (1)
2 variable . . . . (2)
3 following . . . . (2)
4 shrinking . . . . (2)
5 before . . . . (2)

6 horizontal . . . . (3)
7 bend . . . . (3)
8 eventually . . . . (3)
9 indeterminate . . . . (4)
10 hide . . . . (4)

Swallow Showers

Below you will find a list of statements extracted from an advertisement on Swallow Showers from a colour magazine. Decide what are the facts about the shower and what is advertising jargon and write a paragraph which might be useful in providing information to a member of the public who may be interested in buying the shower.

* Feel as fresh as a daisy every time.
* Our prices are very competitive.
* There are seven models to choose from.
* The shower is fitted with an anti-scald device so that both young and old can use it with complete confidence.
* Swallow Showers Ltd. have a nationwide reputation and offer a reliable after-sales service all over the country.
* We have hundreds of satisfied customers.
* For the truly discerning, a Swallow shower is one of the better things in life and a real luxury.
* Come on, spoil yourself! Wash away those early-morning blues!
* A five-minute shower costs approximately one penny.
* Our showers are advertised on television.
* The shower can be installed the same day as you receive it.
* A Swallow shower will add class to your home and your neighbours will envy you.
* Both parts and labour are guaranteed for one year.
* The shower has been passed for safety by the Electricity Council.
* You only heat the water you use, so save money.
* You know it makes sense to buy our superb showers.
* Have friendly early-morning get-togethers!
* You do not need a tank.
* The shower is available in 10 modern colours.
* Your bathroom will look very special.
* Swallow showers are fitted with a water-temperature control.
* Stop that annoying queue outside the bathroom every morning!
* The family that has a Swallow shower is a happy family.

Hand Tools in Woodwork

1 There are more than 73 different kinds of hammer, many with specific trade applications, and there are basic rules to bear in mind when using, caring for and buying a hammer for whatever purpose you may need it. Hammers are dangerous tools when used carelessly: you must never, for example, hold the handle too close to its head, because it reduces the force of the blow. The hammer must be held at such an angle that its face and the surface of the object being hit will be parallel. This will distribute the force of the blow over the full face and prevent damage both to the hammer and the object. A well-made hammer has a head secured to the handle with three wedges, two of steel and one of wood, expanding the handle so that it provides a tight fit, otherwise a loose head may fly off and cause damage. A pull of more than 4 tonnes should be necessary to separate the head from its handle. It is essential when buying a hammer to select the best quality that you can afford; one with a forged-steel head will last for many years, but a cheaper cast one will be prone to shattering and will not give long service. The balance of a hammer is important, too: for best results the hammer should be able to stand on its claw and come to rest without toppling over. The quality of the face or striking head of the hammer will tell you whether it is well-made or not: it should be slightly domed with its edges chamfered or rounded off so that, if by chance a nail is hit at an angle, it will still go in straight. To care for your hammer, you must ensure that its face is free from grease, as a slippery hammer will cause the nail or pin to bend. Wooden handles should be rubbed periodically with raw linseed oil. Make sure that the handles are not split or damaged in any way as they will cause cuts and splinters; never repair a wooden handle; in fact, always replace it.

2 There are specialist hammers for woodwork which can be obtained with heads of varying weights—depending on the purpose for which they are required—but on the whole, there are two basic types: the **claw hammer** and the **cross-pein hammer.** The claw hammer is a must if you do a lot of woodwork as it performs a dual function—it both drives nails in and pulls them out. It weighs from 448–560 g and is provided with either a steel or a wooden shaft, the former being much stronger but having the disadvantage of its plastic or rubber sheath covering becoming slippery when wet or hot and inclined to mark the work if laid down carelessly. The claw hammer has a hammer face which drives in the nail and a cut-away section or claw which tapers to a fine V shape, capable of extracting fine pins or nails. The nail is hooked into the V and, keeping the handle almost upright, you pull, taking the precaution of placing a scrap of wood underneath the hammer to protect the surface of your work. Hold your hammer with your fingers underneath and your thumb along the side or top: the thumb should rest on the handle and never overlap the fingers. For headless nails, you should use **pincers** which open like a pair of scissors to grip the nail and use a series of short, sharp pulls; otherwise you will enlarge the hole when the nail is extracted.

The cross-pein hammer is very useful for small pins and tacks. It has a tapered end or pein which is used for starting off the pin. The pin is held between the fingers and gently tapped; once it is capable of standing on its own, you can drive it home with the hammer face. The lightest version of the cross-pein hammer is the **pin hammer**, which is used on very light and small pins which would be bent by a heavier model. Otherwise, it is used in exactly the same way.

Used in conjunction with the above hammers, are the **pin-push** and the **punch**. The pin-push is quick to use, being particularly suitable for fixing pins into hardboard or thin ply. A panel pin fits into the end tube and is driven home by pressing down on the rounded shank, where an inside spring is compressed and released automatically.

The punch is used for driving headless nails or panel pins below the surface of the timber so that they are invisible, the hole they made being filled with plastic wood afterwards. There are many kinds of hand punches designed to do a variety of jobs, most being made of tool steel and about 11 cm long. Their point can vary in size from 1.5 mm to 4.5 mm. It is recommended that you use a size smaller than the diameter of the nail head so that the hole is not larger than is necessary. The part held in the hand is octagonal in shape or it may be knurled or roughened, which prevents the tool from slipping around in the hand. You must use it with care, ensuring that it does not slip when you hit it, as you want to avoid injury to your fingers and to your work. Both of these hazards can be surmounted by holding the punch at right angles to your work and striking the punch squarely with your hammer. Punches are usually hollow-ground at the tip so that they locate centrally on the nail head and stay there; the punch is tapped with the hammer and the nail or pin is driven in below the surface of the timber.

Should the point of the punch break off, it can be reground and tapered along its length. Remember, though, that although you can strike a punch or a chisel directly with a hammer because they are tempered, being tough but not too hard, you must never strike hardened steel surfaces which are not tempered, as small pieces of steel may break off and an injury to the eyes or damage to the work may result.

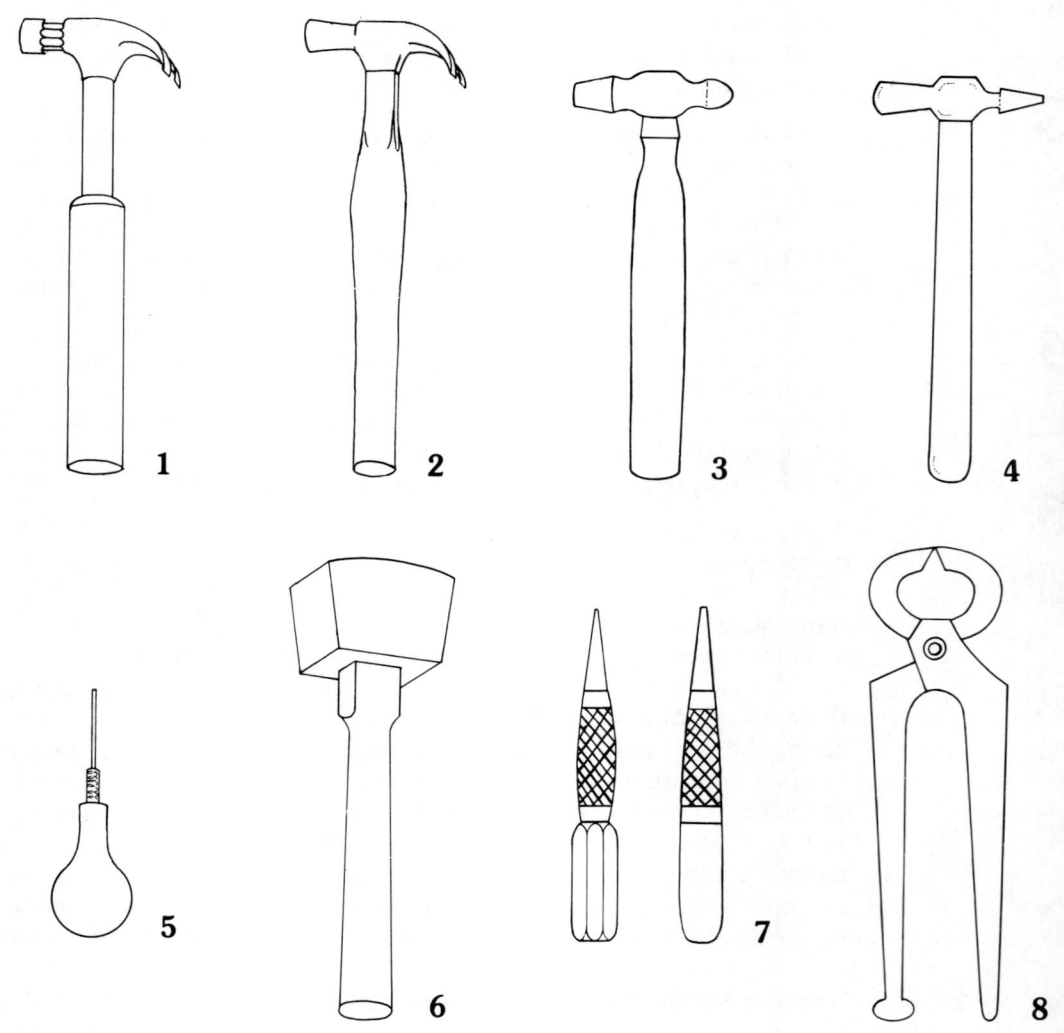

QUESTION 1

Give a word or phrase from the passage which is equivalent in meaning to the following: (the paragraph numbers are given).

1	precise .... (1)		6	double .... (2)
2	spread .... (1)		7	together with .... (4)
3	disposed to .... (1)		8	prevent .... (5)
4	from time to time .... (1)		9	risks .... (5)
5	generally .... (2)		10	overcome .... (5)

QUESTION 2

Look at the diagrams on the previous page and, in the table below, label each tool with its name, using X if the tool illustrated is not described in the passage.

1		5	
2		6	
3		7	
4		8	

QUESTION 3

Using a series of numbered sentences, give the appropriate advice to an amateur on each of the following:

1 Buying a woodwork hammer.

2 Using a woodwork hammer.

3 Keeping it in good condition.

(Continued overleaf)

1 When you buy a woodwork hammer you must . . .
a)
b)
c)
d)
e)

2 When you use a woodwork hammer you must . . .
a)
b)
c)
d)

3 To keep your hammer in good condition you should . . .
a)
b)
c)

The Miniature

Put the missing word in each line in the space provided and indicate
the place in the line from which it is missing by using the symbol /.

1 _____ Miniatures were exquisitely painted portraits, frequently no more 3 cm
2 _____ across, which were designed to be worn or carried their owners.
3 _____ They were romantic, intimate objects, delicately painted, and certain periods
4 _____ during the last four hundred years, very fashionable. The art portrait
5 _____ painting began in Europe in the late Middle Ages and was developed
6 _____ England when continental artists, encouraged by Henry VIII, arrived the
7 _____ early years of the 16th century. One of artists was Hans Holbein whose
8 _____ methods greatly influenced the first great English-born miniaturist, famous
9 _____ Nicholas Hilliard. Miniatures were originally in watercolours vellum or
10 _____ parchment (apart those on copper where oils were used) and circular in
11 _____ shape but later during the Elizabethan period they oval and were fitted into
12 _____ lockets. Many miniatures have survived from the 17th century undoubtedly
13 _____ the finest were those of Samuel Cooper, believed by many be the greatest
14 _____ miniaturist ever. During the wealthy and artistic 18th century, art
15 _____ of miniature painting reached its zenith and very fashionable, with portraits
16 _____ framed in precious stones and mounted in elaborate cases; vellum, copper
17 _____ parchment were gradually replaced fine-grade ivory, a more beautiful
18 _____ medium, being more translucent. The elegance of the period reflected
19 _____ in the glowing colours of the miniatures of this time. With advent of pow-
20 _____ dered paint, the artist had fewer technical problems he was relieved of the
21 _____ drudgery of refining his own pigments. During the Victorian period, was
22 _____ fashionable to wear a miniature with a lock of hair on the reverse side the

23 _____ Queen herself wore a bracelet with linked portraits of all her children;
24 _____ there was gradual decline in the quality of miniatures. Landscapes began
25 _____ to appear as background, the portraits larger and rectangular in shape.
26 _____ Many were placed on desks and small tables. The costumes this period,
27 _____ too, were drab and insipid. With the discovery of photography in 1840,
28 _____ miniature gradually ceased to exist which is a great pity. However,
29 _____ the collector this be a good thing because it increases the rarity value of
30 _____ his collection, which shows a steady appreciation in value the years pass

QUESTION

Decide whether the following statements are true or false according to the passage and then complete the table.

	True	False
1 Victorian clothes were decorative and attractive.		
2 The first miniatures were rectangular in shape.		
3 The decline of miniature portrait painting began in 1700.		
4 The early miniatures were painted on paper.		
5 The discovery of photography supplanted the miniature.		
6 Miniatures today are valueless.		
7 During the reign of Elizabeth I miniatures were oval in shape.		
8 The art of miniature painting flourished in the 18th century.		
9 Nicholas Hilliard was a famous continental artist.		
10 The art of the miniature portrait began in England.		

Little Oakham Hall

1 Many secular buildings have survived in Britain from the 13th century onwards, and one of the most attractive, now that it has been restored to its original character, is Little Oakham Hall in Shropshire. Built as a small defendable manor house in the middle of the 15th century, Oakham Hall, with its pronounced vertical emphasis of structure and decoration, is a classic example of Late Gothic architecture, and despite its recent internal modernisation, the house still presents the same front to the world as it did five hundred years ago.

2 Initially the house consisted of the Great Hall, which occupied a north–south axis and extended between two short wings of two storeys, the northern wing comprising buttery and wine store on each side of the kitchen, and the southern wing which was used entirely as a parlour, with a solar and chapel above. An east-facing private room and gallery formed the second storey of the north wing. The Great Hall was the nucleus of all houses at this period and its function remained virtually unchanged for at least three centuries: at one end of the Hall, within easy access of a stairway leading to the solar and private appartments, stood a raised area or dais where the lord and his family would sit, with their retainers' tables ranged lengthways down each side of the Hall. In many houses, an open hearth stood in the centre of the floor but in Little Oakham Hall, three fireplaces, two dating from the early 16th century, were uncovered, hidden behind layers of bricks and plaster, when Nicholas Martin began the renovation in 1975.

3 When he first saw the old house, a year prior to becoming its owner, Nicholas Martin, an architect by profession, was immediately attracted to it in spite of its air of decay and neglect. For nearly twenty years the house had been unoccupied and its garden was completely overgrown. It was, however, in a delightful spot, standing on high ground, with unspoilt countryside all around, and beyond, the hills of Wales. The house presented a challenge to Nicholas Martin, not only because of its physical condition, which would have to be made structurally sound, but also because its interior had been vastly but hideously refurbished by a previous occupant, a prosperous Victorian industrialist. These embellishments would have to be drastically removed.

4 The industrialist was William Hardcastle, who had purchased the property in the summer of 1850. He found it in a state of dilapidation but was quick to realise its potential. He installed sanitation at once and then rendered the oak beams with plaster; the Hall was sub-divided into four rooms—a dining room and library on the east wall and a parlour and kitchen on the west. The former south-facing parlour adjacent to the library had its windows enlarged to admit more light and became a conservatory. The old kitchen became a pantry and the buttery was fitted out as a scullery, with laundry facilities, conveniently situated adjacent to the new kitchen. The upper rooms were converted into bedrooms to complement those in the old chapel and solar. Finally, a long porch was added to the middle of the west wall, making the house T-shaped.

5 Nicholas Martin began by demolishing this porch and then removed all interior Victorian partitions, being careful not to damage the original oak supports. The old oak beams were then stripped of plaster, exposed and treated, and the two 16th century fireplaces were restored to their previous beauty. After electric underfloor heating had been installed, the floors were re-flagged. A sliding oak partition was then fitted across the Hall which would enable it to be divided into two smaller rooms if required. The northern wing has been extensively refitted with the old pantry and the wine store becoming a launderette and cloakroom respectively, while a new fitted kitchen occupies the Victorian scullery. A dining area has been made along the northern side of the Hall.

6 The southern wing of the house, whose windows have been re-mullioned and reduced in size to their former dimensions, is now used by Nicholas Martin as a private workroom and office, with its own entrance. The house is simply furnished throughout, with walls stripped of the layers of Victorian paper, cleaned and sealed; sturdy dark oak furniture is in keeping with the sense of period and skin rugs are scattered over the stone floors. On cool evenings logs burn in the huge grates. In the final stage of development, the overgrown gardens have been cut down, dug over and landscaped in Elizabethan style, with neat lawns and yew hedges. From the outside, the entire house looks very much today as it would have done in the 15th century, a tribute to the vision and restraint of its new owner.

QUESTION 1

Put the following sentences into chronological sequence as described in the passage.

A   The gardens are landscaped.
B   A conservatory is annexed to the house.
C   Nicholas Martin sees Little Oakham Hall for the first time.
D   Three fireplaces are restored.
E   The house becomes T-shaped.
F   The oak beams are rendered over.
G   A Victorian industrialist becomes owner of the old manor.
H   A dining room is built on the north wall.
I   Victorian interior walls are demolished.
J   Sanitation is installed.
K   A manor house is built in Late Gothic style.
L   An architect buys the old Hall.
M   A firegrate is constructed in the centre of the Great Hall.
N   The Great Hall is sub-divided.

Step	
1	
2	
3	
4	
5	
6	
7	
8	
9	
10	

QUESTION 2

a) Draw a ground floor plan of Little Oakham Hall as it would have looked in 1550.

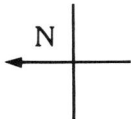

b) Draw a ground floor plan of Little Oakham Hall as it would have looked in 1880.

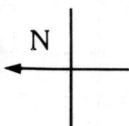

c) Draw a ground floor plan of Little Oakham Hall as it would have looked after the alterations undertaken by Nicholas Martin.

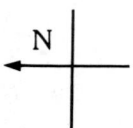

QUESTION 3 ———

Give the words or phrases from the passage which are equivalent in meaning to the following (the paragraph numbers are given).

1	remained . . . . (1)		6	renovated . . . . (3)
2	striking . . . . (1)		7	ruin . . . . (4)
3	at first . . . . (2)		8	permit . . . . (5)
4	practically . . . . (2)		9	robust . . . . (6)
5	before . . . . (3)		10	discipline . . . . (6)

Ashton University

The university of Ashton is situated in attractive rural surroundings just two miles outside the village and ten miles from the centre of Kingston. The square-shaped campus is bordered on its eastern perimeter by the meandering river Ash and to the west by Pilton forest. Open fields and meadowland stretch away to the south for five miles beyond St. Joseph's Road, which forms the southern margin to the campus. In the centre of the forest stands West House, the famous bird sanctuary. Built in 1947, Ashton University has developed considerably and has an excellent reputation for Medicine. Originally, the twin Science and Engineering blocks in the north of the campus were square-shaped, and their present oblong shape results from their extension in 1968. Occupying an east–west axis, these blocks flank each side of the Union building, which was originally rectangular in shape but now cruciform after its extension in 1969. Standing parallel to the Union building and at right angles to the Science and Engineering buildings is the Administration block which was extensively refurbished inside in 1972, while the L-shaped Arts block which backs on to the river housed the Library in its southern wing until 1970. It is now surrounded by flowerbeds and paved areas and is almost exactly equidistant from the Administration block and the river. The new and impressive circular Library complex which overlooks the forest is to be found halfway between the Science block and the Medical School, the crescent-shaped building to the south. In 1971, the year after the completion of the Library complex, two north-facing lozenge-shaped accommodation blocks were added to the rear of the Medical School as the existing block was found to be inadequate, and two wedge-shaped hospital blocks were constructed in 1973 to supplement the old hospital building on the north side of St. Joseph's Road. Standing on each side of the old hospital building, they are fronted by a wide forecourt just off the road, where ambulances are parked. The two square blocks in the extreme southeast of the campus, where the river bends to the east, are the Jarvis Institute, which houses a very fine treen collection and is open to the public five days a week. Since its foundation in 1949 it has become quite a tourist attraction, which would have delighted its benefactor, Sir Oliver Jarvis, who died in

1966, just after the Medical School was inaugurated. The Institute can be reached by taking bus number 55, which stops just outside the hospital, two minutes' walk away.

QUESTION 1

In the space provided and using the key below:

1. Draw a plan of the university campus prior to 1967.
2. Draw a plan of the university campus after 1973.

Bird sanctuary		Meadowland	
Forest		Road	
River			

1 Ashton University prior to 1967

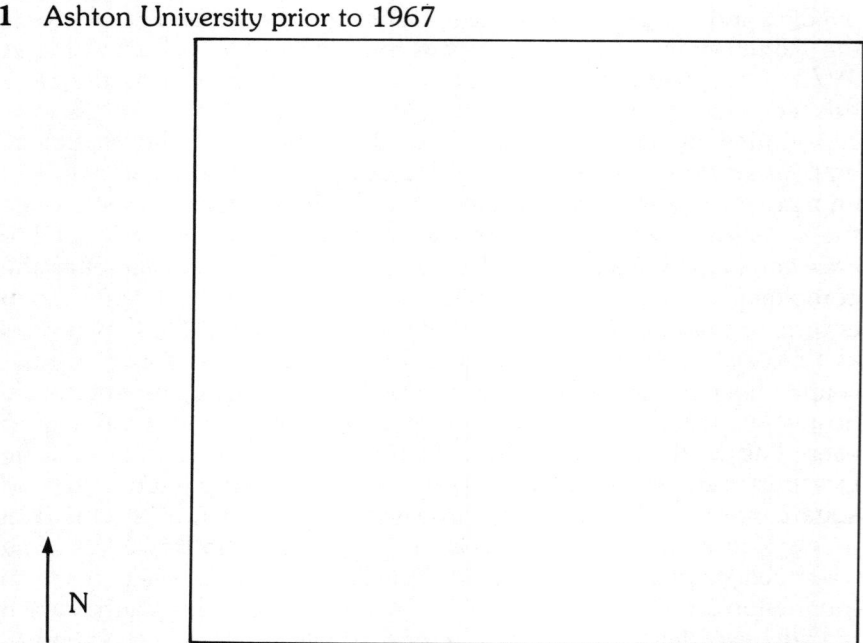

2 Ashton University after 1973

N ↑

QUESTION 2

Put the following sentences into chronological sequence as described in the passage.

A Two new accommodation blocks are built.
B The university is established.
C The Union building is extended.
D The Administration block is extended.
E The Jarvis Institute is built.
F The Science block is extended.
G Sir Oliver Jarvis dies.
H The Administration block is refitted.
I The new library is completed.
J Sir Oliver Jarvis builds the university.
K Two new hospital wings are built.
L The bird sanctuary is built.

Step	
1	
2	
3	
4	
5	
6	
7	
8	
9	

Castles—Part 2

1

The castle was an essential ingredient of the Middle Ages in Europe and was built either by a rich and powerful baron or bishop or a king, either for the protection of the owner and his followers or in order to dominate an area and control a potentially dangerous population.

2

Edwardian castles, which are the finest castles ever built and the highest point of fortress design, were built by Edward I and Edward II after the conquest of Wales in 1282 and show the influence of the Crusader castles of the Middle and Near East. Two main types of castle were introduced into Europe, having their origin in Syria: they were the result of the Crusades, beginning in 1097, when the upper soldier classes of western Europe went to Syria and Palestine on a holy war, passing through Constantinople and the East Roman Empire, where they saw the great fortresses built by the Greeks on Roman foundations. Each type of castle used successive lines of defence, one behind the other, and had frequent bastions for cross-fire. Type A was used if a castle were under attack on all sides which had to be covered equally, one line being completely enclosed by another. There was no keep—the strength of the castle lay in the ring of towers on each curtain wall. Type B was used when one side only was open to attack, so successive baileys faced the direction of attack. The best example of type B is Château Gaillard, built over the Seine in Paris by Richard I of England to guard his duchy of Normandy. The castle was in English hands for only five years, being destroyed by blockade in 1203. The most famous and the best preserved of the Crusader castles is Krak des Chevaliers on the Syrian coast and is an example of type A.

3

Edwardian castles were located on low-lying sites as a rule and concentric in plan for all-round defence, with moats or other water defences surrounding them and loop-holed galleries under the parapet. Their gateways were protected by barbicans or towers. The most famous Edwardian castles were Conway, Caernarvon, Beaumaris, and Harlech and aimed to crush Welsh resistance by blocking all the valley routes into the mountains where rebel forces could hide out.

4 There are some 1500 castles in England today, of which more than 1200 were founded between the 11th and 12th centuries. They were built originally by the invading Normans after 1066 so that they could dominate a territory. They were all private. Castles initially appeared in Europe in the 9th century as a result of the Viking raids on northern France and had at first a purely defensive role: Charlemagne had died in 814 and by 843 his empire had completely disintegrated, with parts of Europe becoming separate units. There was no central authority, so powerful barons took the defence of their territory into their own hands. The first examples of private fortification in England were the Norman castles, and they were to become the forerunners of the great stone castles of the Middle Ages.

5 The first castles were built along the south coast of England and were followed rapidly by castles in the valley of the river Thames. They were called motte and bailey castles, of which no intact example remains, and consisted of a steep conical mound or motte, either natural or artificial, with a flat top on which stood a timber citadel or defence tower raised on posts and surrounded by a timber stockade. At the base of the mound was a further stockade and outer ditch. Since the motte was relatively small in size, stables, byres, soldiers' quarters and other ancillary buildings were sited in the bailey or courtyard. This was an area at the base of the mound whose perimeter was defined by earthen ramparts topped by palisades of timber, behind which was a further ditch, either wet or dry, as an extra line of defence. The mound was connected to the courtyard by a sloping wooden bridge. The orthodox design for this castle was for the motte to be built in a corner of the bailey, giving the castle a figure-of-eight look, but some castles did not follow this stereotype: some had an inner and an outer bailey, others had the motte situated in the centre of the bailey which could be circular, oval, triangular, quadrilateral, lobed, polygonal or crescent-shaped. The original castle at Windsor, for example, had its motte in the centre of two baileys, while the castle at Lewes had two mottes separated by a central bailey. Brinklow castle in Warwickshire, which was in existence by 1130, had its motte topped by a defensive tower and was entirely surrounded by a ditch and inner stockade at its base. To the south-west it had two four-sided baileys, an inner and an outer, each stockaded on the outside only, the inner side being merely ditched. The baileys were joined by a wooden bridge and the inner bailey was connected by a second wooden bridge to the motte. Both motte and baileys were further enclosed by an outer ditch for added protection. (In Scotland it was customary for the motte and bailey to be undivided by a ditch, standing together on a raised mound. The motte had its wooden tower within a palisade and the entire bailey area was surrounded by yet another palisade.) At the beginning of the 12th century, rough stone replaced the internal wooden walls in the motte and bailey castle: they were called 'curtain walls' and by the middle of the century, this was followed by another development in the building of tall walls enclosing the motte. This is called the 'shell keep' castle, necessary when climatic conditions rotted the timber palisades. Around the bailey area, tall stone ramparts, either round or polygonal with timber buildings backed against them on their inner walls, surrounded the total area, leaving a courtyard in the centre. A trench still ran along the whole area on the outside.

6 Prior to the Norman invasion of England, there were very few castles to be found—those that did exist were built during the reign of Edward the Confessor, who ascended the throne in 1042 and introduced Norman architecture; he appointed the Abbot of Jumièges to be Archbishop of Canterbury and established Norman influence before the Conquest. During the Anglo-Saxon period, after the Romans had left Britain, the system of defence was the construction of burhs or stockaded and ditched fortifications for the protection of whole communities against external attack. Although they were primitive, they were successful enough in repelling Viking raids. They consisted of earthworks or enclosures protected by palisades of wooden stakes surrounded by a trench. In southern England the burhs were largely the work of Alfred of Wessex and protected whole districts from attack. Some burhs like London and Canterbury developed into towns and had their own garrison of soldiers.

7 By the 12th century the greatest castles had rectangular stone keeps instead of mottes and each had its own outbuildings. The first stone keep was built in France in 990. Since it would be heavy, the stone keep was built on level ground. The earliest form was the hall keep, which was rectangular in shape and consisted of a great hall and adjacent private chamber on the first storey—the ground floor being used for storage. About 1125 the tower keep developed, with the private chambers being situated above the great hall. Only two stone keeps were built during the reign of William I, the earliest being the White Tower of the Tower of London, which later became a concentric castle after the Crusader model; the other was at Colchester. At first, the stone keep was rectangular in shape with tall, thick walls but this was a considerable drawback in the fact that the enemy could only be reached if the defender were to lean right over the battlements, where he would be exposed to danger. At first the keeps were inhabited by the owner, his family, and retainers, but later keeps were used only as

a last resort, and living quarters were centred in the bailey. Another weakness in the square keep was the fact that the corners were vulnerable both to mining and to missiles, and when a winding staircase weakened the exterior wall. There were no flanking towers at this time. After 1154, during the reign of Henry II, the polygonal or round keep evolved from the early square keep as it offered no vulnerable angles to missiles and its curved staircase could be built into the wall. The round keep is not to be confused with the mound and ditch of shell keeps because it had neither mound nor ditch, being merely a round tower set on flat ground and enclosed by a bailey wall. If small, the tower was often given the further protection of a stone dome instead of a wooden roof, which reduced the risk of fire. After some time the keeps disappeared altogether and the strength of defence was to lie in separate towers set in the curtain wall.

During the 13th century, defence passed from the passive to the active: castles developed really high curtain walls during this time, with defensive towers set in them, sometimes rectangular but usually circular or polygonal, against the danger of mining. Crenellation was introduced when parapets were indented with alternate upright merlons and crenelles or gaps (a licence to crenellate was necessary during the reign of King John from 1199–1216). Behind the parapet was the allure or wall-walk, where soldiers would keep an eye open for enemy activity. The parapet walls were also pierced with loop-holes to enable the crossbow and longbow to be used against invaders. Wooden shutters were employed in the gaps between the merlons to protect the marksmen. There was also a first attempt to overcome the disadvantage of tall walls, when there was always a blind spot at the foot which could neither be seen nor protected by the defenders. Roofed wooden hoardings were introduced, laid on beams projecting through the parapet on the level of the allure or wall-walk where the enemy could be assailed by molten lead, pitch or stones. The wooden hoarding, however, was easily destroyed by fire or by the natural ravages of the weather so it was soon replaced by permanent stone hoarding or machicolations, where stone corbels were used. These brackets were built out from the walls carrying the battlements, with gaps in them for vertical fire. During the course of the century, machicolation, especially over gateways, was progressively in use, and as archery developed passages were cut into the curtain walls themselves and provided with loop-holes from which to fire. The foot of the walls and towers was strengthened by the addition of sloping buttresses, protecting them from mining and ramming. Gateways assumed more and more importance as the century progressed and

9

were mostly machicolated until they supplanted the keep by mid-century; two great flanking towers called barbicans now protected gateways, and there was an increasing use made of drawbridges, which could be raised or lowered as required. A grating made of oak and covered with iron, called a portcullis, was set into vertical grooves in the walls of the gateway and could be dropped into place, effectively sealing the entrance. Behind the portcullis would be a narrow guard chamber with a further grating behind it where attackers could be channelled with no possibility of escape: over the chamber, the vaulted roof had holes in it which enabled the defenders to make short work of the enemy.

By the end of the 13th century, military architecture had become very sophisticated and therefore expensive. Eventually the great day of the mediaeval stronghold had passed and, by the 15th century, the typical castle of central and southern England was a rectangle of buildings arranged around a central court, as in Bodiam castle, with defensive round towers at the angles and occasionally in the centre of each wall, unless there was a gatehouse. These courtyard castles were set within a lake or a moat. Eventually, during the Tudor period, beginning in 1485, castle building drew to a close, except where coastal defence was needed, and some older castles were allowed to fall into disrepair. With the decline of feudalism and the increasing use of cannon, the emphasis moved away from defence and more attention was paid to comfort—the fortified manor house became popular and the state, now strong, took responsibility for national defence.

QUESTION 1

In the space provided overleaf and using the key below where necessary:

a) Draw a plan of a typical motte and bailey castle as described in the passage as it would look from above.

b) Draw a plan of Brinklow castle as described in the passage as it would look from above.

Stockade	○○○○○○
Ditch	∨ ∨ ∨ ∨ ∨
Rampart	∨∨∨∨∨∨∨∨∨∨
Bridge	=

a) Typical motte and bailey castle

N

b) Brinklow castle

N

QUESTION 2

Put the following sentences into chronological sequence as described in the passage.

A   Permission is necessary to indent parapets for defensive purposes.
B   Moated courtyard castles are built.
C   Internal walls of early castles are rebuilt in stone.
D   Drawbridges and gratings offer increased protection from attack.
E   The tower keep develops, with upper private apartments.
F   The first private fortifications are built in England.
G   Permanent stone machicolations come into use.
H   The motte is entirely ringed by tall, stone walls.
I   Gateways, protected by flanking towers, assume more importance.
J   Ditched and palisaded earthworks offer protection to the public.
K   The highest point of castle building is reached.
L   Greater emphasis is put on comfort as the state assumes responsibility.
M   Tower design evolves to minimise attack from mining and missiles.
N   Hoardings are introduced for vertical attack.
O   The great hall has an adjacent private chamber.

Step	
1	
2	
3	
4	
5	
6	
7	
8	
9	
10	
11	
12	
13	
14	
15	

QUESTION 3

Here are two lists of words: for each word in list **A** there is a suitable alternative in list **B**. Pair them up.

	A	**B**
1	ditch	courtyard
2	bailey	invaders
3	corbels	grating
4	portcullis	stereotype
5	citadel	trench
6	stronghold	surrounded
7	ramparts	palisade
8	timber	brackets
9	motte	defensive tower
10	stockade	wooden
11	attackers	mound
12	enclosed	walls
13	entire	external
14	orthodox	total
15	exterior	fortress

Skenfrith Castle

1

The existing castle at Skenfrith, South Wales, was built by Hubert de Burgh, chief legal advisor to King John and Henry III between 1201 and 1205 and is a typical example of a Norman castle of the period. The original castle occupying the site was a motte and bailey type, fortified by a bank and ditch and erected by the Normans soon after their conquest of England in 1066 in order to control the main routes into Wales. The castle was further developed by Henry II, the first Plantagenet king of England, whose strategy for holding and administering important areas depended on the grouping together of castles so that they were able to support and reinforce each other in times of rebellion by the native population. Skenfrith is one of three such castles on the Welsh borders, and forms, with Grosmont and the White Castle, a triangular defence within four and five miles respectively from each other, controlling the main routes into Wales from England. During the 12th century, it was repaired, but most improvements were made during the 13th century, after which time repair work ceased altogether.

2

Let us describe how the castle looked when at its best; for today, very little of the castle remains to be seen. The castle consisted of a round tower of undressed stone built on a flattened motte, slightly off centre of the bailey, towards the south-west, and was entirely surrounded by a quadrangular curtain wall of undressed sandstone. Bold circular towers projected from each corner of the bailey wall. The castle, roughly rectangular in shape, with its south wall being shorter than any of the others and its east wall on the oblique, has water on all four sides, three by a moat just over 13.5 m wide and the fourth by the west bank of the river Monnow. In the centre of the north curtain wall was the main gate (now destroyed) and against the south curtain wall once stood the Great Hall. Within the west wall once stood a suite of rooms and in the centre of the east wall was a vaulted water gate. In the curtain wall, a sloping gutter carried excess water from the wall-walk and drained it into the river. In the centre of the west curtain wall was a solid D-shaped tower, projecting into the moat, giving further defence. Adjacent to the tower in the south-east corner was a mill, but this is no longer in existence. Skenfrith castle is interesting in that it marks a stage of development in castle design where extra defensive towers were set into the enclosing curtain wall of the bailey so defence could be concentrated, thus marking the beginning of the decline of the central keep in castle architecture.

Having read the description of Skenfrith castle, draw a plan of the castle as it would have looked after completion during the 13th century.

Use the following key:

M	Moat		T	Defensive tower		WG	Water gate			Mill		CW	Curtain wall
K	Keep		MG	Main gate		GH	Great Hall		R	Room		B	Bailey

Flour Milling

1 The grinding or milling of flour breaks down the hard grains of cereals into a powder or meal, and today the word 'flour' is given only to the finer fractions obtained by the use of a highly efficient automated process. Man attempted to produce a form of flour soon after he learned to cultivate the soil; more than 6000 years ago, he ceased to eat grain in its wild state and began to break it up by using two stones, grinding on a flat stone with a ball-shaped stone held in one hand. In some places the meal was pounded by using a pestle and mortar, a method still practised today in some primitive societies. Eventually the saddle quern or hand mill superceded earlier methods, being itself a forerunner of the revolving millstone which was operated by animals. In the 1st century before Christ, water-mills were known to be in use, when the current of a stream turned a wheel which revolved the millstones. During the 12th century it was discovered that wind would turn a wheel if sails were attached to it, so for the next 600 years or so windmills became a familiar sight in many countries. Steam eventually overtook windpower, however, at the end of the 18th century, and flour meant for human consumption was ground by the use of steam power, the first successful steam mill being erected in London in 1784. The coarser flour used for animal foodstuffs continued to be produced by windpower. Forty years after its invention in Hungary in 1840, the roller mill was in operation in all large mills, and although not perfected until 1914, produced a finer flour by means of chilled metal rollers in place of the traditional stones.

2 Nowadays, the entire process of milling uses advanced electrical machinery, greatly improving the quality of the flour produced. Before the milling process itself can begin, however, the wheat must be cleaned and conditioned, when specialised machinery removes all impurities like dust, chaff, other cereal grains and seeds; particles of metal are removed by magnetic separators and perforated rotating sieves remove large debris, while smaller particles are taken out by indented cylinders or discs. Light particles are sucked out by air currents and heavy particles, like stones, are removed by the use of water, when they sink to the bottom. The wheat is then washed with clean, running water and dried in a spin drier. Next comes the

3 conditioning process, which varies depending on the quality of the wheat: for example, if the grain is hard and flinty like North American wheat, it must be dampened before being milled, whereas English and European wheat requires drying out before milling can take place. Once the conditioning has been completed, milling can begin.

Wheat grain consists of about 85% starchy material called endosperm, the inside part of the wheat kernel, 2% embryo germ and 13% husk or bran, which is the coat of the wheat kernel. The first step is the separation of the bran from the kernel by passing the grain through a series of fluted rollers, about 254 cm in diameter and between 508 cm and 1524 cm in length, each pair having successively finer flutes and a smaller distance between the rollers. The material is then sifted on woven-wire, nylon or silk sieves of varying mesh sizes; the bran coats are separated and extracted to be later used for animal foodstuffs, while the finer particles, called semolina, goes on to the purifiers, where it is repeatedly sieved and passed through various pairs of smooth-reduction rollers which grind it more and more finely. It is subjected to the combined effects of a powerful centrifugal force and an air current. The two forces act in opposite directions, thus dividing the semolina into fractions with higher and lower protein content as the starch granules, being larger than the protein granules, are separated. In these final stages, the product may be treated in one way or another to improve its appearance, when it is exposed to one or more approved gases to lighten its colour; its baking qualities, by the minute addition of potassium bromate; and its nutritive value by the addition of iron and other vitamins. Any bran remaining at this stage will resist the bleaching action. The final reduction rollers are smooth, producing a very fine ground material which is thoroughly sieved. Only the substance passing through these sieves is accepted as flour. Eventually, after blending has taken place, the flour is bagged off and weighed or filled into bulk waggons automatically.

QUESTION 1

Put the following sentences into chronological sequence as described in the passage.

		Step	
A	Windmills become very popular.	1	
B	The roller mill is invented.	2	
C	Fully automated electrical machinery is in operation.	3	
D	Man eats his grain whole.	4	
E	The first steam mill is erected.	5	
F	Water-mills are in use.	6	
G	The roller mill is further improved.	7	
H	Man begins to grind cereals.	8	
I	The roller mill is in full operation.	9	
J	The handmill evolves into the revolving millstone.	10	

QUESTION 2

Look at the diagram opposite, which represents the processes of flour milling, and then complete the table, using the following words:

wheat grain; chaff; potassium bromate; bran; semolina; stones; iron; gases; flour; metallic particles.

1		6	
2		7	
3		8	
4		9	
5		10	

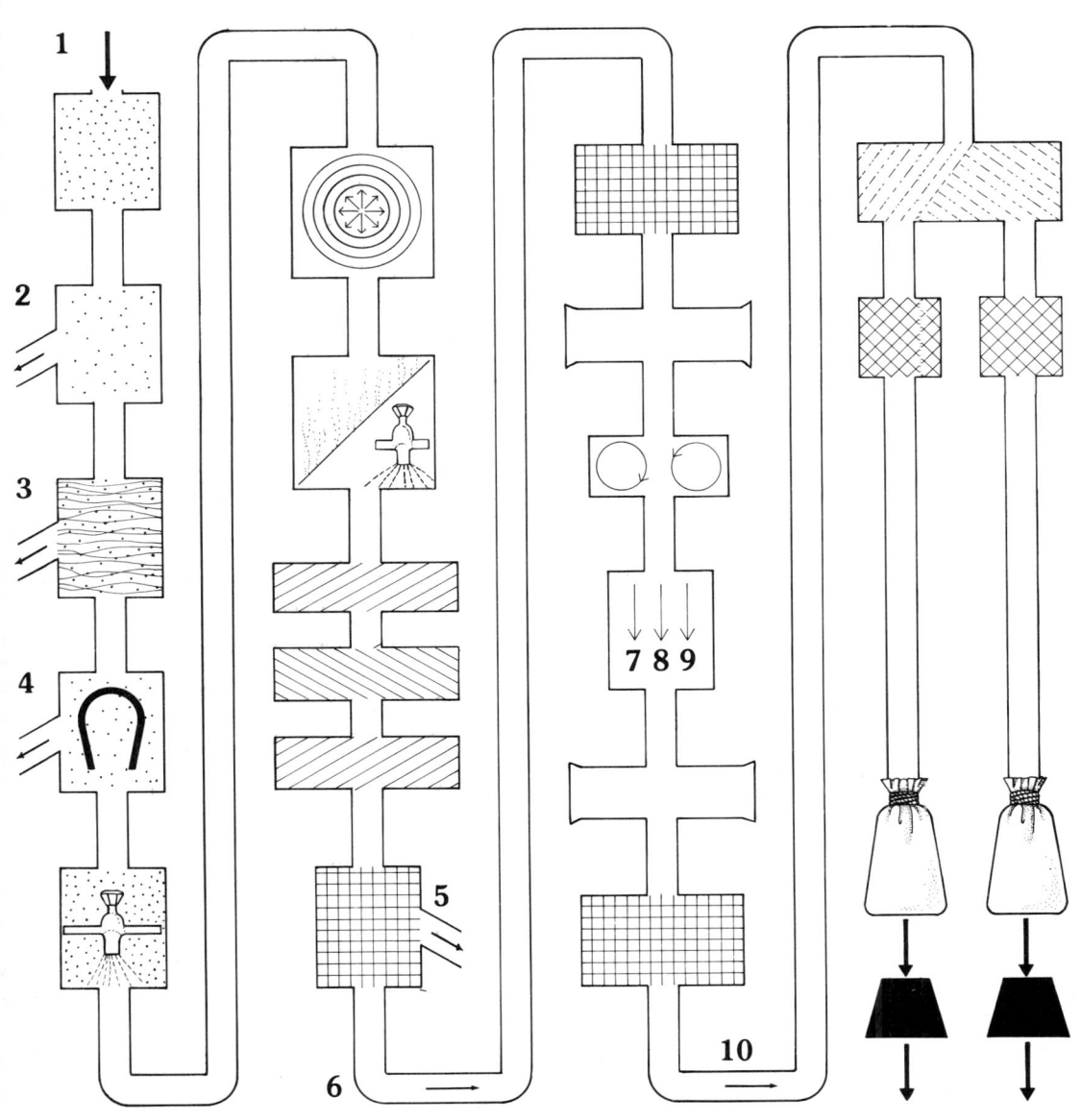

The Solar System

1 The Sun, its planets and their moons, together with the asteroids and comets *constitute* the Solar System, which lies in one of the spiral arms of the Milky Way, the cluster of millions of stars which forms our own Galaxy. There are nine known planets in the Solar System, the Earth being the largest of the inner group, and they all rotate around the Sun, a dense, *roughly* spherical mass of glowing, pulsating matter 1 384 000 km across and the only star in the Solar System. It is 4½ thousand million years old, which is young compared with the age of the Universe, and is composed largely of hydrogen. At its centre, the temperature is 13 million degrees centigrade. It was not until the development of atomic physics in the 20th century that it became clear that the Sun *converts* its mass into energy by atomic reaction, as it had done already for 4½ thousand million years and as it will continue to do for yet another 10 thousand million years. 99.8% of all matter in the Solar System is concentrated in the Sun, leaving only 0.0006% to make up the four inner planets and their moons, while Jupiter—the largest of the planets—takes up 70% of the total planetary mass.

2 The planets of the Solar System are the only planets that we have as yet been able to observe. They appear to shine, but they have no light of their own—they are merely reflecting light from the Sun. When compared with the stars they are cold and, unlike the stars, they cannot produce heat and light by atomic reaction. The nearest planet to the Sun is Mercury, which orbits at an average distance of 5 600 000 km. There is virtually no chance of ever finding life on this planet, which lost its atmosphere early in its history. Mercury, which completes its orbit once every three months, has a cratered surface rather like the Moon but it does not have large desert plains. Its diameter is only 2/5 that of the Earth and it is *perpetually* dry. Because it lies closer to the Sun than the Earth does, we can only see it in the evening sky or the morning sky. When it is to the east of the Sun it rises and sets after it so is called the evening star; when it is to the west and rises and sets before the Sun it is called the morning star. The ancient Egyptians called it Horus and Set respectively, while the Greeks called it Hermes and Apollo. It has no moon.

3 Earth's nearest neighbour, the planet Venus, is named after the goddess of love and, until the Russian probes landed on its surface, it was thought to support life; but a more inhospitable and hostile environment would be difficult to imagine. The surface of Venus consists of rocky desert and its face is completely *obscured* by dense clouds of sulphuric acid which insulate the planet and keep the temperature very high. The *excessive* heat *liberates* carbon dioxide from the surface rocks, saturating the atmosphere with 97% carbon dioxide. Venus is the easiest planet to identify since it is, after the Sun and the Moon, the brightest object in the sky; it is a brilliant yellow-white in colour and can be observed even in daylight. Like the Moon, it has a crescent phase when viewed from the Earth: when it is farthest it seems very small and as it approaches it grows larger but the area illuminated by the Sun is increasingly that which is turned away from us and all we are able to see is an elongated diminishing crescent, thin and bright.

4 The Earth is the third nearest planet to the Sun. Oblate in shape, it is surrounded by a belt of radiation because of charged particles from the Sun being trapped in its magnetic field. The Earth is the sole planet of the Solar System where life as we understand it exists. It formed about 4500 million years ago and life probably appeared about 570 million years ago, with Man emerging about 4 million years ago. Life has been present, therefore, for only 12.5% of its history, and Man for only 0.9%. Civilisation has been present for a mere 0.0001% of its history. Earth's satellite, the Moon, has a diameter of 3476 km and its distance varies from the Earth from 363 million metres to 406 million metres. It is covered with large craters, some with diameters of up to 200 km.

5 Mars, the red planet, has a mean distance of 228 million km from the Sun and is just over half the size of Earth and seventh in order of size of the nine planets. When viewed through a telescope it reveals dark markings on a red-ochre surface material, probably limonite (only on Mars and Mercury can we actually see a solid surface); and several observers have reported seeing a network of straight lines on the surface of the planet; Schiaparelli called them canals—but they are probably an optical illusion, since the photographs sent back by the Mariner probes show no sign of canals, natural or otherwise. Because Mars' axis of rotation is not perpendicular to its orbital plane, but inclined at an angle of $24.936°$, it gives rise to the phenomenon of the seasons, as on Earth. The dark markings near the Martian equator change with the seasons, as do the white polar caps of ice or frozen carbon dioxide, which shrink in summer and expand in winter. Mars has obviously had an active

6   geological history as can be seen from its cratered surface. It has two moons, Phobos and Deimos.

Between Mars and Jupiter revolve numerous chunks of rock called asteroids, some too small to be seen but others fairly large; the largest, Ceres, discovered in 1801 by Piazzi, is 670 km across. The only asteroid visible to the naked eye is Vesta, because of its brightness. Some astronomers believe that there is a second belt of asteroids beyond the orbit of Pluto, but there is little evidence as yet to support this theory.

7   Beyond the asteroid belt lies the planet of Jupiter, the king of the planets and the largest planet of the Solar System, with a diameter eleven times that of Earth. It is more than five times as distant from the Sun as is the Earth and was, until the recent Voyager mission, the most distant planet to have been visited by a space craft. Through a telescope, Jupiter appears as a disc crossed by several dark bands which change position from month to month, indicating that different parts of the planet rotate at different speeds. It cannot, therefore, be solid. It has 14 satellites, four of them the same size as our Moon.

8   At a mean distance of 1425 million km from the Sun lies Saturn, the second largest planet of the Solar System, with a diameter 9½ times that of Earth. It, too, has been visited by the Voyager space probe. It is the most beautiful of all the planets to observe through a telescope. It is surrounded by a *unique* system of rings—five of which have been defined—which lie together as a result of the planet's gravity. It is likely that the rings are composed of ice particles. From time to time, however, the rings disappear in our telescopes for a short period and this is thought to be as a result of their extreme thinness—just 15 km or so thick. Saturn, which has the lowest density of all the planets, just 70% that of water, has 10 named satellites.

9   The third largest planet in the Solar System was discovered in 1781 by Sir William Herschel, although he did not at the time know it was a planet. Uranus has a mean distance of 2870 million km from the Sun and is 3¾ times larger than the Earth. When seen through a telescope it seems featureless. Uranus has five known satellites, which follow a precise orbit around its equator but which sometimes appear to follow a circular and at other times an elliptical path. Unlike other satellites, too, they move north and south of the planet rather than east—west.

10   Some 1600 million km beyond Uranus lies Neptune, with a diameter 3½ times that of the Earth. It was discovered in 1846 by J.G. Galle and was a triumph for theoretical astronomy. Neptune has two moons—Triton, which has a circular, retrograde movement; and Nereid, which

has the most eccentric movement of any moon in the Solar System. Both Uranus and Neptune are very cold, with temperatures about −160° to −170° C and are similar in size and composition, but while Uranus may be easily seen, even by using binoculars, Neptune appears very small in all but the largest telescopes. It is hoped that both Uranus and Neptune will be reached by the Voyager craft in the near future providing that the funds are available.

11 Pluto is to be found 1600 million km beyond Neptune and is the outermost planet of the Solar System but because its orbit is so eccentric, it is at perihelion closer to the Sun than Neptune. It is believed to be smaller than both Uranus and Neptune but its exact size, composition and atmosphere are not known but it is unlikely to be more than 6000 km across. It is believed to be the coldest planet, with an estimated surface temperature of about −230° C, and its year is 247.7 times as long as that on Earth. It was discovered in 1930 by accident, when observers were studying disturbances in the orbit of Neptune.

12 The Solar System, however, consists of more than planets and asteroids; apart from gas and dust particles, there are the comets. The comets are tenuous bodies composed of swarms of dust-like metallic particles which move around the Sun in parabolic, elliptical or hyperbolic orbits. The particles are invisible until they approach very near the Sun or when the Earth crosses the path of one of them. When they pass near the Sun, the frozen gas within the particles is heated and made to glow by solar radiation; the gases are pushed out and the ionised particles form a long, glowing tail which *precedes* the comet. Some comets are periodic in character and their next sighting can be fairly accurately *predicted*.

13 We cannot fail to be impressed when we see the vast distances in the Solar System: from the Earth to the Sun, for example, the distance is almost 4000 times greater than a journey around the Earth; the distance from the Sun to Pluto is equivalent to 150 000 trips around the Earth. Astronomers measure some distances in light seconds or minutes: light travels at 300 000 km per second, therefore the distance from the Earth to the Sun can be calculated as 8½ light minutes and the distance from the Sun to Pluto is 5½ light hours away. Such distances appear immense, but they are a speck when we compare the Solar System with the size of space. The diameter of the Solar System is some 1 1200 million km yet it is only a small part of the Milky Way, the central plane of our Galaxy. To the nearest star to the Sun there is a distance of 417½ million million km or 4½ light years; but even that distance is not great in our Universe. Within our Galaxy are stars like Sirius, the brightest star in the sky, which is 8 light years away; Vega, 26.5 light years away;

Arcturus, a red giant star, 36 light years away; the double star Capella is 45 light years away and Aldebaran, the brightest star in the constellation Taurus, is 68 light years away. Then there are Spica; Antares, a red supergiant, 480 times larger than the Sun; and Rigel, the quadruple star and the brightest in Orion at 220, 400 and 900 light years distant respectively. We have not yet exhausted the description of our Galaxy. The Sun, which moves through space at 250 km per second (which would take us once around the Earth in 2½ minutes) takes 225 million years to complete one orbit of our Galaxy—yet ours is by no means the only Galaxy in the Universe; in the vastness of space there are millions of other Galaxies, thousands much larger than our own.

--- **QUESTION 1** ---

Look at the diagram and give the names of the planets as described in the passage and indicate the position of the **asteroids** by the following symbol:

1		6	
2		7	
3		8	
4		9	
5			

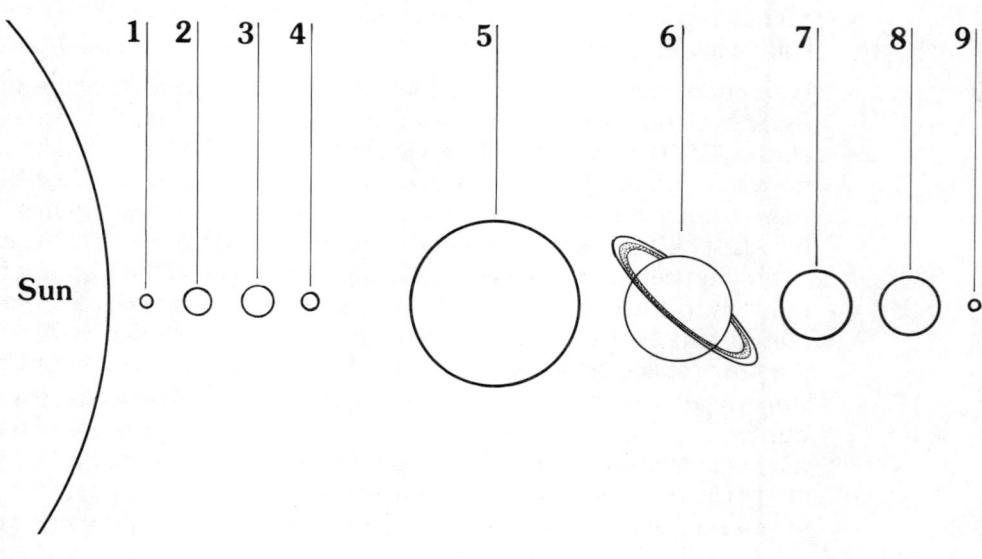

QUESTION 2

Some words in the passage are set in italics. Give their correct meaning in sequence from the list of definitions given to you.

1 .... 6 .... releases   forecast
2 .... 7 .... occasionally   extreme
                                  hidden   goes in front of
3 .... 8 .... changes   almost
                                  make up   constantly
4 .... 9 .... singular   single
5 .... 10 .... follows

QUESTION 3

In the left-hand column there is an incomplete statement; choose the statement in the right-hand column which is most suitable to complete it, then complete the table on page 169.

1	This planet has 13 moons and is unlikely to be solid.	A	It was discovered in the mid-19th century as a result of theoretical calculation.
2	These rock-like bodies of varying size revolve between Mars and Jupiter.	B	It is called the Solar System and consists of nine planets, a group of asteroids and comets all rotating around a single star.
3	When viewed through a telescope, this planet appears to have a solid, red-ochre cratered surface.	C	It has the lowest density of all the planets and has 10 named moons.
4	This is a very cold planet with two moons, one of which has the most eccentric orbit of all moons in the Solar System.	D	It is 11 times larger than the Earth and 5 times further away from the Sun.

5	The planets are quite unlike the stars as they are cold and cannot produce heat and light by atomic reaction.	E	It has white polar caps which change with the seasons and dark markings near its equator.
6	This planet is surrounded by rings of ice particles which make it beautiful when seen in a telescope.	F	Those of the Solar System are the only ones ever to have been observed by Man.
7	This group of celestial bodies lies in one of the spiral arms of the Milky Way.	G	It has five known moons which follow an erratic path unknown in other moons.
8	These are composed of swarms of metallic particles which move around the Sun in different orbits.	H	It is oblate in shape and surrounded by a belt of radiation.
9	This planet is completely obscured by dense clouds of sulphuric acid, and its atmosphere is composed of 97% carbon dioxide.	I	It is composed largely of hydrogen and converts its mass into energy by atomic reaction.
10	This is the sole planet in the Solar System where life is known to exist, although only present for 12.5% of its history.	J	It completes its orbit once every three months and has no atmosphere.
11	This planet, 3¾ times larger than the Earth, was discovered in the late 18th century.	K	As they approach perihelion, they glow and form a long tail which precedes them into space.
12	The only star in the Solar System reaches a temperature of 13 million degrees centigrade at its nucleus.	L	Discovered in 1930, it is believed to be the coldest planet of all in the Solar System.

13	This is the innermost planet of the Solar System and can be observed only at night or in the morning.	M	It is brighter than any of the other planets and is easy to identify.
14	This is the most distant planet in the Solar System and has a very eccentric orbit.	N	It is 480 times greater in size than the Sun.
15	This star is a red supergiant, and 400 light years from the Sun.	O	The largest was discovered in 1801.

1	
2	
3	
4	
5	
6	
7	
8	
9	
10	
11	
12	
13	
14	
15	

The Earth

1

The Earth is the largest inner planet of the solar system and the only planet where life, as we know it, exists. It is an oblate spheroid in shape, flattened a little at its poles. Although it shares many characteristics with Mercury, Venus, Mars and the Moon, such as its comparable size, its density and composition and its position in space, it is very different in so many other ways. It has never been scarred by *excessive* volcanic activity, and it has a plentiful supply of water; in fact, 72% of Earth's surface is covered by water.

2

The Earth rotates on its axis once every 23 hours 56 minutes and revolves around the Sun once every 365 days, 6 hours, and 9 minutes. It has only one satellite, the Moon, and receives its light and energy from its parent, the Sun; in fact, it receives more light in 13 seconds from the Sun than it does from the Moon in one whole year. Earth's average distance from the Sun is 149 million km and the plane on which it revolves is called the plane of the ecliptic. Its axis is at 66.5° to this and stays *practically* parallel to its original direction all the time. Therefore, the poles which face alternately towards and away from the Sun *give rise to* the seasons.

3

The Earth has a magnetic field, but its magnetic poles do not *coincide* with the axial poles, nor are they constant. Radiation surrounds the Earth, probably because the charged particles from the Sun are trapped in this magnetic field. It is believed that the Earth and other planets were hurled away from the Sun about 4500 million years ago. The molten material was hot and gaseous but as it cooled it threw off material into space and formed the Moon. As the molten globe gradually cooled, its lighter *constituents* rose to the top and formed a blackish lava above which rose solid masses occupying about a quarter of the surface. As the Earth cooled still further, great quantities of steam formed from the combining of hydrogen and oxygen, condensing into water which filled the hollows in the crust, forming seas and oceans. Then the exposed igneous rocks began to be weathered by wind, rain and frost, and their sediments started to accumulate in the seas and rivers. The heavy mass of sediment pushed the shallow ocean beds down further during the millions of years that

4

followed until at length parts of the semi-plastic subcrust of the Earth was pushed up until it poured over the land surface. The seas began to rise, forcing up the sediments which, as a result of heat and pressure, were fused into layers.

Earth is divided into three main zones: the atmosphere, which extends 20 times as high as the highest clouds, and protects us from the harmful rays of the Sun and extremes of temperature; the hydrosphere or waters of the Earth, whether solid, liquid or gas, including the water of the atmosphere and water on the surface of the planet in the form of seas, rivers and glaciers; and the lithosphere, the solid body or rock of the planet, which is further subdivided into the core, the mantle and the crust. The core is the inner nucleus of the Earth, with a diameter of 700 km and a temperature of 3000° K. The central core is a solid nucleus of iron and nickel surrounded by a molten liquid mass; the mantle, which is solid, with a thickness of about 2800 km lies between the core and the crust, the latter being the outer layer of the Earth where human life exists. It is 35 km thick, a little less under the oceans, and is composed of three types of rocks—igneous, sedimentary and metamorphic. Igneous rocks are the result of the cooling and *subsequent* solidification of molten material or magma from deep below the surface of the Earth. Volcanic rocks and rocks which *extrude* below the thin crust of the Earth's surface are igneous rocks. If the cooling of these rocks takes place on the surface of the Earth, it is fairly rapid, so it *inhibits* the growth of large crystals and the rocks become fine-grained and smooth in texture; but if it occurs within the Earth, the process is much slower and the rocks formed will be coarse, with large mineral crystals. All rocks on the surface of the Earth are subjected to erosion by wind, or weather, or by chemical action, and the resulting sediment is *deposited* in lakes, rivers and low-lying areas. Over a period of time it accumulates and is consolidated by pressure and cemented by chemical action, forming layers or strata of rock, quite different in character from igneous and metamorphic rocks. It is only in sedimentary rocks that we can follow the geological history of the Earth by the fossil remains found in them. Both igneous and sedimentary rocks may be changed into new forms as a result of being subjected to intense heat and pressure. During the process of metamorphism, the original rock undergoes physical or chemical changes, which drastically alter its texture and colour. Metamorphic rocks are characterised by the obliteration of both former fossils and stratification. They are also much harder than the original rocks from which they developed and in many cases the minerals in them have been flattened out and arranged in parallel bands running through the rock.

5

The seven continents float on a number of semi-plastic plates on the crust of the Earth, which are constantly in motion. When two plates collide, one edge is forced under the other causing ocean trenches, earthquakes, and arcs of volcanic islands, as well as mountain ranges. Both biological and geological evidence demonstrate that the continents were once joined together in different *configurations* and were formed from a single landmass.

QUESTION 1

Some words in the passage are set in italics. Give their correct meaning in the order in which they occur from the list of definitions given to you below.

1	6	earlier encourages
2	7	prevents shapes
		virtually designs
3	8	later placed
4	9	extreme cause
		meet ingredients
5	10	pour forth

QUESTION 2

Complete the sentences below with information taken from the passage.

1 Igneous rocks can have either a very smooth or a rough texture because . . .

2   The Earth has only one satellite, the Moon, which...

3   When subjected to intense heat and pressure, both igneous and sedimentary rocks...

4   The core of the Earth has a diameter of 700 km and is composed of...

5   There are seasons on Earth because...

6   Fossils are never found in igneous rocks...

7   Earthquakes and volcanic islands are created as a result of...

8 Sedimentary rocks were formed when...

9 The seven continents are in constant motion because...

10 Sedimentary rocks are different from both igneous and metamorphic rocks because...

11 The oceans were formed when...

12 The Earth is not a true sphere, because...

13 Mercury, Venus, Mars and the Moon are similar to Earth in...

14 The charged particles from the Sun...

15 Igneous rocks were formed when...

The Greenhouse

1 The greenhouse is a common feature in many town and country gardens in Britain and is indispensable to the gardener, as it provides near-perfect conditions for plants, both edible and ornamental, all year round, irrespective of the weather. There is a greenhouse to suit every requirement, heated or unheated, small or large, permanent or portable, standard or specialist, decorative or functional. Most greenhouses, however, come in two basic materials, wood and aluminium, each possessing advantages and disadvantages: wood is warmer in winter but is prone to decay unless regularly maintained; aluminium does not deteriorate but conducts the cold inside in winter; wood takes screws and nails easily; aluminium requires special fixing devices or free-standing units. A greenhouse should always be situated on a level site on a north–south alignment to take full advantage of the sun and should be provided with a hard walk-way of slabs, concrete or bricks to facilitate access. The door should be able to accommodate a wheelbarrow with ease.

2 There are six types of permanent greenhouse, including the miniature version, the most popular being the **span-roofed type**. We will call this type **1A**. It is free-standing with glass running vertically up both sides to a central ridge and can be obtained made entirely of glass or with a timber or brick base up to about 76 cm. As light comes from both directions, pot plants grow more evenly in this type of house but it is advisable to site it away from trees and buildings which may obstruct the light. Staging or shelving can be erected on one or both of the sides, but in summer it will be necessary to protect plants from scorching by using blinds or whitewash. A type which has become very popular in recent years is type **1B**. It is very decorative in design and is ideal as a garden feature but it is very practical, too. It is **multi-sided** in construction with ventilators at ground level and a Perspex dome at the top to control the flow of air. All areas are accessible from one central spot in this house and it makes the maximum use of floorspace. A variation of this type is the circulaire or **curved-sided** model, which has each light at an angle to catch the sun's rays. Neither type of greenhouse should be sited near a wall or corner, as the many angles would encourage the growth of weeds, and plant debris would accumulate. The **Dutch-light** type consists of a series of glazed lights attached to a skeleton structure, with sides sloping down at an angle from a main centre beam. We will call it type **1C**. A model which has become less fashionable nowadays is the **three-quarter span type**, which we can classify as **1D**; a cross between a span-roof type and a lean-to, it has a wall on one of its sides and is free-standing. It is particularly suitable for fruit growing, and peaches and vines were usually grown in this type of house as a good height is available for training them against the wall. Since the wall is lower than the house, the short-span ridge allows more light and can be hinged back for ventilation. Staging can be erected inside. The **lean-to** model is less expensive, as it is usually attached to the side of a house or building, which tends to make it warmer than other types, so more attention must be paid to ventilation. Since it admits light on one side only, it should preferably be sited facing south. This model, which we will call **1E**, can double as a sun lounge or conservatory, with tall plants growing on the wall side and smaller ones placed on the glass side. Care must be taken when erecting this type as the damp-course of the house adjacent must not be covered.

3

All these greenhouses must be adequately ventilated and be constructed, where appropriate, of good horticultural glass. They must never be sited in low-lying areas, which could be frost pockets, and must be protected from cold winds without being obstructed. If space is at a premium, however, the gardener will find the miniature greenhouse, which we will call type **1F**, the most useful. This greenhouse can occupy a very small area and is often placed on a balcony or patio. The **cold-frame**, which is its technical name, is useful for the propagation of half-hardy vegetables and protecting delicate plants over the winter. The cold-frame should be sturdily constructed with a sloping top to enable rainwater to run off and should slide or lift open for access to plants. When fixed into position, the cold-frame should have plenty of room around it and should heating be required, wires buried below the soil level or around the inside perimeter of the frame can easily be installed. Ventilation is achieved by propping open the top with a stick, or by sliding the doors across.

4

A second category of greenhouse is the mobile type called a **cloche**. We will classify it as type **2**. It is extremely useful in that it occupies very little space and is cheap to buy or make. Cloches extend the season of many crops by protecting them from frosts and can be used in succession, being moved when and where required. Cloches are not usually heated, but if placed in position ten days or so before the seeds or plants are to be put in, the soil will be warmed sufficiently to encourage germination. There are five main types of cloche; type **2A** is usually made of toughened plastic or rigid polythene and is tunnel shaped. It can be whitewashed in summer to avoid scorching delicate plants; although after some time, the plastic will become opaque. Watering often presents difficulty in the early stages as the cloche will have to be lifted but this will not be necessary once the roots have spread out a little. Type **2B** is shaped similarly to **2A**, but is constructed from sheets of plastic over a metal frame or series of hoops. It is ideal for salad crops and offers excellent protection against birds and frosts. A larger version is available, type **2C**, with a doorway made of strips or concertina-shaped plastic, which functions as a curtain. This model is cheap and easy to erect and will give good service for up to three years before breaking down under the ultraviolet light. Like all plastic constructions, too, this model has the disadvantage of being unstable in windy conditions. Two further models are **2Di** and **2Dii**, the **large** and **lower Barn** types, which are essentially a number of pieces of glass held together in a barn-shape by wire, their size depending on the crop to be covered. The large barn type has sides about 31 cm high and reaches about 48 cm at the centre and is useful for taller crops like strawberries, peas, and dwarf beans; the lower Barn cloche is about 33 cm high and is able to accommodate up to three rows of lettuces in winter and cucumbers in summer. Both types are easily moved when required. A slight variation on this model is type **2E**, which is tent shaped and made of two sheets of glass about 22 × 60 cm, clipped together at the top by galvanised wires. Whatever model is used—large or small—to protect and propagate plants, it must be remembered that when ideal conditions are provided for crops then they are also ideal for pests and that garden hygiene must be fastidiously maintained, with regular spraying throughout the year; pots should be scrupulously clean, the soil sterilised, and the inside woodwork scrubbed annually with a good insecticide. Locks and hinges should be oiled regularly and the glass cleaned.

QUESTION 1

Give the word or phrase in the passage that means the following:

Paragraph One

1 essential ....
2 independent ....
3 has tendency to ....
4 degenerate ....

Paragraph Two

5 minute . . . .

6 situate . . . .

7 burning . . . .

8 rubbish . . . .

9 substitute . . . .

Paragraph Three

10 precious . . . .

11 growth . . . .

Paragraph Four

12 movable . . . .

13 hard . . . .

14 cloudy . . . .

15 every year . . . .

─────── **QUESTION 2** ───────

Study the greenhouse models on pages 179–181, and then complete the table. If any model is not described in the passage, use an X.

1		10	
2		11	
3		12	
4		13	
5		14	
6		15	
7		16	
8		17	
9			

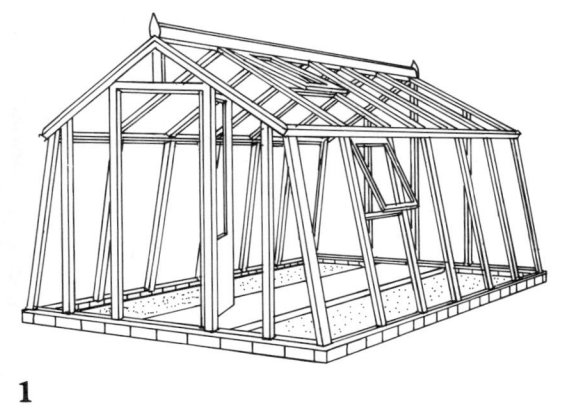

1

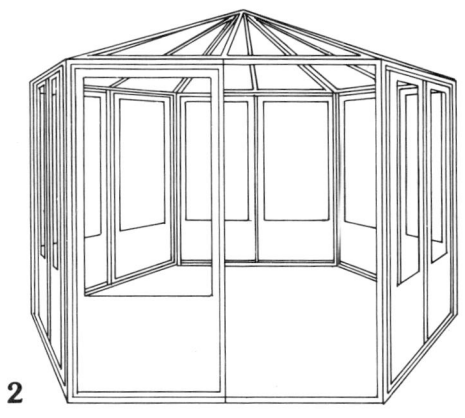

2

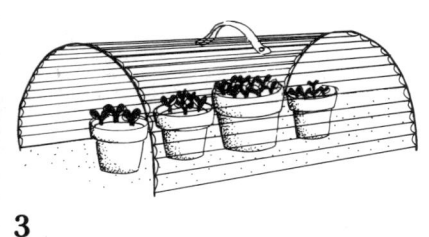

3

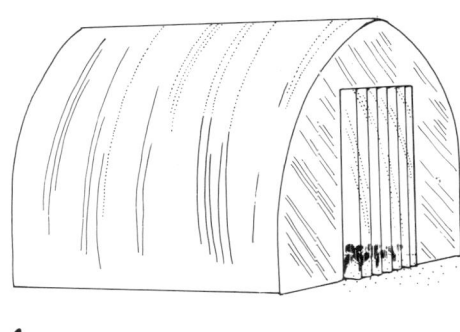

4

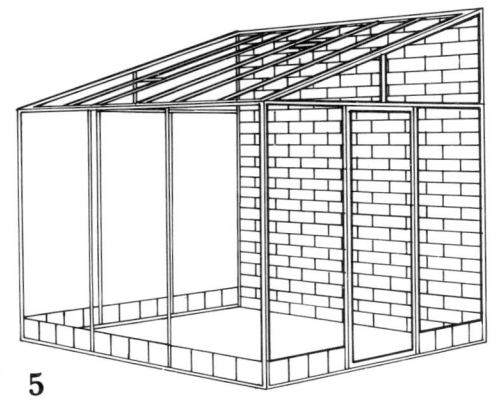

5

6

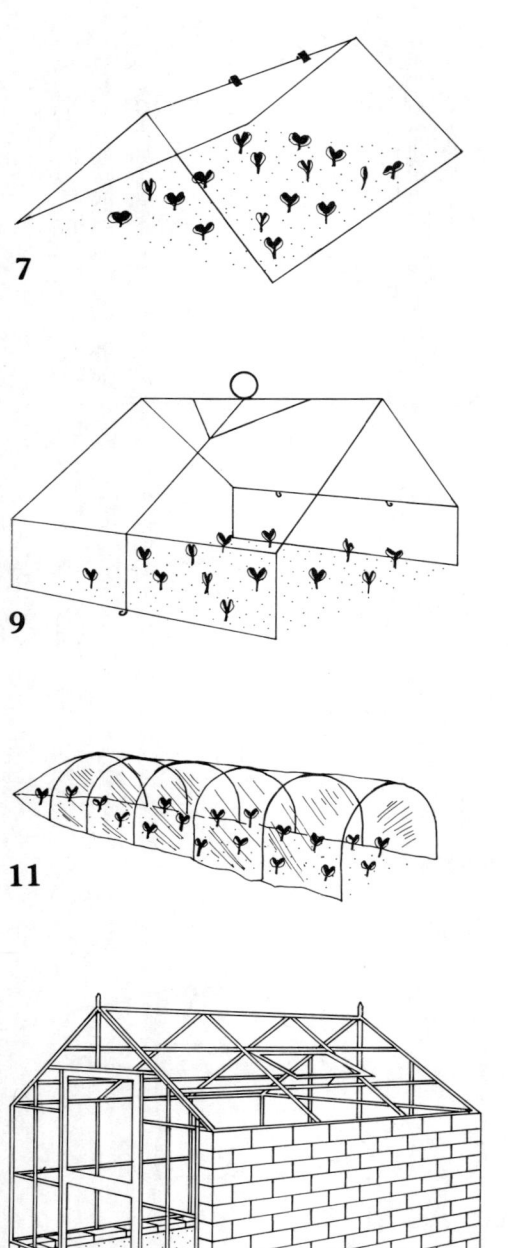
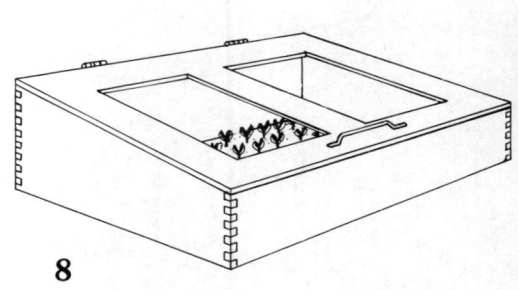
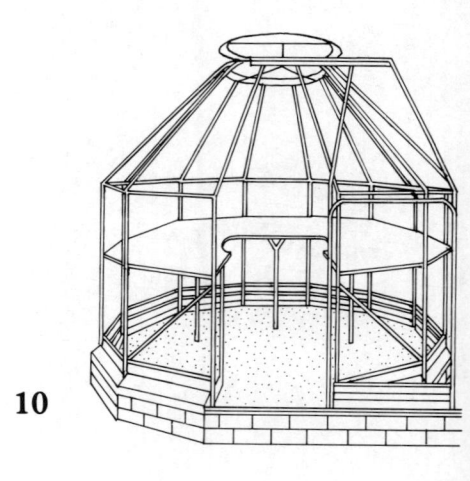
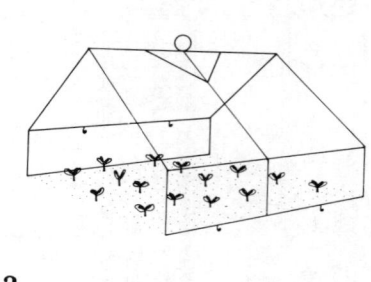

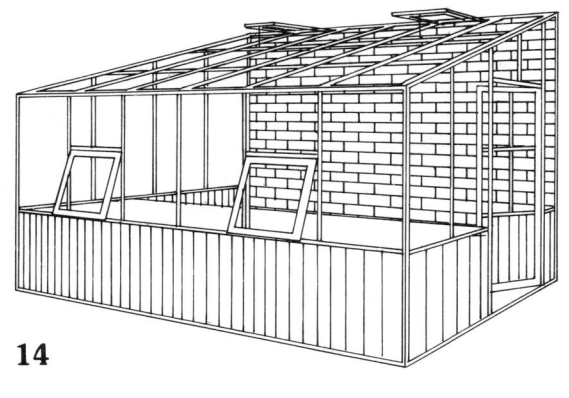

14

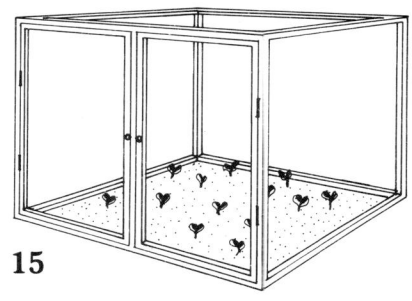

15

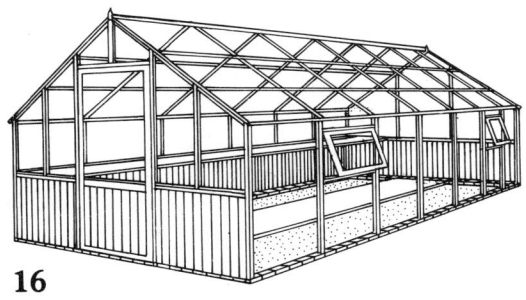

16

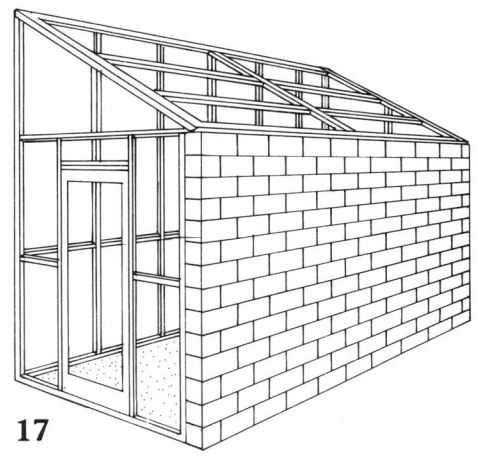

17

Ribblesdale House

1 Minutes away from the river and situated in the heart of the rolling Pennine Hills stands the distinctive and attractive Ribblesdale House, home of the painter Mortimer Eastwood and his family. Facing a row of picturesque Georgian cottages, Ribblesdale House, built of local blue limestone with warm, brown sandstone quoins, conveys a sense of the past; yet within the house, the 20th century is very much in evidence, with warm-air central heating, launderette and sauna. Ribblesdale House is a splendid example of conservation and restoration.

2 It was just over two hundred years ago that Ribblesdale House was built by a prosperous local landowner, on the site of a derelict 14th century manor house whose history has long since perished with the passage of time and whose moat has vanished into the undulating fields, but whose old walls are still to be seen bearing witness to another age. The house was originally constructed in 1760 on a traditional four-square plan, three storeys high, with stables and outbuildings in a courtyard to the west. The ground floor comprised a kitchen and dining room on the west wall, with adjacent parlour facing north, and study. Three bedrooms and a nursery occupied the middle storey, while the top floor accommodated servants. To the west, a square scullery, with an outbuilding to the north, faced the kitchen and two stable blocks, at right angles to the south wall, stood opposite each other, with cobbles between them.

3 The house presented a challenge to Mortimer Eastwood, returning to his native Lancashire after many years in Australia and the Far East, so, after becoming its new owner in 1967, he took the advice of a local builder on the restoration. While he aimed at the complete modernisation of the house, he was anxious not to detract in any way from the character. His achievement is remarkable; from the outside it is impossible to ascertain what is original and what is modern. The structural work took six years and fell into place neatly with the minimum of inconvenience to the family, and taking advantage of the weather for external work Mr Eastwood made gradual progress. He is particularly proud of his initial work, the installation of warm-air central heating, which is very cleverly routed; its existence, in fact, can only be detected by the unobtrusive floor outlet grilles. It took only the summer months to install.

5 Since the approach to the house was rather cramped, Mortimer Eastwood, having completed the installation of central heating, replaced the low-frontage wall and shrubbery by granite flags obtained from the back of the scullery; then the old, brown paintwork added fifty years ago by a previous owner to protect the house from damp, was sandblasted away to reveal the original limestone, and all the glazing bars were replaced to give a finer sense of scale to the Georgian building. The outside scullery and outbuilding were combined to form a launderette and sauna respectively and were annexed to the house using the brick from the kitchen wall which was demolished for the purpose. Extra bedrooms were made in the attic by enlarging the roof lights. Two existing bedrooms were given bathrooms *en suite*. The entire re-roofing and re-pointing took place the following summer in 1972.

In order to take full advantage of the clear north light, Mortimer Eastwood had appropriated the old parlour for his studio that first winter, and the adjacent dining room became his library. Physical and visual connection between the former kitchen and study has been achieved by breaking into the thick dividing wall and making an arch, with new pine units fitted into the kitchen section and the simply decorated living section maintaining the harmony of materials and design. This most recent phase of development is a constant delight to the Eastwood family, as they can enjoy the extensive views to the south. The ample garage was constructed by the simple expedient of spanning a slated roof over the sound remains of the old stables to the west and apart from the pointing, which was done in 1973, took place in one operation with the flagging of the front of the house. The existing cobblestones were sound, so they were left *in situ*.

QUESTION 1

Read the passage on Ribblesdale House and complete the table on the next page, showing the alterations carried out in sequence by Mortimer Eastwood.

A The exterior walls were sandblasted.
B The stables were built.
C Flagstones were removed from the yard.

D	The kitchen was taken out.
E	Bathrooms were built in the attic.
F	House walls and roof were made good.
G	The house was painted brown.
H	The sauna was installed.
I	The garage walls were built.
J	A living area was established along the south wall.
K	The frontage was cleared and paved.
L	Central heating was installed.
M	The attic was converted.
N	The launderette was annexed to the kitchen.
O	A studio was built.
P	The kitchen wall was removed.

Step	
1	
2	
3	
4	
5	
6	
7	
8	
9	
10	

QUESTION 2

1 In the space below, draw a plan of the ground floor of Ribblesdale House, including any outbuildings, as it would have looked in the late 18th century.

↑
N

2 In the space below, draw a plan of the ground floor of Ribblesdale House as it would have looked after the alterations undertaken by Mortimer Eastwood.

↑
| N

--- **QUESTION 3** ---

Give the appropriate word or phrase in the passage which is similar in meaning to the following (the words are in sequence).

1 carries . . . .

2 affluent . . . .

3 demolished . . . .

4 included . . . .

5 intended . . . .

6 guess . . . .

7 complete . . . .

8 took possession of . . . .

9 plan . . . .

10 solid . . . .

Windmills and Watermills

1 It could be said that the development of civilisation has taken place in response to man's need to improve methods of agriculture. Since earliest times, he has needed to invent new methods of harnessing natural power to relieve him of the slow and laborious toil necessary for his survival. Primitive man ground his grain by pounding it between two stones to produce a form of flour but in the course of time this crude method was superseded by working a rubbing stone backwards and forwards across a saddle-shaped stone base called a saddle quern—a task performed by the womenfolk. Many centuries later, the rotary quern or handmill replaced the saddle quern; it consisted of two circular stones mounted on a central pivot, the upper stone being made to revolve by a handle on the side. It was from such early beginnings that the revolving millstone developed, and during Roman times a more sophisticated version of the rotary quern appeared: operated by asses or slaves, a hollow stone shaped like an hour-glass revolved on a conical stone base, the grain being fed through a hole in the centre. The friction caused by turning the stone round ground the grains as they filtered between the two stones, and the meal ran down the sides, where it was collected.

2 The windmill and watermill were man's earliest engines and his only ones for many centuries. The first known reference to a watermill dates from the century preceding the birth of Christ, and it has become known as the Greek mill. The upper stone was driven from below by a vertical spindle, on the lower end of which was a wooden rotor or impeller. There was no gearing and both rotor and running stone revolved at the same speed. This horizontal mill required a fast-falling mountain stream for it to function efficiently. It later became popular in many European countries from the Baltic to the Mediterranean but it is particularly associated with Norway and Sweden, where it was further developed and called the Norse mill. It consisted of two elements, a basement or underhouse through which the stream flowed and an upper meal house. The most basic mills used the walls of the banks of the stream but later examples were built of rubble or masonry. The upper structure was a rectangular hut of stone or timber with gable ends and a simple pitched roof, sometimes of thatch. It was often possible to situate a number of mills, one below the other, along the banks of a mountain stream. The mill had no gearing and its basic mechanism was that of the early Greek mill from which it developed: a vertical wooden shaft with paddles at the end formed the horizontal wheel of the mill. The shaft terminated in an iron spindle which passed through the bearing in the bed stone (the lower fixed stone) to support and drive the runner stone above it. A square wooden hopper hung from the rafters to feed the grain down to the stones.

3 Also appearing during the Roman period was a second basic type of mill—the vertical mill, and this is the direct forerunner of the modern mill. It seems likely that it originated in Persia. It consisted basically of a vertical water-wheel fitted with blades or paddles which turned in the current: one type was fitted with undershot wheels, when the current acted against the flat paddles, and another with overshot wheels, where the water was delivered over the top of the wheel and the paddles retained the water, whose weight drove the wheel round. This was a great advance over the Greek mill because gearing was introduced. A toothed pinion was keyed to the same horizontal axle and a larger toothed gear wheel was mounted on the vertical spindle of the millstone. It was often used for irrigation, and where no water was available, draught animals were used. The mill, however, met with a great deal of opposition from the Romans because they believed spirits lived in water and were not to be used to serve man. It was only with the advent of Christianity that milling became a respected way of life. The water-mill has survived in Britain for nearly 2000 years and was certainly introduced by the Romans, and it would appear that it was used both for grinding corn and for raising water.

4 A simple expedient for coping with the seasonal fluctuation in water levels was the floating mill, a barge moored on a river, powered by undershot wheels which remained above the water. There were two kinds; one mill had two water-wheels mounted on the sides of the barge, and the other had just one. In both types, the millstones had a simple roof to protect them. Another type of mill used by the Romans was the edge-runner mill, and it did not use water power but animals or slaves to drive it. It was used for crushing olives, from which olive oil was extracted, and consisted of a pair of broad stone wheels mounted on a horizontal axle which projected on either side of a vertical shaft. The shaft rotated, causing the wheels to revolve, the edges of the stones providing the cutting surface.

5 Windmills were first used for milling grain or lifting water in Persia about 7 AD, and they can still be found today in Seistan but they are considerably different in design from the windmill that became so

widespread in Europe from the 12th to the 19th century. The Persian mills had vertical, not horizontal, shafts and the sails rotated on a horizontal plane, rather like a helicopter, driving a single pair of stones directly, without gears. They stood in a long row of stationary open-roofed buildings with inlets for the wind extending along the whole of the building and with similar outlets on the opposite wall. Windmills were probably introduced into France and Britain by the Crusaders, and they were in use here by the early 12th century. During the Middle Ages the mill was a simple structure, often no more than a rectangular hut covered by daub and wattle. The mechanism was very much like that of the Roman vertical mill. From the 13th century onwards, there were many references to mills in title deeds and illustrations of them in illuminated manuscripts.

One of the earliest windmills known in Europe is the post mill—some, indeed, being carefully preserved until this day. The post mill is essentially an adaptation of the watermill, where wind is utilised instead of water. It is box-like in form, made of a heavy wooden frame and mounted on a massive vertical post upon which the whole mill, including its sails, gearing, and millstones, could be rotated on a vertical plane to catch the wind. It was turned into the wind by a tail pole pulled by the miller, and this tail pole was sometimes combined with the steps which led into the mill building. The vertical post rested on two horizontal cross-trees, the main horizontal members of the underframe, placed at right angles to each other and supported at their ends by piers of brick or stone. The entire weight of the mill was transferred to these piers by four diagonal struts or quarter-bars, fixed into the post and resting on the cross-trees above the piers. The whole framing of the mill was covered by weatherboarding, often painted white. In some variants of the post mill, the whole substructure, comprising post, cross-trees, and quarter-bars, was buried in the ground, presumably for greater stability. No examples of this early post mill, often called the sunk post mill, now work. The early open trestle mill was similar to the sunk post mill but it was raised on piers above ground level. From the 18th century onwards, the post mill was provided with a round house, a stationary building made of brick, stone or wood and, although having no structural significance, protected the underside of the mill and acted as a store. The post, which passed up through the lower floor of the mill body, socketed into the crown tree, a horizontal beam which is the principal framing member of the mill body and from which the whole structure of the mill is supported. The sails were mounted on a wooden or cast-iron windshaft which inclined at an angle of 10–15° to the horizontal, carrying a large toothed gear wheel called a brake wheel. This was connected to the first driven gear in the mill which drove the vertical shaft. A handbrake fitted on the rim of the brake wheel could stop the mill. Sometimes a smaller but similar wheel could be mounted further back on the windshaft to drive additional stones in the tail of the mill. Until 1745, mills had to be turned by hand but in that year, Edmund Lee patented a fantail device, a small auxiliary windmill with sails set at right angles to the sails of the mill. It was mounted on the ladder or tail pole, and was geared to wheels which ran on a circular track around the base of the mill, hence slowly moving it round into the wind automatically.

7 About the middle of the 14th century, the tower mill evolved in western Europe and appeared in England in the 17th century. The earliest known illustration of a tower mill is contained in a 15th century French manuscript. It was a development of the post mill, and in it the machinery is contained in a round or octagonal body with the cap at the top carrying the sails. The mill is stationary and enables more space to be given to machinery and storage, but the top or cap of the mill rotates, carrying the windshaft, which in turn supports the sails. An iron track or curb secured to the top of the tower enables the cap to move round; in the early tower mill, a rack was fixed around the curb; a gear attached to the cap carried it round on wheels, with a chain hanging down to the ground. By pulling on this chain, the cap could be turned. With the introduction of the fantail, however, a small auxiliary windmill was placed behind the cap at right angles to the sails. When the sails face the wind, the fan is stationary but when the direction of the wind changes, it turns. It is geared to the rack around the curb and turns the cap until it faces into the wind again. The internal construction of the tower mill is very similar to the post mill except that the brake wheel drives an intermediate gear or wallower at the top of the vertical shaft which conveys the power to the millstones on the first floor of the mill. The second floor carries the hoppers, open wooden containers, which discharge the grain to the stones. The upper floors are used for storage. The body of the tower mill proper is built of stone or brick, in which case it is usually round, but timber towers can be found and they are tapering and polygonal. They are a variant of the tower mill and are called smock mills. Sometimes they can have brick bases.

8 The combination mill is often found in the eastern counties of England. This is part tower and part post mill, its post mill body having been removed from its substructure and mounted on a short tower, with curbs at the top, enabling it to turn.

189

QUESTION 1

a) Draw a saddle quern as described in paragraph 1, as seen from the front.

b) Draw a rotary quern as described in paragraph 1, as seen from the front.

c) Draw the hour-glass shaped handmill as described in paragraph 1, as it would appear from the front.

d) Read paragraph 3 on the vertical water-wheel. Draw (a) an undershot wheel and (b) an overshot wheel to illustrate the difference.

   (a) undershot wheel   (b) overshot wheel

e) Read paragraph 5, where the early windmills are described. Draw the Persian vertical windmill, as it would appear from the front.

QUESTION 2

Look at the illustrations of windmills and watermills below and overleaf. Give each one its name as described in the text using the following words: floating mill, combination mill, Norse mill, tower mill, smock mill, open trestle mill, post mill, sunk post mill, Roman edge mill. Also label all of the arrows using the following words: cross-tree, piers, tail pole, struts, ladder (steps), round house, fantail, runner stone, shaft, bedstone, meal house, wallower, stones.

1 ....
(a) ....
(b) ....
(c) ....
(d) ....

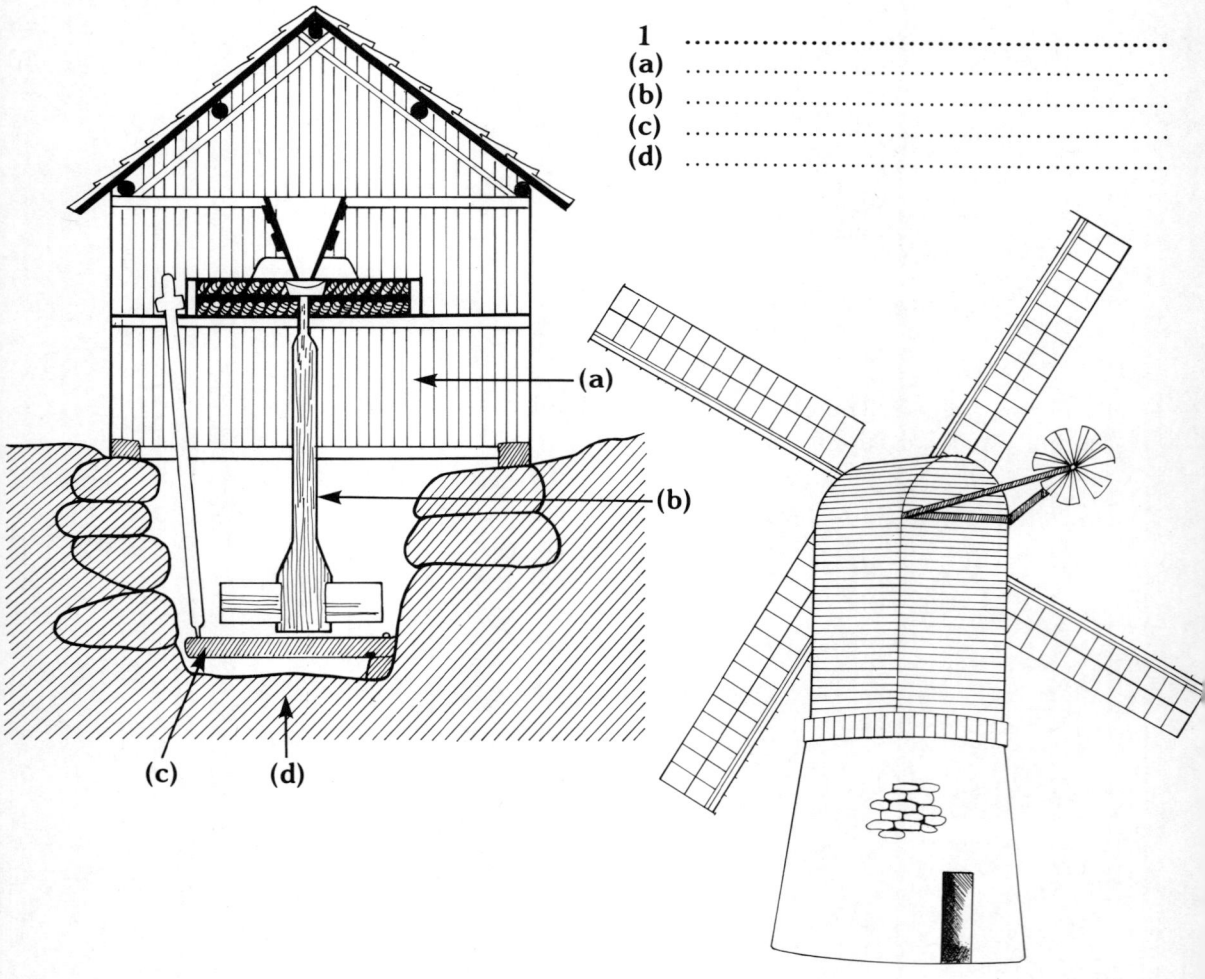

2 ....

192

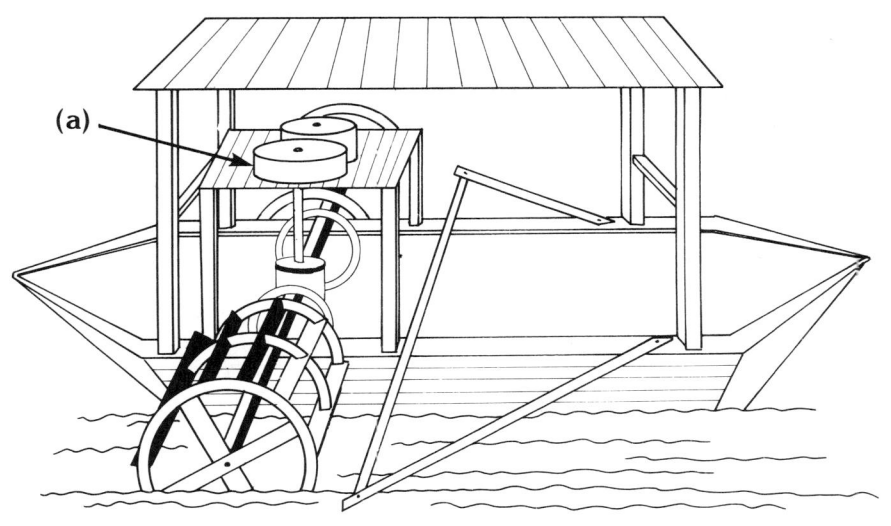

3 .... (a) ....

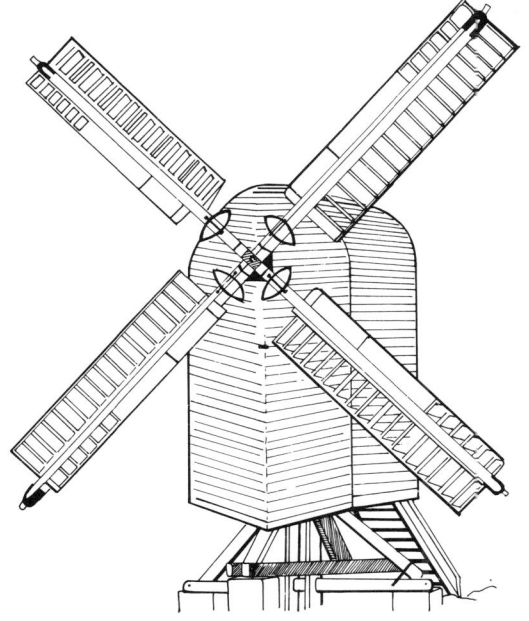

4 ....

5 ....

(a) ....

(a)

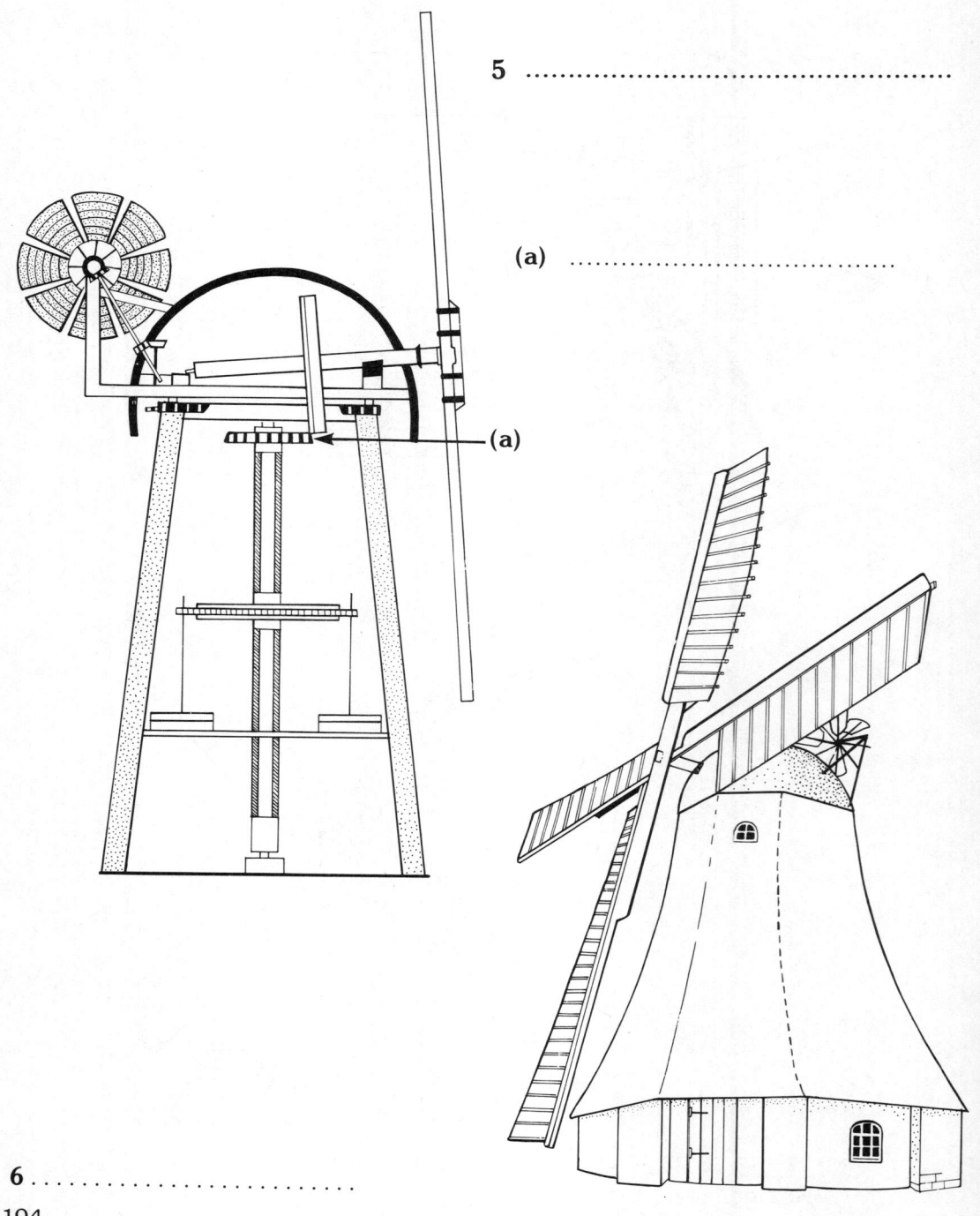

6 ....

7 ....
   (a) ....
   (b) ....

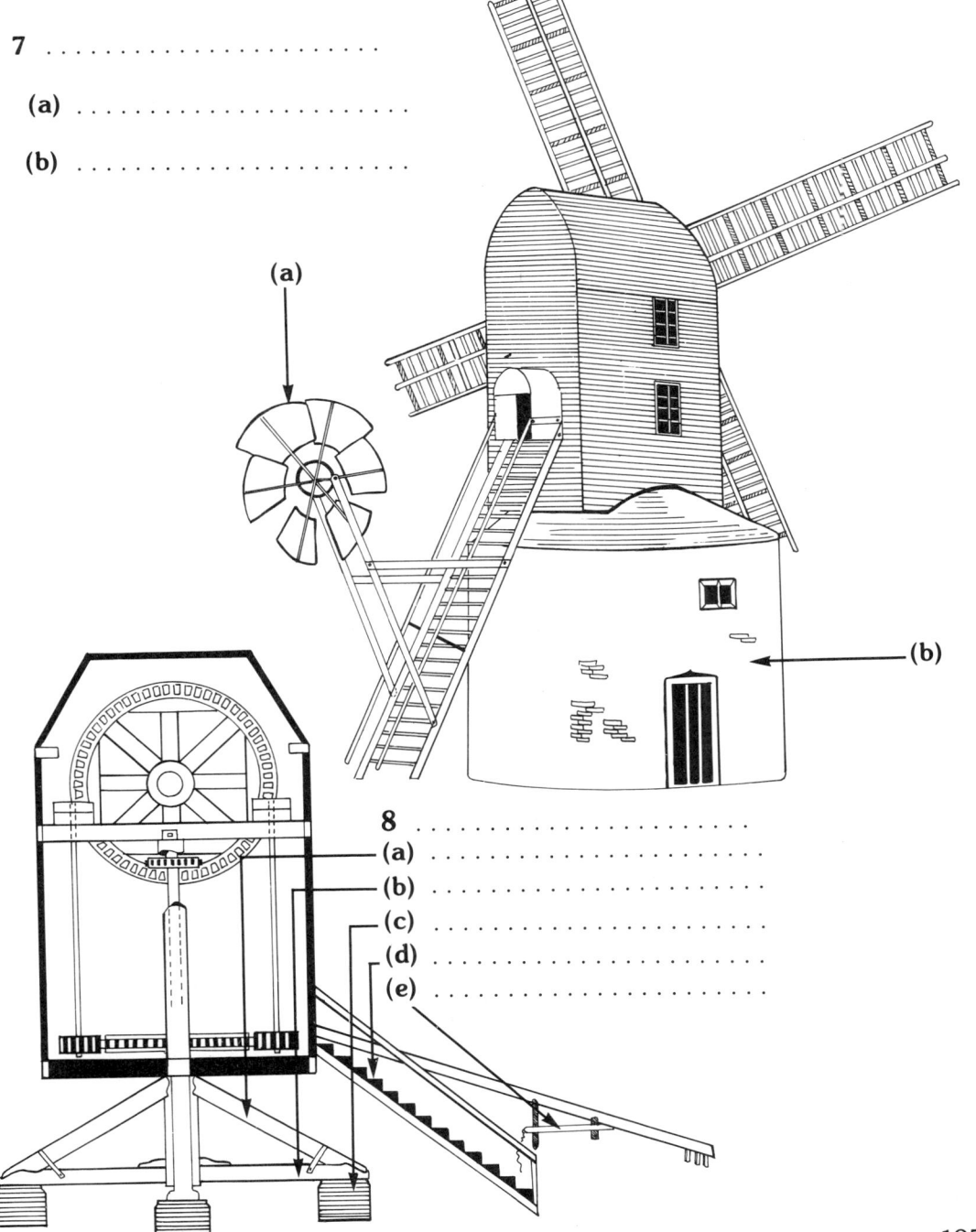

8 ....
   (a) ....
   (b) ....
   (c) ....
   (d) ....
   (e) ....

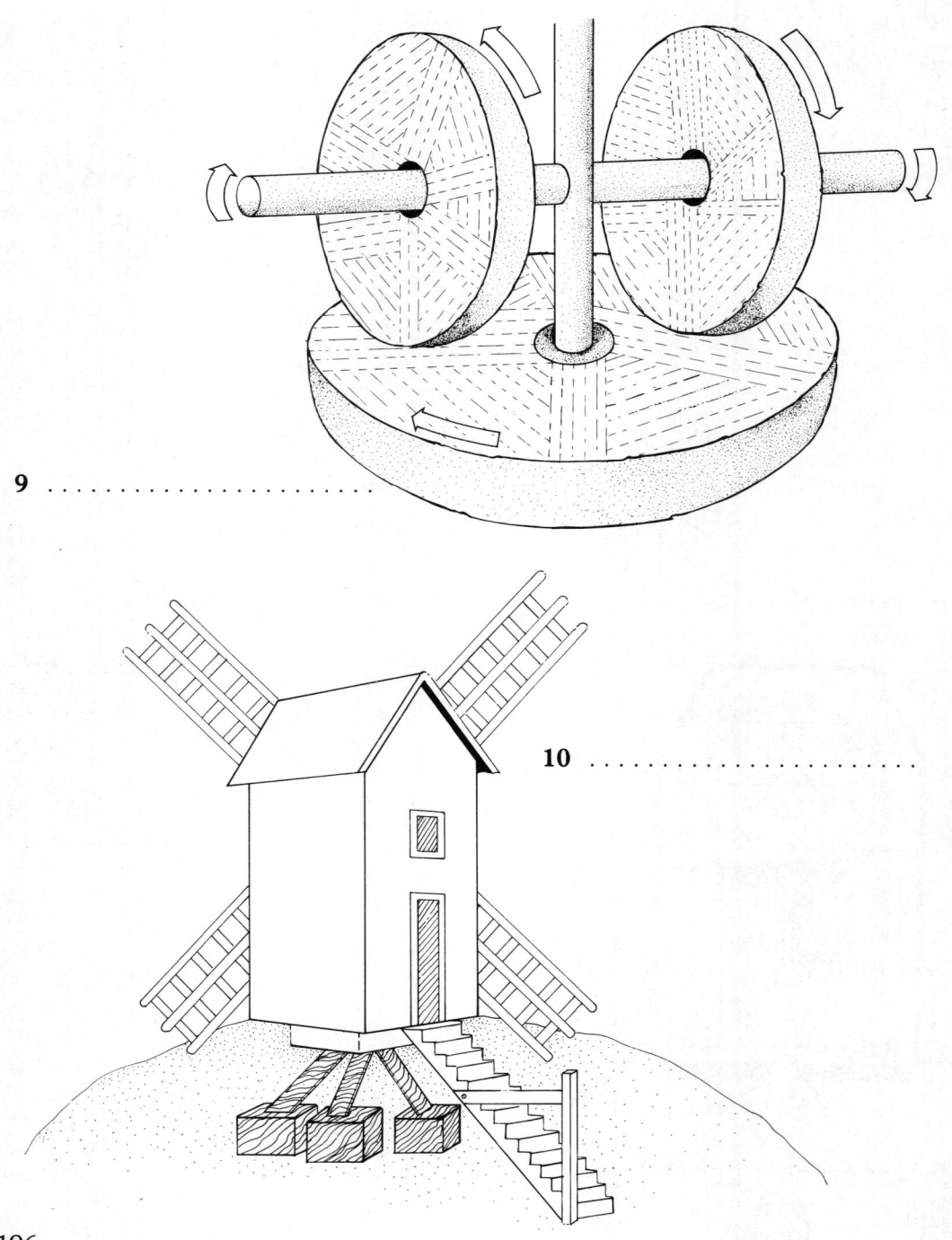

9 ....

10 ....

Probing the Universe

1 When Yuri Gagarin, the Russian cosmonaut and the first man into space, piloted Vostok 1 on 12th April 1961, he began another era in Man's age-long curiosity about the universe around him. Later that same year, Alan Shepherd piloted the first American spacecraft, and within the decade, the first man would walk on the Moon.

2 Man has always needed to understand the heavenly bodies; in fact, astronomy is one of the oldest sciences. The first people known to have studied the heavens were the ancient Egyptians, who knew the positions of the constellations and the courses of the planets. Actual observations of the stars are recorded in the tomb of Rameses VI, of the XXth Dynasty (1202–1102 BC). Two calendars were kept by the ancient Egyptians, the official calendar of 365 days which lost a day every four years but kept the date by the days of the month; and the solar calendar of 365¼ days by which the dates of astronomical importance, like eclipses and agricultural festivals, were kept. Their year was divided up into 12 months and each month into three weeks of 10 days each; the beginning of each week was indicated by the rising of a star called the decan star and star maps and decan lists were kept for astrological purposes, like the casting of horoscopes.

3 After the decline of the ancient Egyptian civilisation, the science of astronomy was neglected for a thousand years or so until it was revived by the Greeks. In Phoenician and early Grecian times, sailors found that different groups of stars could be seen at different latitudes; they noticed, too, that during the lunar eclipse, the Earth's shadow on the Moon was always curved, indicating that the Earth was a sphere. Certainly by 400 BC this was acknowledged by Greek astronomers. The behaviour of the celestial bodies puzzled the Greeks, and they tried to find the right answers. In the 3rd century BC Aristarchus suggested that the planets, including the Earth, orbited the Sun; but hundreds of years were to pass before this observation was accepted. Four hundred years later, in the 2nd century AD, Ptolemy, the greatest of the Greek astronomers, stated that the universe must be ordered in circles since it was made by gods and the circle was the most perfect mathematical form. He believed that the Earth stood

4

motionless while the Sun went round it with each planet moving around the Earth in a large circle as well as moving in a small circle. This geocentric cosmology was to dominate western scientific thinking until the Copernican revolution of the 16th century. The father of systematic astronomy was Hipparchus who compiled the first catalogue of the stars. He was able, just after 200 BC, to estimate the distance of the Moon from the Earth, which has proved to be just 1% different from today's estimate.

After the Greeks, there was again a period of decline in the science of astronomy in Europe; the Arabs took up the subject, giving it a terminology, and it was eventually returned to Europe after the Moorish conquest of Spain. By the Renaissance it was again flourishing in Europe and the Ptolemaic cosmology was once more challenged. In 1543, the Polish astronomer Copernicus published a book in which he attempted to overthrow the geocentric model of the universe in favour of the heliocentric. His ideas had been published earlier in 1510 in an abbreviated form but now that he was near death he was persuaded to publish his work in full. He stated that the Earth orbited a motionless Sun which meant that he had to reject scholastic physics and postulate a much greater scale for the size of the universe. The idea that the Sun was the centre of the universe and not the Earth went against the judgment of antiquity and caused a great deal of antagonism and psychological unease from both astronomers and the Church, who believed Ptolemaic theory more consistent with Biblical revelation. Ptolemaic theory also gave more accurate mathematical results and Copernicus was not able to explain why planets should be attracted to the Sun. In 1575, the Danish astronomer Tycho Brahe began to build an observatory at Uraniborg and was able to make the most accurate naked-eye observations to date. In 1601, Kepler became his assistant and, after his master's death, was able to use Brahe's data to calculate an elliptical orbit for Mars, and in so doing made two fundamental changes to the theories of his predecessors: the ellipse replaced the current circular model, thus presupposing that planets moved around their orbits at varying speeds. The abandonment of the Greek idea of the perfect geometrical universe had begun, although Kepler still adhered to the Greek idea that planets moved around their orbits on heavenly spheres. After Kepler's death, astronomy and astrology became independent subjects, and his three laws of planetary motion enabled astronomers to deduce a great deal about the physical properties of the stars. Kepler believed that a planet moves around the Sun in an elliptical orbit with the Sun at one focus of the ellipse, thus rejecting the Greek notion that (a) the line joining the Sun to the planet sweeps through an equal area in any given period of time, so that a planet close to the Sun would have to travel faster than when at a greater distance; and (b) the square of the period of rotation about the Sun is proportional to the cube of the mean distance from the Sun. It was the formulation of these laws which made Newton's Law of Gravitation possible. In 1687, Newton published his *Principia* and found the answers to Kepler's theory of elliptical orbits. All planetary bodies move in accordance with the laws of physics. Newton maintained that every particle of matter attracted every other with a weak force that varied depending on the distance that separated them; that every particle continued in a uniform state of motion unless a force, such as gravity, acted to change it. The gravitational pull of the primary body continually pulls the orbiting planet to the Sun or the satellite to the planet. At the same time as Kepler published his first two laws in 1609, a mathematician at the university of Padua in Italy, Galileo Galilei, took a most important step in the history of observational astronomy, which resulted in the biggest impact being made on the science. The previous year, a Dutch lens grinder named Lippershay had invented spectacles and the telescope. By applying the telescope to the heavens, Galileo saw the planet Venus and noted its phases. He realised that it orbited around the Sun. He observed sunspots and four bright satellites around Jupiter. Copernicus had been right.

5 The first discovery of a new planet to be made in recent historical times was the discovery of Uranus in 1781 by Sir William Herschel who pioneered the building and use of reflector telescopes. The first indication of the chemical composition of the stars was given by Joseph von Fraunhofer, a German optician, when in 1815 he successfully mapped the dark lines that appear on the surface of the Sun. In 1861, with a much improved spectroscope designed by Bunsen and Kirchhoff, spectroscopic analysis began; then, in 1868, Sir Norman Lockyer discovered a line in the solar spectrum which could not be related to any known element at that time. Three years later he called it helium after *helios*, the Greek word for the Sun.

6 The science of atomic theory has made possible the enormous advance in astronomy in modern times; in fact, more advance has been made in the last 30 years than in the previous 3000. We now understand how stars shine—we know that they are vast thermonuclear reactors. The new chemical-atomic theory began when the English Quaker John Dalton compiled and published the first table of comparative atomic weights in 1803, when he stated that the particles or atoms of different elements were distinguished from each other by their weights: hydrogen and helium had light atoms, whereas lead and

mercury had heavy ones. The publication of his atomic theory in 1810 made the study of chemical reactions precise enough to be useful to astronomers. The notion of atoms, however, was not new; it had first been suggested by the Greek philosopher Democritus, who lived in the 4th century BC. He said that all matter was composed of particles so small that they could not be divided up. (We now know this to be untrue; atoms are themselves composed of yet smaller fragments.)

7 The invention of the radio telescope has considerably widened astronomical knowledge. In 1932 an American radio technician, Karl Jansky, was investigating static in short-wave radio receivers when he found a steady signal in the decametre waveband. The emission came from the Milky Way. Jansky was not an astronomer, however, and he did not realise the significance of his discovery. Subsequently Grote Reber, an American amateur astronomer, built a 9.5 m radio telescope in his back yard in 1937 and was able to detect several sources of radio waves beyond the Milky Way. The outbreak of the Second World War halted any further development of radio astronomy for a while, although work on radar during the war was later found to be useful in astronomy. When the war ended, giant radio telescopes were built, transforming the whole subject area. In 1955 the largest steerable telescope in the world, 76.2 m in diameter, was completed at Jodrell Bank, pioneered by Sir Bernard Lovell and now operated by the University of Manchester.

8 Radio telescopes are able to detect objects that are too distant to be seen through an optical telescope and they are not affected by the dust and gases that obscure so much of space. Bright stars are not radio objects, but there are many objects that can be detected only by their emitted radio waves. The giant radio telescope at Cambridge has detected nebulae 5000 million light years away. We have learned from the radio telescope that the Milky Way has a spiral shape, and other celestial objects have been discovered like pulsars and quasars— the most energetic objects known in space. One quasar has been known to flare 10 thousand times brighter than the Milky Way Galaxy! Should we one day encounter life on other planets, then it will probably be with the radio telescope that we shall communicate with them.

9 The first artificial Earth satellite, Sputnik I, went into orbit on 4th October 1957, closely followed in the next month by Sputnik II. The first object to reach the Moon from Earth was the probe Lunik II in September 1959. In 1962 John Glenn orbited the Earth three times in the first Mercury craft to be boosted by an Atlas rocket, and in June

1963, Valery Bykovsky set the five-day endurance record in space. The following year, Alexei Leonov completed the first space walk. On July 20th 1969, Neil Armstrong became the first man to set foot on the Moon, the climax of an intensive American space programme. For the next few years several manned and automatic probes were launched into space; on the Apollo 15 mission, a lunar-roving vehicle collected a wide range of samples for analysis; Apollo 16 brought back over 91 kg of Moon rock and in December 1972, the last lunar landing was made by Apollo 17. The planets have been studied by automatic space probes—the Mariner series studied Mars, Venus and Mercury, and the Pioneer series have investigated the outer planets. The Russians have sent soft-landing missions to Venus and Mars. The Mariner 9 mission to Mars in 1971 was the first space probe to be put into orbit around another planet, and the American Viking probes that soft-landed on the planet in 1976 confirmed that Mars was marked by excessive volcanic activity, that it was red in colour and that it most certainly does not support life as we know it. In 1980, pictures of Saturn were returned to Earth from the Voyager spacecraft which had been launched three years earlier. It is hoped that by the year 2000, Voyager will have visited even the outermost planets of the Solar System.

10

We are now able to observe the celestial bodies with orbiting observatories that are sent out into space and relay astronomical information back to Earth: artificial satellites have been used for reconnaissance; surveying; studying the electromagnetic and gravitational fields which surround the Earth; in communication when relaying television signals, and in meteorological observation.

11

The enormous advances made in modern times in our space research have led many people to wonder whether it will be possible in the foreseeable future for Man to explore other planets. At the moment the answer must be no: the distances are so immense, and no spaceship yet constructed could withstand such journeys. Even if they were able to travel at the speed of light, it would take 136 years to make the return journey to Aldebaran, whilst a return journey to Antares would take about 800 years; and these are not great galactic distances but a minute fraction of the distance across our own Galaxy. A return journey to Andromeda, the nearest other spiral galaxy, would take such a spaceship about 4 million years!

QUESTION 1

Put the following sentences into chronological sequence as described in the passage.

		Step	
A	A giant radio telescope is built.	1	
B	The science of spectroscopic analysis is born.	2	
C	The first artificial satellite goes into orbit.	3	
D	The most accurate naked-eye observations are made.	4	
E	The first estimation is given for the distance to the Moon.	5	
F	The sky is seen for the first time through a telescope.	6	
G	The first historical discovery of a planet takes place.	7	
H	A dying man rejects the judgment of antiquity.	8	
I	The telescope is invented.	9	
J	The first artificial satellite orbits a planet other than Earth.	10	
K	The first publication of atomic theory.	11	
L	The answer is found to why planets move in elliptical orbits.	12	
M	Foundation of the geocentric model of the universe.	13	
N	The publication of the first table of comparative atomic weights.	14	
O	The earliest acknowledgement that the Earth is spherical.	15	
P	A new element is discovered on the Sun.	16	
Q	The first object from the Earth reaches the Moon.	17	
R	Radio waves are first detected.	18	
S	Confirmation that the red planet is dead.	19	
T	Accurate map is made of dark bands on the Sun.	20	
U	Man enters space for the first time.	21	
V	An endurance record is set in space.	22	
W	The first suggestion that the planets orbit the Sun.	23	
X	The first human being lands on the Earth's satellite.	24	
Y	Man walks in space for the first time.	25	

QUESTION 2

In the left-hand column there is an incomplete statement; choose the statement in the right-hand column which is most suitable to complete it, then complete the table overleaf.

1	As a result of the first space probe to be put into orbit round a planet other than Earth and the subsequent soft landings five years later,	A	This idea was violently opposed on mathematical, traditional, and theological grounds.
2	The earliest known people to study the stars and planets were interested in astrology and	B	and shortly afterwards a new element was discovered in the Sun.
3	Spectroscopic analysis began in the middle of the 19th century.	C	This meant there could be no doubt that planets orbited the Sun.
4	It was known as long ago as 400 BC that the Earth was a sphere and	D	they kept two calendars, one for official use and one for noting important astronomical dates.
5	Using the data left him by his employer he was able to calculate an elliptical orbit for Mars and	E	we know without any shadow of a doubt that it does not support life on its surface and that it has had an active geological past.
6	The book published by this great scholar appeared in the middle of the 16th century and attempted to replace the old geocentric idea of the universe with the idea that the Sun was at the centre with the other bodies revolving around it.	F	in doing so he caused two fundamental changes to be made to traditional astronomical theories, discrediting the Greek idea of a perfect, geometrical universe.

7	The idea of geocentric cosmology was the peak achievement of Greek astronomy and was adhered to for over a millenium.	G	sailors found that they were able to see different groups of stars at different latitudes and they observed the curved shadow of the Earth on the Moon.
8	A steady signal picked up on a short-wave radio receiver was a discovery whose significance was not immediately recognised.	H	It is of vital importance to astronomers, because it enables them to understand the chemical composition of the stars and the atmosphere of the planets.
9	By using a new invention he was able to observe the planet Venus and see that it had phases like the Moon.	I	It was to lead to the growth of the science of radio astronomy, which has made us aware of bodies 5000 million light years away.
10	The discovery of the construction of matter began in the first decade of the 19th century.	J	The idea of the Universe was that it was constructed in a perfect mathematical pattern of circles within circles around a motionless Earth.

1		3		5		7		9	
2		4		6		8		10	

Rose Cottage

1 Rose Cottage is the home of Bill Matthews and his wife and stands in a leafy and secluded lane in the picturesque Cambridgeshire countryside. Built of flint with red brick quoins, it is a pretty, thatched cottage, rectangular in shape, occupying a low-lying position in half an acre of land. It is almost completely hidden from view behind tall hawthorn hedges. Originally a farm-labourer's cottage dating from the 18th century, the house has been totally renovated within the last four years by Bill Matthews and his sons. All the work having taken place within the existing structure, it is a fine example of what can be achieved with the minimum capital outlay and an abundance of patience and imagination. Bill Matthews decided that he wanted to retire to the countryside after a lifetime of hard work in the city, and when he saw the cottage, he knew it would suit him admirably; the price was right and his sons were anxious to help, so he went ahead.

2 The cottage consisted of two storeys, with two rooms on each storey: on the ground floor, a pantry occupied the north wall, with parlour adjoining; and upstairs, two bedrooms completed the living quarters. A single-storey lean-to, which had served as a cowshed, stood on the west wall, and beside this, two derelict outbuildings which had stored fodder for the animals. The entrance to the cottage was in the middle of the south wall and was enclosed by a porch. There was a diminutive plot of land at the rear but at the front of the house, a wide lawn, very overgrown and neglected, sloped down to the entrance.

3 They found that the cottage had no damp-course and that the roof leaked badly. There was no electricity or water laid on. Bill Matthews was fortunate in finding a local builder who was able to assist them in stripping and re-thatching the roof, but the most pressing problem was the installation of a damp-course, so it had to receive precedence. The floor was of uneven stone flags over eleven and a half centimetres of brick, which would have been a daunting task to excavate, so a damp-proof membrane was laid over the existing flags, topped with a layer of screed and the entire area re-floored. At the same time, an electric cable was installed under the floor, as it was the least obtrusive form of central heating. The house was connected to mains water and

4 electricity as soon as the roof was finished. Up until then, the sole source of light had been oil lamps.

A dividing wall was then constructed across the lean-to, using flint from the porch, which was demolished for this purpose, and a fully-fitted kitchen and bathroom were established, while the pantry became a dining room and the parlour a south-facing sitting room. To give an illusion of space, the wall between them was opened up beforehand and the living area enlarged. All the rotten timbers were replaced where necessary, but the upstairs floor-boards were sound so they were sanded and sealed. One of the bedrooms was fitted with twin beds in case guests came to stay. The bedrooms were reached by a new wrought-iron staircase, which had been rescued from a demolition site, and this was fitted after the installation of the damp-course and prior to the re-thatching of the roof.

5 It was decided to locate the entrance on the north wall, in order to take full advantage of a private garden at the rear of the house, so a new front door in sturdy oak (another find) was let into the middle of the north wall, turning the cottage round from front to back. The new back door gives immediate access to a paved area, used for eating out in the summer months. A considerable garden, on two levels and linked by terraces, ascends gently towards the rear, its shrubs providing an effective screen for privacy. All indoor walls were whitewashed, with the exception of the outside walls of the kitchen and bathroom, which were cladded with tongued and grooved boarding to disguise their unevenness. This was done as soon as they were converted, prior to the conversion of the parlour. The most recent undertaking has been the establishment of a garage in the old outbuildings, which forms an unbroken line with the south wall of the house.

6 The cottage is simply but tastefully decorated throughout with the white walls, not only making the most of the natural light (Bill Matthews was reluctant to alter the dimensions of the original leaded casements) but acting as relief to the heavy dark beams and occasional piece of antique furniture. The basic colour scheme has been chosen from the warm end of the spectrum, being particularly effective in the north-facing kitchen and dining room, which receive little sunlight. The gleam of copper pans and a profusion of potted plants add the final touches to a cottage which is perfectly tailored to suit the simple lifestyle of a couple who have richly deserved their retreat.

QUESTION 1

Give a word or phrase from the passage which is equivalent in meaning to the following words (the numbers of the paragraphs are given).

1	isolated	(1)	6	priority	(3)
2	accomplished	(1)	7	formidable	(3)
3	eager	(1)	8	decayed	(4)
4	scanty	(2)	9	conceal	(5)
5	urgent	(3)	10	shine	(6)

QUESTION 2

Put the following statements in the order in which they happened, in the table below:

A   Guests come to stay.
B   A kitchen and bathroom are annexed to the east wall.
C   The water is connected.
D   The roof is replaced.
E   A new staircase is fitted.
F   The lean-to is divided into two.
G   A garage is provided.
H   Ugly walls are hidden from view.
I   Bill Matthews builds a lean-to.
J   A door is made in the north wall.
K   The living area is opened up.
L   The porch is pulled down.
M   Oil lamps are fitted.
N   The upper rooms are dealt with.

Step	
1	
2	
3	
4	
5	
6	
7	
8	
9	
10	

QUESTION 3

1 Draw a plan of the ground floor of Rose Cottage before it was modernised.

↑ N

2 Draw a plan of the ground floor of Rose Cottage after it was modernised.

↑ N

Bacteria and Viruses

1. Bacteriological technique was founded by the German medical scientist Robert Koch in 1881 when he announced a method of obtaining pure cultures of different organisms. (He was in 1905 to receive the well-deserved Nobel Prize for Medicine.) It is that branch of the biological sciences which is concerned with the study of the lowest forms of life, especially those that produce disease in man and animals. There are many such micro-organisms, among them fungi, spirochaetes, amoebae, parasites, worms, bacteria and viruses: but the most virulent are the latter two.

2. Bacteria are tiny living things that can be observed with an ordinary microscope; they are extremely small: a speck of dust could carry thousands. Since they are microscopic they are measured in micrometres (μm) and range in size from 0.3 to 30–40 μm. The anthrax bacterium is the largest known disease-producing bacterium, discovered in 1865, and its life history and method of reproduction (by spores) were described by Koch in 1876. It looks like chains of cylindrical rods. Viruses are much smaller than bacteria and can only be observed under an electron microscope, which uses a magnetic field instead of a glass lens and a stream of electrons instead of a beam of light. Viruses are neither animals nor plants but represent the intermediate stage between living organisms and non-living organic matter. They are capable of being produced in crystalline form and, when thawed out, still retain their toxic properties. They grow only on living cells, whereas most bacteria, being saprophytic, can exist independently and can be cultured in a laboratory. Many dangerous diseases are produced by viruses, such as: typhus, yellow fever, sandfly fever, glandular fever, poliomyelitis (an infection of the motor nerves, or nerves of movement), and encephalitis (infection of the brain, first noted in Vienna in 1916 and reaching epidemic proportions two years later in London). Foot and mouth disease, fatal to animals other than man, is also caused by a virus. Rabies or hydrophobia is a disease, nearly always fatal, caused by a virus and transmitted to man via an animal bite, usually from a dog which is driven mad by the disease. If the symptoms have developed in man there is no hope of cure, but it is possible to prevent

3

the progression of the disease as soon as possible after the bite by using an anti-rabies serum. In July 1885, Pasteur successfully treated a boy who had been bitten by a rabid dog. Three years later, the Pasteur Institute was founded in Paris as the centre of the production of the rabies vaccine. The common cold and influenza are still difficult to treat with vaccine. With some virus diseases, a first attack will give immunity for life—measles, chickenpox, mumps and smallpox being examples; with others, vaccination can lend protection for only a limited period.

Bacteria were first observed in 1676 by van Leeuwenhoek while he was constructing a simple microscope. They appear to be unicellular organisms which are different from plant and animal cells in that they have no distinct nucleus; they are similar to plant cells, though, in that they are surrounded by a rigid cell wall. It is difficult to classify bacteria, since they are so various in their many characteristics, but it is possible to divide them according to their behaviour into three groups: the saprophytic species that absorb food from dead or decaying matter and thus contribute to the natural cycle of life and death; the pathogenic species which produce toxins, and therefore disease; and the symbiotic species which use a body as a host but which offer some advantage in return, such as the build-up of vitamin B2 in the intestine or the ability to aid digestion by breaking food down. We may classify the lower groups of bacteria, called bacteria proper, according to their shape—coccoid or ball-shaped, rod-shaped, helical, part helical, curved or thread-like. The spherical coccoid cells occur in characteristic arrangements on one, two or three planes of division. Occupying one plane of division are the **cocci** which live singly, **diplococci** which live in pairs, **staphylococci** which cluster together like a bunch of grapes and **streptococci** which are found in chain formation. The latter two are responsible for local infections such as boils and for deep-seated spreading infections such as broncho-pneumonia, tonsillitis, inflammation of the skin (erisipelas) and inflammation of the membranes surrounding the brain and spinal cord (meningitis) respectively. **Tetrads** are coccoid cells to be found in plates of four at right angles on two planes while **sarcinae**, first noticed by Goodsir in 1842, look like two tetrads superimposed. They are to be found in cubical packets of eight on three planes. **Bacilli** are bacteria that are rod-shaped or cylindrical in shape with rounded ends. The tetanus bacillus which was discovered by the Japanese Kitasato in 1889 looks like a drumstick or rod with a small knob at one end—its spore—while the bacillus causing typhoid has short fine hairs or threads scattered all around the outside of its cell wall. The anthrax bacillus grows in long chains of cylindrical rods and produces spores which are very difficult to destroy. Another group of bacteria are **vibrios** which are short and curved, looking rather like commas. In 1883, Koch discovered the vibrio which causes cholera. There are further bacteria that are elongated and twisted or wavy in shape, one group are called **spirilla** and the other, **spirochaetes.** Spirilla are rigid, helically-coiled rods, usually with **flagella** at each extremity which enable them to move. Spirochaetes are spiral cells which are flexible, thin and hairlike and can be divided into three classes of pathogenic types—**borrelia,** which has very thick, large, open coils, **treponema,** whose coils are shorter and thinner, rather like a corkscrew, and **leptospira** with the finest coils and a hook on one or both extremities. All three classes move by rotating around their own long axis. The last class of bacteria are the mould-like **actinomyces** which are often found in soil and include some pathogens. Although there are different shapes of bacteria in this group, all are filamentous and characterised by their interlacing pattern of growth which looks like a tangle of threads. The name we give to the tangle of threads is a colony or mycelium.

4 Bacteria can be classified according to their motility or power of movement; some are incapable of movement but others, like spirilla and the typhoid bacillus, move with flagella—or threads—attached to them, either in tufts on one or both extremities or all around the cell wall respectively. The flagella can be short or long, wavy or straight. Spirochaetes are motile without possessing flagella; they move by twisting round and round. Bacteria reproduce in two ways, either by simple fission when they split in two, or, less commonly, by spore formation. If the organism has flagella, it is always the non-flagellated end that bears the new flagella after division. Spore formation will take place only in favourable conditions. It will form at the tip of the parent cell, when it is called terminal; or in the middle, when it is called central; or at a short distance from the end, when it is called sub-terminal. Each organism produces only one spore.

5 The method of taking food is also a way of classifying bacteria; those that obtain energy by oxidising substances they have built up from inorganic matter are called autotrophs; those that need organic material for survival are heterotrophs; bacteria needing oxygen for survival like the tetanus and tubercle bacilli are called aerobic and flourish in a well-aerated environment like a lung, while bacteria that will grow only in the absence of oxygen and are killed in its presence are called anaerobes. A suitable environment for them would be in the intestine or in the dead tissue of a lacerated wound. Such organisms aid decay. All bacteria require the presence of carbon dioxide for growth, some as much as 10%. All bacteria enjoy warmth to some degree and all need water; four-fifths of the bacterial cell is composed

of water. Generally speaking, warm, moist conditions are ideal for bacteria; for organisms which infect man and animals, the ideal temperature is between 35–40 °C and above this, growth will cease. Certain bacteria prefer a much higher temperature; they are called thermophilic and they heat manure and hay. Intense cold does not destroy bacteria but both strong sunlight and pure oxygen do. X-rays do not affect them. Boiling usually kills them, except for the cholera vibrio which is destroyed by drying. The most difficult to destroy is anthrax, whose spores are unaffected by boiling, drying and freezing (unless, in the latter case, it is done over and over again) but it is destroyed by steaming at a temperature of 120 °C over a period of three days, half an hour at a time.

Bacteria cause disease by infecting or destroying the tissues in which they live. In the human body this can result in fever, delirium, paralysis and many other effects. Some dangerous diseases transmitted by bacteria include plague, diphtheria, whooping cough, yaws, leprosy, tetanus, pyaemia, septicaemia and meningitis. Infected food or drink can cause typhoid, the milder paratyphoid, dysentery (not the amoebic variety), diarrhoea, undulant fever, salmonella poisoning, vomiting, botulism (a form of food poisoning), and—from the milk of an infected animal—tuberculosis, a disease whose bacillus was discovered by Koch in 1882. Anthrax can be caught by eating the flesh of an animal which had previously eaten spore-infected grass, whilst cholera is transmitted by flies or infected water.

It was not until the 19th century, however, that bacteria were at all associated with disease. Round about 1865, Pasteur made the first study of the way in which micro-organisms multiply and cause infection. He developed a form of vaccination, using dead anthrax germs, to give immunity from the disease, following the example of Edward Jenner who introduced cowpox vaccine to fight smallpox in 1796. The idea of vaccination was not new; among Eastern nations it had long been established practice and it was in 1717 that Lady Mary Wortley Montagu introduced the idea from Turkey into England where, in 1853, as a result of its efficacy in controlling smallpox, it was enforced. In 1878, Koch came to the conclusion that when certain diseases were present in the body, then certain bacteria were also present, either in the body itself or in its discharges and that, were an uncontaminated bacterium to be injected into a healthy individual, he too would develop the same disease. A Royal Commission was set up in England in 1889 to examine the objections to vaccination which some people still held, and after seven years its findings were made known. Its conclusions as to the value of vaccination in the case of smallpox were favourable, and it was acknowledged that vaccination diminished the likelihood of being attacked by the disease and, where disease was present, rendered it less severe. With the advent of the National Health Service in Britain in 1948, vaccination against smallpox ceased to be compulsory and opinion was still divided. Today, however, anyone who is travelling overseas without a valid International Certificate of Vaccination may find himself refused entry to many countries.

8 Bacterial infections differ from virus infections in several respects: they have a shorter incubation period, and a first attack does not render immunity. Bacterial diseases are also responsive to antibiotics and sulpha drugs, whilst many virus diseases are resistant. The first sulpha drug was synthesised in 1908 but not used against streptococci until 1935. It is now used against many other bacteria. Inoculation is usually effective against bacterial infection but virus diseases are only occasionally treated in this way.

9 Bacteria can be classified as to whether or not they react to the Gram stain—a deep-purple dye of gentian violet, iodine and alcohol, first described by its inventor, J.H.C. Gram, in 1884 and used to identify bacteria. It is a very useful method of staining because it renders the outline of the bacterium and its structure more visible under the microscope. Some organisms will retain the violet stain, in which case they are called Gram positive; others will not and are termed Gram negative. Two other staining processes are Neisser's method for identifying diphtheria bacteria, in which a blue stain is applied for half a minute and then a brown stain is applied for one minute; the bacilli will then show up as an organism stained brown with the blue dots at either end, identifying it clearly; and Ziehl-Neelsen's method for recognising tuberculosis, where the tubercle is stained red then washed clear, then counterstained blue for half a minute. By this method, any tubercle bacilli will be stained red but other organisms, if present, will be blue as the acid treatment will remove the red stain from all organisms other than the tubercle bacillus which are acid-fast.

10 There are four ways of observing bacteria. They can be placed on a glass slide and stained in the appropriate way (methods of staining bacteria were described by Koch in 1877); they can be cultivated in a special nutrient medium which will allow certain characteristics to be seen, for example, when the addition of sugar can show the readiness of the organism to ferment it. Agglutination is another method of observing the behaviour of bacteria; a fluid medium containing bacteria is exposed to a known serum. If reaction takes place, the bacteria will go into

11

clumps or agglutinate, so identifying themselves; if agglutination does occur, we can be sure that it is the same type of organism as that which caused the formation of agglutinin in the serum we have used. In order to establish this, the use of a microscope is not always necessary because if the experiment takes place in a test tube, the clumped bacteria will sink to the bottom of the tube and be seen clearly with the naked eye. A final study of the organism may be made by injecting it into an animal and noting the effects produced, whether harmless or deadly, and whether it produces local infections such as boils.

Bacteria can be useful to man, too. Numerous organisms known as chromogenic bacteria are able to produce various coloured pigments, the most common colours being red, blue, yellow and purple; some, especially those living in sea-water, are phosphorescent; many bacteria produce other substances through fermentation such as alcohol, lactic and butyric acid. Another group of bacteria produce a mould from which antibiotics can be made. This mould was first noticed in 1911 in Scandinavia but it was Sir Alexander Fleming who used its properties in the new drug penicillin in 1928, causing a revolution in therapeutic medicine. The drug, however, was difficult to produce in large quantities and it was not until 1940 that Chain and Florey, applying new methods of production, were able to manufacture it on a much larger scale.

QUESTION 1

Put the following sentences into chronological sequence as described in the passage and complete the table below.

A   The bacillus causing tuberculosis is identified.
B   An epidemic takes place in London.
C   Smallpox vaccination is no longer obligatory.
D   Methods of staining bacteria are outlined.
E   A centre is set up for the production of rabies vaccine.
F   Bacteria are observed for the first time.
G   The cholera bacillus is identified.
H   The idea of vaccination reaches England.
I   New techniques are laid down in the science of bacteriology.
J   The anti-rabies serum is used for the first time.
K   Bacteria are identified by a new stain.
L   The first antibiotic is produced.
M   The tetanus bacillus is identified.
N   Sulpha drugs are used against a form of bacteria.

O Smallpox vaccination is necessary.
P The causes of infectious disease are studied for the first time.
Q A vaccine is used against smallpox for the first time.
R The life history of the largest bacillus is explained.
S International recognition is given to a great scientist.
T A disease affecting the brain is recognised in Vienna.
U Bacteria arranged on three planes are seen for the first time.
V Sulpha drugs are introduced.
W The results of seven years of research are made known.
X The growth of a mould is first noticed.
Y An antibiotic is extensively produced.

Step		Step		Step		Step		Step	
1		6		11		16		21	
2		7		12		17		22	
3		8		13		18		23	
4		9		14		19		24	
5		10		15		20		25	

QUESTION 2

Give the appropriate name to the eighteen illustrations of bacteria on page 215 or where appropriate answer the question below the illustration.

1 ....   7 ....   13 ....
2 ....   8 ....   14 ....
3 ....   9 ....   15 ....
4 ....   10 ....   16 ....
5 ....   11 ....   17 ....
6 ....   12 ....   18 ....

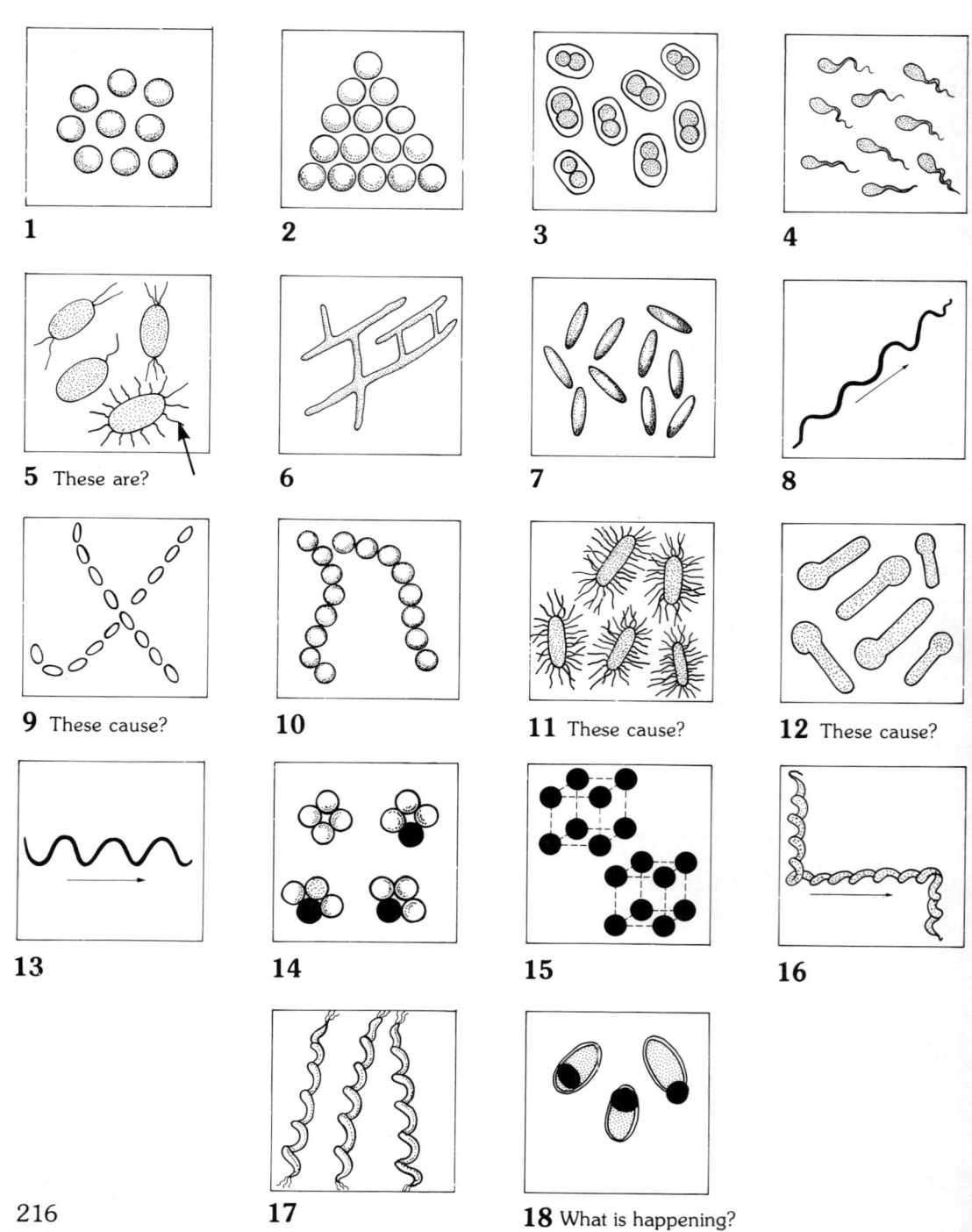

1
2
3
4
5 These are?
6
7
8
9 These cause?
10
11 These cause?
12 These cause?
13
14
15
16
17
18 What is happening?

QUESTION 3

In the left-hand column there is an incomplete statement; choose the statement in the right-hand column which is most suitable to complete it, then complete the table overleaf.

1	This bacterial disease takes many forms, one of which is transmitted to man through the milk of an infected animal.	A	There was an epidemic of it in London two years after its discovery.
2	It was in 1911 in Scandinavia that this mould was found growing on a type of bacteria.	B	It was first noticed in 1883 and drying is the method of destroying it.
3	This is a dangerous virus disease but recovery from it usually means a lifetime immunity.	C	Its bacillus was first noted in 1882 and it can be recognised in a laboratory by alternate staining with red and blue dyes.
4	First noticed in Vienna in 1916, this virus disease causes acute inflammation of the brain.	D	Seventeen years later, a drug was produced which was to revolutionise therapeutic medicine.
5	This micro-organism is comma-shaped and very dangerous, being transmitted to man by flies or infected water.	E	Under the microscope it appears round in shape and arranged in a chain formation.
6	This disease is nearly always fatal and it is transmitted to man by the saliva of an infected animal.	F	A vaccine was introduced in 1796 to fight its effects, as a result of which most countries nowadays insist on its being carried out before entry is permitted.
7	This micro-organism causes a spreading infection either under the skin, in the bronchial tubes, or the brain, or spinal cord.	G	It is treatable by a vaccine developed by Pasteur, provided it is applied immediately after contact.

8	This bacillus has the appearance of a chain of rods and was first observed in 1865.	H	It was discovered the same year as the Royal Commission was set up to investigate vaccination.
9	These micro-organisms grow only on living cells and are observed by means of an electron microscope.	I	It reproduces by spores and is transmitted to man via the animal infected with it.
10	This bacillus is shaped like a drumstick and needs oxygen for its survival.	J	A first attack of certain diseases in this group can give immunity for life, but with others even antibiotics are ineffective.

1		3		5		7		9	
2		4		6		8		10	

Bonding

Bonding is the term given to the arrangement of bricks in a wall, and there are many varieties of **bond**, each used for particular purposes; some bonds are very attractive in appearance and are used for decorative effect, others are selected for economic reasons, where fewer bricks are used. Where strength and stability are called for, walls of double thickness are required and the most satisfactory bond will be chosen. Whichever bond is being used, there are certain general rules which will apply when constructing a wall which govern not only the structural but also the decorative aspects: the weight of the bricks must be distributed evenly throughout the length of the wall, and to achieve this the vertical joints must be **staggered** so that the downward pressure produced by the weight of the bricks, together with any other structure like a roof, is spread over the wall as a whole, otherwise uneven settlement and cracking will result. The main rule in bonding is that the vertical joints of one **course** must coincide exactly with those in the next course but one, i.e. all alternate cross-joints must be kept vertical. Unless completely unavoidable, vertical joints in one course must never be allowed to fall above vertical joints in a course immediately below. All transverse joints must continue unbroken across the width of the wall unless stopped by the centre of a **stretcher**, and at all times, the **lap** must be correctly formed or the wall will look uneven and inaccurately laid. This can be achieved by starting a stretcher course with a three-quarter **bat** or by introducing a **closer** next to the **quoin** header. On no account may a closer be built in the face of a wall unless it is next to the quoin **header**. (The words given in bold typeface are explained on page 224.)

Here are some varieties of bond in general use.

English bond This is the strongest bond and is used for walls 23 cm thick. It consists of alternate courses of stretchers and headers and has two variations: type (a) which is the most common, has a closer placed next to the quoin header to form the lap and prevent continuous vertical joints; and type (b) which uses a ¾ bat on the stretcher course at the quoin instead.

Flemish bond	This is more attractive and economical than the English bond but less strong because of the large number of short, continuous joints. It is constructed by placing a header next to a stretcher on each course, the header in one course centred in a stretcher in the course below to form the lap. As in English bond, it is used for walls 23 cm in thickness. A closer is used next to the quoin header to even up the bond and form the lap.
Stretcher bond	This consists entirely of identical courses of stretcher faces laid end to end so that the next brick laid is in the middle of the brick in the course below, joint staggering being achieved by using ½ bat at the quoin. It is the simplest and most widely used bond in modern building and is used in walls a half brick in thickness.
English garden wall bond	This is also known as Sussex bond. It is less strong than English bond, as it is only one brick deep, but it is more economical. It consists of three courses of stretchers (or five if desired) to one course of headers, the header in one course being laid over the centre of the middle stretcher in the course immediately below. Closers are used in every header course to form the lap. Since this is essentially a decorative bond, it is permitted to use bricks of a different colour on header courses.
Header bond	This is satisfactory for walls one brick in thickness and consists entirely of headers, with ¾ bats being used at the quoin on alternate courses to form the bond. It is used for footings and in curved walls.
Dutch bond	This is similar to English bond in that it consists of alternate courses of headers and stretchers but it has no closers in the header course, the bond being formed by starting each stretcher course with a ¾ bat. In addition, a header is placed next to the ¾ bat on alternate stretcher courses.
Monk bond	This usually consists of two stretchers to one header in each course. The header is laid centrally over the cross-joint between the two stretchers in the course below. The bond may be made to look like an elongated Flemish bond (it is sometimes referred to as Flying Flemish bond) by blinding out the joint between the two stretchers. On long lengths of wall, it is an effective bond to use as it appears to have fewer cross-joints to distract the eye.
Flemish garden wall bond	This is used on walls one brick in thickness and is similar to Flemish bond, but the number of stretchers to each header in each course may be increased either three to one or five to one. Each header is placed over the centre of the stretcher in the course below.

QUESTION 1

Read the descriptions of the various types of bond and look at the bond types below and overleaf, and then complete the table with the appropriate name. If any type has not been described, use an X.

1		6	
2		7	
3		8	
4		9	
5		10	

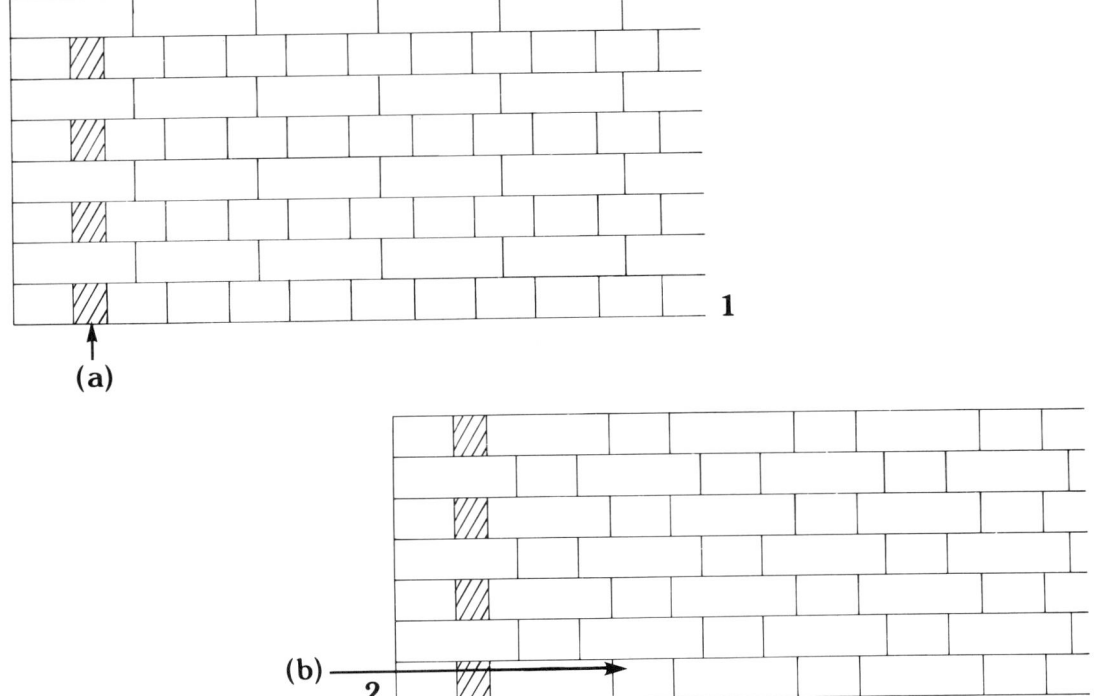

221

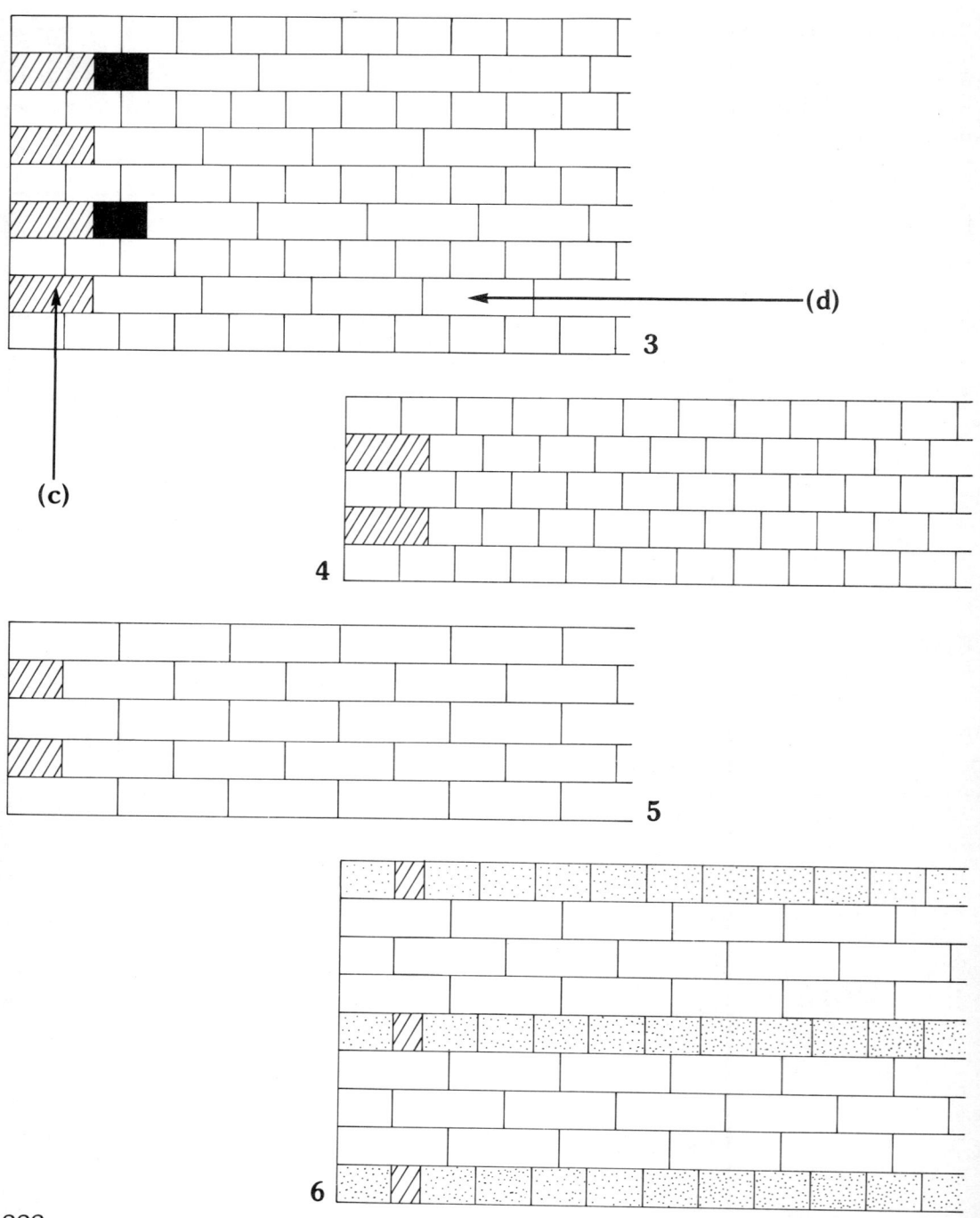

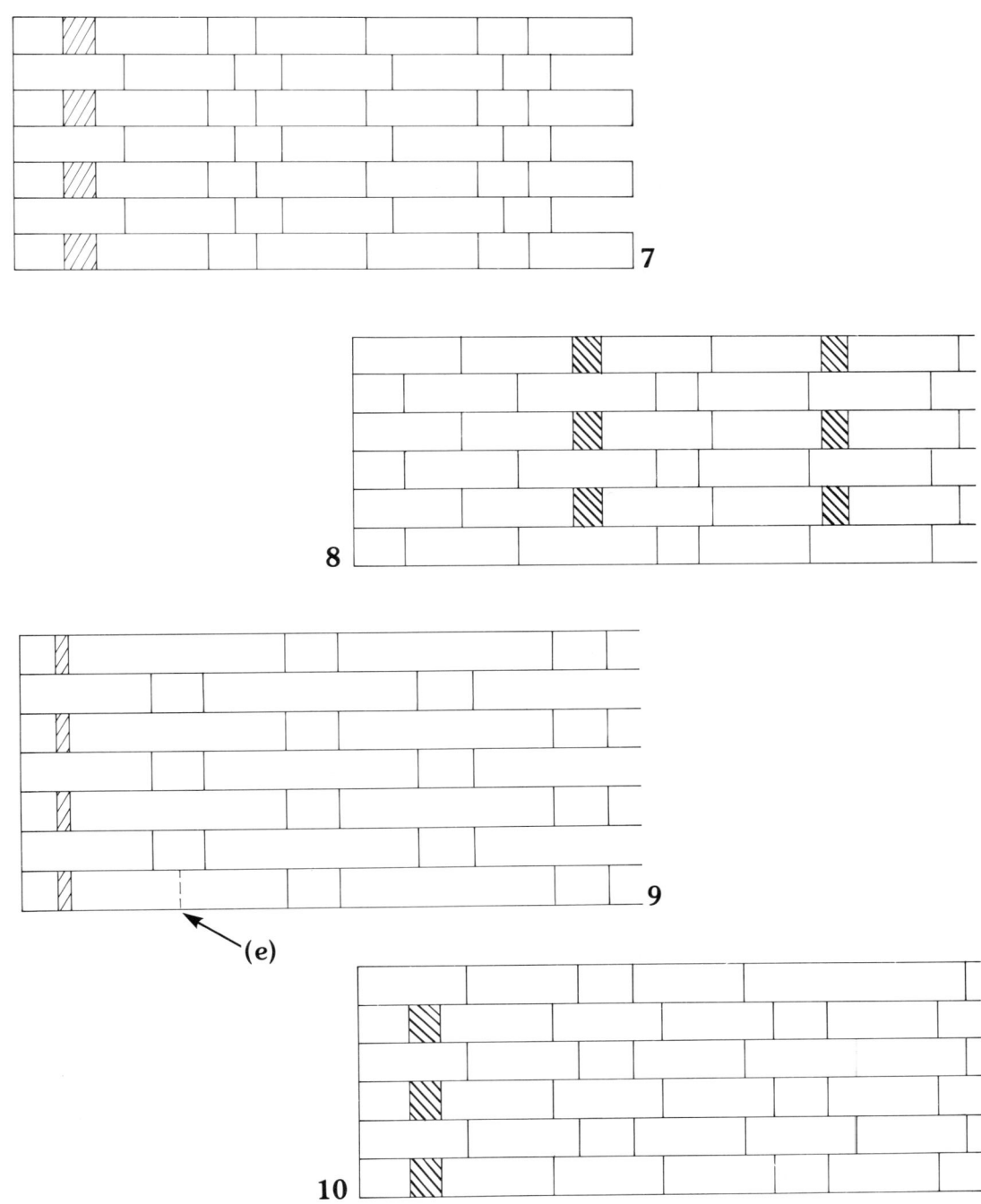

QUESTION 2

Look at the arrows (a), (b), (c), (d) and (e) overleaf, and then complete the table with the appropriate technical term. These terms are given below.

Bat	Part of a brick cut across its width, e.g. ½ bat, ¾ bat
Blinding out	Making a joint invisible by the use of a mortar the same colour as the brick
Bond	A pattern or recognised arrangement of bricks in walls
Closer	A part brick, cut along its length and used near quoins to even up the bond
Course	A horizontal layer of bricks
Header	A brick laid with its ends parallel to the wall face
Lap	The horizontal distance which one brick projects beyond a vertical joint in the course immediately below it, varying from ¼ to ½ brick
Quoin	A corner
Staggered	Arranged in a zig-zag pattern
Stretcher	A brick laid with its long sides parallel to the wall face

(a)		(d)	
(b)		(e)	
(c)			

Bodiam Castle

Look at the diagram of Bodiam castle overleaf and, using the table and key below, give a description of the castle suitable for insertion into a guide book on British castles. Begin with the following sentence:

Bodiam castle, on the south-east coast of Britain, is set in the middle of an artificial lake, surrounded by green banks. It has two entrances, the main one on the north wall.

Key

⊡⊡⊡⊡⊡	Portcullis or heavy timber grating
DB	Drawbridge
T	Towers
WG	Water gate
ωωωω	Machicolation

Date of construction	1385 AD
Period of history	Early in the reign of Richard II
Built by	Sir Edward Dalyngrigge, soldier from the French wars
Dimensions	Walls: 12½ m high; towers 18⅓ m high; depth of lake 2½ m.

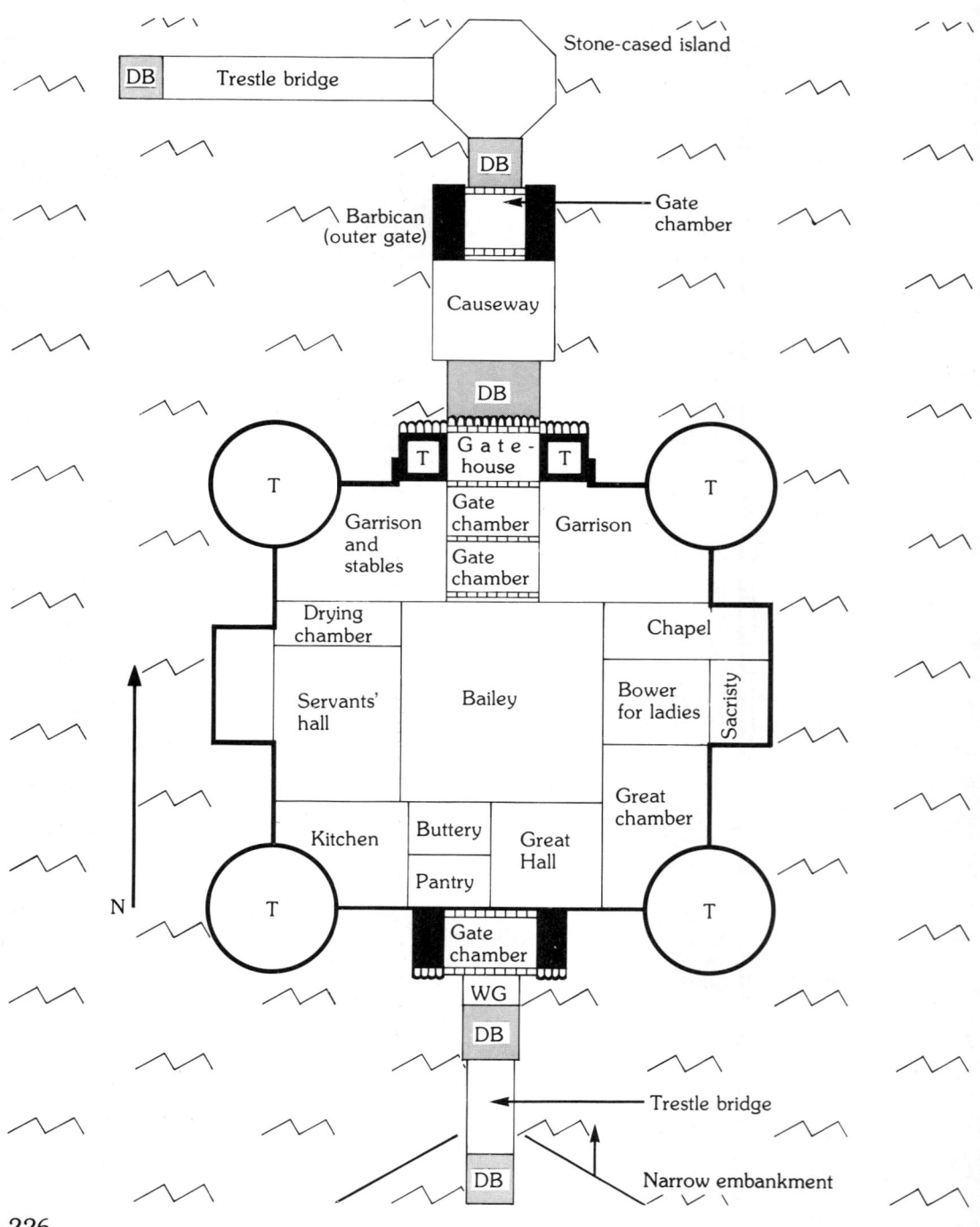

The Development of Archaeology

Put the missing word in each line in the space provided and indicate the place in the line from which it is missing by using the symbol /.

1 _____ Our picture of Man's remote past derived from the study
2 _____ of archaeology, and cannot begin to understand his emergence from
3 _____ savagery unless we can appreciate what archaeology to tell us.
4 _____ It was in 1836 that curator of the National Museum of Antiquities
5 _____ in Copenhagen put forward his hypothesis there were three main Ages
6 _____ in the development early Man's history—Stone Age, Bronze Age
7 _____ and Iron Age—thus providing a framework the study of prehistory
8 _____ which has survived this day. The man responsible for introducing the
9 _____ word 'prehistory' was Sir John Lubbock, book *The Origins of*
10 _____ *Civilisation,* which published in 1870, was the first study of
11 _____ Man's beginnings. He divided the Ages of Man four parts: Palaeolithic,
12 _____ Neolithic, Bronze Age and Iron Age. His book, was written before
13 _____ many of the great archaeological discoveries been made, and today
14 _____ we find it rather narrow and simplistic. It was the Renaissance
15 _____ an interest was born in the history of ancient civilisations and
16 _____ during the 18th century Roman and prehistoric remains collected
17 _____ avidly but without any attempt classification or dating. The
18 _____ publication of Darwin's *The Origin of Species* in 1859 caused quite
19 _____ controversy the age of mankind, and in the seventy-five years which
20 _____ succeeded it a revolution place in our knowledge of our earliest
21 _____ beginnings. Flint handaxes, which been discovered in the gravel

22	_____	beds at Hoxne in 1790 and later in northern France, were accepted as
23	_____	evidence of the antiquity of the human race the publication of
24	_____	Darwin's book. In the middle of the 1870's, amateur archaeologist
25	_____	named Schliemann unearthed nine cities, buried on top of the other,
26	_____	in western Turkey and thus found the legendary Troy. The opulent
27	_____	decadent civilisation of Crete was brought to life Sir Arthur Evans
28	_____	in 1899. Sir Arthur, who was thirty-nine years old Schliemann died,
29	_____	was to spend a total of thirty-five years excavating same site at
30	_____	Knossos, uncovering a world hitherto hidden Greek culture. He
31	_____	called it the Minoan. The foundations modern excavation were laid
32	_____	down Pitt Rivers, who paid great attention to the accuracy of plans
33	_____	in his explorations in Dorset from 1887–1898, it is to Flinders Petrie
34	_____	that we owe the arrangement of the prehistoric material Egypt which
35	_____	established the science of Egyptology in 1901. Petrie made first
36	_____	scientific explorations in England and published book on Stonehenge,
37	_____	but 1880 he was in Egypt where he was to dig for forty-six years.
38	_____	He became authority on the pyramids, those sublime monuments to
39	_____	death, and his scientific publications amount to ninety volumes. Is
40	_____	often called the father of archaeology. The key the language of
41	_____	the ancient Egyptians was provided in 1822 the Frenchman Champollion
42	_____	in his famous letter, when his solution the riddle of the hieroglyphs
43	_____	opened the doors of Egyptian antiquity making it possible only for us
44	_____	to understand the ancient world of the Nile Valley, also the first
45	_____	beginnings of our culture. The roots of European civilisation are there.

QUESTION

Put the following sentences into chronological sequence as described in the passage and then complete the table below.

A   The dating of Roman remains begins.
B   The science of Egyptology is established.
C   Darwin starts a controversy.
D   Greek mythology is discovered.
E   A number of flint tools are found.
F   The first study of Man's beginnings is made.
G   Eight cities are found on the same site.
H   An important site is uncovered in Turkey.
I   A Danish scientist puts forward a theory.
J   The Minoan civilisation is revealed.
K   A letter provides the key to the past.
L   Excavation becomes a science.
M   The earliest collections are made of prehistoric remains.

Step	
1	
2	
3	
4	
5	
6	
7	
8	
9	
10	

Exeton

Give an account of the growth of Exeton from the 15th century to the present day, using the maps below.

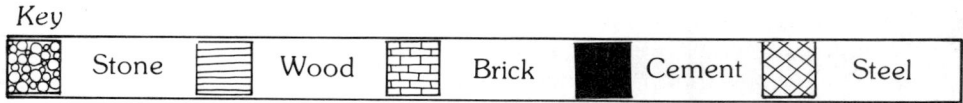

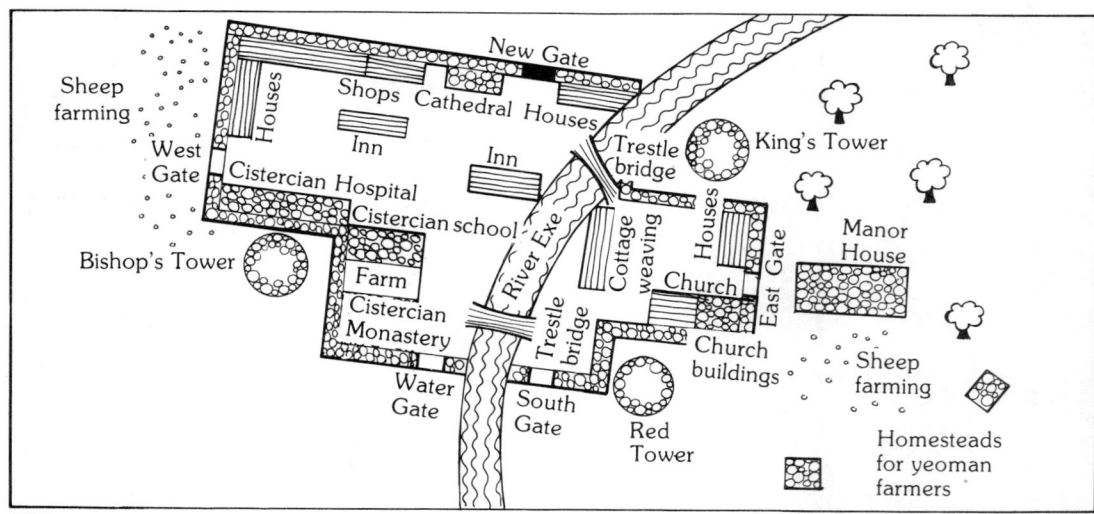

15th century

Walls principally dating from early 14th century on Roman remains of 200 AD

18th century

20th century

Clinic
Golf course
Residential housing
Leisure Centre
Civic Centre

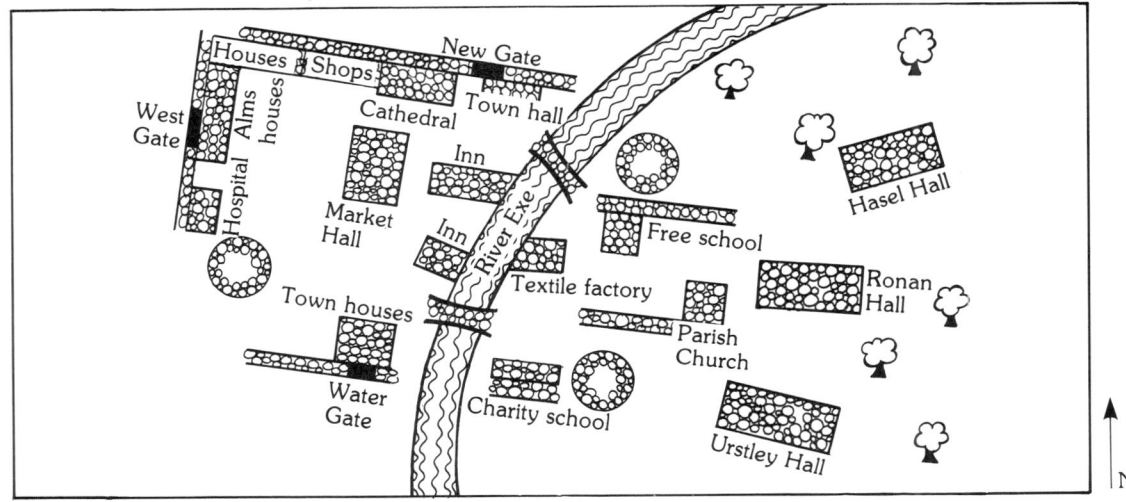

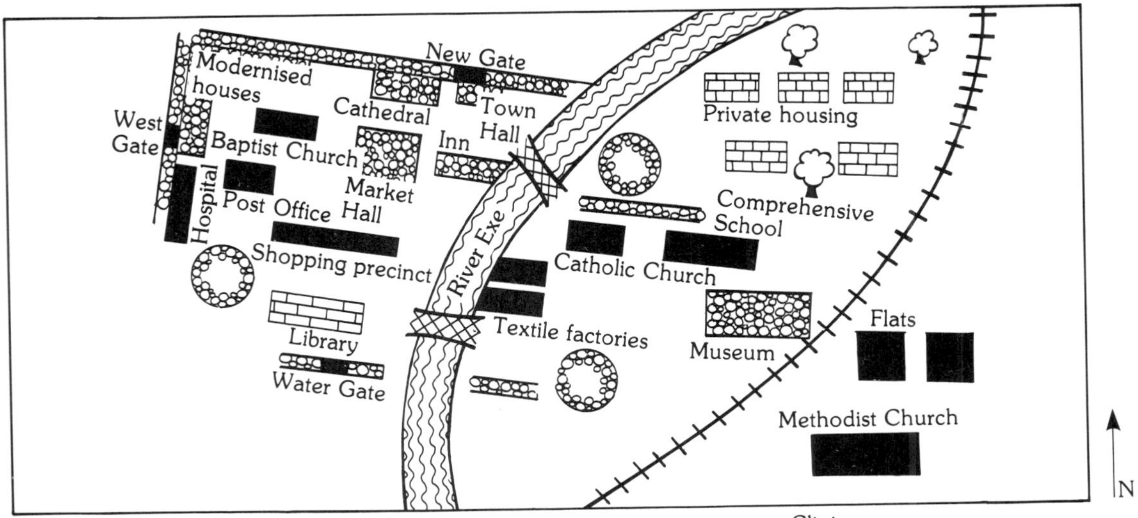

The Methods of Excavation

1 Every archaeological site presents its own particular problem in the strategy of its excavation; each site is unique and no one set of precepts will govern the method of excavation of all types of site. However, it is safe to say that there are seven standard methods appropriate to certain site types on land. Firstly, we have to determine the characteristics of the site in question, whether it is flat or contoured, whether composed of one layer or stratified, whether accessible or not. Its size is also an important factor: some sites can extend for several kilometres and their wholesale excavation would be impossible. Some sites are threatened by proposed roadworks or building programmes, and such rescue excavations must be rapid and selective (unlike research excavations, which can be more thorough), often being conducted under emergency conditions and with limited funds. The stability and type of soil on the site must also be taken into account when the excavation method is to be decided.

2 Let us examine some site types in more detail. A remarkable feature of Neolithic culture in western and north-western Europe was the barrow or ceremonial burial ground. It consisted of a raised mound of earth or stone, circular, rectangular or cruciform in shape depending on the date of its construction, with many layers, each containing artifacts appropriate to the period. The relative stratigraphy is vital here so the quadrant method is used, which has two variations depending on the size of the site. The first, we will call it **Method A1**, is used when the mound is relatively small, without pronounced contours. The site is divided into four sections by two baulks at right angles to each other, each about 60 cm thick. The removal of each quarter would reveal both the vertical and the horizontal sections, giving a better interpretation of the stratigraphy. If the mound is particularly extensive or contoured, then **Method A2** would be used, with a further subdivision into eight triangular sections, forming a star shape. Each section would be excavated separately, then the baulks themselves would be excavated.

3 During the 3rd and 4th centuries BC a large number of hill forts or fortified enclosures were built in Britain. They consisted of a single rampart or wall, sometimes of stone but usually of earth, reinforced with timber and protected by a single ditch. Their large enclosures were places of refuge or centres of resistance to warring tribes. Although their name suggests that they were to be found exclusively on hills, they are in fact found along coastlines, on plateaux and in valleys. Total excavation of this type of site would be impossible because of the extensive territory, so **Method B** or the linear method is used, as it is on all such sites, like roads, walls and dykes. A cross-section of the wall is obtained by the digging of one or more trenches at right angles to the structure, revealing a vertical cross-section which will provide the archaeologist with data on the method and period of its construction. This method, however, has the disadvantage of providing evidence relating only to the sectioned part of the rampart, and more extensive trenching may be needed to give a fuller picture. In some situations, a trench is all that is possible for sheer practical reasons where the site is inaccessible as in a town site, where part of a Roman wall is uncovered sandwiched between two other structures, or when the site is under impending threat from the bulldozer.

On relatively flat sites where there is little or no surface contour and there are no great depths, the grid system is used, which we will call **Method C**. A system of trenches is dug, each at right angles to the other, creating squares varying in size from $3\frac{1}{2}$ m to 7 m, each square separated from its neighbour by a narrow baulk which is finally removed and excavated. This method is particularly suited to large sites, and the system of trenching can be extended if required. As in all horizontal excavations, each section is drawn on the site plan until a cumulative section is obtained.

The grid system cannot be used, however, on sandy soils or gravel, as it is too severe and would destroy fragile evidence, and where the baulks would prevent such evidence from being detected. On a one-layered horizontal site, **Method D1** is preferred, when the turf and topsoil would be removed to show soil marks where organic material has been destroyed and there are no structures remaining. Careful horizontal scraping of the surface would disclose colour differences in the soil and reveal the position of post holes and other decayed timber structures. Some soil colour changes may be made visible by the use of ultraviolet or infrared light or enhanced by chemical treatment or filters of various colours. This method is particularly important in that it attempts to reconstruct events from soil evidence alone but because it is largely manual, it is very slow and would not be used in salvage or rescue excavations where rapid mechanical methods would have to be employed with the resulting loss of evidence. However, **Method D2** is the basis of the large investigations of sand and gravel sites which form a large percentage of rescue excavations in lowland Britain. Time and cost effectiveness are major considerations on threatened sites, and a thorough excavation is not possible. On large horizontal sites where the stratification is shallow, the site is stripped of its turf and topsoil to a few centimetres of the subsoil (or occupation layer) by bulldozer to enable the archaeologist to recover a broad picture of the site as a whole and salvage any evidence before it is too late.

Method E is the planum method, which is used on difficult rescue sites where the stratification is discontinuous and irregular in composition and thickness. It is used on stone-free soils and where there are no existing structures. In the method, each layer is removed a centimetre at a time, in a series of horizontal slices, taking care that no interleaved layer, however small, is missed. The method can be adapted to fit any surface contour and any size of site, from a pagan Saxon village to a post hole, although at no time is it possible to see the site in its entirety because of the confusion of the chronology of the layers. Any finds are plotted on to the site map, and it is possible to obtain a general pattern, if not a complete one, of various features.

QUESTION 1

Read the description of the following site types and determine which method of excavation, according to the passage, would be most appropriate, and then complete the table on page 236. If you think that the site type has not been described, use an X.

1. Roman roads were long causeways fanning out from London in all directions. They were originally planned to speed the movement of legions of soldiers but eventually they were significant in the development of towns. Constructed on a base made of large stones embedded in sand and covered with gravel varying from 45 cm to 90 cm in thickness, they extend for several kilometres in some areas. The most active period of road building in Britain was in the 1st century after the Claudian invasion and was complete by the 3rd century.

2. Large slabs of stone have been set on edge to form walls for this circular, raised burial place on the coast of Scotland. Other slabs have been laid across the top to form a roof and the entire structure is covered with mounds of earth or turves. It contains the remains of a family of the Neolithic period.

3. This large and complicated masonry structure lies under a continuous layer of plough soil, rubble and debris, with deposits of later timber buildings in evidence. Total excavation of the site is required in order to understand its history and methods of construction.

4   This mound or mortuary enclosure is deeply contoured and rectangular in shape. It was once surrounded by a wooden fence, a bank and ditch and covered with turves, giving it the appearance of an artificial hill nearly 100 metres long. It is situated on high ground and probably dates from 3300–2000 BC with the strong possibility of a rich and rewarding research excavation.

5   This Celtic fortified village was built on a very steep slope and consists of a large central enclosure with an annexe to the south, probably intended for livestock. Its outer ramparts cover a total area of 18 hectares and turn inwards parallel to each other to form a narrow entrance which would have been guarded. Such forts are common in Europe.

6   Dating from about 5000 BC and therefore belonging to the Neolithic period, this settlement consists of a number of dwellings stretched along the shores of a lake and resting on strong stone piers. The houses would have once stood well above the water-line and would have had strong timber frames, clay floors and walls of wattle, that is, woven twigs covered with clay. The roofs were made either of rushes or reeds, since they would have been available on the site and in plentiful supply. Transport was probably by canoe, although the remains of narrow bridges indicate that there was some connection with the land, and the settlement may have been a defensive one.

7   This single-layered horizontal gravel site has been accidentally uncovered by excavations for a roadworks programme and indicates a complex of Roman and sub-Roman banks and ditches about 3½ m below the modern road surface.

8   Threatened by the construction of a motorway, this large, stone-free stratified site has been detected by crop marks from the air. Although there do not appear to be any structures still remaining, a rescue excavation is thought to be justified because of the possibility of uncovering evidence from the discontinuous layers which have been occupied not only by prehistoric man but by the Romans. The site was abandoned as late as the 13th century.

9   This research site is found on a long stretch of river gravel where there was a prehistoric settlement. Although no surface features or structures can be detected, its position on the distribution map indicates that it merits further investigation in that it may yield evidence which will reconstruct the movement of a group of people and their migratory habits.

10 A large, flat-bottomed broad-beamed cog or high-sided merchantship of the 14th century has been uncovered whilst dredging operations have been taking place in a harbour on the Baltic coast. Constructed of heavy overlapping planks in the clinker tradition, it is in an excellent state of preservation, being 23 m long with a maximum of 7½ m in width and has a castle or raised platform on the deck from which it could launch attacks if threatened.

1		6	
2		7	
3		8	
4		9	
5		10	

QUESTION 2

Give another word or phrase from the passage which has the same meaning as the words below (the numbers of the paragraphs are given).

1. instructions .... (1)
2. entire .... (1)
3. essential .... (2)
4. illustration .... (2)
5. shelter .... (3)
6. approaching .... (3)
7. harsh .... (5)
8. delicate .... (5)
9. improved .... (5)
10. done by hand .... (5)

QUESTION 3

In the boxes below, draw a plan (as seen from above) of the following excavation methods.

Method A1

Method A2

Method B

Method C

Pyramids and Ziggurats

1

The ziggurat was an important element in the temple complexes of Mesopotamia, today called Iraq, a civilisation which *embraces* the Sumerians (the first civilisation in the history of man, some 5000 years ago) the Akkadians, Babylonians and the Assyrians. The ziggurat was a high, terraced, artificial tower or platform with thick walls built of sun-dried brick with an outer casing of stronger fired bricks, and it dominated the centre of every large city. Crowning the *diminishing* terraces of the ziggurat was a temple or shrine which served not only for religious ritual, where annual human sacrifices were made to fertility gods, but for civic needs, too. It was from the top of the ziggurat that the Babylonians were able to study the movement of the heavenly bodies, and they are known to have been expert astronomers. Every ziggurat had its angles oriented to the cardinal points of the compass, and quite often its sloping sides were terraced with plants and trees. Access to each ascending layer was by means of a triple stairway or, as in the Assyrian version, arranged on a narrow spiralling ramp. The most famous ziggurat is that of Etemenanki, known as the Tower of Babel and described by Herodotus when he visited Babylon in 450 BC.

2

During the period of Mesopotamian history, the plan of the ziggurat underwent several changes in design. The earliest, which we will call **Type 1**, belongs to the period 3500–3000 BC. They were usually flat-topped, one-storeyed, rectangular mounds with battered or sloping sides decorated with shallow buttresses on all sides except the south-east. The temple stood on the top of the mound. There were four entrances, the most important being placed asymmetrically on one long side. All angles were oriented to the compass points. By the third millennium BC it was usual for the ziggurat to have two or more tiers, each with battered walls on which flattened columns called pilasters were attached. The mound was provided with three very steep stairways on one of the longer sides, two adjacent to the ziggurat and one on its axis. All stairways *terminated* on a landing in the centre of the structure. We will call this triple-stairway ziggurat **Type 2**.

3 By the 13th century BC **Type 3** had developed; the rectangular shape was replaced by the square shape and the number of tiers increased to four or five. In the Neo-Babylonian period, after the Assyrian invasion, it even reached seven tiers. The walls in this type were *rigidly* vertical and the entire structure more delicate in design, with each tier mounted on a plinth, and shallow buttresses projecting slightly from the walls. The first tier, which was usually the shallowest, had recessed stairways on each front leading to the first tier, but the second tier could be reached only from a stairway on the south-west side. The other tiers were reached on the south-east, that is, the principal side.

4 **Type 4** is *typically* Assyrian in design, tall, with battlemented cresting on the walls, as on palaces and towers, reflecting the *martial* nature of the Assyrian people. It was square in shape, its corners still adhering to the compass points, and had seven tiers, each one panelled and painted in different colours. At the top was a shrine. On each side of the structure, a continuous ramp, some 183 cm wide, acted as a stairway, winding around from the bottom to the uppermost tier. During the second half of the Assyrian period, about 1000 BC, ziggurat building began to be replaced by the building of palaces. By 612 BC, however, the Assyrians had been defeated and Babylon again became the centre of a great empire extending from the Persian Gulf to the Mediterranean, and an enormous amount of rebuilding took place. This is when the Tower of Babel was constructed by Nebuchadnezzar II, based on earlier models but much more *grandiose* in size and design.

5 The Egyptian pyramids are massive stone structures built by living pharaohs to contain their bodies after death and today they stretch from the west bank of the Nile delta for more than 160 kilometres. There are sixty-seven of them around Cairo alone. They began to be built during the IVth Dynasty (3998–3721 BC) and continued to be built during the Vth and VIth Dynasties (3721–3335 BC) when a whole range of pyramids, although smaller in size, were erected. Pyramids were not isolated structures but stood in a walled enclosure and contained a number of subsidiary buildings, such as smaller, secondary pyramids to house relatives and mastabas for the nobility and an offering chapel on the east side with a mortuary temple for worship of the dead. A canal connected the Valley building with the Nile, which enabled the dead king to be transported to his last resting place.

6 The faces of the pyramid *adhere* to the compass points, unlike the ziggurats whose angles do so, and were not for public use but for the glorification of a king. Ziggurats were constructed by a succession of rulers and were constantly renovated and kept in good repair, unlike the pyramids which were allowed to deteriorate. Ziggurats were not tombs but temples for the living; pyramids were monuments to death and constructed out of vanity. Great labour and expense was incurred in the building of the pyramids and several devices employed to conceal and protect the tomb chamber which contained priceless funerary goods, although *to no avail*. During the chaos of the VIth Dynasty, pyramid building had to be abandoned because no precaution could prevent the looting of the tomb chamber, and eventually rock-hewn tombs took their place when stairs, corridors and passageways were cut into the mountain itself and extended to a depth of 96.25 m below the valley floor. The mortuary temples themselves were often situated on the other side of the mountain and contained no funerary goods.

7 It was in the IIIrd Dynasty, about 4000 BC that the mastaba was transformed into the step pyramid, when the step pyramid of King Zoser was planned and put into effect by the great architect, astronomer, priest, writer and physician, Imhotep, who was later, in the XXVIth Dynasty, to be deified. It was the world's first large-scale monument in stone, and from this remarkable invention, the huge pyramids of Gizeh developed. There were five stages in the construction of the stepped pyramid. Initially it was an unusual square mastaba which was enlarged, though still remaining square. The third phase was the addition of nearly 9 metres to the eastern side, making a base for a four-stepped pyramid. Enormous further additions were made to its sloping sides until the structure became rectangular in plan, then the first step of the pyramid was made by yet more extensions on all sides. On the north and west sides further extensions were added until finally the structure became a six-stepped pyramid. King Zoser was buried in a granite chamber under the pyramid. A network of connecting passages containing eleven members of Zoser's family led off the tomb chamber to all points of the compass while a large complex of temples and royal buildings, also built in stone, surrounded the pyramid. Around the entire complex stood an enclosure wall over 9½ metres in height. The tomb of Zoser was the first of a long series of pyramids built during the Old and Middle Kingdoms.

8 The *transition* from a step pyramid to a true pyramid is illustrated by the pyramid of Meidûm. It was probably begun as a seven-stepped pyramid but was then heightened by 13.75 m to form an eight-stepped pyramid, of which only three survive in this modern age. As each step was added, its sides were filled in and made smooth with limestone. At first, the sides were very steep at the nucleus (75°) but the final pyramid has sloping sides of 51°. The tomb chamber had a corbel roof, corbelling being the earliest experimental device for constructing arches or vaults. (A corbel vault is built of horizontal courses of stone or brick, each course projecting from the one below, which is partly embedded in the wall and partly projecting from it to support its weight. The Egyptians knew how to construct an arch but did not attempt to use it in stone.)

9   The tomb chamber was at ground level in the heart of the structure, which is attributed to Senefru, the last king of the IIIrd Dynasty. The Meidûm pyramid is the connecting link between the stepped and the sloping outline of the pyramid. Two other pyramids at Dashûr are also associated with Senefru and appear to have been conceived as true pyramids, although only one was completed as such. The Bent or South Pyramid, square in plan, was constructed about 2723 BC. It is *peculiar* in that the angle of its inclination changes about halfway up from 54° in 4.57 m at the base to 43° in the upper section, possibly because of hasty completion. It has two entirely independent tomb chambers, one reached from the northern side and one from the west, both with corbelled roofs on all four sides. Surrounding the pyramid was a double-walled rectangular enclosure with a complex of buildings, but the Bent pyramid was eventually abandoned and never reached completion. The Second or North Pyramid at Dashûr is the first structure to have been designed and completed as a true pyramid. It is noted for the shallow angle of its sides, similar in fact to the upper portion of the Bent Pyramid, 43° in 10.97 m instead of the customary 52°. It is here that Senefru is buried.

10   The second king of the IVth Dynasty was Cheops (Khufu), who was the son of Senefru, and his pyramid is the largest and most northerly of the Gizeh complex. This magnificent structure represents the peak of all pyramid building. Two million large blocks of limestone, some weighing between 15 and 20 tons, were used in its construction, which took twenty years. The pyramid of Cheops demonstrates the power of the second civilisation— the first being the Sumerian— in the whole of human history. It is still largely *intact*, except for the fact that its tip has flattened out. All four sides face the compass points, because, like all great buildings in Egypt, it is oriented by the Nile, which runs due north at this point, and each side forms an equilateral triangle making an angle of slope of 51° in 15.86 m. There are three separate internal chambers: the subterranean chamber, the Queen's chamber with its vaulted roof, and the King's chamber, the first two being abandoned eventually in favour of the latter, where the tomb of Cheops is laid. The entrance to the tomb is on the north side, just off centre at about 16.77 m vertically from ground level, and leads to a corridor sloping at 26° to the first rock-cut chamber. This, however, was discarded, and another corridor was cut in the ceiling of the first, about 18.50 m from the entrance, and rose to 21.35 m from the ground where it entered the Queen's chamber, only to be abandoned in its turn. The approach was sealed off and the ascending corridor extended into a corbelled vault 214 cm wide and 229 cm high opening into the Grand Gallery. The King's chamber leads off the Grand Gallery and is lined with granite, with a granite-lined vestibule in front of it.

11

Three massive granite slabs slot into the walls at the side and seal the chamber. Above the King's chamber are five tiers of stone beams, spaced out, one above the other, and leading from it diagonally on each side to the outer casing of the pyramid are two very narrow shafts or passages, perhaps for ventilation purposes or perhaps to *enable* the spirit of the dead king to come and go as he wished. A further narrow shaft links the initial subterranean chamber with the entrance to the corridor which leads to the Queen's chamber.

12

The pyramids were always oriented with their faces to the cardinal points of the compass, so that the north-east/south-west diagonal of Cheops, if extended, would coincide exactly with that of the pyramid of Chephren (Khafra) who was the third king of the IVth Dynasty whose pyramid is only slightly smaller than that of his predecessor, although it has a much steeper slope—52° in 610 cm. There is only one chamber at the core of the pyramid, situated partly in the rock and partly built up, but it has two entrances, both on the northern side, one through the granite casing of the pyramid and the other through a subterranean passage which joins the first halfway along. It is an extremely solid pyramid with much of the original limestone at the tip preserved, as are some of the other buildings in the pyramid complex.

13

To the south-west of this pyramid stands the pyramid of the pharaoh Men-Kau-Rê or Mycerinus, a successor of Chephren and the fourth king of the Dynasty. It was completed by his son and, although much smaller than the other pyramids at Gizeh, is better finished. Its sides slope at 51° and even today, much of its outer casing is still preserved. Its entrance is on the north a few feet above ground level and slopes downwards entering the centre one of three subterranean chambers, one above the other, in direct vertical line with the apex of the pyramid. A blind passage with no external outlet lying parallel to the entrance

14

passage leads into the smallest and uppermost of the three chambers while the third and lowest chamber which is larger than either of the others leads off the central chamber.

During the Vth and VIth Dynasties, the principal pyramids, all built at Saqqâra and Abusir, were smaller in size and inferior in construction but conformed to the regular design. After the VIth Dynasty there was nearly a century of *anarchy* in Egypt and many tombs and pyramids were robbed and desecrated; it was only in the second half of the XIth Dynasty that more settled conditions returned and the first king of the XIth Dynasty built a small pyramid and, for the first time, a burial chamber situated beneath the cliff face. This new architectural *concept* was used to full effect by the beginning of the XVIIIth Dynasty (1587–1375 BC) for royal persons, when rock-cut graves became the accepted custom of burial.

(Please note that all dates given are those based on Petrie's chronology.)

QUESTION 1

Put the following sentences into chronological sequence, based on information in the passage.

A The tower of Babel is built by King Nebuchadnezzar II.
B A square ziggurat with four or five tiers and vertical walls is built.
C The first large-scale monument in stone is built.
D The Assyrians are defeated
E A one-storeyed rectangular ziggurat with sloping walls is common.
F There is a transition from the step pyramid to the true pyramid.
G Palaces replace ziggurats in popularity.
H Herodotus visits Babylon and reports on what he sees.
I A rectangular ziggurat has two or more tiers and a triple stairway.
J The highest point of pyramid building is reached.

Step	
1	
2	
3	
4	
5	
6	
7	
8	
9	
10	

QUESTION 2

In the passage, fifteen words or phrases are set in italics. From the list below choose the fifteen most suitable alternatives and write them out in the order in which they appear in the text.

1	9	allow	complete
2	10	unusual	flamboyant
		most important	noble
3	11	war-like	is composed of
4	12	getting smaller	precisely
		rising	activity
5	13	idea	development
6	14	prevent	characteristically
		without result	disorder
7	15	came to an end	conform to
8			

QUESTION 3

Look at the diagrams of pyramids and ziggurats overleaf. In each case decide whether the structure is a pyramid or a ziggurat, and give its name or type, as described in the text, in the table. Pay careful attention to the compass points.

1		7	
2		8	
3		9	
4		10	
5		11	
6		12	

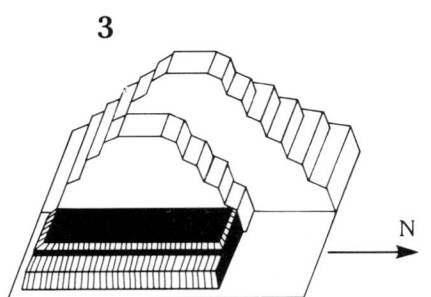

245

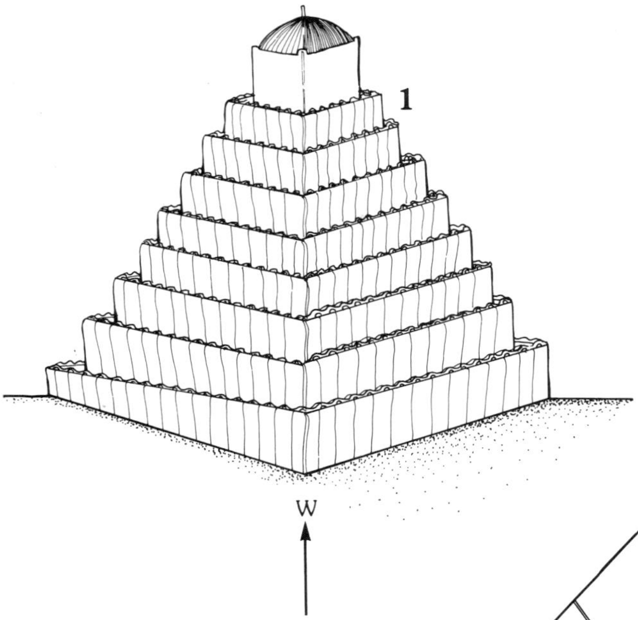

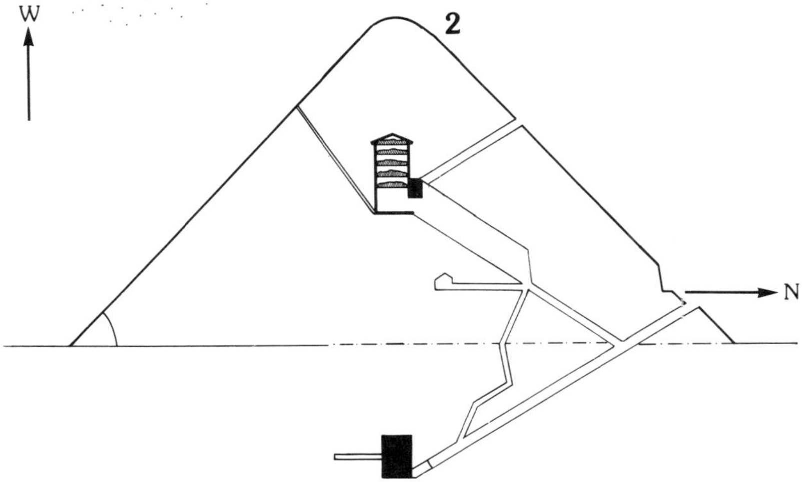

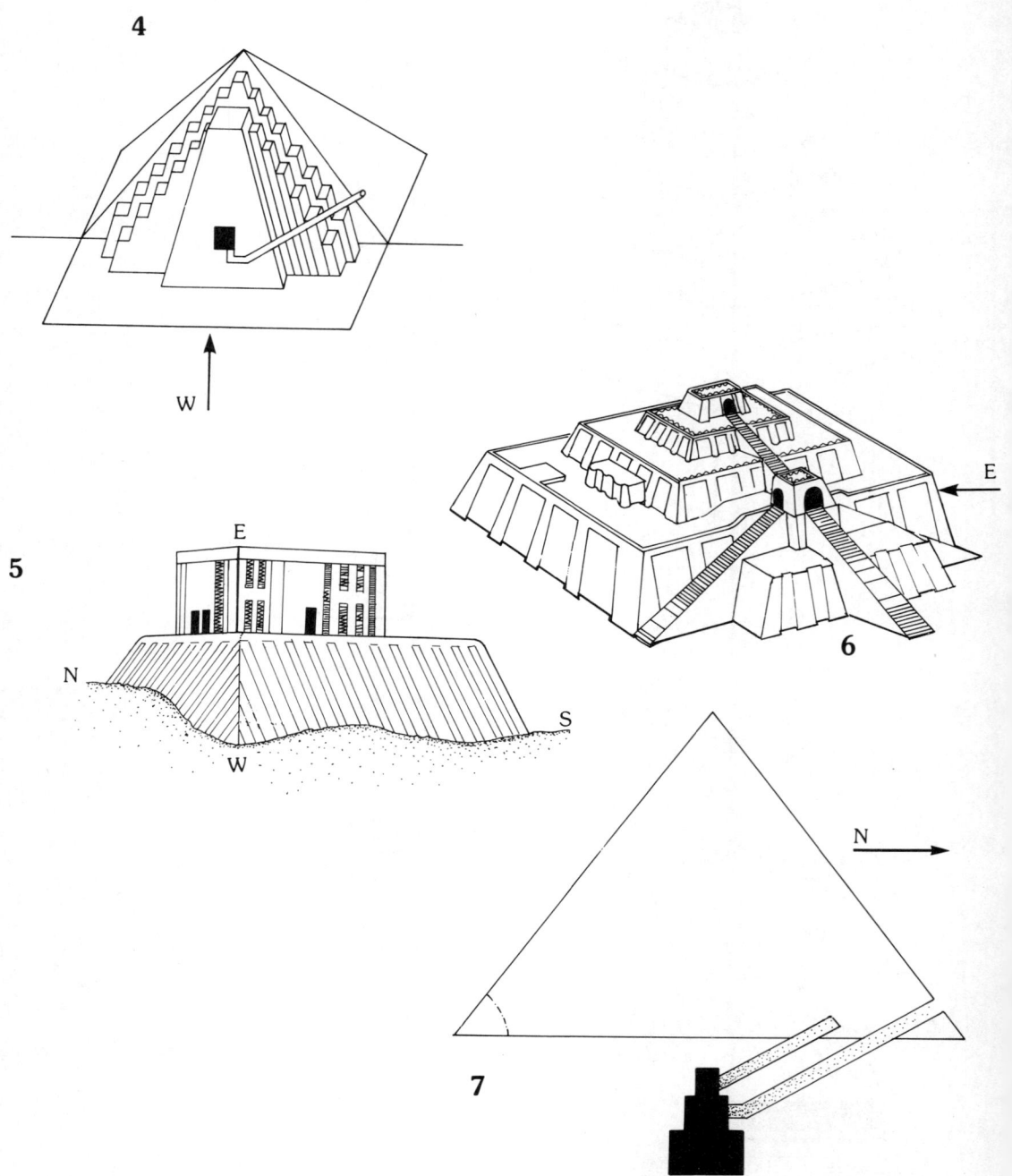

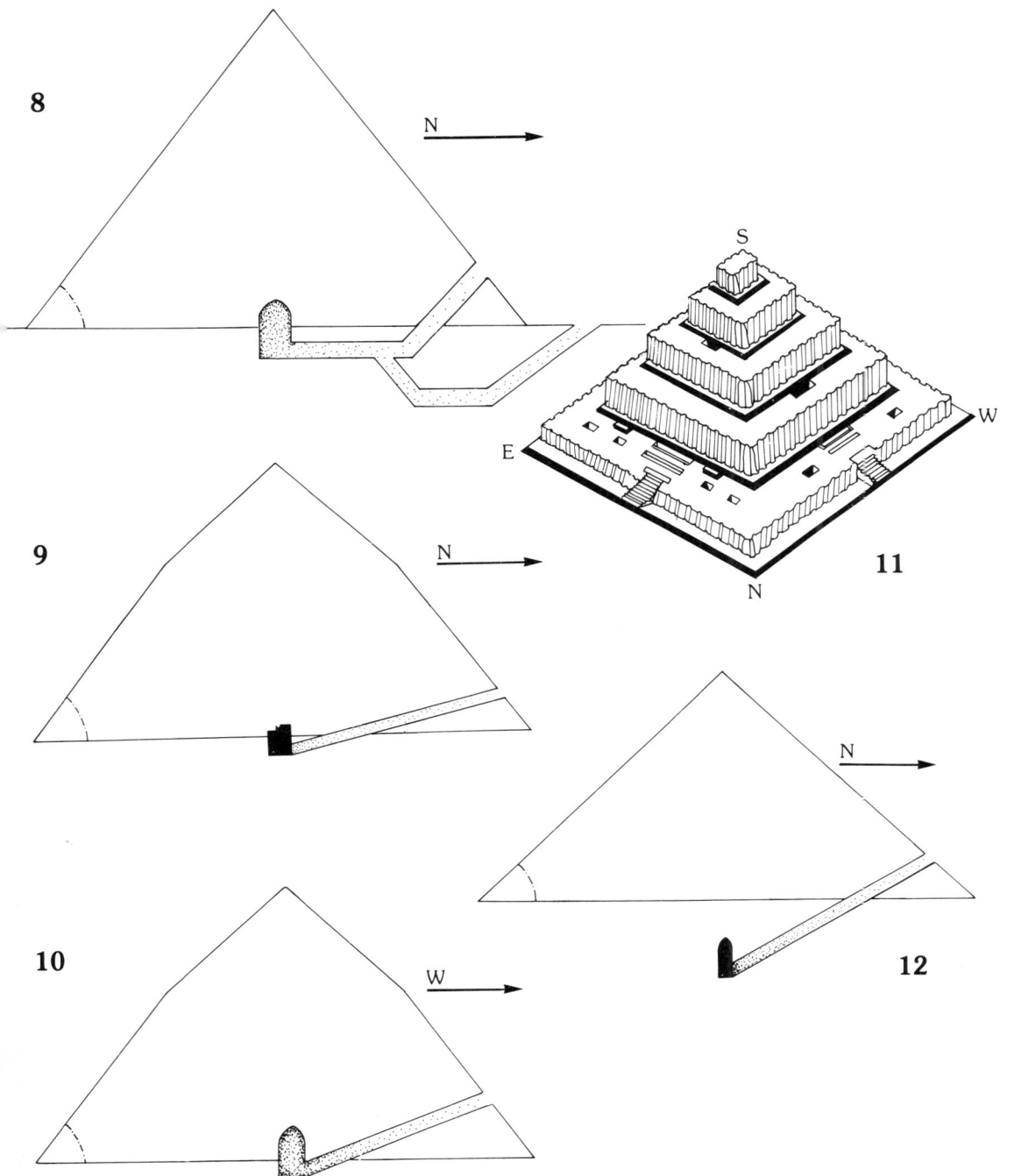

The Process of Excavation

1

There is more to excavation than merely digging a hole in the ground in the hope that some still-preserved traces of ancient cultures can be discovered. Inexperienced people should never attempt to excavate a site, however enthusiastic they may be, as valuable evidence can so easily be overlooked or even destroyed in the process. After all, excavation is essentially destruction, and although it is becoming much more scientific it is an attempt at obtaining evidence that can never be repeated. It is of the utmost importance that every last scrap of evidence is extracted from the site, as there will be no second chance. There must be no margin for error.

2

Before the excavation can even be considered, there must be some justification for it: perhaps some visible feature or indication of man's former presence which will make the effort and expense of excavation worthwhile, and such evidence is usually obtained from the distribution map or inventory of sites compiled from the preliminary field survey. Before the archaeologist begins to dig, therefore, he has some firm prospect of uncovering evidence of earlier cultures and whether these are within his area of interest, or whether the data to be uncovered could contribute to a more complete understanding of finds made on sites already investigated by himself or others. The basic methods of excavation are the same, irrespective of the size of the site, and these are governed by the principle of stratigraphy: this refers to the fact that when the geological layering of the earth took place, it did so in a definite sequence—the bottom layer was laid down first, then came the second layer, then the third, and so on, so that the lower strata, or layers, are older than the upper ones. Such time horizons provide the archaeologist with a framework for dating the remains that he uncovers. Without the stratigraphical reference, the material that is found is scientifically useless; it must be placed in a context. The real value of structures and artifacts, therefore, lies in their relationship to time, and great care must be taken so that the excavation programme is conducted scrupulously.

3

With the smaller type of site, the excavation programme begins with the marking out of the trenches. This is done by placing wooden or metal pegs into the ground with string stretched tautly between them so that the area is divided up into squares or rectangles of a certain size at right angles to each other, once the area of the site has been selected and a plan drawn up of the proposed trench structure. It is also important to decide, at this point in the programme, where the dump is to be placed, because the large quantities of excavated earth will have to be carried away from the site as the work progresses and then replaced at the end of the excavation programme. If the site is situated on a slope, even more thought must be given to the position of the dump as it would be a waste of energy and resources to haul tons of earth uphill after months of exhausting work. Having marked out the site into a grid system, the excavator then places a series of individually lettered or numbered markers at fixed intervals along the site, establishing a grid of points which will be recorded on the site plan and from which it will be possible to indicate where finds were made.

4 Now the turf is removed and stored in a suitable place, for it will have to be replaced when the programme is completed, and the excavation proper can proceed. The lines of string which acted as guides in the turf-removal process can be disposed of, and then the whole site sectioned into areas. Each of these sections will be excavated separately. A trench is usually dug by three people, depending on its size, and is heavy work, demanding patience and skill It is the pickman who initiates the procedure by loosening the earth over a given area to a depth of a few centimetres, and the excavated earth is carefully removed at frequent intervals by men with shovels, each keeping a watchful eye for artifacts or finds, however small, that may come to light. If the earth is not removed at frequent intervals, it will accumulate and may contaminate lower layers. No work will be allowed to begin on the second layer until the first layer has been thoroughly examined and set aside and all finds recorded on the site plan. Once the first layer has been exhausted and all debris removed, work on the second layer can go ahead.

5 As each layer is excavated in turn, its number is recorded in the site notebook, a brief description made of the soil type and any finds noted, prior to their being placed in metal trays with the appropriate identification marks or labels to be referred to later when the report will be written. Nothing, however small, can be neglected: even the grains of plants can tell the expert the dietary habits of the people of that site; human remains could illustrate religious practices or rituals, while fragments of pottery would indicate that the site was unlikely to be Anglo-Saxon, as they used pottery very rarely. Any structures found are dealt with differently: they are drawn to scale on the trench plan

6

and usually photographed so that their stratigraphical position relative to the site is made clear.

The final section drawing can be attempted only when the entire excavation is complete. The sequence of strata is shown, each layer numbered separately and drawn up on squared paper. This is done by using a vertical line of dots to represent different levels, repeated at regular intervals and eventually joined up until a total visual record is provided of the stratigraphical pattern of the site. This section drawing, which is the most vital record of the excavation, is then furnished with a key to indicate each geological feature and complements the records in the site notebooks, showing not only the position of each trench but, where possible, which side of the trench is being represented. Once the digging and recording have taken place, the trenches are refilled and the turf placed in its original position so that no signs remain of the long months of excavation. It is, however, by no means the end of the exercise: months, if not years of intensive study await the director of the programme and those specialists who will assist him in the interpretation of the evidence. The subsequent publication of his research will depend on the comparisons made about the significance of that particular site in relation to others previously excavated and whether any conclusions can be drawn about the specific area of archaeology to which it belongs.

QUESTION 1

Give a word or phrase in the passage that has the same meaning as the following: (the paragraph numbers are given)

1	simply	(1)	9	begins	(4)
2	greatest	(1)	10	collect	(4)
3	mistake	(1)	11	emptied	(4)
4	previous	(2)	12	rubbish	(4)
5	add	(2)	13	before	(5)
6	in spite of	(2)	14	eating	(5)
7	tightly	(3)	15	at length	(6)
8	itself	(4)			

250

QUESTION 2

Put the following sentences into chronological sequence, as described in the passage.

A The turf is removed from the site.
B A field survey is undertaken.
C The string guidelines are disposed of.
D The complete stratigraphy of the site is available.
E The trench plan is proposed.
F The trenches are refilled.
G The initial loosening of the upper layer begins.
H A place is selected to dump the debris.
I The trench plan is marked out.
J The site is selected.
K Conclusions are drawn as to the significance of the evidence.
L The turf is replaced.
M The report appears in print.
N A grid of points is established.
O The evidence will be studied for a long period.

Step	
1	
2	
3	
4	
5	
6	
7	
8	
9	
10	
11	
12	
13	
14	
15	

Ancient Jewellery

1 Since earliest times man has needed to satisfy certain needs—the need to adorn and beautify his body, demonstrate his rank and wealth, express his love or respect and ward off evil influences or danger. For this he has used objects which he considered precious, either for their intrinsic value or for the degree of artistry which enriched and fashioned them. We call these precious ornaments jewellery and the way in which we use jewellery today is very little different from the way in which man used it in earliest times. Virtually all jewellery from the distant past available to us today has come from tombs containing funeral treasures and, fortunately, many such tombs have been found intact. The development in the forms and craftsmanship of the jewellery expresses the way of life and cultural awareness of the age in which it was created.

2 The earliest evidence of man's intense interest in jewellery has been found in excavations of the **Palaeolithic** period from 40 000 to 10 000 years ago and in the cave paintings of that time. The first jewellery was made from the animal and vegetable world and required a minimum of processing; coloured feathers, horn, skins, teeth, bones and seashells were chosen because they were part of the hunting and fishing life of the first men and they probably had a ritual more than a decorative significance. The next phase in man's development was his discovery of minerals—he was attracted to brightly-coloured pebbles and gradually learned how to pierce them so that they could be worn around his neck and ankles. Then he was able to polish and shape the pebbles. There was little variety of design over these millennia and it was not until the early Neolithic period that regional or individual styles began to appear and then semi-precious stones such as cornelian and serpentine began to be used in the making of pendants and beads. Eventually gold was discovered in Asia Minor.

3 There are several terms used in the fashioning of jewellery which have been known and used since ancient times. *Repoussé* is a technique particularly suited for impressing delicate designs on to sheet metal; the decoration is punched and hammered on to the metal from the reverse side with horn, bronze, wood or copper hammers. The relief is then finished off on the right side by chasing, that is, given further definition with engraving tools. Less prominent relief designs can also be obtained by using a cameo or intaglio stamp, a method especially suited where repeated patterns are needed. Mycenaean relief beads were made by this method. *Filigree*, or the technique of making and using lengths of gold wire obtained by stretching narrow strips of sheet metal, has been known since ancient times and was very popular in Classical Greek jewellery. The wire was made by rolling strips of metal, usually gold or silver, into a spiral and then it was applied as a decoration to the ornament but during the Roman period a drawplate for drawing the wire evenly was introduced. (The drawplate was not widely used until the Middle Ages.) Genuinely ancient pieces of jewellery can be authenticated by examining the wires used—if there are longitudinal striation marks present in the wire, the ornament cannot be earlier than Roman. The ancients used wire singly or twisted together then soldered on to a backing of sheet gold. They also made elaborate chains with wire such as looped chains. Single looped chains were obtained by folding each separate link into two, making an ellipse. The next loop was then threaded on to this double loop and was itself folded into two and so on. The double looped chain was made by passing successive links through the looped ends of the two preceding ones. Chains have been found which were up to eight links across by using this method. A similar technique to filigree is *cloisonné*. It involves punching a design lightly on the back of the gold sheet and then soldering strips of gold on the front, following the outline. This forms cells or pockets which are filled with a cement-like paste providing a bed for the glass or stones which are inlaid. In the best work, the stones or pieces of glass are shaped exactly to fit. The technique of embedding a decorative material into another substance so that both surfaces are completely level is called *inlay*, the most exquisite examples of which were uncovered in the tomb of Tut-Ankh-Amon. Here, coloured stones or glass were fixed to sheet metal, usually gold, by using filigree and cloisonné and the background filled with grains of gold. These globules of gold are the technique of *granulation*. It is one of the oldest techniques in the art of jewellery making and, together with filigree, came into use during the first millennium BC. The globules of gold are applied directly on to the sheet metal following the shape of the design, either free-hand or by using the transfer method. In some of the oldest examples, the globules measured only 0.4 mm across although in Etruscan work, they were as little as 0.25 mm across. It was the Etruscans who developed granulation to its highest level between 7th–6th centuries BC although after this period it began to decline. By 1000 AD it had disappeared.

Completely round ornaments such as human or animal heads were made by hammering a piece of sheet gold into hollow sections and using an alloy such as gold and silver or gold and copper as a *solder*. This has a lower melting point than the metal. In antiquity, hard solder was used and belonged to the most highly-developed phases of the goldsmith's art. Solder was used in Mesopotamia from the 3rd millennium BC and in the Minoan civilisation in the 2nd millennium. Since all metals oxidise when they are heated, thus preventing the solder from covering the joint, a material called a flux is used which enables the solder to flow. Today we use borax but in ancient times, natron or the burnt dregs of wine were used. *Enamelling* involves the use of powdered glass coloured with metal oxides diluted with water and adhesive applied to certain parts of the ornament that have either been cut lower or have been surmounted by a raised rim of gold, silver or copper. The glass is heated and adheres to the metal and crystallises as it cools. When it is smooth it can be either translucent or opaque. The art was practised by the Assyrians and Egyptians and was introduced into Europe by way of Greece.

4

Egypt was the richest gold-producing country in the ancient world and this greatly enhanced her power and prestige. The finest Egyptian metalwork was in gold and its delicacy of craftsmanship has never been surpassed. Silver was at first very rare and was more valuable than gold until it was imported in large quantities during the 18th Dynasty and even then it was not used for adorning the body but for trinkets. It was only when Egypt became poor under Roman domination that silver was used for personal jewellery. Most of the jewellery that has come to us from ancient Egypt has been uncovered from tombs where it was intended to protect the dead person on his journey through the underworld. In addition to its ornamental value, Egyptian jewellery had a religious or symbolic purpose. It used a limited repertoire of motifs which emerged again and again. A popular motif was the *scarab*, a beetle symbolising rebirth; it was used as an amulet and incorporated into pectorals and rings. The scarab was carved or cut to represent a beetle on its upper side while its flat underside was engraved with hieroglyphs. Other motifs were the sacred cobra or *uraeus*, the emblem of supreme power and protector of the king and normally found in the centre of the king's mitre; the falcon, which was the symbol of the god Horus and of the king himself and the *udjat* or eye of Horus. The *ankh* sign, the symbol of life, can often be recognised in ancient Egyptian jewellery—it is a T shape surmounted by a loop with an elliptical knot where the bars are crossed. In addition to a number of hieroglyphic signs, flower shapes were also common: papyrus and the symbol of resurrection, the lotus flower. The gods were also represented. The jewellery of the ancient people of Egypt used three predominant colours—red, blue and blue-green, represented by cornelian, lapis lazuli and turquoise or vitreous pastes imitating them. There were various kinds of neck ornaments in ancient Egyptian jewellery and among these the collar and the pectoral were the most important items. The collar was worn at all periods and by both sexes. It had amuletic powers and consisted of rows of beads made of glass, glazed faience, lapis lazuli, turquoise or steatite which were held together by connecting spacer bars. The collar was worn across the shoulders and chest. Small amulets sometimes replaced the beads during the Middle Kingdom and terminals in the shape of falcon heads were added. At the back of the neck a counterpoise matching the collar hung down. There were two other collar types, one consisted of a number of strings of beads collected together and threaded through several circular spacer beads and the other consisted of up to four rows of closely-strung biconical beads. The pectoral or breast ornament is what we mostly associate with Egyptian jewellery. Although it developed in design from its origin before the Old Kingdom, its usual form was an openwork design inlaid with lapis lazuli, cornelian and other stones showing either the king engaging in some activity or it carried some symbolic meaning. The openwork panel was enclosed in a rectangular frame and was repeated in repoussé on the back. One of the finest examples of this form of ornament is the pectoral of the noble-woman Sit-Hathor-int and dated 1840 BC. It was found in the tomb of her father Sesostris II by Flinders Petrie in 1913 and shows two falcons which are each resting one foot against palm branches. A god kneels in the centre of the branches, supporting them with outstretched arms. Above the branches two sacred cobras with ankh signs hanging from their necks, hold the royal emblem or cartouche of Sesostris. This pectoral is unusual, however, in that it is not enclosed in a rectangular frame as was the custom during the Middle Kingdom. The biggest collection of gold and jewellery ever discovered was that from the tomb of Tut-Ankh-Amon, the young king of the 18th Dynasty, one of the most brilliant periods in the history of Egypt. The tomb was crammed with exquisite objects which illustrated the high degree of craftsmanship of the time and the wide variety of techniques employed. The finest jewellery of ancient Egypt, however, is undoubtedly that of the 12th Dynasty when the spiral design in gold wire was a popular motif for decorating small objects such as scarabs and when the technique of granulation was probably introduced into Egypt. (At a much later date, it was to be the characteristic decorative technique of Etruscan jewellery.) The most important items of Egyptian jewellery from a historical viewpoint are four rosette bracelets in twisted gold from the tomb of King Zer, dating from about 4000 BC because they are the first to show the craftsmanship of the Egyptian jeweller—already at this early period, they knew how to use solder, so skilfully that there was no sign of solder visible, according to Petrie.

5

The greatest and richest archaeological discovery since the tomb of Tutankhamen in 1922 was that of the Royal Tombs of Ur in Sumeria, the legendary home of Abraham, which were excavated by a team directed by Sir Leonard Woolley in 1926. The **Sumerians** lived in southern Mesopotamia in the regions of the Tigris and Euphrates rivers from 5000 BC and were the first known civilisation. In the Royal Tombs, dating from the 3rd millennium BC were the bodies of soldiers of the guard, grooms, drivers, women attendants and courtiers, all richly dressed in ceremonial costume. Also found were the skeletons of the oxen which had pulled the funeral cart of the dead rulers. The orderly arrangement of the bodies showed that there had been a sacrifice on a grand scale and that there had been no resistance. In the tomb of Queen Shub-ad, Woolley uncovered a rich array of funerary gifts including several goblets, plates and bowls, all of gold or silver. The body of the Queen was covered with a garment made of beads of gold, lapis lazuli, cornelian, agate and chalcedony, edged with a fringe of small tubes of gold, lapis lazuli and cornelian. A headdress which had probably been worn over a thickly-padded wig was discovered. It consisted of three diadems of decreasing diameter, one on top of the other, mounted on a gold band. The lowest was made of large interlocking pendant discs while the other two were of gold willow leaves in groups of three and of thin gold beech leaves, respectively. Willow leaves in groups of three and beech leaves, all with their veins realistically drawn, was a popular motif in Sumerian jewellery as were circular and disc shapes, small joined hoops and tubular shapes. They were found in necklaces, earrings and bracelets, interspersed with semi-precious stones. The naturalistic animal motifs showed that the Sumerians had a thorough knowledge of anatomy. They were also familiar with a wide range of technical processes—soldering, repoussé, alloys, stonecutting, filigree, inlay and enamelling.

6

The dominant centre in the Aegean Bronze Age for the making of jewellery was the island of Crete. It was there that the **Minoan** civilisation began in 2500 BC and ended about 1475 BC with the Mycenaean invasion. The island was settled about 2800 BC by immigrants from Asia Minor who brought with them techniques inherited from the peoples of Mesopotamia. The name Minoan was coined by Sir Arthur Evans who excavated the greatest Minoan palace at Knossos from 1899 to 1934. King Minos was the legendary ruler of

Crete. During the excavation, ornaments and pins of gold wire were found, crowns of leaves made from sheet gold, beads of gold, amethyst, cornelian, crystal, steatite, faience and shell, as well as a wide range of intricate and beautiful pendants, many in animal shapes. A typical pendant from the middle Minoan period, that is, 17th century BC, was in the shape of two bees whose curved bodies were in profile, enclosing an irregular circle. In the middle of this irregular circle a honeycomb of granulated gold was held by the bees' legs. Spreading out on each side were their tapered wings, each with indented edges. Three discs with edges of granulated gold were suspended from the pendant with gold wire, one on each wing and the other from the point of intersection of the bees' bodies. The upper part of the pendant consisted of two beads, one of which was set in a larger bead of gold wire. In all, the pendant was 46 mm high. Another typically Minoan pendant was hammered and embossed from sheet gold and showed a crouching goat with three small gold discs hanging from its legs.

7

The Minoan civilisation was brought to an end when the Mycenaean Greeks invaded the island and brought their own civilisation which lasted until 1100 BC when it was itself destroyed by the Dorian invasion. The most important elements in jewellery making during the **Mycenaean** period were the development of the technique of granulation, the use of *stamping* for mass production and the introduction around 1450 BC of enamelling. Stamping was used in the making of relief beads, a typically Mycenaean item of jewellery. The beads were made by stamping a piece of sheet gold into a hollow hemisphere and then a flat piece of gold was soldered on to the back, the depression having been filled for strength. The beads, which were pierced and attached to a chain, were decorated with motifs from marine life such as shells, with intertwined ribbons, geometrical scrolls and rosettes of various shapes. By the 15th century BC the beads were manufactured very widely and are probably the earliest example of mass-production in jewellery. The beginnings of Mycenaean jewellery were found in the Shaft Graves at Mycenae by Heinrich Schliemann in 1876, just three years after he had uncovered the palace of King Priam at Troy in north-west Asia Minor. The tombs were those of the Royal House of Mycenae and dated from 1600 BC. From seventeen tombs, 13½ kilograms of precious metal, largely gold, were brought to light, including oval-shaped diadems of sheet gold, decorated with delicate spirals or circles in repoussé, bracelets of thin strips of sheet gold decorated with rosettes, hooped earrings in gold or silver wire, pendants, 8750 little rings, pins and buttons from sheet gold, stamped with stylised butterflies or an octopus. Very often several metals would be used on one object—one bracelet found consisted of bands of gold and silver and gold foil; in the centre of the bracelet was an ornament in the shape of a flower with sixteen fluted petals and a centre of gold and bronze. The Mycenaean civilisation was destroyed by Greek tribes and there was a decline in the arts for four hundred years—the Greek Dark Ages. Many of the art forms of the Mycenaean civilisation were preserved in Cyprus which was settled by them in 1400 BC and from there both form and techniques were re-introduced into Greece.

The greatest exponents of the art of granulation were the **Etruscans**: they could produce grains as small as 0.14 mm in diameter. They are believed to have originated in Asia Minor but they colonised Italy about 900 BC and settled in Tuscany in central Italy. The height of their civilisation was about 500 BC but they were absorbed by the Romans within two hundred years and the Roman Republic supplanted them as the main political influence in Italy. The Etruscans preferred to work in gold and in that medium they produced some of the finest jewellery ever to be made, especially during their early period. The characteristic items of Etruscan jewellery were the baule earring, the fibula and the bulla. The baule earring looked like a bag and consisted of a strip of gold bent into a cylinder and closed at the ends with discs. A hook was fitted which could be inserted into the ear but this was hidden by a metal plate. The entire earring, which was an Etruscan invention, was covered with filigree and sometimes with enamel. The baule earring, however, was eventually replaced by the hoop earring with one end terminating in a human or animal head. The fibula was another typical item of Etruscan jewellery, not original but borrowed from an earlier Italian model although transformed as a result of the craftsmanship of the Etruscan jewellers into a work of art. It was used for fastening clothes and had two main forms, the leech and the serpentine, although both operated on the same principle—that of the safety-pin with a sprung wire or pin hooking into a clasp or catchplate. Fibulae, so-called because their shape resembled the fibula or outer bone of the leg, were made of sheet metal, both silver and gold and were richly ornamented with powder granulation along the bow and foot either in animal shapes or in geometric designs. Some more elaborate fibulae terminated along the catchplate in animals' heads in the round. The bulla was the most popular form of pendant; suspended from a chain by means of a broad cylindrical loop, it was worn by both sexes around the neck and was intended to ward off the evil eye with the charm inside it. The bulla was made of sheet gold, round, oval or heart-shaped and decorated with granulation, filigree and repoussé work in the form of subjects from Greek mythology. During the Roman period, the Etruscan bulla became very popular and was worn by boys until they reached manhood and girls until they married—either singly or strung in a necklace. Necklaces were also popular with the Etruscans—they were of beads, scarabs or pendants. Amber was used, as was glass and faience, a white paste of powdered quartz, shaped and covered with a blue glaze to imitate precious stones. Faience had been invented by the ancient Egyptians during dynastic times. (The scarab had probably been introduced by the Phoenicians from Egypt but the Etruscan scarab was not engraved on the underside as the original Egyptian one had been.) The finest Etruscan necklaces, however, were those made of gold. They consisted of pendants in the shape of acorns, flower buds, pomegranates and heads of the water spirit, Silenus, attached to cross-linked chains suspended from a collar some six links across. The pendants, several of which were combined on the necklace, were decorated with fine granulation. Since granulation died out before 1000 AD we have no idea what method the Etruscans used. Hard colloid has been suggested but this is, strictly speaking, not a solder at all but a type of glue used in decorative work.

Another great era for the production of jewellery was the **Hellenistic** period when vast areas of the East came under Greek control as a result of the conquests of Alexander the Great in the latter part of the 4th century BC and an abundance of gold from the conquered territories provided the impulse to create beautiful objects. Although Greek sculpture had been magnificent, goldwork and jewellery had been neglected and was in any case restricted by monetary laws during Classical times. The Hellenistic period began politically with the accession of Alexander the Great and continued with the Greek expansion into Asia Minor. Gold jewellery became plentiful and its production flourished not only in Alexandria and Antiochia, the two centres of the Hellenistic world from where it was exported to all parts of the empire, but also in the workshops of Asia Minor, Central Asia, Syria, Southern Russia, Northern Italy and Greece itself. It was very different from jewellery of the preceding Classical period. Hellenistic jewellery was more lavish and elaborate as well as being more plentiful. An important technical innovation was polychrome when stones and glass were used in the form of inlays, showing a Persian or Indian influence. Stones and glass had previously been very rare in Greek jewellery. Red garnet was the favourite stone followed by amethyst, cornelian, pearls and chalcedony with the occasional use of emerald. Colour became the dominant feature in Hellenistic jewellery. A new type of enamelling was introduced called dipped enamel in which a metal core was dipped in molten glass and then shaped to the required shape by standard techniques used in glassmaking. Earring pendants were usually made by this method. A new motif of the Hellenistic period was the Heracles knot which looked like a reef knot and this was used as the centrepiece in necklaces, pendants and diadems. A popular bracelet type was in the form of a coiled serpent with a Heracles knot in the centre. The knot was imported from Egypt where it had had a magical significance. Necklaces were popular during the Hellenistic period and there were many forms. Two of the most widespread consisted of a chain ending in animal heads which were connected to garnets and funnel-shaped spacers; and the strap necklace was decorated with many tiny pendants in the shape of two-handled jars, spearheads, pinecones or female heads, sometimes alternating with stones or vitreous paste. The tiny gold pendants were attached either directly or by means of gold chains. There were usually between one and three rows of tiny pendants in the necklace. The Hellenistic earring was very different from the earrings of **Classical** times, which had been three main types: the disc type in silver or gold, sometimes enamelled which looked like studs and covered the base of the ear; earrings with pendants in the shape of an inverted cone and decorated with filigree and granulation; leech-shaped earrings and the boat shape with a hooped top, frequently hung with pendants in the form of buds or shells. Sometimes a figure sat in the boat which was suspended from an enamelled rosette. The entire earring was covered in filigree. In the succeeding period, more lavish earrings became fashionable; these consisted of plain or twisted hoop earrings with the heads of lions, dolphins, goats and a wide variety of other animals, or clasp or stud type with either a carved head in low relief (medallion) or a rosette, suspended from which were gold figures of dancers, sirens or cupids. They were also often given an amphora (a two-handled vase) or a bunch of grapes. An earring uncovered from a tomb in Judea dating from the 2nd and 1st centuries BC is a typical example—the disc was shaped like a rosette from which hung a stone set in gold. Two gold spirals on the lower end of the stone held an amphora from which a bead was suspended. The earring was covered with granulation and filigree.

10

The beginnings of iron-working seem to have taken place among the Hittites in Anatolia around 1500 BC and from there spread over the Near East and the Aegean, reaching the south of Italy by the 9th century. It was not until 700 BC that it eventually reached northern Europe, spread by the migrating tribes of the earliest European iron age culture—the **Celts**. The pre-Christian or pagan culture of the Celts is in two parts, the Hallstatt culture and the La Tène culture. The Hallstatt culture, named after the Austrian cemetery of Hallstatt near Salzburg, spread to occupy much of central and western Europe between 700 and 500 BC until it eventually reached eastern and south-eastern England. It seems that the Hallstatt people traded their salt, which was the foundation of their economic wealth, with the Greeks and Etruscans who provided them with wine and pottery. The La Tène culture originated in western Switzerland and imposed itself on that of the Hallstatt around 500 BC and during the following three hundred years it covered practically the whole of France and extended from Ireland to Asia Minor. The most common field monuments of the Celts were the fortified enclosures known as hillforts which were built throughout the Iron Age and ceased when the Romans invaded territories occupied by the Celts; in Britain, after 43 AD. The remains of these forts are now grassy banks and ditches. The Celtic style expressed itself essentially through the working of metals from iron to gold, although bronze was more highly prized by the British Celts because it was not in great supply. The bronze was sometimes cast and sometimes wrought but it was at all times decorated with great skill with chasing, engraving and enamelling in bright colours. Separate pieces were riveted together as the Celts did not use solder. They did not use stones in pagan times apart from amber and that only rarely. Among the earliest Celtic jewellery found in Britain are bead necklaces of amber, glass and jet and lunulae. These were found in Ireland and were crescent-shaped gold plates, decorated with fine lines in a zig-zag pattern around the horns and edges, meant either to be worn around the head like a diadem or around the neck like a torc. Apart from the crescent shape, the broken circle or penannular shape was a characteristic of Celtic jewellery and can be seen in the magnificent collars or torcs. These were worn by men around the neck and consisted of a bar or ribbon of twisted metal curved into a loop with terminals decorated with simple hemispherical forms or ornamented with motifs in the form of animal heads or spiral scrolls. Torcs were often of bronze but sometimes of gold or electrum. One of the most beautiful was found in Snettisham in Norfolk and was made of eight twisted strands of electrum, each strand itself consisting of eight fine twisted wires. The thick hoop-shaped terminals were decorated in an abstract relief design of rough geometric patterns. Bracelets and armlets were also penannular and similar in design to the torcs. Other typical Celtic ornaments were brooches, early ones being rather like safety-pins and later ones penannular in shape, consisting of a broken ring along which moved a pin which was longer than the diameter of the ring. The pin was pushed through the fabric at one end of the ring and pushed under its exposed part then turned, so that the brooch was held by the weight of the fabric. It was worn with the pin pointing diagonally upwards. The brooch was at first simple in design but became increasingly elaborate until the gap in the ring closed. The brooch, which seems to have been invented by Celts in Britain, was fully developed during the Christian period but much later, during the Middle Ages, it died out except in remote areas. The decorative forms in Celtic art are distinctive—at first they were the zig-zag design, the spiral and the swastika, an ancient Bronze Age symbol but during the La Tène period, scrolls, flowing lines and trumpet shapes replaced them. Human, animal and bird motifs became stylised into abstract or geometrical patterns.

After the withdrawal of the Roman legions, Teutonic tribes invaded Britain and the Celts fled to western Scotland and Ireland where their culture continued and developed under the influence of the Christian church when elements of Italo-Byzantine art were introduced. The most characteristic pattern became interlaced work, at first an under and over plait but later the lines became broken. This produced the effect of knots which became increasingly complex. Another pattern was the Greek key pattern but it was slanted at 45° to make it more harmonious with other motifs. During the 8th century in Ireland, Celtic metal-work reached a high degree of perfection, with extensive use of enamelling in bold reds, yellows and blues. Plating, gilding, chasing, engraving, chainwork and filigree were also boldly used. *Niello*, a matt black material, in a powdered state, was put into a decorative pattern which had previously been engraved into gold or silver. When the object was heated, the powder melted and was smoothed out. Niello later became very popular during the Middle Ages and although it had been used on metalware such as plates during the Hellenistic and Roman periods, it had not been used on jewellery before the 4th century AD. Towards the end of the 10th century, however, Celtic art began to decline and in Europe was either forgotten or absorbed into mediaeval art.

QUESTION 1

Indicate whether the following statements are true or false according to the passage:

	True	False
1 Polychrome was a characteristic of Hellenistic jewellery.		
2 The bulla pendant was used as a talisman.		
3 Relief beads were made by stamping.		

4	During the Classical period in ancient Greece, gold jewellery was plentiful.		
5	Torcs were an essential ingredient of Etruscan jewellery.		
6	Silver was more valuable than gold in 15th Dynasty Egypt.		
7	Niello was used in jewellery in 250 BC.		
8	Solder was used by the Celts.		
9	The finest jewellery of ancient Egypt was that of the 12th Dynasty.		
10	The Etruscan scarab pendant was engraved on the underside.		
11	The ancient Egyptians used a drawplate to draw wire.		
12	The British Celts prized bronze above gold.		
13	Precious stones were common in early Celtic jewellery.		
14	Regional styles in jewellery-making began in Palaeolithic times.		
15	The ankh sign was popular in ancient Egyptian jewellery.		

QUESTION 2

In the left-hand column there is an incomplete statement. Choose the statement in the right-hand column which is most suitable to complete it, then complete the table on page 265.

1	The earliest forms of jewellery were made by Palaeolithic man many millennia ago	A	They wore torcs and lunulae in broken circle and crescent shapes, decorated with zig-zag lines or spirals.
2	These people first settled in central Italy and within a hundred years were producing superb jewellery in gold, bringing the technique of granulation to its highest level.	B	This technique has been known since the 3rd millennium BC although the Celts used riveting instead.

3	This bead is probably the earliest example of mass production in jewellery becoming popular during the 15th century BC.	C	Gold was plentiful and jewellery became lavish, colourful and elaborate.
4	This technique involved stretching lengths of sheet metal into wire which was then applied to jewellery as a form of decoration.	D	Using materials from the animal and vegetable world that required a minimum of processing.
5	These Iron Age people made field monuments or fortified enclosures known as hillforts.	E	The falcon, the cobra, the eye of Horus, the ankh, the lotus flower and the sacred beetle were characteristic motifs.
6	The first known civilisation was that of the Sumerians dating from 5000 BC.	F	Their most characteristic earring consisted of a strip of gold bent round into a cylinder so that it looked like a bag.
7	After the accession of Alexander the Great, vast areas of the East came under Greek control.	G	It was made from sheet gold, stamped and formed into a hollow to which a flat piece was soldered and then it was filled, pierced and attached to a chain.
8	Cells or pockets are formed by soldering strips of gold on to sheet metal which has been given a relief design.	H	The Romans introduced a drawplate so that it could be drawn evenly and this enables us to date the ornament.
9	Completely round objects were made by joining two hollow sections together using an alloy as a solder.	I	Archaeological excavation has shown that they were familiar with a wide range of technical processes but they also practised human sacrifice on a large scale.
10	In addition to its ornamental value, the jewellery of this people had a religious and symbolic purpose.	J	Cement-like paste is then added to form a bed for the glass or stones to be laid into.

1		3		5		7		9	
2		4		6		8		10	

---QUESTION 3---

Put the following sentences into chronological sequence as described in the passage.

A The Minoan civilisation begins in Crete.
B Schliemann uncovers the Shaft Graves at Mycenae.
C The ancient Egyptians are first using solder.
D Celtic metalwork reaches a high level of perfection in Ireland.
E Evans begins to dig in Crete.
F The Royal Tombs of Ur are excavated.
G The Hellenistic period begins under Alexander the Great.
H Petrie finds a chest ornament.
I Jewellery is made from teeth, bones and shells.
J The Mycenaeans invade Crete.
K The first known civilisation begins between the Tigris and Euphrates rivers.
L Crete is settled by immigrants from Asia Minor.
M The Dorian invasion of Crete takes place.
N The Romans conquer Britain.
O The palace of King Priam is discovered at Troy.

Step		Step		Step		Step		Step	
1		4		7		10		13	
2		5		8		11		14	
3		6		9		12		15	

---QUESTION 4---

Look at the diagrams of jewellery overleaf, decide which culture they represent and complete the table.

265

1		11	
2		12	
3		13	
4		14	
5		15	
6		16	
7		17	
8		18	
9		19	
10		20	

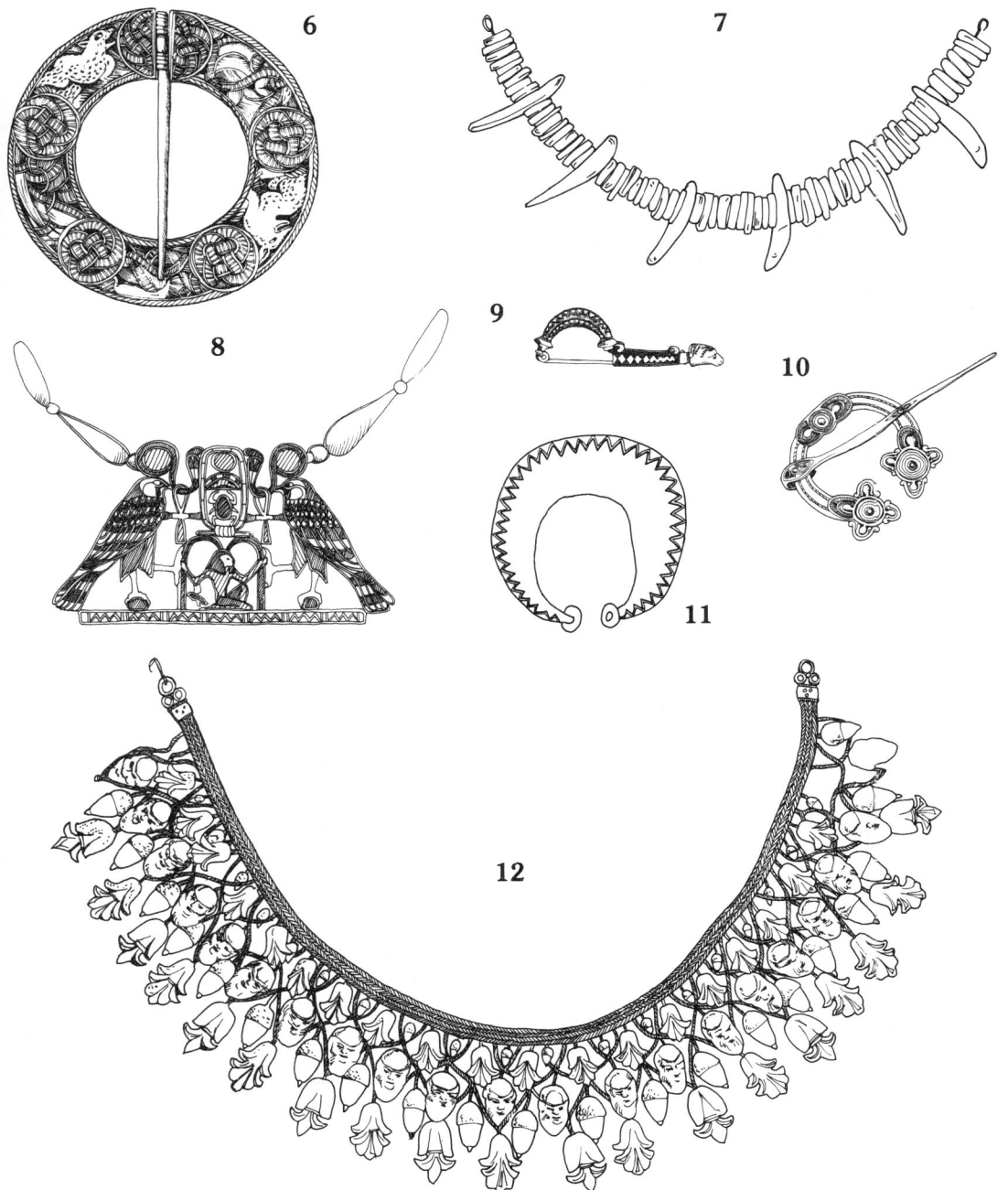

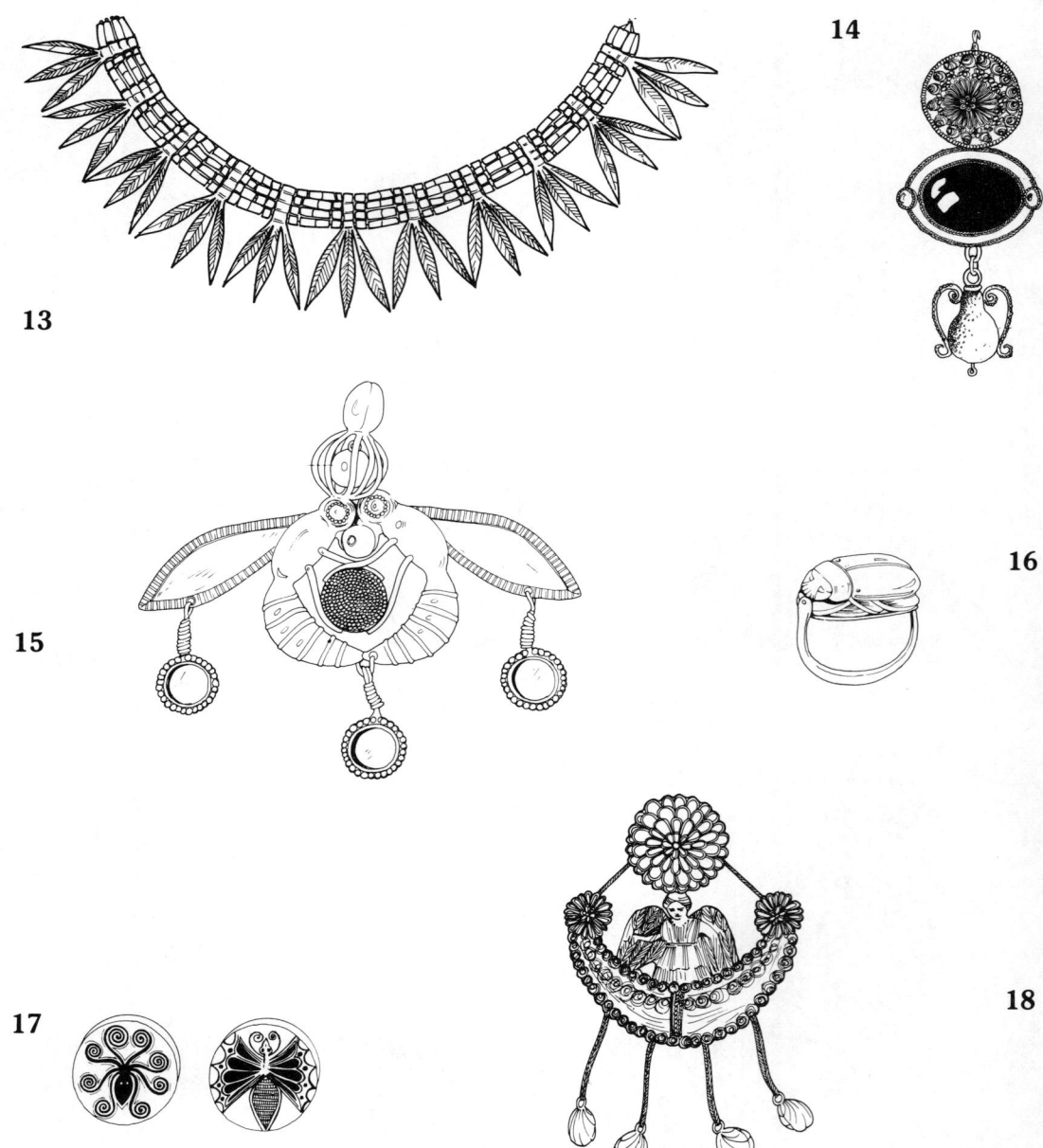

19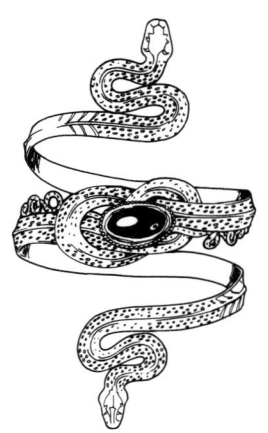

20

Gold

Use the following notes to write a descriptive paragraph on **Gold**.

amalgamation method—mercury combines with the gold from the crushed minerals then distilled to release gold

melting point 1063° C

in Middle Ages alchemists believed it had magical properties

about ⅔ of gold supply used in coinage or bullion

modern methods of extraction more efficient

not dissolved by hydrochloric acid

softness counteracted by presence of other metals

unattacked by air, water or hydrogen sulphide

one of the oldest metals used in the Arts

soluble in aqua regia

good conductor of heat and electricity

ancient peoples used to make jewellery out of natural gold

its colour markedly affected by presence of other metals

about ⅓ of gold supply used in Arts

converted into chloride by chlorine gas or solution

amalgamation = the combining of metal with mercury

natural gold malleable—easier to work

precious metal

ancient peoples ground auriferous rock to powder—washed with water—
over sheep's fleece—gold particles sank to bottom—held by grease in
wool—lighter debris floated away—dry fleece shaken—recovered gold
melted into ingots

lettering of books—decoration of porcelain

can be beaten to sheets 1/000 mm thick

main countries producing gold—South Africa, USSR,
Brazil, Chile, Peru, Mexico, United States, Australia

today best known and most efficient method of extraction is cyanide process

alchemists tried to change other metals into gold

panning—prospector would stand in shallow water of river bed—flat
dish used to separate heavier gold particles from lighter sand

extraction of gold has undergone many changes over centuries

ancient Egyptians used sluice to recover gold—shown in paintings
during 18th Dynasty

chlorination—chlorine gas or solution converts gold from powdered
rock into chlorine—chlorine removed by washing—gold precipitated

discovery of gold prehistoric

aqua regia = mixture of nitric and hydrochloric acid

sluice = powdered auriferous rock washed in artificial water course
made of sloping wooden channels with obstacles to catch gold particles

cyanide process—ground gold-bearing rock put in dilute solution of
cyanide and sodium—gold dissolved—run into long boxes filled with
powdered zinc—gold precipitated as black mud—dried and treated with
dilute sulphuric acid to dissolve zinc—recovered gold fused into
ingots—later refined

most malleable of all metals

amalgamation method suitable for rich ores only

chlorination—modern method of refining gold

boiling point 2660° C

auriferous rock = rock containing gold

chemical symbol for gold Au

ores containing sulphides require chemical treatment—chlorination method suitable

amalgamation used for centuries

until the 19th century—panning was used

Sumerians in South Mesopotamia mined gold—4000 BC

not dissolved by nitric acid

has always been sign of power and wealth

Dale Village

Look at the diagram overleaf and then answer the following questions:

─────────────────────────────── **QUESTION 1** ───────

Direct your friend by car from the junior school to the castle, where you have arranged to meet him.

─────────────────────────────── **QUESTION 2** ───────

You are staying in Dale village, where you attend the local technical college. Write a letter to your family describing the village.

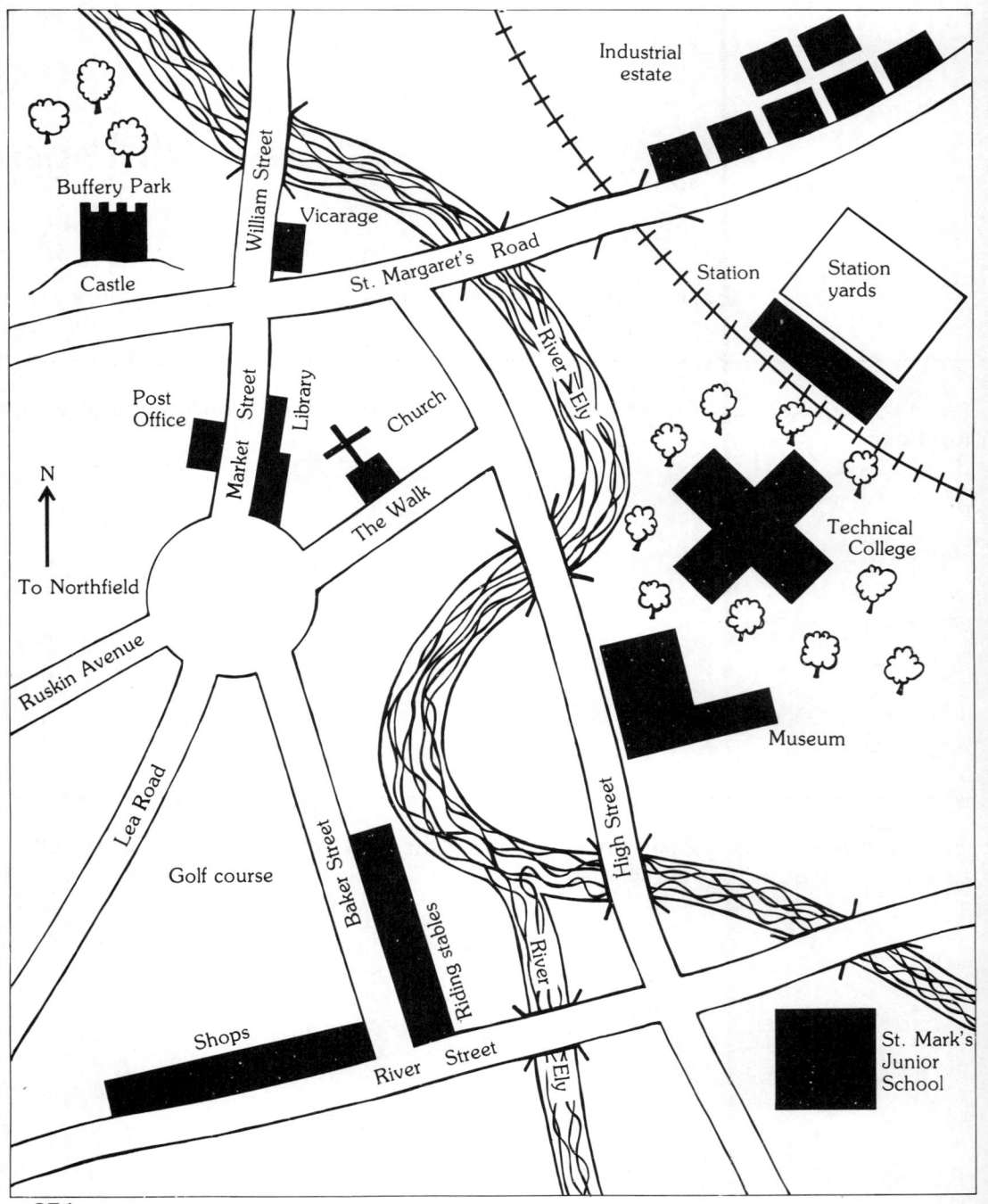

The Lion

Read the following notes on the lion and write a description suitable for inclusion in a junior encyclopaedia.

lions live in groups

now largely found south of Sahara

carnivorous mammal

hunts at night

hunts in groups only to catch large prey

will attack man in certain circumstances, especially if desperate for food

will eat carcass left by other animals, even if badly decomposed, when necessary

lions practically disappeared from Asia

Somali lions smaller/ no mane for lions from Senegal

will eat small animals— even grass if old and feeble

mane grows from 3rd to 6th years

cubs have dark stripes and faint spots

'King of the Beasts'— agile, lithe

lions roar at night

young called cubs

lions usually have long mane

one of best known species of cat family

lions sleep during the day

lioness excellent mother

live up to 20 years in captivity

unlike other cats, does not climb

have powerful canine and cutting teeth like all cats

prey include zebra, antelope, wild pig

dangerous if wounded

lions usually tawny in colour but can be light or dark brown

found mainly in hot climates

lioness will brave great danger to obtain food for cubs

all lions have strongly curved claws and short muzzle

A Landmark in Archaeological History

1 When Howard Carter met Lord Carnarvon in 1907, four years after being made Inspector of Lower and Middle Egypt, he entered into a partnership that was to last for several years, excavating in the Valley of the Kings along the west bank of the Nile which reached a splendid and triumphant climax in November 1922 with the discovery of the burial treasure of the boy king, Tut-Ankh-Amon. This pharaoh of the XVIIIth Dynasty reigned for a mere nine years but he is significant to the study of Egyptology because his is the only mummy to be found with its wrappings intact in the sarcophagus and the tomb where he was buried about 1350 BC. The archaeological value of the find is incalculable but what is equally amazing is that it was found at all. The area along the Nile was believed by many experts to have been exhausted; for over a century, excavations had been conducted by adventurers, collectors and archaeologists, and as early as 1200–1090 BC during the XXth Dynasty, there is evidence that grave robbers, often including priests, were active. The flamboyant and extraordinary Italian, Belzoni, had ransacked the area with scant respect for scientific consideration during 1817, then in the middle of the 1840's Richard Lepsius uncovered more than 30 pyramids hitherto unknown. A decade later, Mariette (whose body was returned to Egypt after his death) excavated and catalogued 141 sphinxes and temples.

2 This did not, however, prevent Loret, two years before the turn of the century, from discovering the tomb of Amenophis II (the pharaoh who died in 1420 BC) and thirteen other royal mummies; nor the American Theodore Davis, who received permission to excavate in the Valley of the Kings in 1902, from discovering others such as the tomb of the sport-loving Thothmes IV, of Siptah and of the pious reformer Horemheb, who died without issue. The year prior to Carter's meeting with Lord Carnarvon, Davis had found a blue, varnished pitcher in the Valley of the Kings which bore the name of Tut-Ankh-Amon, and the year after the meeting, he was able to find the mummy and tomb of Amenophis IV, alias Akhenaten, the heretical and self-centred pharaoh, husband to the beautiful Nefertiti who bore him six daughters, one of whom, Anches-en-Amon, was the wife of Tut-Ankh-Amon.

3 Howard Carter had first come to Egypt in 1890 and two years later, in the capacity of draughtsman, accompanied Sir Flinders Petrie to Beni

Hassan and El Bersha. Petrie had already been in Egypt for some years, beginning in 1880 when he was able to disprove conclusively the notions and speculative theories of Piazzi Smyth regarding the unit of measurement employed in the building of the Great Pyramid. Petrie was to spend a total of seventy years in the study of archaeology, forty-six of them in Egypt. He brought a system of sequence dating to the Ist and IInd Dynasties, 3000 years BC, and is remembered today for his work in transforming the science of archaeology and developing a technique for excavation which is still being used.

4

It was Napoleon Bonaparte, however, who was to initiate the interest in Egyptology. Accompanying the Emperor on his fruitless campaign of 1798 was the artist Denon, who made many fine drawings of what he saw of the antiquities of the ancient world. In the years 1809–1813, a very costly publication, Jomard's *Déscription de l'Egypte* was issued, stimulating further interest in Egyptology and resulting in men like Belzoni going to collect all they could find, from scarabs to obelisks, without the least regard for their archaeological significance.

5

It was not until 1822, exactly one hundred years before Carter's discovery, that the mute world of Pharaonic writing was given expression when the young Frenchman, Champollion, in his famous letter, announced that he had unlocked the secret of the hieroglyphs on the Rosetta Stone, a black basalt block which had already been unearthed in 1799 four or five miles north-west of the port of Rosetta. With the understanding of the hieroglyphs, the dead world of ancient Egypt came alive.

6

The fifth Earl of Carnarvon had first become interested in excavation during a winter convalescing in Luxor after a serious automobile accident in 1900 in Germany. Three years later he visited several sites and saw an opportunity of combining his passion for objects of art with the excitement of excavation. However, he lacked expertise and went to Professor Maspero, director of the Department of Antiquities, for advice. Maspero recommended Howard Carter, an expert who lacked financial independence but who had worked with Petrie and Davis and was a reputable scholar. It was a good partnership. For a number of years they achieved very poor results and were hampered by the outbreak of the First World War, when Lord Carnarvon was forced to return to England and Carter for six solitary seasons was to persist in his excavations, finding little of consequence. Finally, he decided to devote one more season to the Valley, and his persistence was rewarded. One day in November 1922, the first of a series of stone steps was uncovered near the tomb of Rameses VI in the centre of the

7

Valley, leading to a sealed doorway. Carter examined the seal and found it to be that of the royal necropolis. He bored a peephole in the door and inserted an electric torch, finding that the passage was filled with rubble. With great self-discipline, Carter sent off a telegram to his patron and waited for his arrival on the 23rd November before progressing further. The first stone was removed on the 25th, and two days later they were in the Antechamber, which was packed tightly with scores of objects, some familiar and some new and strange. Most of the smaller objects and all of the larger ones bore the name of Tut-Ankh-Amon. Under one of the three couches they noticed a small, irregular hole in the wall. There was another sealed doorway beyond, and when they inserted their electric torch they found another chamber, smaller than the first, even more crowded with objects.

This room, afterwards called the Annexe, was in a state of indescribable confusion. Every inch of the floorspace was crammed with beautiful things. Excited and bewildered, Carter and Carnarvon were entirely unprepared to deal with such a multitude of objects, many of which were in a highly perishable condition, so they decided to make provision for a darkroom, a laboratory, and a safe place to preserve and catalogue the objects. The tomb was resealed with a heavy steel gate and was not opened up again until December 16th when Carter was more prepared with photographic equipment, chemicals and packing boxes. On the 22nd, the tomb was opened to the press, and three days later the first object was removed from the tomb. By the middle of February, the Antechamber had been cleared out and the door to the burial chamber was breached, revealing a wall of gold, which proved to be the shrine, an enormous structure that almost filled the entire chamber and which was to reveal a succession of no fewer than four shrines, one within the other, concealing the stone sarcophagus of Tut-Ankh-Amon. It would take several seasons to catalogue the objects. Before the excavation was complete, however, on 6th April, 1923, Lord Carnarvon, simultaneously with the failure of every electric light in Cairo, suddenly died before he had had the chance of looking upon the face of the young king whose discovery his generosity and persistence had made possible.

QUESTION 1

Read the passage carefully and fill in the table overleaf, indicating whether the statement is true or false.

		True	False
1	Champollion found a black stone.		
2	The Earl of Carnarvon spent 1915 in Egypt.		
3	A mummy, buried in 1420 BC, was discovered.		
4	Horemheb had many sons.		
5	Akhenaten had six daughters.		
6	Tut-Ankh-Amon was related to Amenophis IV.		
7	Petrie discredited Smyth's theories.		
8	Belzoni conducted scientific experiments in the Valley.		
9	Carter achieved excellent results before 1922.		
10	Carter was working in Egypt in 1880.		

QUESTION 2

Put the following statements into chronological sequence with the dates they took place in the second column.

		Step	Date
A	A young boy king dies and is buried.	1	
B	The excavators are exhausted in the Nile Valley.	2	
C	The tomb of Tut-Ankh-Amon's father-in-law is discovered.	3	
D	The language of the hieroglyphs is understood.	4	
E	Mariette dies in Egypt.	5	
F	Petrie confirms Smyth's theories.	6	
G	The lights go out in Cairo.	7	
H	Napoleon's expedition to Egypt takes place.	8	
I	Lord Carnarvon has an automobile accident in Luxor.	9	
J	An American archaeologist has permission to excavate.	10	
K	Howard Carter arrives in Egypt for the first time.		
L	A staircase is uncovered in the middle of the Valley.		
M	An expensive series of books is issued.		
N	Tomb robbers are very active.		
O	Carter meets his future benefactor in London.		

QUESTION 3

Give the word or phrase from the passage that has the same meaning as the words below. The paragraph numbers are in brackets.

1	only	(1)	11	evolving	(3)
2	important	(1)	12	begin	(4)
3	complete	(1)	13	unsuccessful	(4)
4	beyond compare	(1)	14	expensive	(4)
5	hardly any	(1)	15	silent	(5)
6	previously	(1)	16	recovering	(6)
7	also known as	(2)	17	skill	(6)
8	role	(3)	18	distinguished	(6)
9	hypothetical	(3)	19	crowded	(7)
10	used	(3)	20	broken open	(7)

The Mastaba

1

The mastaba was an ancient Egyptian tomb or funerary mound, usually rectangular in shape, with battered or sloping sides and a flat roof covering a burial chamber below ground where a king or important official would be laid to rest. Over the centuries of ancient Egyptian history, the mastaba became more and more complex in design and structure until it *evolved* as a royal tomb into the great pyramids of the IIIrd to the VIth Dynasties.

2

There are five main mastaba types, beginning in the Ist Dynasty with the lined tomb, which is the earliest form of mastaba; *prior* to this, in the pre-Dynastic period, the dead were *simply* laid in desert cemeteries called pit graves, which were holes in the ground covered by mounds of sand and surrounded by circles of stones. The earliest mastaba was used for the burial of nobles and had an inside lining of brick, transforming it into a tomb, topped by a flat wooden roof or by one of arched brick. *Eventually* thick internal walls sub-divided the pit into several rooms, often exceeding twenty, the centre ones being used to house the sarcophagus and the others the funerary offerings which the Egyptians believed would be necessary to the deceased in his after-life. This chambered tomb was rectangular and single-storeyed but it covered a wider area and had a wooden roof supported by timber posts. Debris was piled on top, forming a superstructure which was held in place by thick walls of sun-dried brick. In the earlier version, the walls were ribbed with alternate vertical projections of buttresses and recesses but the plain-wall type became more popular. Each had battered walls at 75° and was surrounded by an enclosure wall. During the IInd and IIIrd Dynasties, the mastaba became oriented on a north/south axis with the long, east side facing the Nile. The system of chambers was more deeply sunk than ever before and into solid rock. A stairway and ramp led from the top of the north end of the super-structure to connect with a series of vertical shafts leading directly to the tomb chamber itself. This was lined with stone and surrounded by *secondary* chambers for the funerary offerings. Heavy stone blocks called portcullises were placed at the foot of each shaft after the burial to seal off the entire tomb area, then the shaft was filled in to the top with rubble and debris. The battered walls were completely plain, except that, facing the Nile on the long east side were two recesses, one on the northern end and one to the south, the former being an entrance and the latter a false door with a table beside it for offerings to the deceased. It was believed that the spirit of the dead man would use this false door to come and go as he wished and take the food laid out daily for him.

3 Two or three hundred mastabas of the IVth and Vth dynasties *adjoin* the great pyramids of Gizeh. They show a marked difference in design from the earlier mastabas, being constructed *largely* of limestone instead of brick and having two important innovations: one was the inclusion of a small offering chapel either inside the structure or added on at the side towards the southern end, making the mastaba L-shaped; while the other was having a much more deeply sunk tomb chamber which was approached from the northern end of the structure from a long vertical shaft connected to a short horizontal passage adjacent to the tomb. The sides of the mastaba were battered as before and the two recessed doors maintained on the long east side as in the earlier type.

4 By the VIth Dynasty the mastaba had become increasingly *intricate* in design, with the chapel or offering room assuming more importance, often being a series of rooms inside or adjacent to the structure, with highly decorated walls, either painted or in relief sculpture. Tall pillars were arranged along the sides of the offering room and were used also to support a roofed entrance to the south of the building. A *shrine*, called a serdab, became the most important room in the whole complex, where principal offerings were made. A serdab containing one or more statues of the dead man would be found behind the offering room, completely sealed off except for slits in the wall from where they could have been observed. A second serdab would stand alongside the entrance. More pillars decorated a court area to the east, which had a central stairway, and the court was connected by a long passage to a small chamber, behind which stood the offering room. In the offering room, a tall upright slab of stone called a stele stood along the west wall, bearing religious *inscriptions* and the name of the dead man, with a table beneath it for offerings. The tomb chamber itself was at a much lower level to the south of the structure and to the west of the offering room. It was approached by means of a diagonal corridor which joined the stairway descending from the pillared court in the storey above.

QUESTION 1

Look at the diagrams (pages 284–287) and label each one in the table, using one of the following phrases for each answer. If it is none of these, put X.

shaft-chapel type
brick-lined type
pit grave
serdab type
chambered type
stairway/ramp type

1		7	
2		8	
3		9	
4		10	
5		11	
6			

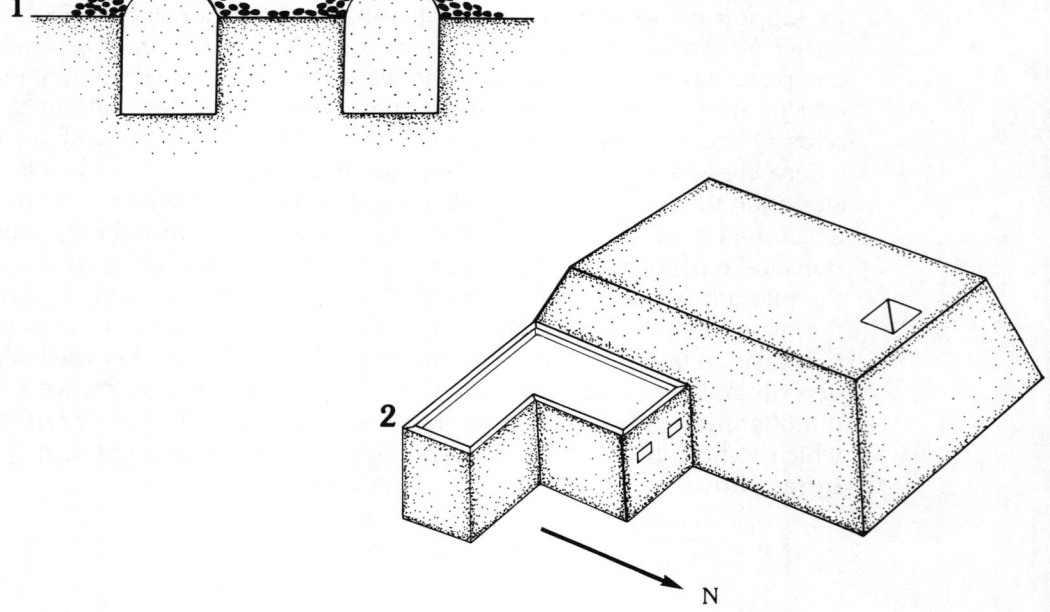

284

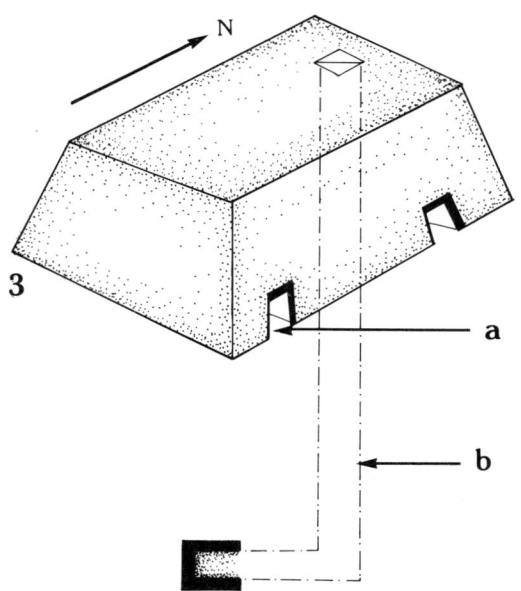

Number	Name of feature
3a	
3b	

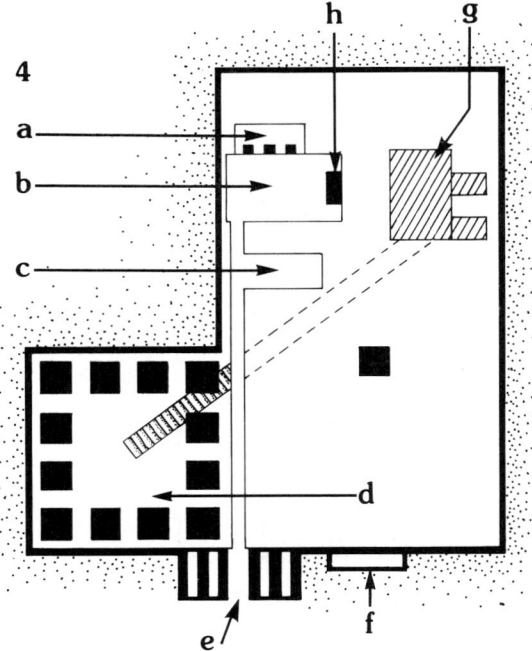

Number	Name of feature
4a	
4b	
4c	
4d	
4e	
4f	
4g	
4h	

5

Number	*Name of feature*
5a	
5b	
5c	
5d	
5e	

6

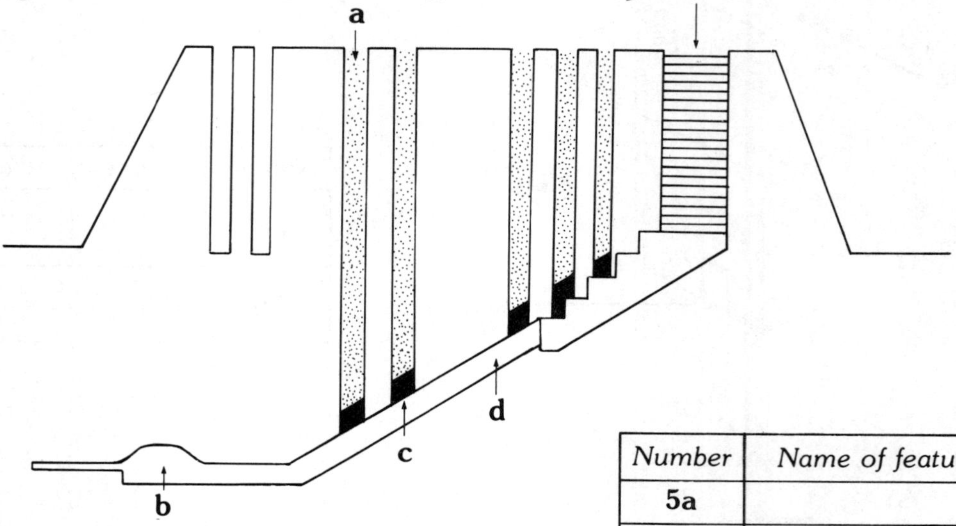

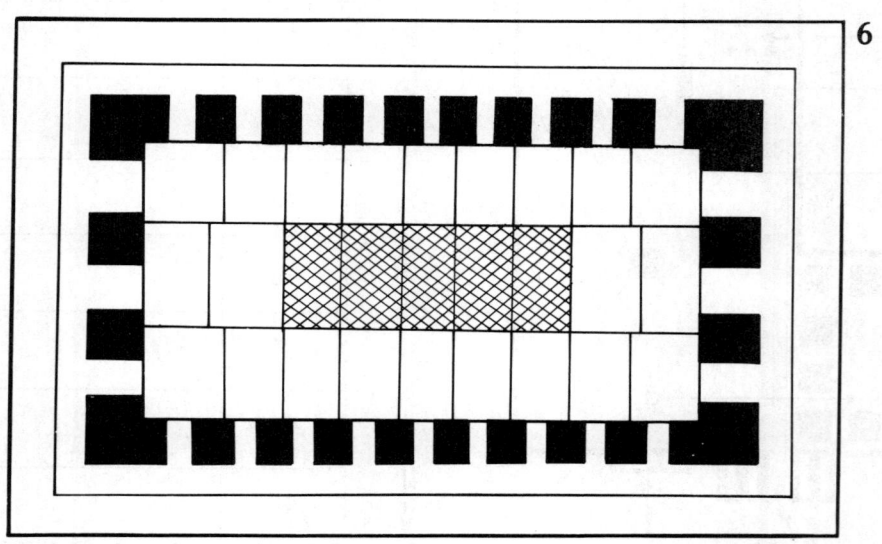

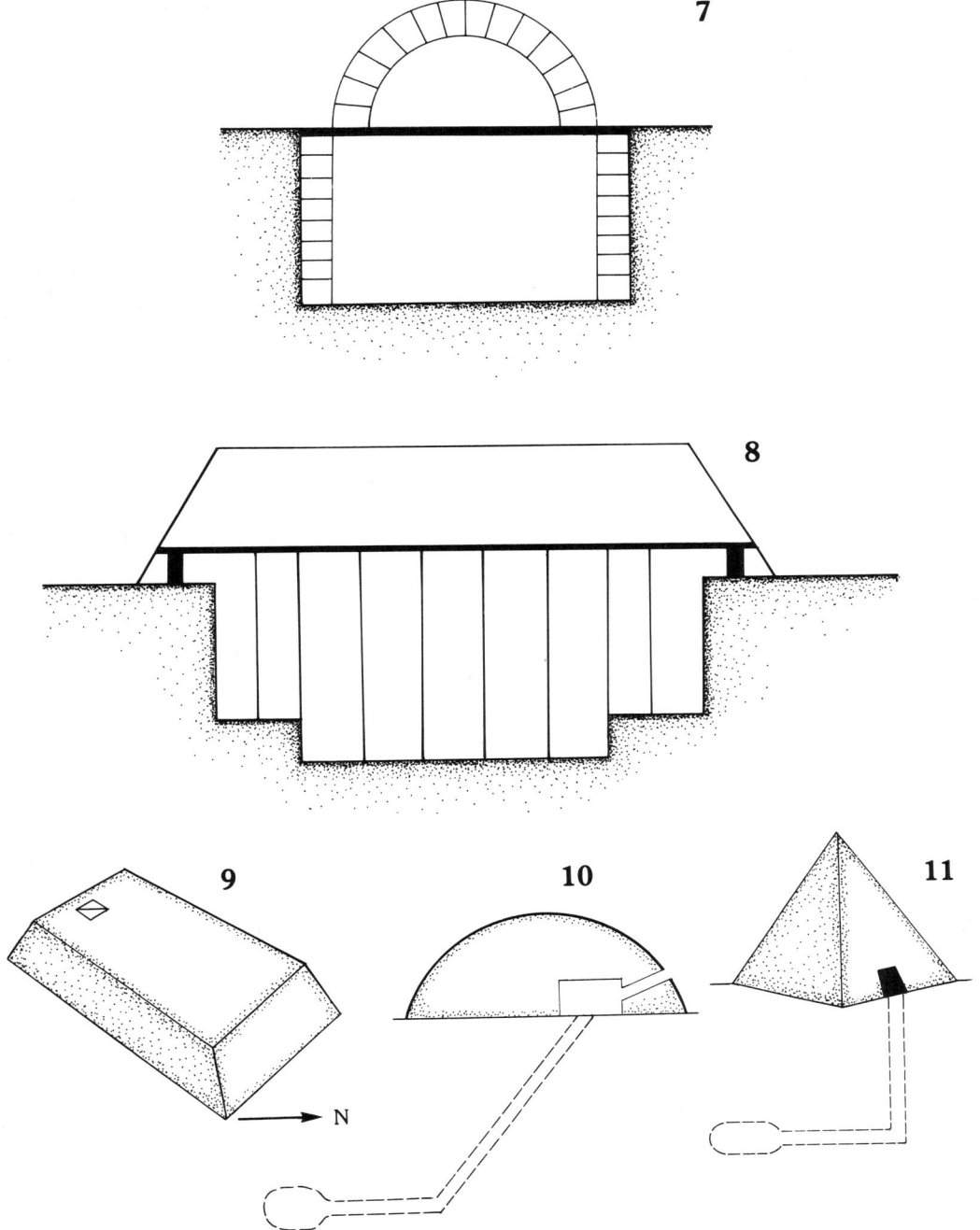

287

QUESTION 2

Some words in the passage are set in italics. Give their correct meaning in sequence from the list of definitions given to you.

1	6	merely		after this
2	7	stand beside		pictures
3	8	complicated		two other
4	9	writings		previously
5	10	subsidiary		enormously
		developed into		after some time
		holy place		easily
		predominantly		

QUESTION 3

Give the correct names to the numbered features in the separate tables below diagrams 3, 4 and 5.

Bricks and Bricklaying

1 **Types of bricks**

Most of us are aware of what a brick is; we know that it is usually rectangular in shape, reddish in colour, and employed in the building of walls. Bricks are made from clay as a rule, their colour and texture depending on the district from where the raw material is obtained. There are hundreds of varieties of brick types, each depending on its function, what it is made of, and the manner in which it is made. Facing bricks, for example, are used for external brickwork, so they should be attractive in appearance and have good weathering properties; they can be either rough or smooth in texture, hard or soft, and can range in colour from red to yellow, brown, purple and black. Bricks that are to be rendered over or plastered are cheaper than facings and are called commons. These can occasionally be used for visible work if they are of the requisite quality. Extra-hard bricks that are impervious to water are often used for underground structures where strength and durability are essential and are called engineering bricks. Fire bricks are made from special clays and should be able to withstand high temperatures; they are very hard and have a close texture. They never have a frog or recess in either face. The glazed brick is made from a similar type of clay and is glazed either by salt in the final stages of burning or by being dipped into a specially prepared clay.

QUESTION 1

Give a word or phrase from the paragraph which has the same meaning as the following words (the list of words occurs in sequence):

1. used ....
2. outside ....
3. graduate ....
4. from time to time .....
5. can be seen ....
6. necessary ....
7. impenetrable ....
8. permanence ....
9. bear ....
10. last ....

2 Brick shapes

When bricks are cut or made in certain shapes they have special names. A *frog*, for example, is a brick with a shallow recess on either one or both of its faces, which can be rectangular, triangular or trapezoidal in section. A *bat* is a part brick cut across its width so that it is possible to have a half bat or a three-quarter bat. If cut on an angle across the width it is called a mitred bat, and if the cut brick is cut at an angle which is more than half its size it is called a large mitred bat. A brick cut across its length is called a *closer* and is used to even up the spacing in a wall; if cut in two it is called a queen closer while a king closer has one corner cut away up to half its width. A bevelled closer is cut at an angle from one corner to the other to half the width. The sharp right-angled edges of the bricks are called the *arris*.

── QUESTION 2 ──

Referring to the paragraph above, study the brick shapes in the diagrams below, and then complete the table opposite.

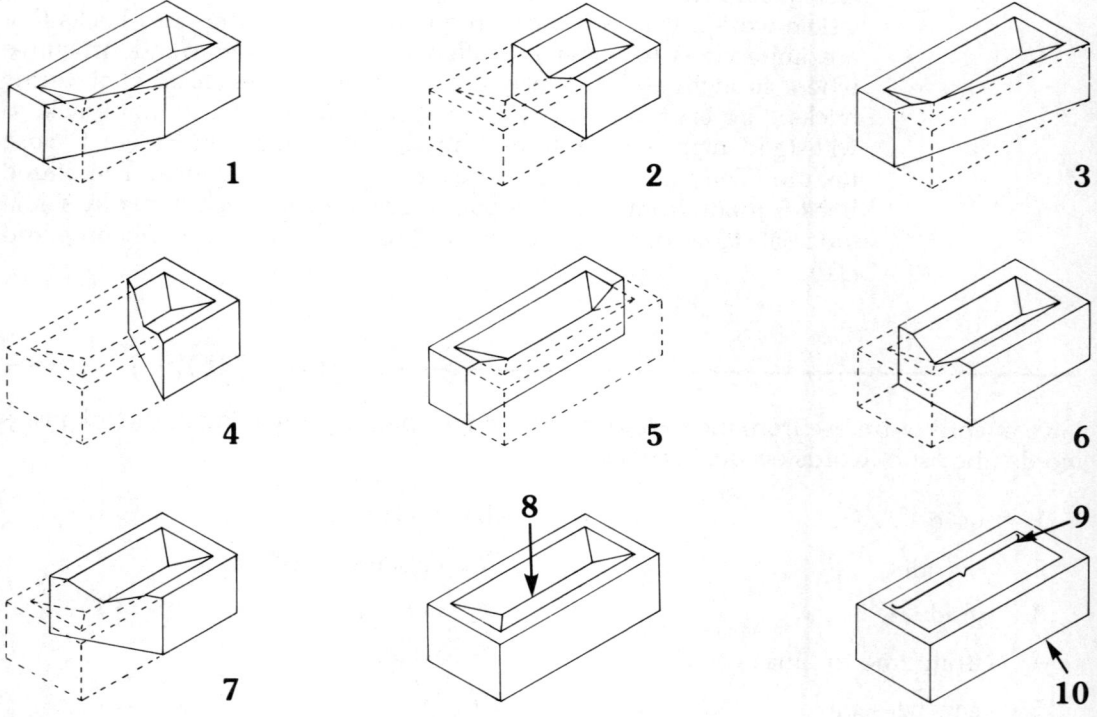

1		6	
2		7	
3		8	
4		9	
5		10	

3 **Brick positions**

When the bricklayer is laying bricks, he has a special name for each, depending on its position or function. A row of bricks is called a *course* and a brick that is laid with its long sides parallel to the wall face is called a *stretcher*. Mortar, once between the bricks, is called a *joint*, while the alternate rows of bricks in an unfinished wall are known as *toothing*. The terminal part of the wall with all the bricks flush with each other is a *stopped end*. When bricks form a corner they are called *quoins* and bricks introduced at right angles to a wall to give it strength are called *piers*. A *header* is a brick whose end lies parallel to the wall face while the *closer*, cut across its length, is used near a corner to even up the bond.

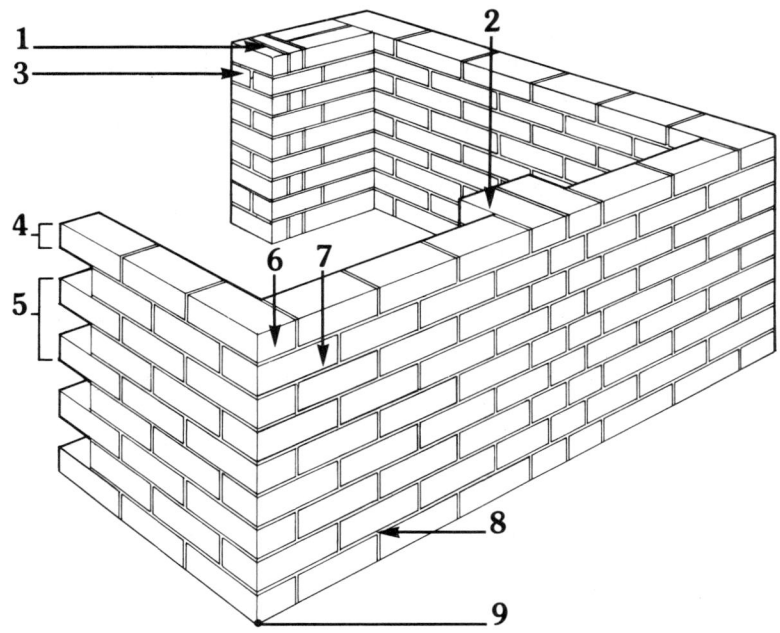

QUESTION 3

Look at the diagram of the wall on the previous page, and then complete the table with the names appropriate to their position in the wall.

1		6	
2		7	
3		8	
4		9	
5			

4 Tools

The bricklayer has his own specific tools, which are not as numerous as in other trades. We will describe some of the most common of them. The trowel is the principal tool used by the bricklayer who becomes very skilled in its use. It consists of an elongated lozenge-shaped steel blade to which a wooden handle is attached by means of a curved metal shank. When the bricklayer grips the trowel, his thumb should rest on the uppermost part of the shank and his fingers should be under the handle. There are two types of trowel, the *pointing trowel* and the brick trowel. The former has both of its edges straight and is available in various sizes, common blade lengths being 75–150 mm. It is used for pointing and jointing. There are two types of pointing trowel, the dotter, which is used for cross joints and the larger bed jointer, which, as its name implies, is better suited for longer joints. The *brick trowel* has both a curved and a straight edge and is used by the bricklayer for lifting the mortar from the mortar board and spreading it where required, for forming joints between bricks and for collecting surplus mortar squeezed from between the bricks which are being laid. Its blade length varies from 225–350 mm and is obtainable in both left- and right-handed versions. Its straight edge is used for scooping up mortar and its opposite or curved edge is for 'cropping' or cleaning up bricks once they have been cut. It is important to remember that a trowel handle must never be allowed to wear smooth but must be roughened by a piece of glass paper or a brick, and in no circumstances should mortar be permitted to harden on the blade. Used in conjunction with each other for the accurate cutting of bricks are the *bolster* and the *club hammer*, the former being a cold chisel with a flat, sharpened blade ranging from 50–100 mm, the larger size being the most suitable. The latter is a hammer whose steel head weighs from 0.90 kg to 1.35 kg. It has chamfered or bevelled edges so that the bricklayer will not injure his hand if he misses the tool he is striking. The *brick hammer* is shaped differently, having one square head used for hitting nails or forcing bricks and another chisel-shaped or with a flat edge, which is used for trimming the rough face of a brick, particularly if it is very hard, when it has already been split by the bolster. It is possible to obtain this hammer with either a short or a long blade head. The *comb hammer* is a more modern version of the brick hammer but used for the same purpose. In place of the chisel end there is a slot where a detachable comb or blade can be inserted, and some types have two slotted ends, one for a chisel blade and the other for the comb blade. It is efficient because it is not necessary to sharpen the blades as they get worn, as they can be replaced.

The bricklayer will test the brickwork for straightness both vertically and horizontally with a tool called a *spirit level* which consists of a hardwood case, in the centre recess of which is a glass tube filled with alcohol save for a small bubble of air. When used horizontally, the bubble shows in the centre; when used vertically there is at least one small spirit tube fixed at right angles to its length. The correct vertical plumb is obtained when the bubble shows in the small tube at the bottom. The spirit level can also be used on the rake, when it gently taps back any brick that is out of line and where the bubbles, of course, will have no significance. The small, pocket-sized *boat level* has an identical use to the spirit level and is used in the same way, except it is used in confined spaces. As its name denotes, it is shaped like a boat and normally contains one tube for uprightness and one for levelling. Both of these tools have superseded the *plumb line*, which is an excellent tool for keeping brickwork upright. It is a long piece of wood, about 1.5 m long and 2.5 cm thick, with a hole near the bottom in which a lead plumb bob is suspended from a cord fixed to the top of the rule and passing down a middle cut or groove extending along its length. A wire hoop or bridle passes through the rule just above the opening to control the line in windy conditions. A *line and pins* are used to make sure that a course of bricks is true and should always be used on any work over 1.2 m in length. Usually made of nylon thread, the line, about 3 knots long (i.e. 11 m), is wound around two flat, steel blades, clockwise on one and anticlockwise on the other. The blades are stuck into upright mortar joints on each corner of a wall and pulled taut to give the true guideline. Some bricklayers, however, prefer to use a pair of *L-shaped corner blocks* made of hardwood with a groove in them which clip on each end of the wall to hold the line (which passes down the saw cut on each block and is secured on to screws on the side of the block) as they are more efficient and convenient than the line and pins and they avoid damage to face work which the pins cause as they are driven into the joints. Another method for holding a long length of line to prevent it from sagging is the *tingle plate*. It is made from a piece of thin metal such as brass, copper or zinc, measuring about 5 × 10 cm. It has three prongs or nibs which support the line at intervals of about 7 metres or less on windy days. The tingle is placed flat on each course over a brick called a tingle brick and weighted by a loose bat. As each course rises, so the tingle brick will be raised to support the line along the course following. A square piece of plywood about 200 mm square with a handle screwed to the underside is called a *hawk* and is used for carrying small quantities of mortar on the occasional repair job. It is also available in aluminium, which makes it light and convenient to use. For calculating that all corners are accurate, the bricklayer uses the *large square* which is essentially three straight pieces of wood in the ratio 3:4:5 screwed firmly together. It measures about 75 × 45 × 60 cm. The *gauge rod* makes sure that the courses are rising evenly. It is made from a straight piece of timber with saw marks every 76 mm (which is the height of the brick plus the mortar bed) and is used vertically. A piece of plysheet about 67 cm square fixed to a row of timber battens will carry reserve mortar. This is called a *spot board* and is laid out on the site along the building line, alternating with piles of bricks and dampened in warm weather to prevent the mortar from drying out. The *hod*, used for carrying up to a dozen bricks at a time or small quantities of mortar, is a three-sided metal or wooden box, available in several sizes, fixed to a wooden pole and carried on the shoulder of the bricklayer. A very useful time-saving tool is the *bat and closer gauge* which is used for marking off bricks with great accuracy without the need for a measuring rule each time. It is made from oak and should be treated with care. It measures about 202 × 75 × 20 mm, its longer cut being equal to the width of a brick and the shorter equal to half the width.

QUESTION 4

Look at the diagrams of the tools opposite and overleaf and give them their correct names from the information you have just read by completing the table on page 298. They are not drawn to scale.

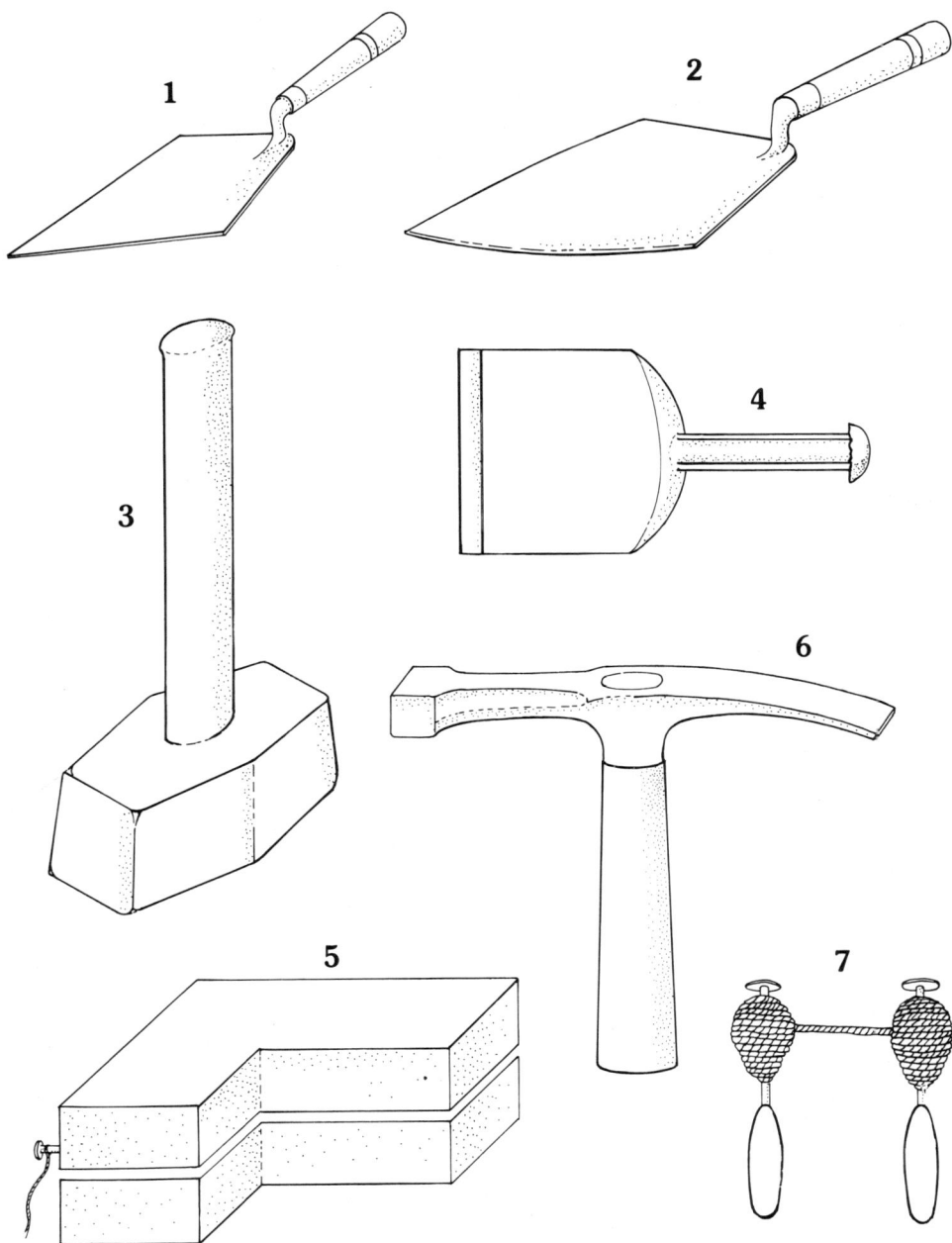

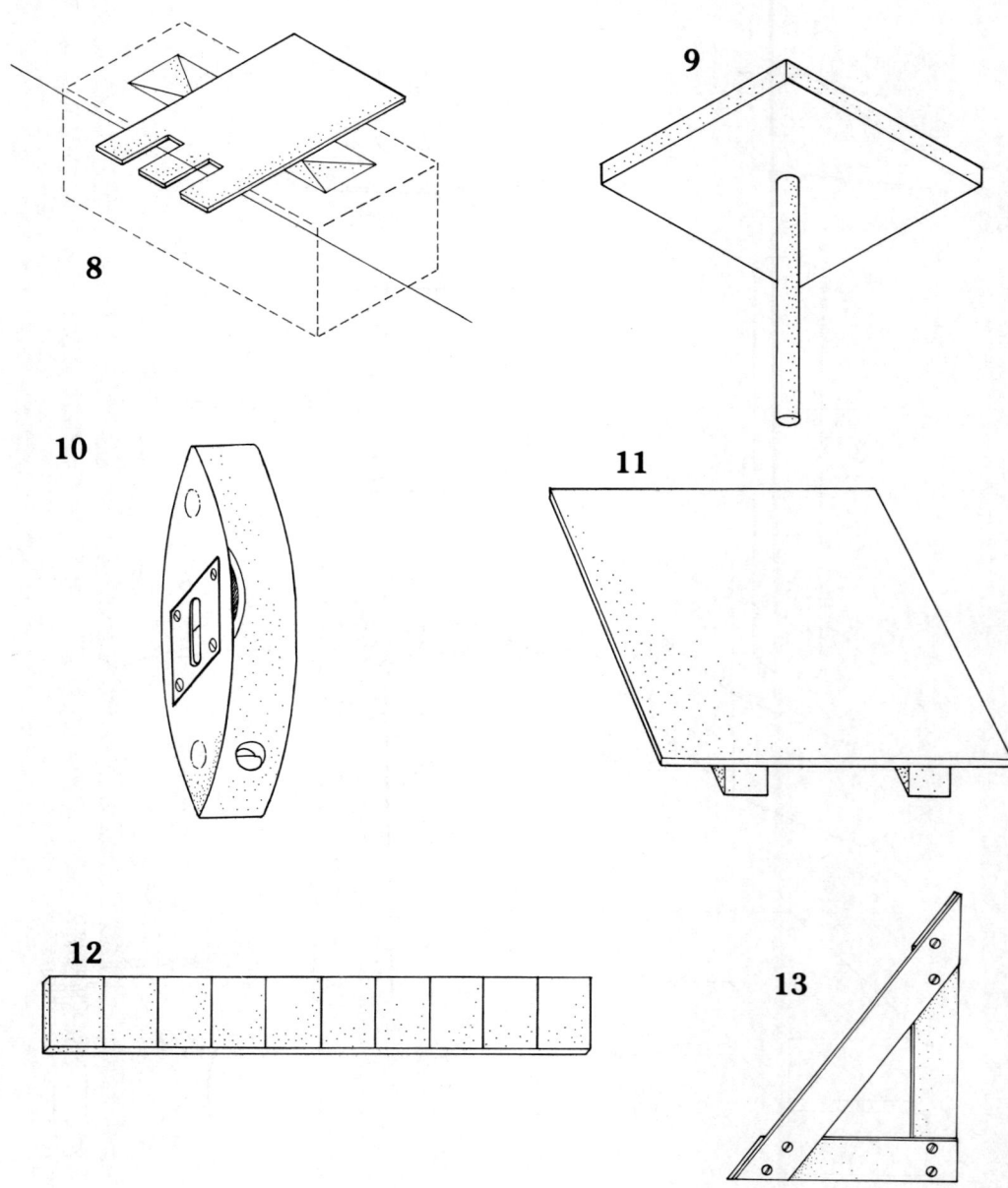

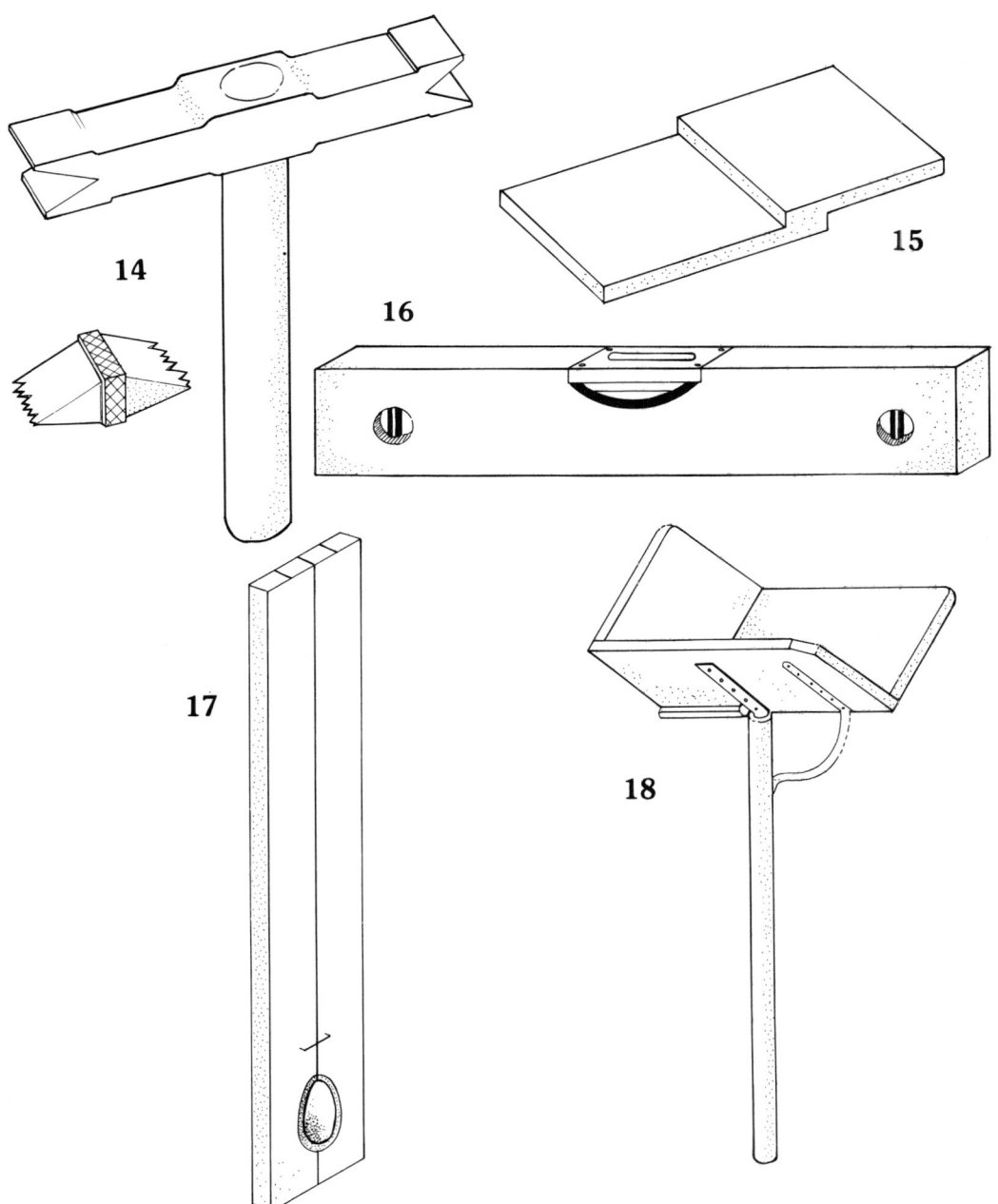

1		10	
2		11	
3		12	
4		13	
5		14	
6		15	
7		16	
8		17	
9		18	

QUESTION 5

Here are two columns, each containing data about tools used by the bricklayer but they are not in order. Match them up and give the name of the tool being described in the table on page 300.

1	This small flat tool is useful for supporting long lengths of the line at regular intervals along the wall face, being held in place by a loose brick.	A	It can be used both vertically and horizontally for plumbing for uprightness but can also be used for tapping bricks gently into line.
2	The secret of quick bricklaying is to be found in the correct handling of this tool. The widest part of its blade is called the shoulder and varies in size with the pattern or type. It is used for lifting mortar from the mortar board and spreading it across the face of the bricks and between the joints.	B	To cut the brick accurately, it is necessary to stand it on its edge and mark it, then treating the other edge similarly. It is then given a sharp blow with the sharpened edge of the chisel. If laid on its back, a brick will break unevenly across the centre.
3	This tool has a steel head varying in weight from 0.90–1.35 kg and is used for precision cutting of bricks.	C	Made from thin metal, it has three prongs or nibs and the line is passed under the outer nibs and over the centre one.

4	This tool ranges in length and has two sizes, each with a different name. It is used for jointing after the brick has already been laid.	D	Its bob is usually about 2 kg in weight and pear-shaped. The hole at the bottom must always be larger than the bob so that it can swing and strike the true vertical.
5	These hardwood corner pieces clip on to each end of the wall to hold the line which acts as a guide when laying bricks.	E	It is also used for collecting surplus mortar squeezed from the bricks. Its cutting edge is to be used for rough cutting only and never where the brick edge is visible.
6	This tool is not used very much nowadays but it is very reliable and never needs re-adjusting, nor is it easily damaged like a spirit level. It is used vertically.	F	On no account should a brick be laid touching the line—the bottom edge of the brick should be kept flush with the top edge of the course below and lines should never have knots in them.
7	This tool is available in a number of lengths, depending on the size of the work in hand and is available with either a fixed or an adjustable bubble tube, the latter being preferable as being easier to adjust. Accuracy is ascertained by making sure that the bubble is between the lines.	G	The smaller version is called a dotter and its larger one a bed jointer, both with straight edges.
8	Should it become damaged, it can be repaired by unravelling a portion of the line from each end, forming a small hole about 50 mm from each end. The ends can be threaded into each hole and pulled taut so that the unravelled portions come together.	H	They are L-shaped and have a groove in them through which the line passes.

No.	Letter	Name
1		
2		
3		
4		
5		
6		
7		
8		

Allergies

An allergy is a state of abnormal sensitivity by the body to various substances or physical agents that, in the doses causing a reaction, are harmless to normal people. A minute dose is all that is needed to produce a reaction in the sensitive individual. Histamine is released from the cells of the affected tissue, causing inflammation and reaction, with leakage of the small blood vessels and spasms of muscles.

A TYPES OF ALLERGY

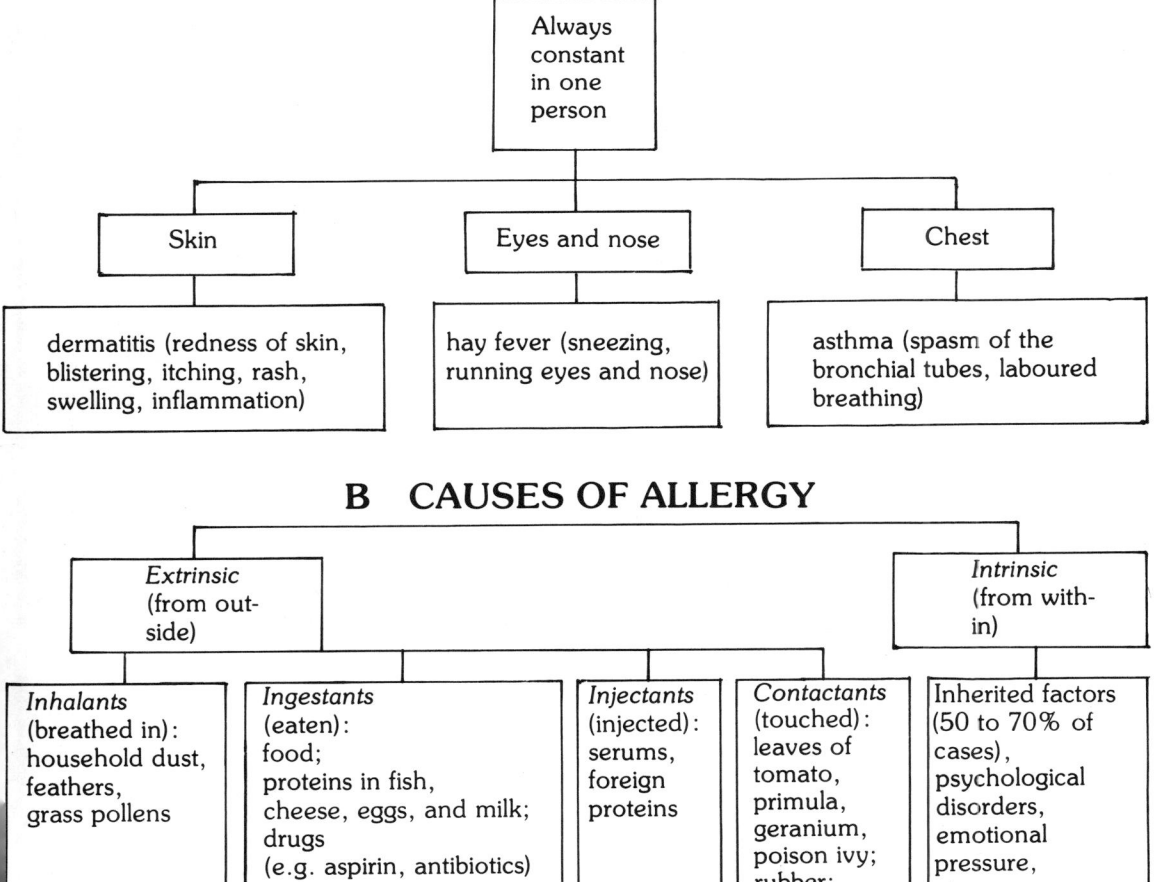

B CAUSES OF ALLERGY

C TREATMENT

| (a) Prevention of further contact with allergens. | (b) Desensitisation by means of minute injections of the specific allergen, in amounts which do not cause a reaction, increasing in dosage to achieve immunity. | (c) Use of anti-histamine drugs in all cases except asthma. | (d) Injections of adrenaline to relieve spasms—but this is not curative. Cortisone is given as a last resort. There is a large psychological factor in asthma, which is not greatly amenable to medication. |

VOCABULARY USED

Allergic	The state of being affected with an allergy.
Allergic reaction	The response to an allergen.
Allergen	A substance which causes a reaction. It is often a protein.
Antibodies	Proteins made by special white blood cells in the body to fight allergens.
Toxic	Poisonous.
Histamine	A strong chemical released from the cells of an affected tissue, causing reaction.
Anti-histamine	Drugs which relieve the symptoms of an allergic reaction by opposing the effects of histamine released by the body cells.

QUESTION

Using the information in the tables above, write a description of Allergies suitable for inclusion in a medical textbook for general use.

AURAL TESTS

Traffic Accident

Listen to the account of the accident. The statement will be read twice. You will then have 5 minutes to answer the question.

―――――――――――――――――――――――――――― QUESTION ――――

Label the vehicles shown on the drawing:

| D | Dolomite | A | Alpine | M | Marina | H | Horsebox |
| E | Escort | X | Vehicles not mentioned | | | | |

Also label:

S   Stables   N   Nurseries   Clifford Road   Shoesmith Lane

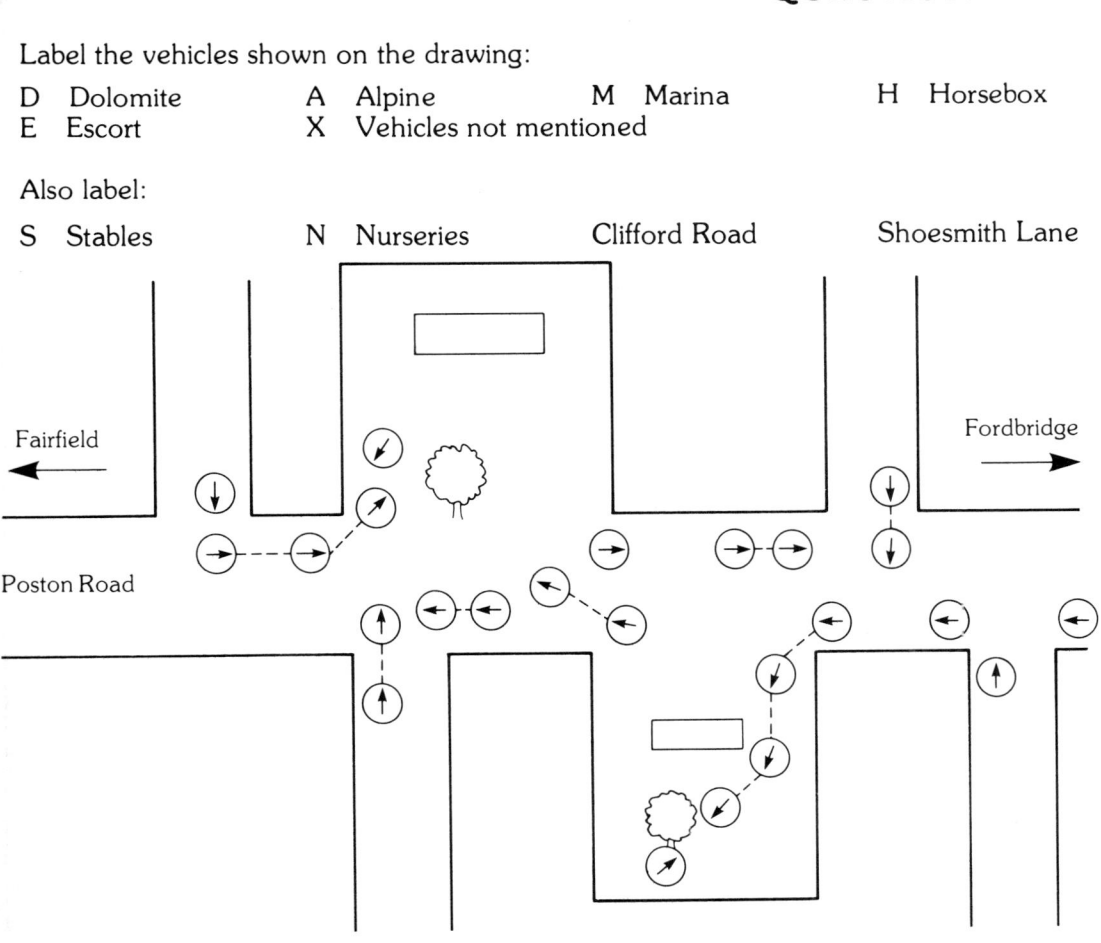

305

The Life Cycle of the Frog

Study the following 15 statements; then listen to the account of the life cycle of the frog. It will be read twice and you may take notes. You will then have 5 minutes to complete the table.

— QUESTION —

Complete the table showing the stages of development in the life cycle of the frog. The first stage has been done for you.

A   The tail of the tadpole decreases in size and its mouth enlarges.
B   The lungs begin to form.
C   The egg subdivides and becomes curved in shape.
D   The tadpole begins to breathe like a fish and its mouth forms.
E   The tadpole becomes a carnivore.
F   The tadpole attaches itself to a water plant.
G   The hindlegs appear.
H   Adult female frogs lay their eggs in water.
I   The young tadpole has a tail and hatches.
J   The forelegs appear.
K   Complete metamorphosis takes place.
L   The external gill slits disappear and the tadpole breathes air from the surface.
M   The frog climbs out on to dry land.
N   The toes begin to form.
O   The tail is digested by the body.

Stage		Stage	
1	H	9	
2		10	
3		11	
4		12	
5		13	
6		14	
7		15	
8			

Blakeley Castle

Listen to the directions on how to get to Blakeley Castle and the neighbouring church; they will be read twice. You may take notes during the first reading.

---------- QUESTION 1 ----------

Draw the route on the map overleaf during the second reading of the directions.

---------- QUESTION 2 ----------

The names of places mentioned in the directions are listed below. Complete the table. If a place was not described, mark it with an X.

Grammar School	Sportsground	Signpost

Library Complex	Fire Station	Technical College

General Hospital	Post Office	

1		6	
2		7	
3		8	
4		9	
5		10	

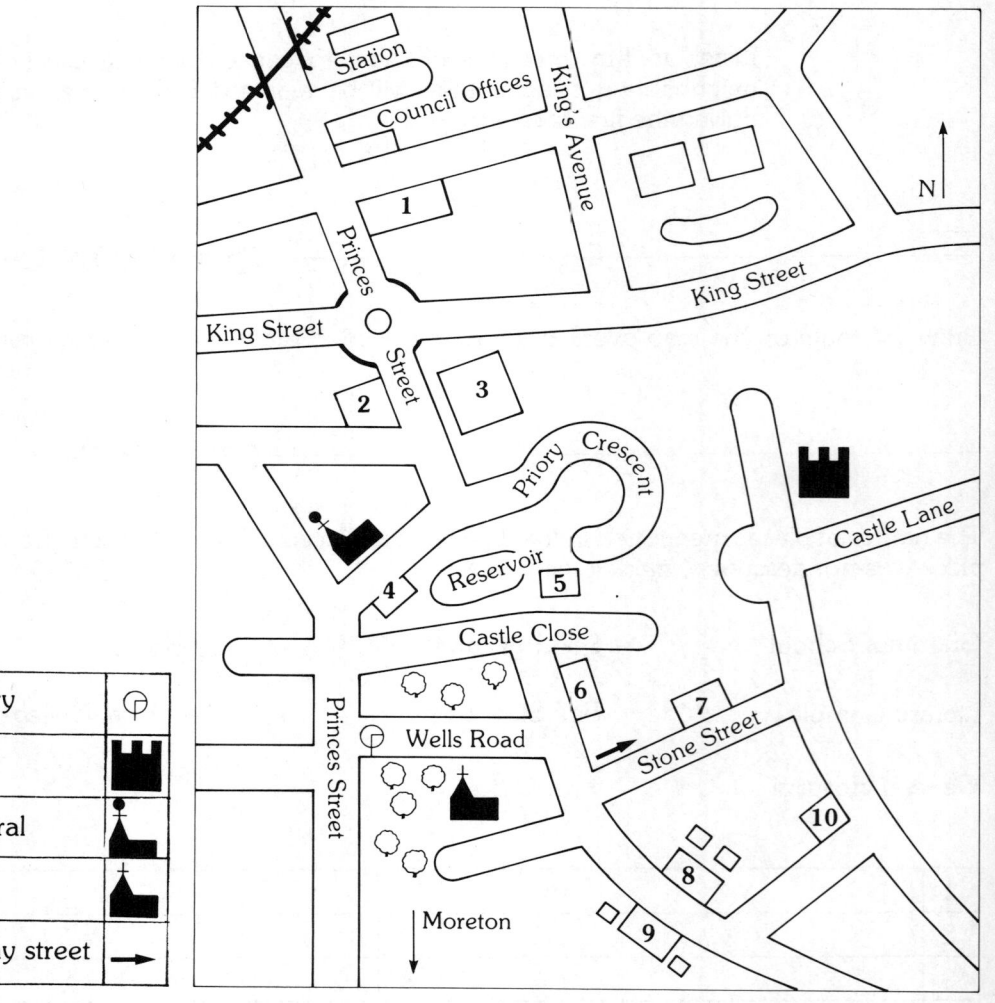

St. Dane's Church

Listen to the letter in which David gives his friend John directions to St. Dane's Church and the George and Dragon Hotel. After the second reading you will have 10 minutes to answer the question.

QUESTION

Mark the following on the map overleaf:
1. The route to the church.
2. The route to the George and Dragon Hotel.
3. Priory Road.
4. Hudson Street.

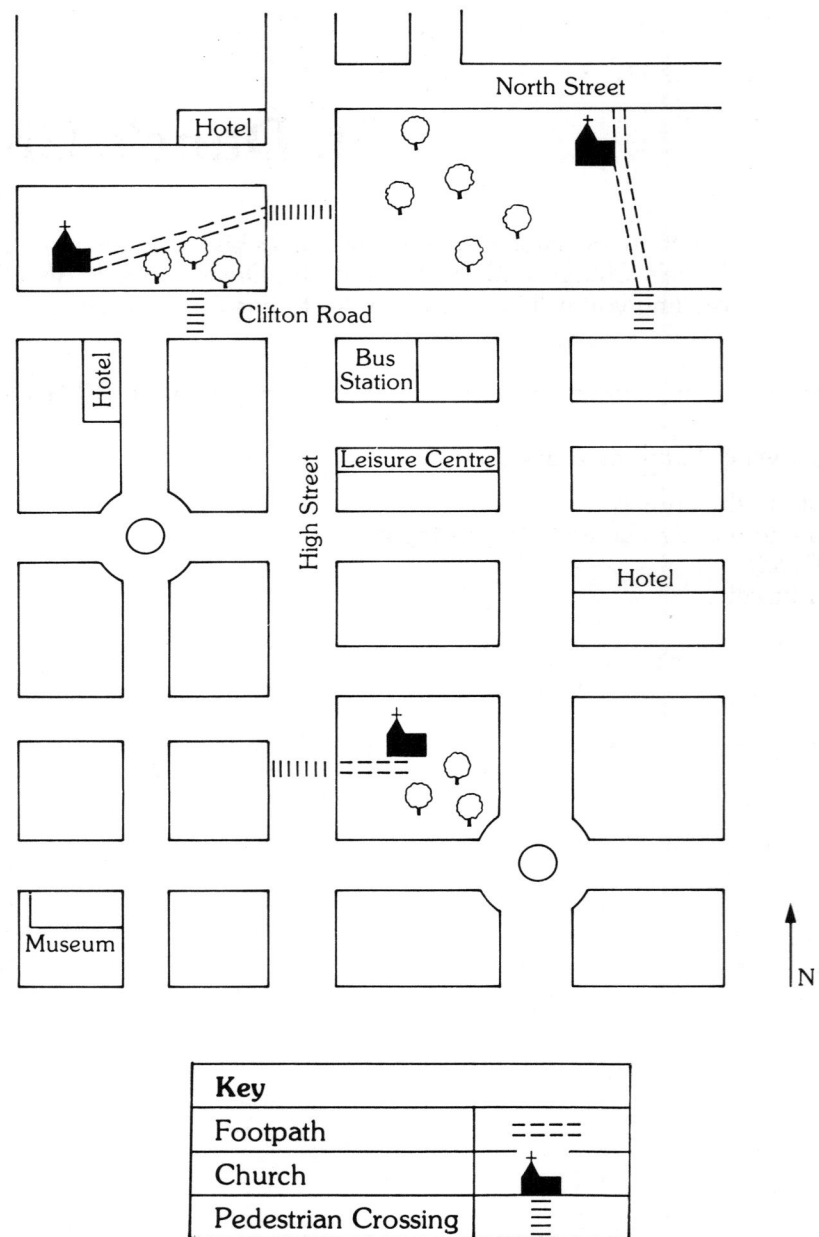

The Regional Exhibition Centre

Listen to the directions given to motorists on how to approach the Regional Exhibition Centre. The directions will be read twice. You will then have 10 minutes to answer the questions.

―――――――――――――――――――――――― QUESTION 1 ―――――

Draw the routes on the map overleaf as follows:
　From the north, use a solid line _____
　From the south, use a broken line __ __ __ __ __ __ __
　From the east, use a dotted line . . . .
　From the west, use a line of asterisks * * * * * * * * * *

―――――――――――――――――――――――― QUESTION 2 ―――――

The places mentioned in the directions are listed below. Complete the key to the map. If a place was not mentioned, mark it with an X.

　　　　Safari Park　　　　　　　　Green Dragon

　　　　Beacon Reservoir　　　　　Telephone Exchange

Key	
1	
2	
3	
4	
5	

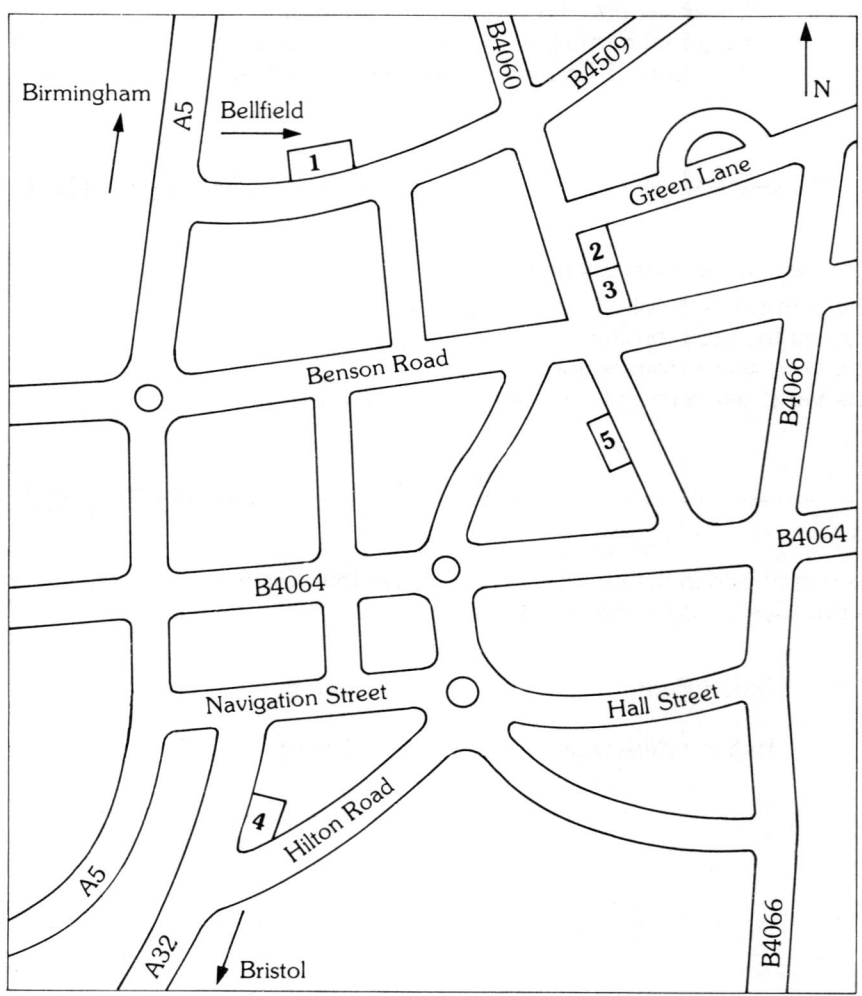

Bees—The Honey Bee

Study the following statements. After hearing the passage on bees, in particular the honey bee, you will be asked to match up the two halves of the ten statements. The passage will be read twice and you may take notes. You will have 7 minutes to complete the table overleaf.

QUESTION

Complete the table by matching up the two halves of the following ten statements.

1. Nectar is sucked up from the flower by the bee:
2. Bees collect pollen in pollen baskets on their legs or on their body hairs,
3. Some bees lay their eggs in the nests of other bees,
4. Only the honey bee makes a honeycomb for the community;
5. She is the central figure in the community and the largest,
6. The drone is alone in not having a sting,
7. The worker bee has a sting, but she can use it only once;
8. There is no difference between the larvae of worker bees and queen bees, just after hatching;
9. The solitary female bee provides the larvae with pollen and nectar,
10. The worker bee performs special dances

A. the latter are fed a special food and develop differently.
B. but is unable to do anything but lay eggs.
C. which is thus transferred from flower to flower, fertilising them.
D. and has no social function except to fertilise the queen.
E. it is later brought up as honey.
F. because they are unable to collect pollen to feed to their young.
G. then flies away and leaves them for ever.
H. which tell the other bees where there is a source of food and how much is there.
I. it is a double layer of hexagonal cells, arranged vertically and made of wax.
J. she then dies, because it is barbed and cannot be retracted.

1		6	
2		7	
3		8	
4		9	
5		10	

The Honey Bee Community

Study the following 16 statements; then listen to the account of the establishment of a honey bee community. It will be read twice and you may take notes. You will then have 10 minutes to complete the table overleaf.

--- QUESTION ---

Complete the table showing the correct sequence of events as they occur. The first step has been done for you.

A   The old queen once again leaves the hive with a large number of workers.
B   Eventually a new site is selected and the swarm moves in.
C   The fertilised queen returns to the nest.
D   Some larvae are fed a special food.
E   Unfertilised eggs are laid in the larger cells.
F   Scouts search for a new nest.
G   The wax is formed into a comb by the older workers.
H   A newly hatched queen emerges and kills all her competitors.
I   The old queen leaves the hive with a large number of workers.
J   The younger workers seal up holes in the new nest, leaving just an entrance.
K   The queen lays fertilised eggs in the smaller cells.
L   They form a swarm and settle on a branch.
M   The workers feed the larvae.
N   The new queen takes her mating flight.
O   The younger workers begin to weave threads of wax.
P   The drone dies after fertilising the queen.

315

1	I	9	
2		10	
3		11	
4		12	
5		13	
6		14	
7		15	
8		16	

The Castes of the Honey Bee

Study the drawings **A–F**. Then listen to the description of the different castes of the honey bee; it will be read twice and you may take notes. You will have 5 minutes to identify the following: the queen, the drone, the worker.

--- QUESTION ---

Complete the table overleaf by identifying the queen, the drone and the worker from the following drawings. If a drawing does not represent any of the castes described put X in the table.

A
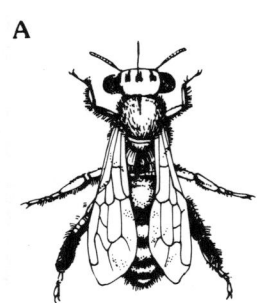

B
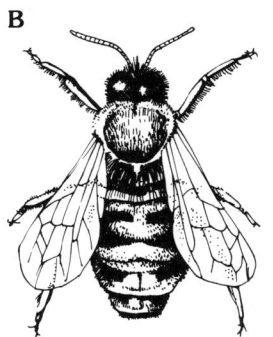

C
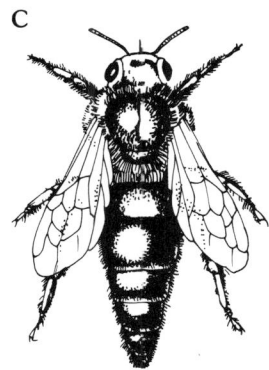

317

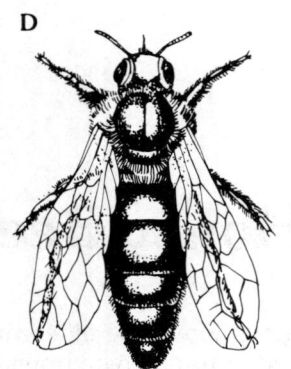

A		D	
B		E	
C		F	

The Worker Bee

Study the drawing of the worker bee and then listen to the passage. It will be read twice and you may take notes. You will then have 5 minutes to complete the table.

Before the reading starts, you will have 4 minutes to study the diagram and the words you are to use.

---- QUESTION ----

Complete the table overleaf by naming the parts of the worker bee. The words are listed here:

thorax	front leg	hind wing
simple eyes	second leg	front wing
compound eye	hind leg	abdomen
antenna	pollen basket	prong
head	sting	comb

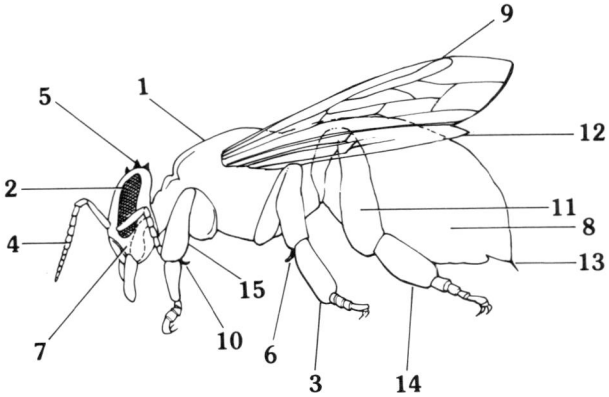

1		9	
2		10	
3		11	
4		12	
5		13	
6		14	
7		15	
8			

A Neolithic Settlement Complex

Listen to the account of a Neolithic settlement complex. The passage is divided into three parts. Each part will be read twice and followed by a question. You may take notes to help you.

QUESTION 1

Draw a plan of the causewayed camp as it would have looked from above. Use the symbols given in the key. You will have 5 minutes to do this.

Key

Ditch	⊂υυυυ⊃
Bank	⅏⅏⅏⅏⅏

↑ N

─────────────────────────────────── **QUESTION 2** ───

Draw a plan of the long barrow as it would have looked on completion from above. Use the symbols given in the key. You will have 3 minutes to do this.

Key

Ditch	v v v v
Palisade	o o o

N

─────────────────────────────────── **QUESTION 3** ───

Put the following ten sentences into the correct sequence in the table.

A   The enclosure was closed.
B   A wooden palisade was constructed.
C   Ditches were dug parallel to the long sides.
D   The eastern end was raised.
E   A site on high ground was chosen.
F   Timber ramps were placed along the sides of the enclosure.
G   The dead were brought to the enclosure.
H   The ramps were removed.
I   A rectangular area was marked out in an east–west direction.
J   The enclosure was covered by a mound of earth.

1		6	
2		7	
3		8	
4		9	
5		10	

Iron Age Village Complex

Listen to the account of the excavation of an Iron Age village complex. The passage is divided into four sections, each followed by a question. After the second reading of each section, you will have 5 minutes to answer the question, before going on to the next part.

QUESTION 1

Complete the table by putting the stages A–J into the correct sequence as described in the passage.

A The turf was removed.
B A team of Government archaeologists was called in.
C Pegs and string were used to divide the site into squares.
D High-altitude photography was carried out.
E A site map was drawn up.
F The site was measured and the position of the trenches decided on.
G Wooden pegs were labelled with letters and numbers.
H The excavation began with the digging of the first trenches.
I The building of a by-pass was proposed.
J Variation in the quality of vegetation was discovered by oblique aerial photography.

1		6	
2		7	
3		8	
4		9	
5		10	

QUESTION 2

Draw a plan of the Iron Age village settlement as it would have looked from above, using the symbols given in the key.

Key

ᴗ	Grain pit
●	Hut
┳	Granary
ⱽ ⱽ	Marshland
= = = =	Trackway
○○○○	Palisade
∣∣∣∣∣∣	Ditch

N

QUESTION 3

Indicate with a tick which of the following huts is typical of the Iron Age following the descriptions given in the passage.

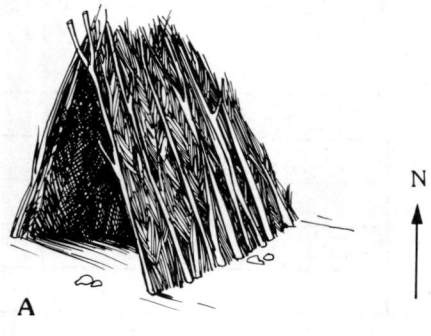

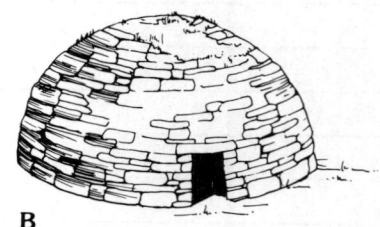

N

A   B

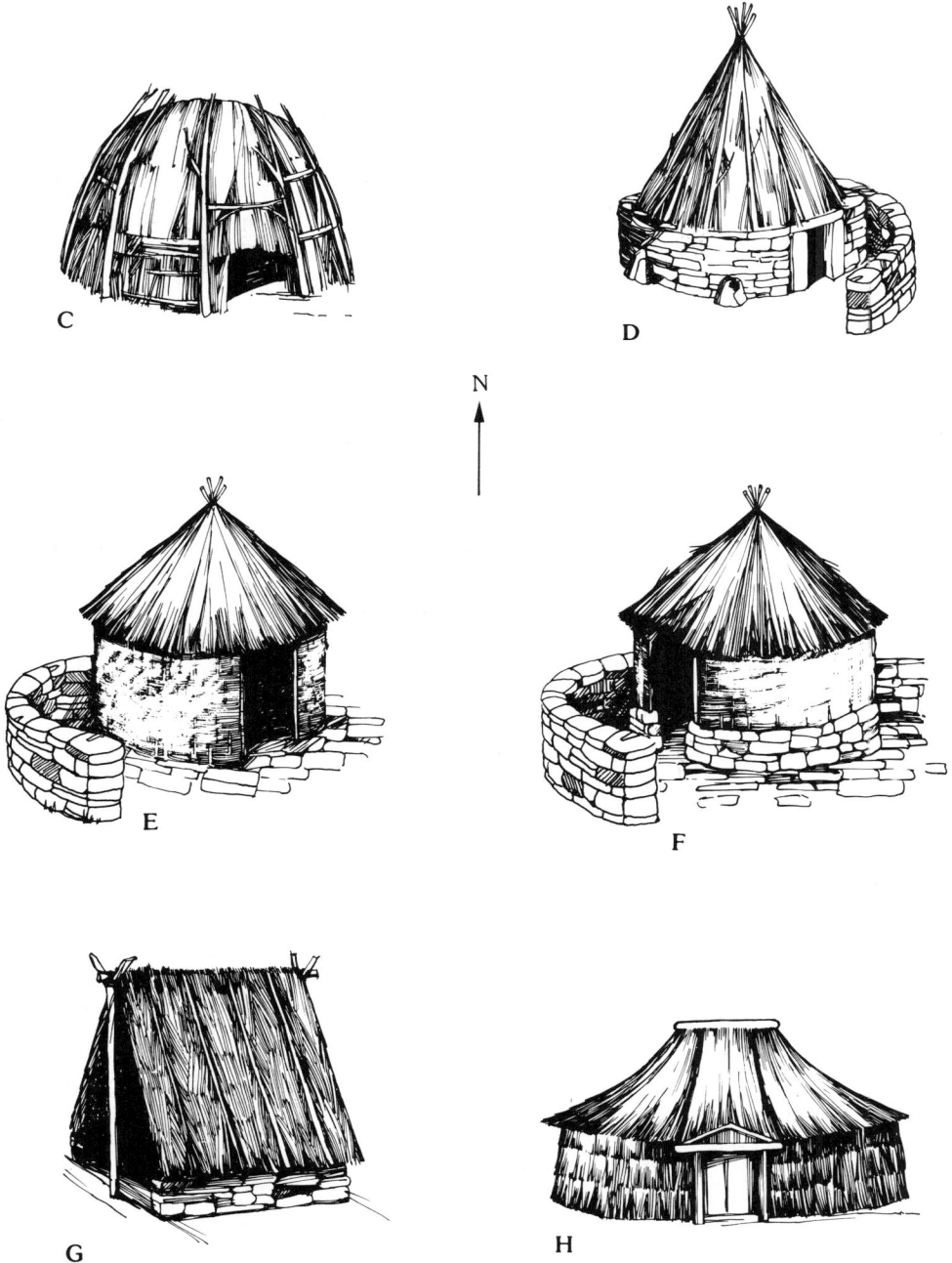

QUESTION 4

Complete the table by matching up the two halves of the following five sentences.

1. Stone benches were placed against the wall
2. Inside the cooking pit would have been a pot with water and meat
3. Clay loomweights were found
4. We know that trading took place with distant settlements
5. This discovery is very important

A. which indicates that the people could weave cloth.
B. because it had previously been thought that this activity began a thousand years later.
C. and covered with heather or skins.
D. which was cooked by dropping hot stones from the fire into the pit.
E. because salt containers were found that had been made some distance away.

1		4	
2		5	
3			

Roman Forts

Listen to the descriptions of three Roman structures, the marching camp, the fort and the fortress. Each section will be read twice and is followed by a question. After the second readings you will be given time to answer the relevant question. You may take notes during the readings.

QUESTION 1

Draw a plan of a marching camp as it would have looked from above, using the symbols given in the key. You will have 4 minutes to do this.

Key

Tents	△
Bank	⬭
Ditch	⊔⊔⊔⊔⊔
Palisade	○ ○ ○ ○
Entrance	E

QUESTION 2 (a)

Draw a plan of the fort as seen from above, using the symbols defined in the key. You will have 7 minutes to do both parts.

Key

B	Barracks
G	Granary
CH	Commandant's house
H	Hospital
HQ	Headquarters
E	Entrance
T	Tower
S	Stables
⊔⊥⊔⊔	Ditch
∴∵∴	Berm

↑
N

QUESTION 2 (b)

Draw a cross section of the wall and ditch, using the symbols defined in the key.

Key

P	Parapet
B	Berm
D	Ditch
W	Wall

QUESTION 3

Draw a plan of a shore fortress, as seen from above, using symbols given in the key. You will have 4 minutes to do this.

Key

Drum towers	○
Ditch	⊥⊥⊥⊥⊥⊥
Entrance	E
Sea	～～～

The History of the Horse

Study the ten sentences below. Then listen to the passage outlining the history of the horse—it will be read three times in all. After the second reading you will have 5 minutes to complete the table. During the third reading you should check your answer. You will then have a further 2 minutes to finalise your answer.

QUESTION

Complete the table by putting the ten sentences in their correct chronological order: that is, in the correct sequence in time in which the events occurred.

A   The use of horses for sport was first recorded.
B   The first horse race was recorded in England.
C   The Greeks are known to have used horses to draw chariots.
D   Horse sports became popular in England.
E   Arab horses were imported into Britain for breeding purposes.
F   Nomadic tribesmen domesticated the horse for the first time.
G   A wild ancestor of the horse became extinct.
H   Horse stealing became a capital offence in England.
I   The Egyptians bred a horse strong enough to be ridden.
J   Horses were used for driving chariots into battle in Europe.

1		6	
2		7	
3		8	
4		9	
5		10	

The Horse—Parts of a Horse

Listen to the explanation of some of the most commonly used terms associated with a horse's body. The passage will be read twice and you will then have 7 minutes to complete the table. You may take notes.

―――――――――――――――――――――――― QUESTION ――――――

Complete the table overleaf by identifying the numbered parts of the horse, using the following words:

dock, knee, girth, fetlock, tail, withers, croup, near-hind leg, hock, mane, near-foreleg, muzzle, off-foreleg, forelock, off-hindleg, back, fetlock joint, hoof.

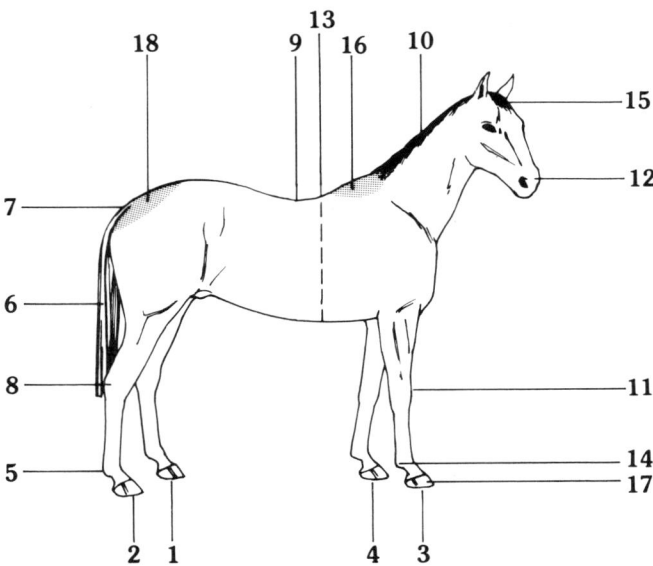

331

1		10	
2		11	
3		12	
4		13	
5		14	
6		15	
7		16	
8		17	
9		18	

The Horse—Colours

Study the drawings A–J of different colour types of horses. Then listen to the description of the classification of horses by colour. The passage will be read twice. After the second reading you will have 10 minutes to identify the colour types and complete the table accordingly.

QUESTION

Complete the table using the following words to identify the different colour types of horses:

skewbald, palomino, dun, piebald, dapple, roan, bay.

If a type illustrated is not described in the passage, put an X in the table.

A		F	
B		G	
C		H	
D		I	
E		J	

A

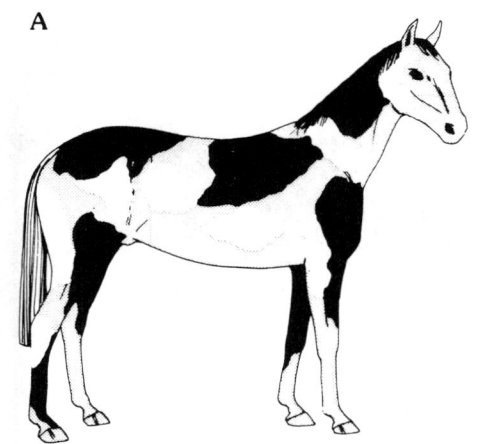

B

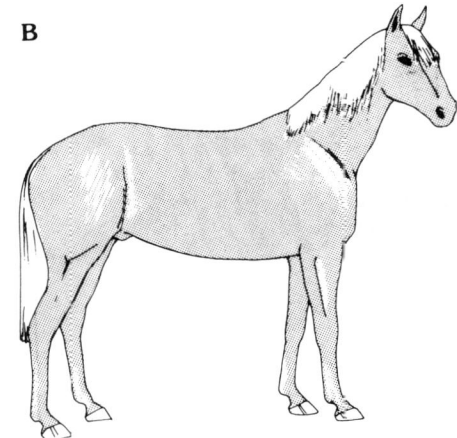

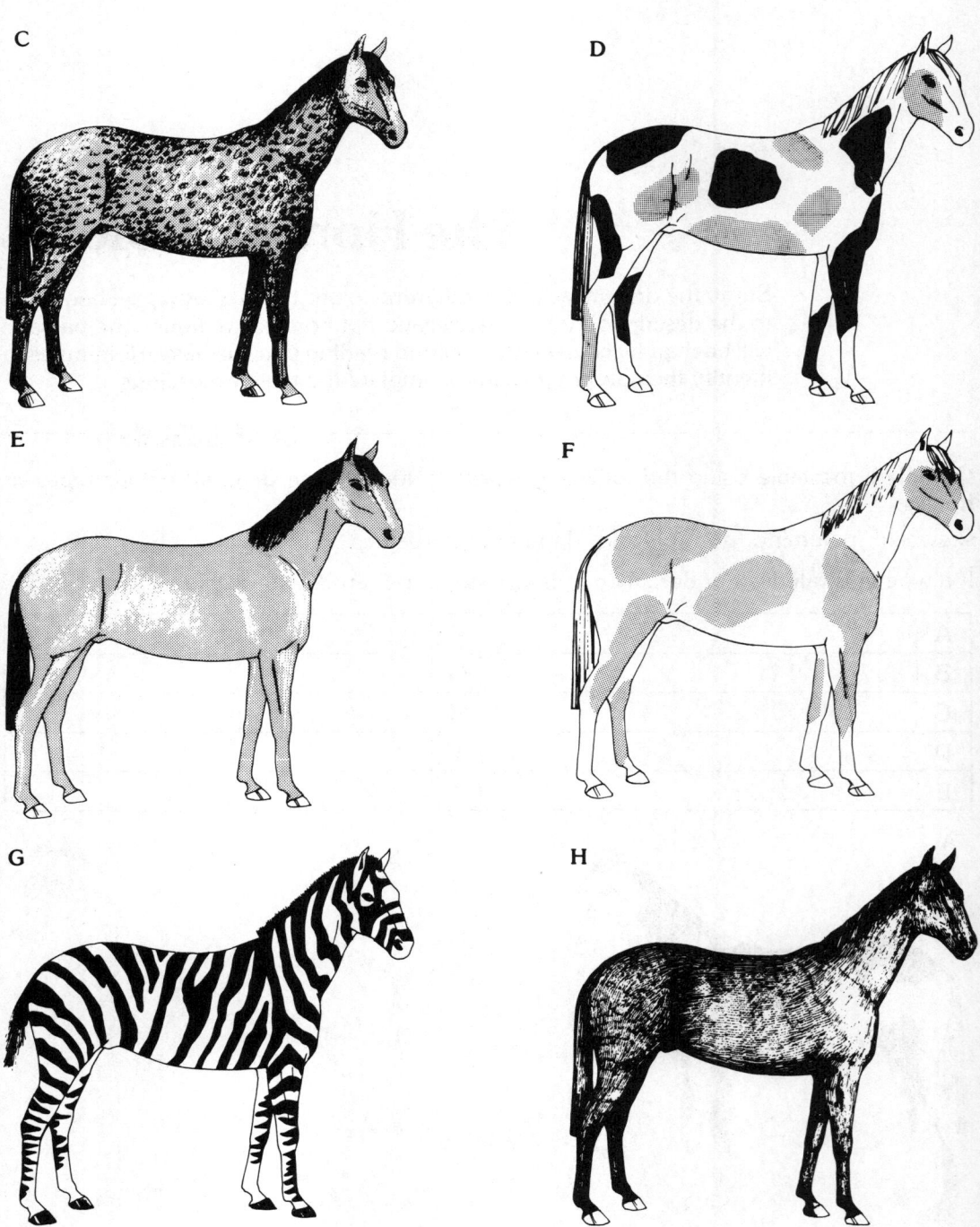

I

J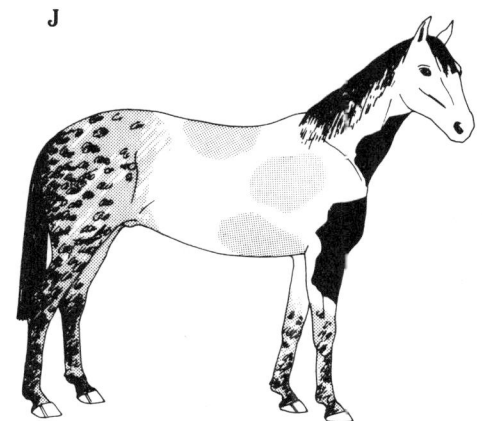

The Horse—Breeds

Study the ten drawings of horses and ponies. Then listen to the description of six different breeds—each section will be read twice. The entire passage will then be read straight through. After the last reading you will have 10 minutes to complete the table.

QUESTION

Complete the table by identifying the different breeds of horse and pony from the drawings, using the names:

Shire, Shetland pony, New Forest pony, West Highland pony, Connemara pony, Exmoor pony.

If a drawing does not represent any of the ponies or horses described, put an X in the table. There may be more than one example of the breeds described.

A		F	
B		G	
C		H	
D		I	
E		J	

337

Wiring-Up a Three-Pin Plug

Listen to the passage which describes the wiring-up of a three-pin plug. It will be read three times in all. You may take notes during the first reading. During the second reading start to complete the table in Question 1—after the reading you will have 10 minutes to finish it. When you have heard the reading for the third time you will have a further 10 minutes to complete the tables in Questions 2 and 3.

QUESTION 1

Complete the table by listing the stages A–O in the correct sequence.

A Remove the fuse.
B Screw down the cord grip.
C Screw the back of the plug into place.
D Connect the wires to the appropriate terminals.
E Loosen the two small screws holding the cord grip.
F Loosen all three terminal screws.
G Pass the cable under the cord grip.
H Loosen the screw in the centre of the plug and remove back.
I Strip back the outer sheathing of cable and apply insulation tape if necessary.
J Tighten the terminals to prevent the wires being pulled out.
K Position the wires against the terminals and cut them to length.
L Twist the core of fine copper wires to avoid loose strands.
M Insert the appropriate fuse.
N Remove coloured insulation from each of the wires.
O Shake the plug to make sure nothing is loose.

1		9	
2		10	
3		11	
4		12	
5		13	
6		14	
7		15	
8			

QUESTION 2

Complete the table by matching up the two halves of the following sentences.

1	Some cable contains only two separate wires, live and neutral;	A	but you must do so if you are using braided cable which tends to fray.
2	The live wire is covered in brown plastic insulation, following an international code;	B	it ensures that the body of the appliance is kept at earth potential.
3	A 13 A fuse is the largest fuse used for a domestic appliance;	C	it is used for small appliances taking a low current, such as a transistor radio.
4	It is not always necessary to use insulation tape,	D	such as PVC, butyl, silicone rubber, or heavy-duty rubber covered in braid.
5	There are two small screws at the base of a three-pin plug;	E	such as black and white television sets, food-mixers, and record players.
6	Cable is covered in different insulating materials depending on its weight and what it is going to be used for,	F	they hold the cord grip over the cable where it enters the plug.
7	The green and yellow striped wire is connected to the earth terminal;	G	it is used for appliances taking a large current, such as colour televisions, vacuum cleaners and electric heaters.
8	3 A fuses are used for appliances that require a low current,	H	it must be connected to the live terminal with the fuse.
9	If the plug rattles when you shake it,	I	you must be careful not to cut the wires with the strippers.
10	When you remove the coloured insulation from each wire	J	it has not been wired-up correctly.

1		6	
2		7	
3		8	
4		9	
5		10	

QUESTION 3

Identify the parts of the electric cable and plug shown in the diagram, and complete the table using the following words:

cable, neutral wire, fuse, cord grip, live wire, sheathing, earth wire, earth pin, neutral terminal, exposed core of fine wires.

1		6	
2		7	
3		8	
4		9	
5		10	

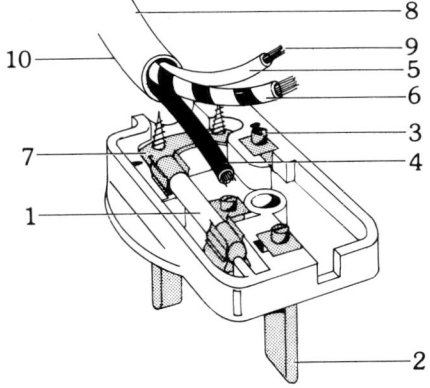

Screws, Nails and Bolts

Listen to the description of screws, nails and bolts, their uses and the tools used in working with them. The passage is divided into three parts followed by a question. Each part will be read twice and you will be given time for the question before the next part is begun. Look at the diagrams in Question 1 before the reading.

QUESTION 1

Identify the parts of the screw as labelled in diagrams A and B and complete Table 1 and Table 2, respectively. If a feature is not described, put an X in the table. You will have 3 minutes to do this.

Use the following words:

head, pitch, slot, thread, root, length, shank, crest and gauge.

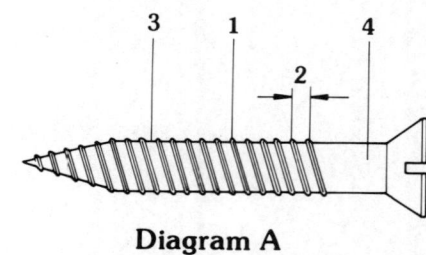

Diagram A

Table 1

1	
2	
3	
4	

342

Table 2

1	
2	
3	
4	
5	
6	

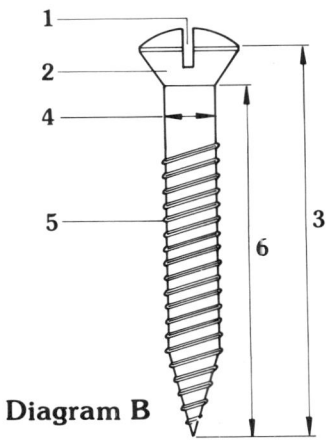

Diagram B

QUESTION 2

Indicate which of the diagrams A–E shows the correct use of a screwdriver by putting either a tick (√) or a cross (X) in the table. You will have 1 minute to do this.

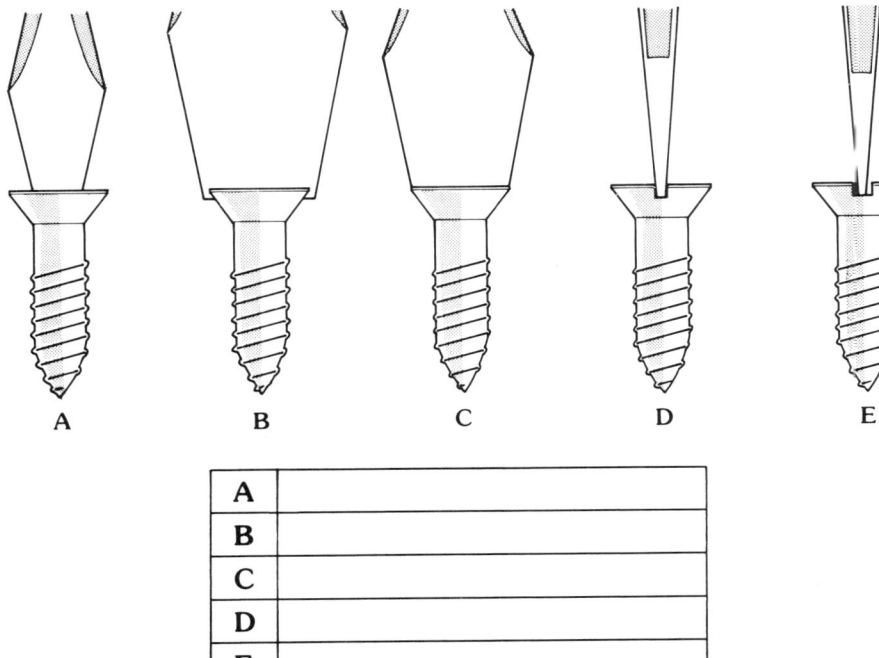

A	
B	
C	
D	
E	

343

QUESTION 3

Study the diagrams A–O of screws, nails and bolts—note particularly their shapes, heads and threads. Complete the table by identifying the diagrams, saying in each case which tool should be used. The diagrams of the different tools are at the end of the question. Use the following words:

Column 1

nail bolt, countersunk screw, raised-head screw, round-head screw, dome-head screw, Pozidriv screw, Philips screw, dowel screw, coach screw, handrail screw, self-tapping screw.

Column 2

pliers, spanner, screwdriver, Pozidriv screwdriver, hammer.

If a diagram does not represent any of the types described, put an X in the table. You will have 10 minutes to complete this section.

Diagram	1—Type of screw, nail or bolt	2—Tool used
A		
B		
C		
D		
E		
F		
G		
H		
I		
J		
K		
L		
M		
N		
O		

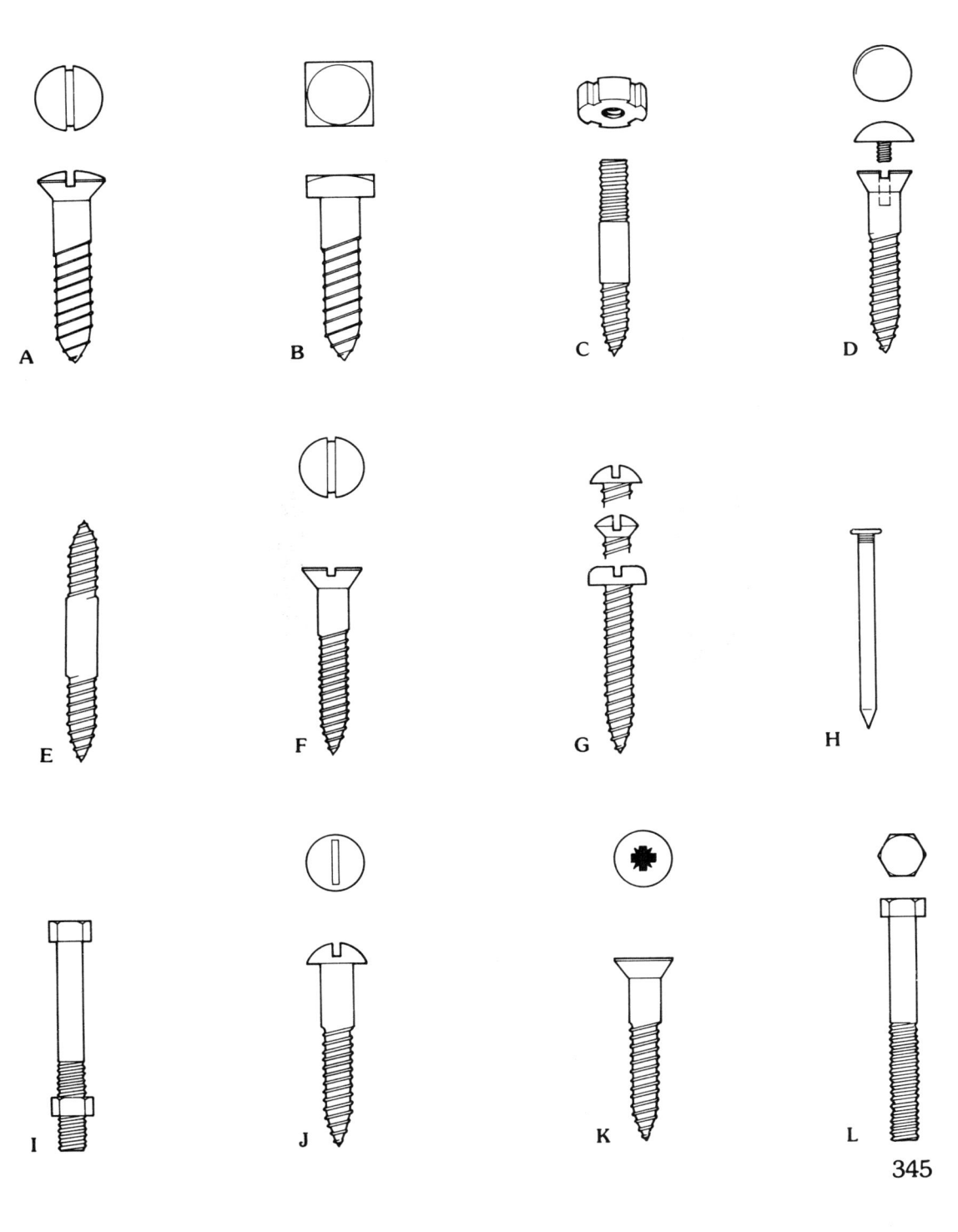

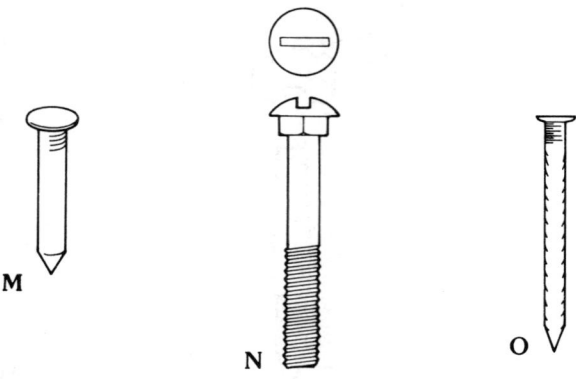

Tools used for fixing nails, screws and bolts

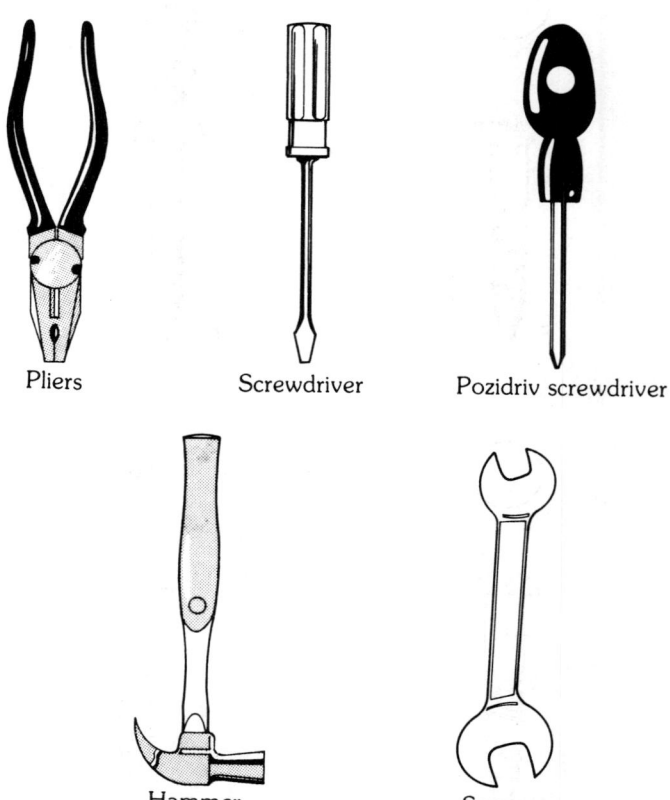

Castleburgh

Listen to the description of the town of Castleburgh and its surroundings, and the discussion of some of the events that have occurred since as far back as the Iron Age. The passage will be read three times in all. After the second reading you will be given 3 minutes to think about the questions and after the last reading you will have 5 minutes to answer the questions. You may take notes during the readings.

Before listening to the passage, take some time to look at the map in Question 1 (overleaf) and read through the fifteen sentences in Question 2.

QUESTION 1

Complete Keys (a) and (b) to the map using the following words:
Key (a) coniferous woodland, natural woodland, moorland, grazing land.
Key (b) mines, hillfort, castle, museum, reservoir, church.

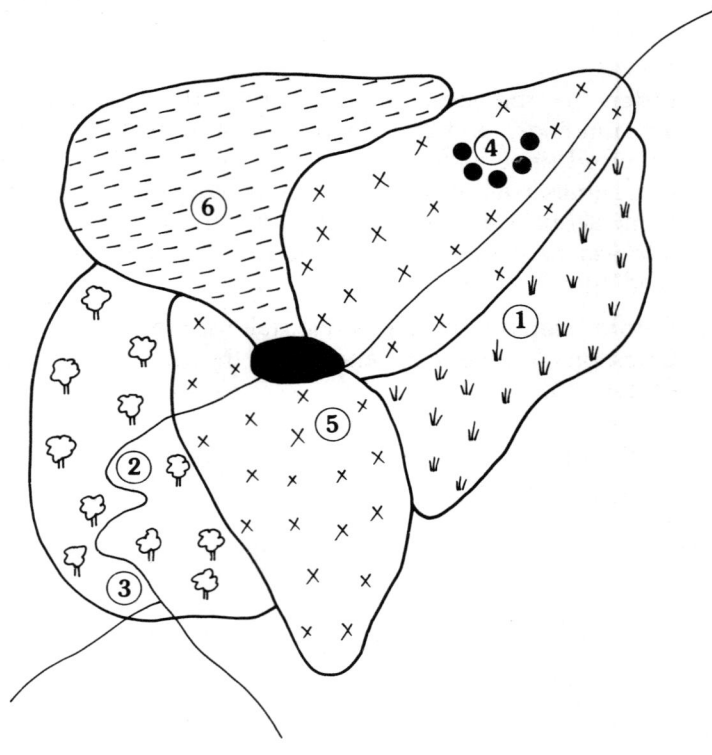

Key (a)

🌳 🌳	
⋎ ⋎	
─ ─ ─	
× × ×	

Key (b)

1	
2	
3	
4	
5	
6	

QUESTION 2

Complete the table by putting the following fifteen sentences in their correct chronological order.

A   The Normans built a castle in the area.
B   The lead mines were closed for economic reasons.
C   The Romans destroyed the hillfort.
D   Christianity came to the north from Ireland.
E   The plague killed half the population of Castleburgh.
F   The Celts built a hillfort.
G   The Saxons built a church in the area.
H   A cottage became a museum.
I   The emperor Hadrian visited Britain.
J   The king of Kent became a Christian.
K   The Dark Ages began.
L   The reservoir was constructed.
M   The Romans had to leave.
N   A wall was built from coast to coast.
O   The Romans came to occupy Britain.

1		9	
2		10	
3		11	
4		12	
5		13	
6		14	
7		15	
8			

St. Mary's Church—Inside

Listen to the description of the inside of St. Mary's Church. The passage will be read twice. You will then be given 5 minutes to answer Question 1 and a further 5 minutes to answer Question 2. Before the reading, look at the words in Question 1 and the sentences in Question 2.

QUESTION 1

Complete the table by identifying the inside parts of St. Mary's Church from the plan, using the following words:

altar, tower, rood screen, font, sacristy, choir stalls, north aisle, porch, chancel, south aisle, nave, pulpit, north transept, altar screen, south transept.

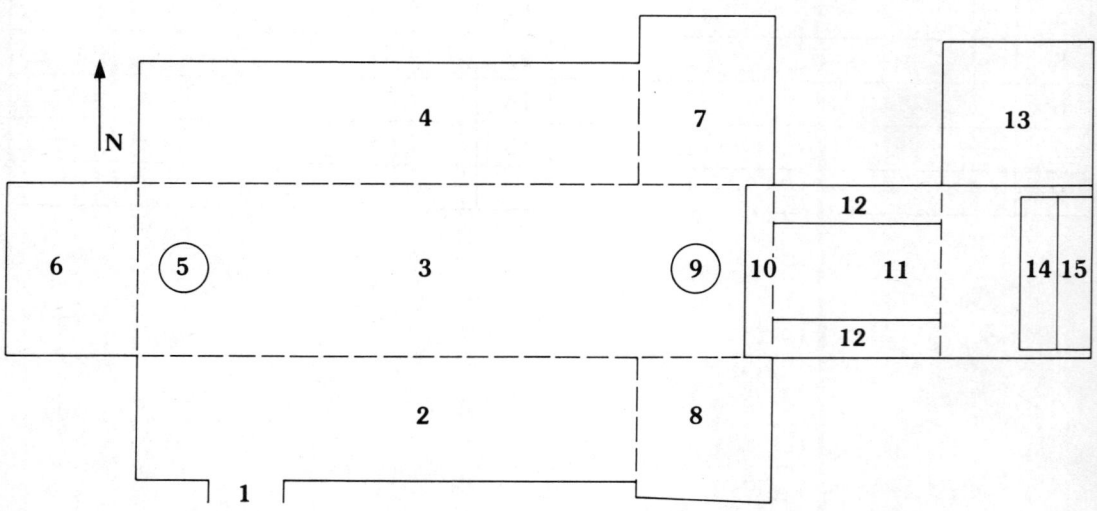

1		9	
2		10	
3		11	
4		12	
5		13	
6		14	
7		15	
8			

QUESTION 2

Complete the table by putting the following ten sentences in the correct chronological order according to the passage.

A   The porch was built on the south wall.
B   The tower was added.
C   The rood screen was given by the carpenters' guild.
D   Elizabeth I ordered rood screens to be destroyed.
E   The east end was squared off.
F   The spire was added to the tower.
G   The original Norman church was built.
H   The priests were no longer separated from the people in the church.
I   The south aisle was widened.
J   There was a further extension outwards from the nave and the windows were widened.

1		6	
2		7	
3		8	
4		9	
5		10	

St. Mary's Church—Outside

Listen to the description of the outside features of St. Mary's Church. The passage will be read twice and you will then have 10 minutes to answer the questions.

QUESTION 1

Complete the table by naming the numbered parts of the drawing using the following words:

parapet, spirelight, finial, louvre, spire, buttress, belfry, tower, weathervane, turret.

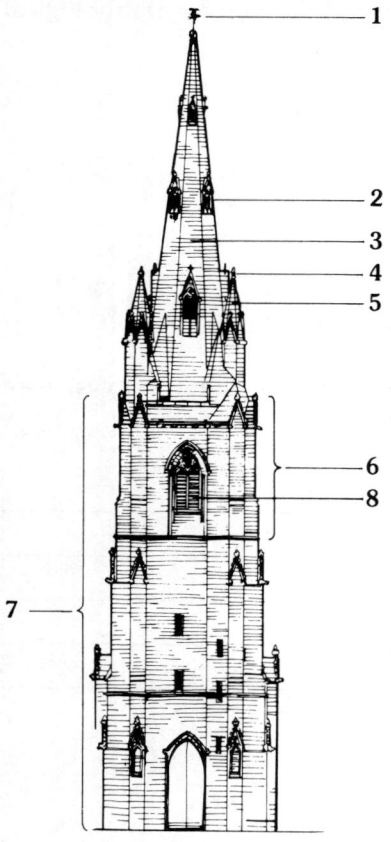

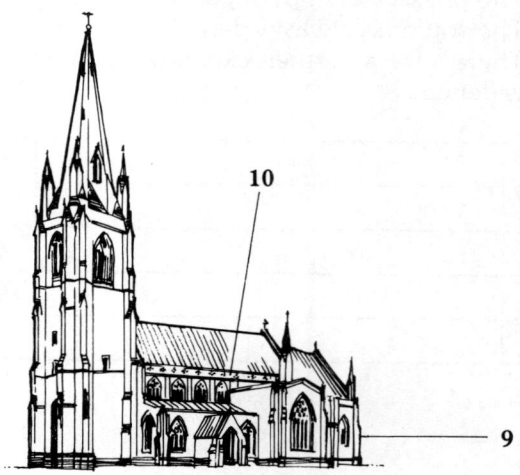

1		6	
2		7	
3		8	
4		9	
5		10	

QUESTION 2

Complete the diagram by inserting the names of the following periods of English architecture in the correct chronological order.

Perpendicular, Norman, Decorated, Early English, Anglo-Saxon, Gothic.

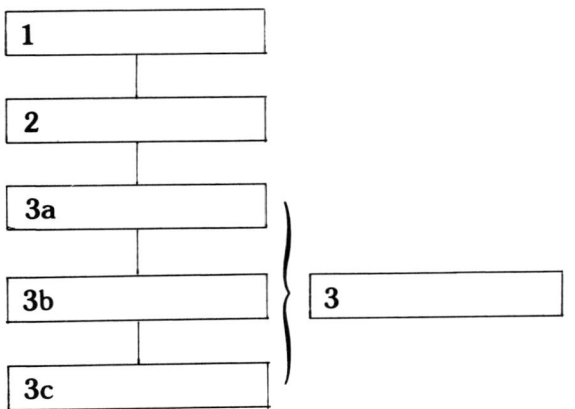

Buttresses

Listen to the description of different types of buttresses. The passage is divided into two parts. Each part will be read twice and will be followed by a question. You will have 10 minutes to answer each of the questions.

QUESTION 1

Complete the table by identifying the buttress types illustrated in the following ten drawings, using the descriptions:

flying buttress, clasping buttress, set-back buttress, diagonal buttress, angle buttress.

If a buttress type has not been described, put an X in the table on page 356.

C

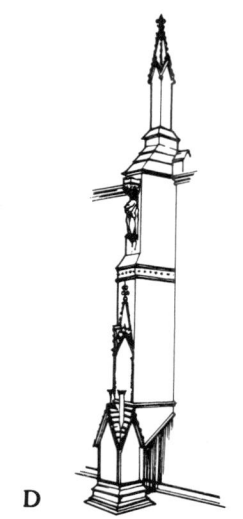

D

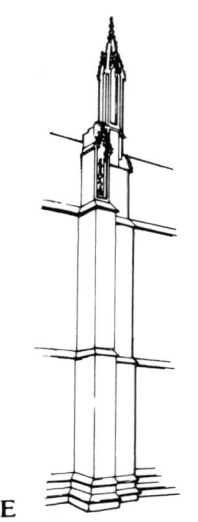

E

F

355

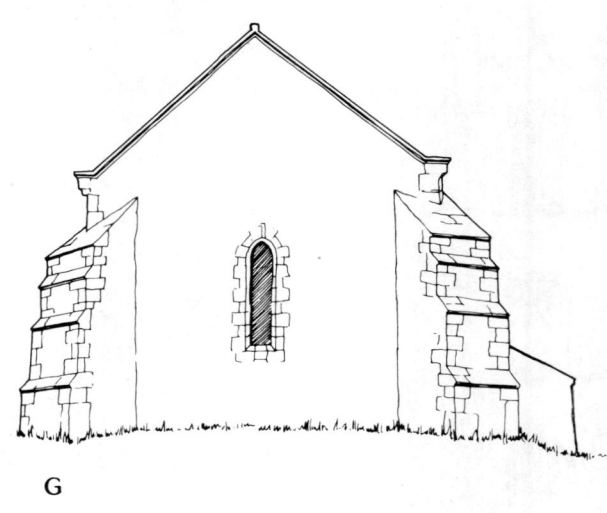

G

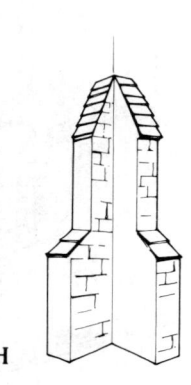

H

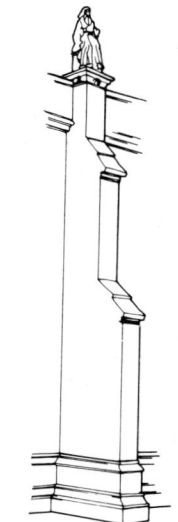

I

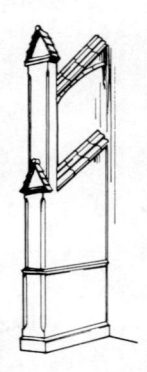

J

Drawing	Buttress type	Drawing	Buttress type
A		F	
B		G	
C		H	
D		I	
E		J	

356

QUESTION 2

(a) Complete table (1) by identifying the period of architecture for the following fifteen buttress types illustrated overleaf. Use the words:

Perpendicular, Early English, Norman, Decorated, Perpendicular flying, Early English flying, Decorated flying.

(b) Complete table (2) by identifying the buttress features a–h shown in the illustrations. Use the words:

pinnacle, finial, capital, plinth, gable, niche, canopy, set-off.

You will have 10 minutes to do both sections.

(1)

A		I	
B		J	
C		K	
D		L	
E		M	
F		N	
G		O	
H			

(2)

a		e	
b		f	
c		g	
d		h	

357

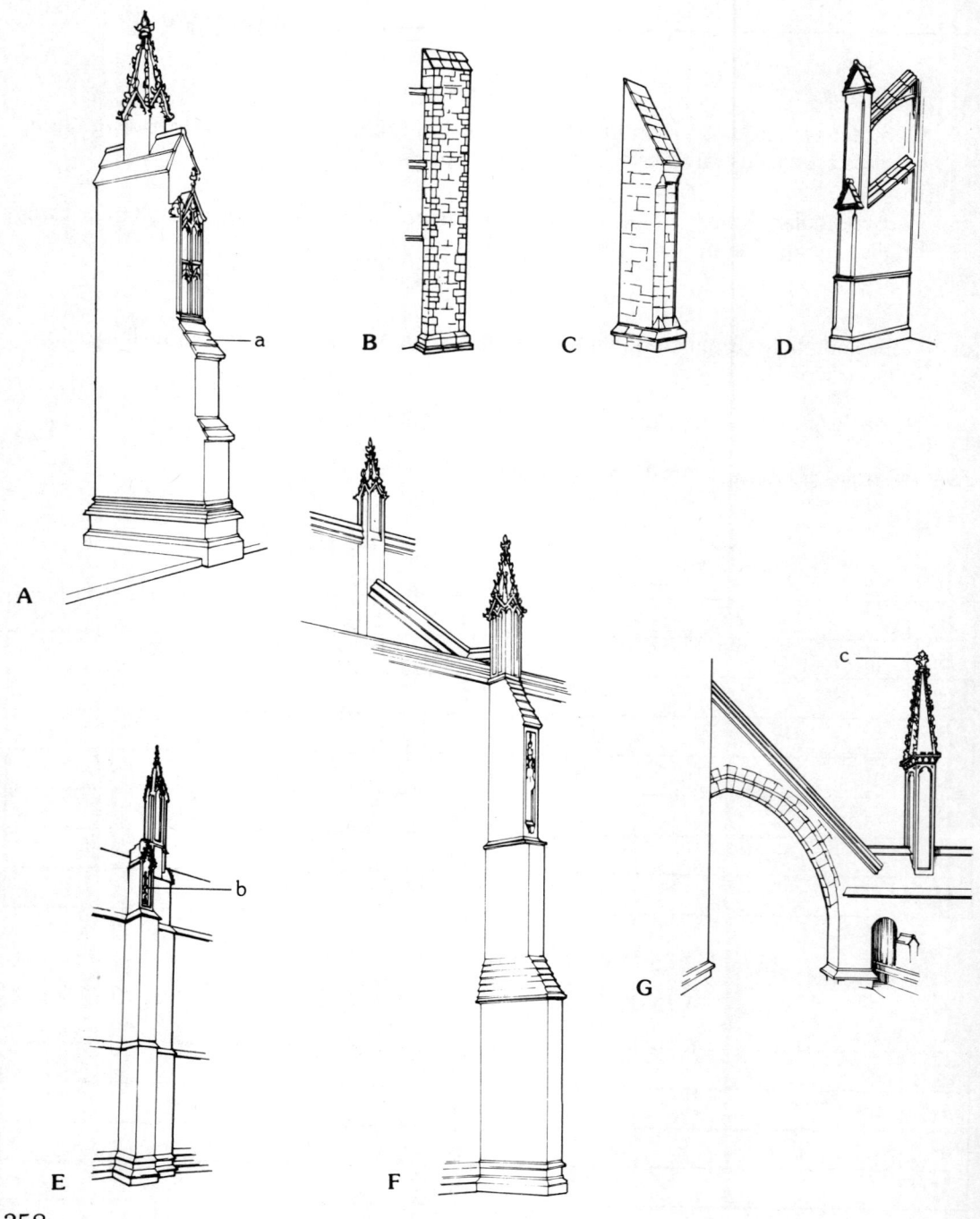

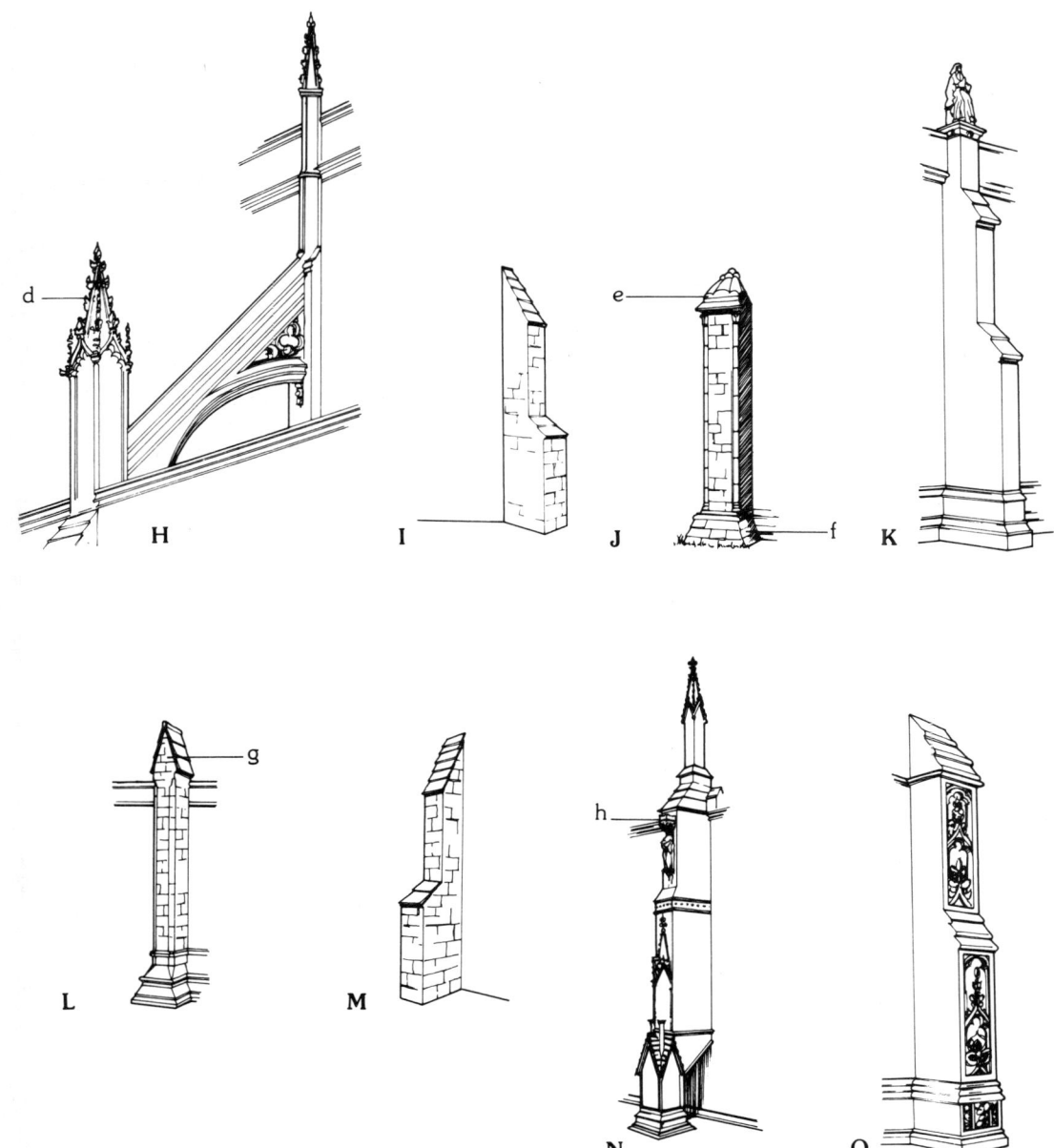

Triangles

Listen carefully to the discussion on triangles. The passage will be read twice. During the second reading complete the table defining all the terms mentioned in the passage. The information you write in this table will help you to answer Questions 1, 2 and 3. After the second reading you will have 15 minutes to answer the questions. A final passage will be read, involving construction using triangles. You will then have 10 minutes to answer Question 4.

TABLE

Term	Definition
Equilateral triangle	
Isosceles triangle	
Scalene triangle	
Congruent triangle	
Acute-angled triangle	
Obtuse-angled triangle	
Right-angled triangle	
Similar triangle	
Base	
Altitude	
Base angles	
Vertex	
Median	
Sides	
Vertical angle	
Centroid	
Incentre	
Circumcentre	
Orthocentre	

QUESTION 1

Look at Figures 1–7. State any conclusions you can draw from the figures in the key below. Figure 1 has been done for you as an example.

Fig.	Conclusions
1	All the sides and internal angles are equal. Angles = 60°. Equilateral triangle.
2	BQ is called
3	
4	If AC is 6 metres, how long is AO?
5	
6	
7	

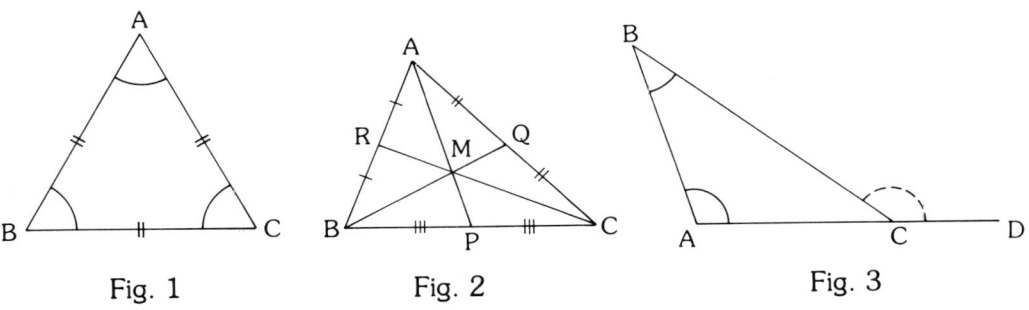

Fig. 1   Fig. 2   Fig. 3

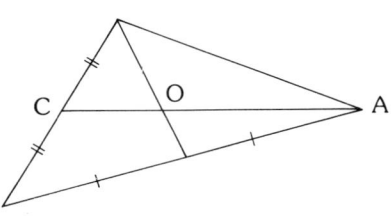

Fig. 4

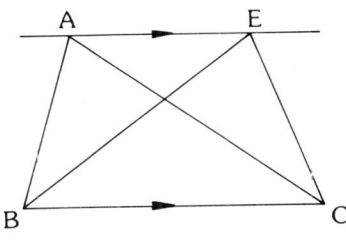

Fig. 5

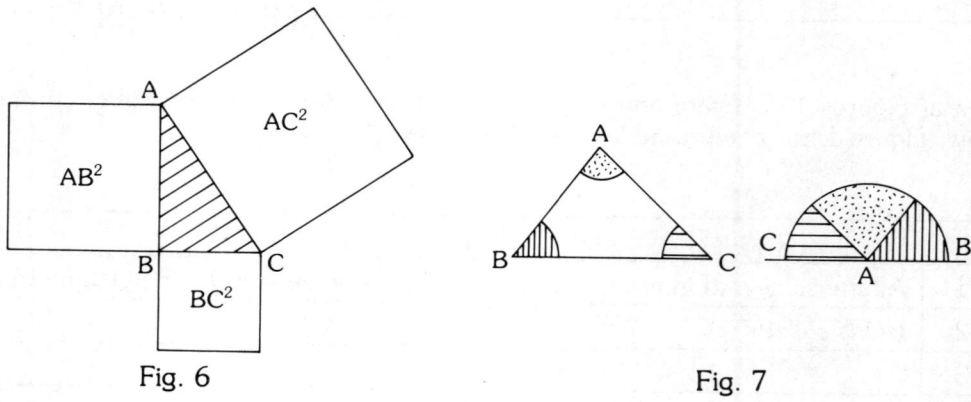

Fig. 6   Fig. 7

QUESTION 2—Triangle types

Look at the following ten triangles. Identify them using the following:

congruent, isosceles, obtuse-angled, scalene, equilateral, similar, acute-angled, right-angled.

There may be more than one example of some of the types.

Fig.	Type	Fig.	Type
8		13	
9		14	
10		15	
11		16	
12		17	

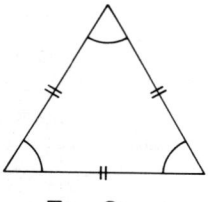

Fig. 8

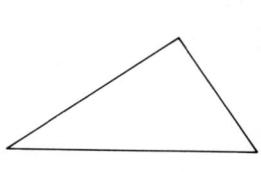

Fig. 9

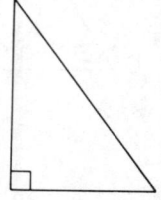

Fig. 10

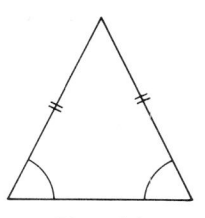
Fig. 11

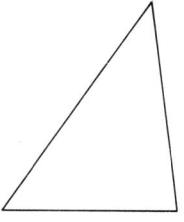
Fig. 12

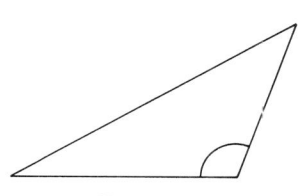
Fig. 13

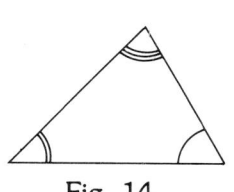
Fig. 14

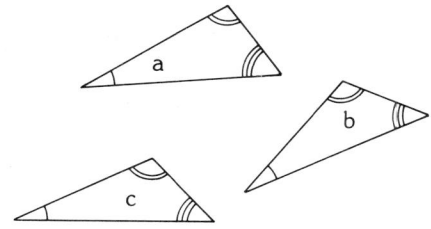
Fig. 15

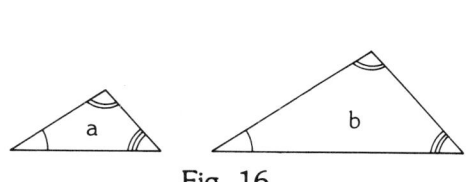
Fig. 16

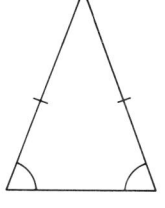
Fig. 17

QUESTION 3—Properties of a triangle

Look at the triangles in Figs. 18 and 19. Identify the properties of a triangle by completing the key below. The first part for Fig. 18 has been done as an example.

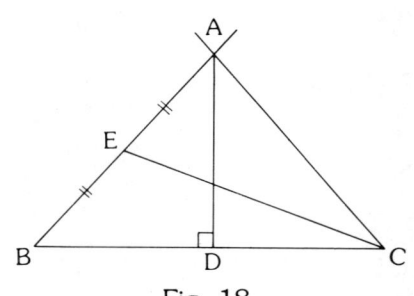

Fig. 18

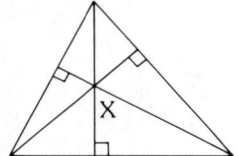 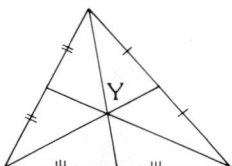 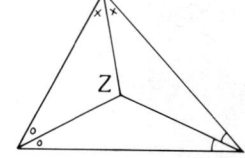 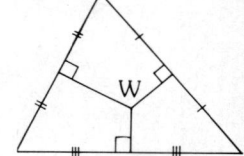

Fig. 19

Fig.		Properties
18	Base Height/altitude Base angle Vertex Vertical angle Side Median	BC
19	Orthocentre Centroid Incentre Circumcentre	

QUESTION 4—Construction

Listen to the passages and construct the figures in the ways described. Identify types, lengths and angles as instructed. For the last figure, use the key shown to shade in the triangles.

△ ABC is ....
∡ ABC measures ....
△ BDC is ....

AD is ....
∡ ADC measures ....
ADC is ....

∡ ADB measures ....

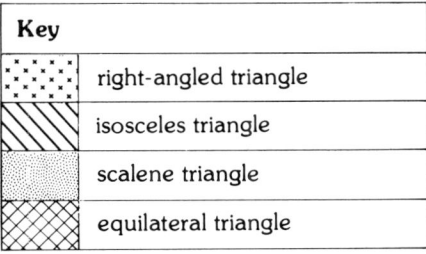

Key	
	right-angled triangle
	isosceles triangle
	scalene triangle
	equilateral triangle

Neolithic and Bronze Age Pottery

Listen to the account of Neolithic and Bronze Age pottery. The passage is divided into two parts, each followed by a question. Each part will be read twice and you will then have 10 minutes to answer the relevant question. You may take notes. During the second reading of the second part you are asked to summarise the information in a table to help you with your answer to Question 2.

QUESTION 1

Complete the table by matching up the two halves of the following ten sentences.

1 Red patches occurred on some early pottery

2 Some early pottery was coarse and heavily pitted

3 Slip is a thin layer of clay added to a pot.

4 The Beaker people appear to have grown more barley than wheat

5 The study of ancient pottery is of great importance

6 We are able to reconstruct pots from shards or fragments of the original vessels

7 Prehistoric pottery was produced by tribes or individual village people, each with its own design,

A because the firing process was not even.

B excluding oxygen in the firing process so that carbon monoxide was predominant.

C because ground shells and pieces of flint and chalk were added to the clay mixture before firing.

D by firing the pot in an oxidising atmosphere.

E which makes it more decorative and less likely to leak.

F but they exhausted the soil of nutrients by such methods and were forced to move on.

G as a result of the widespread destruction of farming land by Neolithic man who did not manure his fields.

8 Prehistoric man was able to make red pottery

9 Neolithic farmers made clearings in the forests so that they could grow their crops

10 A black pot could be made by

H which have remained in the soil for thousands of years but have not decayed because they are extremely durable.

I because it can tell archaeologists how early man lived, moved around and developed his culture.

J and the distribution of such artifacts shows the extent of trade and communication.

1		6	
2		7	
3		8	
4		9	
5		10	

Complete this table during the second reading of the second part of the passage. It will help you with your answer to Question 2.

Name of pottery	Wall type	Base type	Rim type	Decoration
Primary Neolithic				
Peterborough				
Grooved ware (a)				
(b)				
(c)				
Bell beaker				
Barrel beaker				
Long-necked beaker				
Short-necked beaker				

QUESTION 2

Complete the table by identifying the twenty pots illustrated, using the names given in the previous table. If a pot has not been described, put an X in the table.

A		K	
B		L	
C		M	
D		N	
E		O	
F		P	
G		Q	
H		R	
I		S	
J		T	

A

B

C

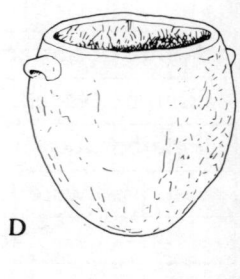

D

368

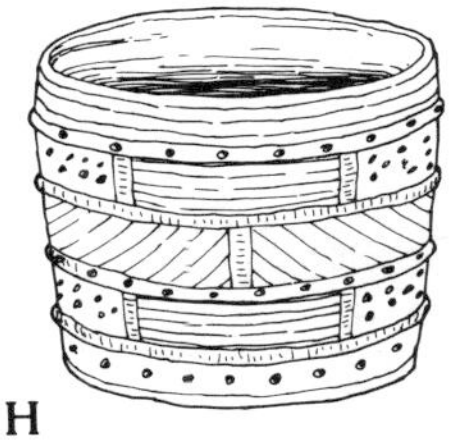

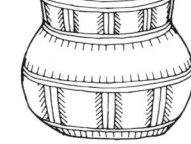

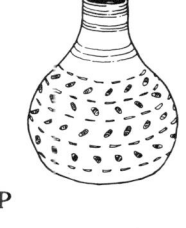

Q

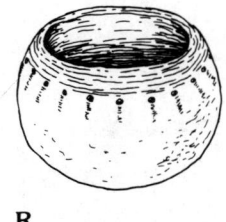

R

S

T

Gears

Listen to the passage describing different kinds of gears—each section will be read twice. While you are listening, summarise the information in the table in Question 1; it will help you to identify the gear types in Question 2. After the second reading you will have 10 minutes to answer Question 2.

QUESTION 1

While listening to the passage, write down the chief characteristics of each type of gear listed in the table.

Type of gear	Characteristic; e.g. spiral teeth, cone-shaped etc.
Straight bevel	
External spur	
Internal spur	
Hypoid bevel	
Single helical	
Worm gear	
Spiral bevel	
Internal helical	
Double helical	
Rack and pinion	

QUESTION 2

Study the diagrams A–Q overleaf and then identify the types of gears illustrated. Use the information summarised in Question 1. If a diagram does not represent any of the types described, put an X in the table. There may be more than one example of some types of gear.

Diagram	Type of gear	Diagram	Type of gear
A		J	
B		K	
C		L	
D		M	
E		N	
F		O	
G		P	
H		Q	
I			

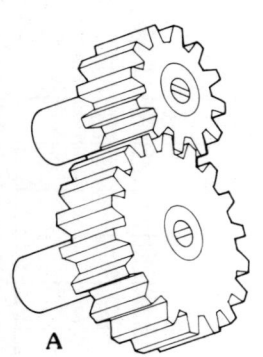
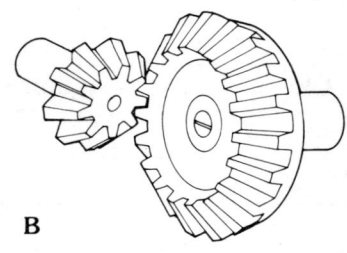
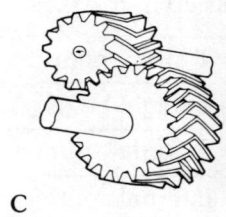
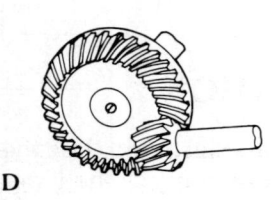
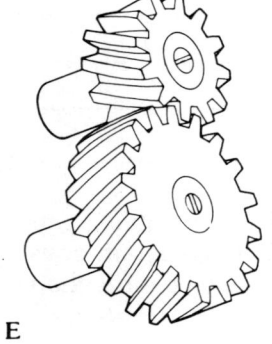
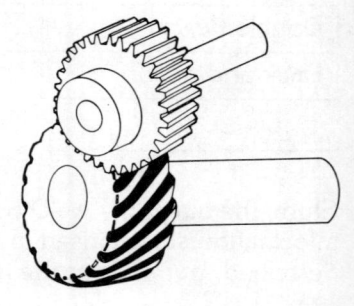

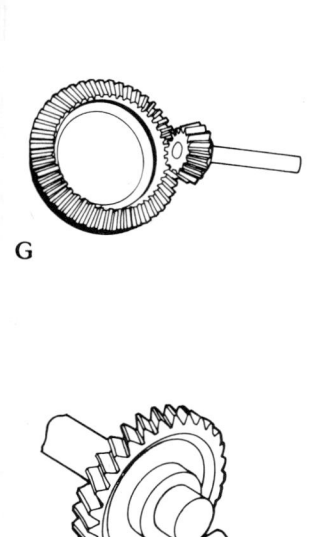

G

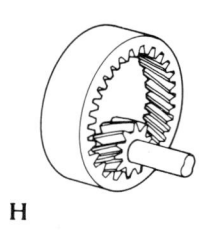

H

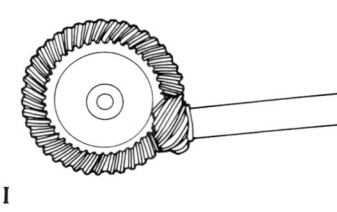

I

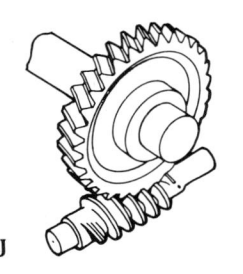

J

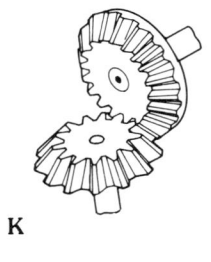

K

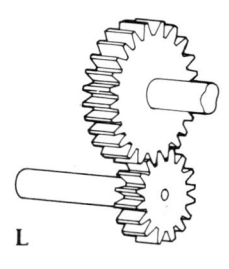

L

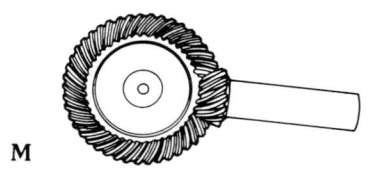

M

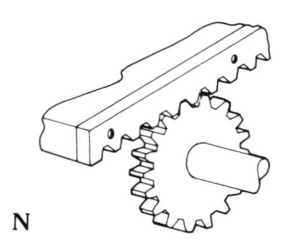

N

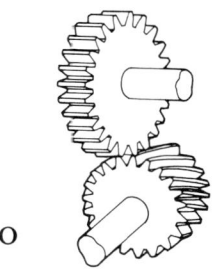

O

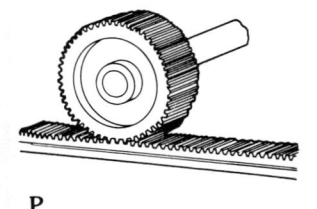

P

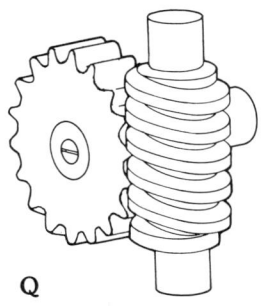

Q

The City of Norwich

Listen to the account of the history of the City of Norwich. It will be read three times in all. After the second reading you will have 10 minutes to answer Question 1, and after the third reading you should answer Question 2. You will have 5 minutes to do this. You may take notes during the readings to help you.

QUESTION 1

Complete the table by putting the following fifteen sentences A–O in the correct chronological order.

- A The cathedral was damaged by fire.
- B The city bought a priory church.
- C Norwich lost half of its inhabitants from plague.
- D A small tribe from East Anglia rose against the Romans.
- E Norwich had its first mayor.
- F More than 30 000 houses were destroyed in Norwich.
- G A stone castle replaced the wooden one.
- H The church of St. Peter Mancroft was built.
- I People from across the sea settled in East Anglia.
- J The cathedral spire was replaced.
- K A former mayor's house became a craft museum.
- L The name of Norwich appeared on coins for the first time.
- M The remains of a Norman castle became a museum.
- N Work began on the cathedral.
- O The people of Norwich were forced by invaders to build a castle.

1		9	
2		10	
3		11	
4		12	
5		13	
6		14	
7		15	
8			

QUESTION 2

Complete the table overleaf by matching up the two halves of the following ten sentences to obtain a coherent statement.

1 Norwich has known great prosperity in its history

2 A subjugated tribe rebelled against their Roman oppressors

3 After the White Tower in the Tower of London

4 This building has been a private dwelling, a prison, and a factory;

5 The grandson of Alfred the Great

6 The Iceni destroyed the Roman administrative centre south of Norwich;

7 Red dye was made from the roots of this plant and sold to clothmakers during the Middle Ages;

8 This museum takes its name from the immigrant weavers who once lived there;

A its magnificent hammer-beam roof and rare 15th century stained glass must be seen.

B it originally belonged to the first Mayor of Norwich.

C but it has also suffered great loss.

D the church of St. John Maddermarket takes its name from it.

E today it illustrates domestic life from the 16th to the 19th centuries.

F but they were defeated and their queen killed herself.

G it was from here that stone was brought to build the cathedral and churches in Norwich.

H it stands in the market place and is now used as a magistrates' court.

9 This church, where Sir Thomas Browne is buried, is the finest in Norwich;

I this castle has the largest keep in England.

10 This building, which was begun in 1407, has been used as a centre of local government and a prison;

J was the first ruler of all England.

1		6	
2		7	
3		8	
4		9	
5		10	

Civilisation and the Natural World

Listen to the description of some of the ways in which humans have domesticated and cultivated the natural world around them. The passage will be read to you in sections which will be repeated once. You will be allowed to make notes to help you. Then you will be asked to answer Question 1, filling in the *centre column* of the table with the *steps* in the chronological order in which they happened. The whole passage will then be read a third time. Then you will be asked to answer Question 2, filling in the *last column* of the table with the number of the *result* statement which matches the step in the centre column. You now have 5 minutes to study the steps. (After Question 1 you will be given 5 minutes to study the list of results.)

QUESTION 1—Steps

You have heard a description of how people have domesticated and cultivated the natural world around them. Now put the sentences below into sequence, showing the chronological order in which they happened. Put them in the centre column of the table.

The Steps
A The silkworm is domesticated in China
B Cattle are domesticated in Greece
C Rubber seeds are smuggled out of Brazil and brought to Britain
D Horses are domesticated in Central Russia
E The first fur farms are established in Canada
F The bee is domesticated in Egypt
G Sheep and goats are domesticated in the Middle East
H The cat is domesticated in Egypt
I Tea is brought to Britain from China
J The dolphin is used in scientific research
K The dog is domesticated

L Wild jungle fowl are domesticated in what is now Pakistan
M Paper is made for the first time in China
N A high-quality linen is used in Egypt
O Wheat is cultivated in the Middle East

	Step	Result
1		
2		
3		
4		
5		
6		
7		
8		
9		
10		
11		
12		
13		
14		
15		

QUESTION 2—Results

Read the statements below which describe the result of each of the steps. Put the number of the statement which matches the step in the last column of the table.

The Results
1 flour is made by grinding the grains and feeding the outer covering to animals
2 it is the most popular and inexpensive source of meat and eggs
3 it is from such plants that we obtain a waterproof material
4 it was used for clothing and for wrapping the dead
5 it makes a pleasant drink but was at first very expensive

6   and since then it has played a large part in the spread of learning
7   it has been trained to hunt antelope in India
8   they draw sledges, guide the blind and are used by the police
9   and since then they have provided people with meat, milk, wool and skins
10 because the animal population had declined and hunting had become expensive
11 they provide people with skins, meat and milk and are used as working animals
12 it was first used to catch rats but then it was worshipped
13 because it can produce and hear sounds at a very high frequency
14 its body produces threads which are woven into an expensive fabric
15 its syrup is used as a sweetener and its wax as polish and for candles
16 the first London coffee house was opened
17 they are used for pulling and bearing loads, for sport and for hunting
18 they were bred to eat on days when the Church forbade the eating of meat